Religious Activism in the Global Economy

Religious Activism in the Global Economy

Promoting, Reforming, or Resisting Neoliberal Globalization?

Edited by
Sabine Dreher and Peter J. Smith

ROWMAN &
LITTLEFIELD
INTERNATIONAL

London • New York

Published by Rowman & Littlefield International Ltd
Unit A, Whitacre Mews, 26-34 Stannary Street, London SE11 4AB
www.rowmaninternational.com

Rowman & Littlefield International Ltd. is an affiliate of Rowman & Littlefield
4501 Forbes Boulevard, Suite 200, Lanham, Maryland 20706, USA
With additional offices in Boulder, New York, Toronto (Canada), and Plymouth (UK)
www.rowman.com

British Library Cataloguing in Publication Data
A catalogue record for this book is available from the British Library
ISBN: HB 978-1-78348-696-0
         PB 978-1-78348-697-7

Library of Congress Cataloging-in-Publication Data
Names: Dreher, Sabine, editor.
Title: Religious activism in the global economy : promoting, reforming, or resisting
   neoliberal globalization? / edited by Sabine Dreher and Peter J. Smith.
Description: Lanham : Rowman & Littlefield International, 2016. |
   Includes bibliographical references and index.
Identifiers: LCCN 2016010347 (print) | LCCN 2016014107 (ebook) |
   ISBN 9781783486960 (cloth : alk. paper) | ISBN 9781783486977 (pbk. : alk. paper) |
   ISBN 9781783486984 (Electronic)
Subjects: LCSH: Globalization—Religious aspects. | Neoliberalism—Religious aspects. |
   Religion and politics.
Classification: LCC BL65.G55 R453 2016 (print) | LCC BL65.G55 (ebook) |
   DDC 201/.7—dc23
LC record available at http://lccn.loc.gov/2016010347

Printed in the United States of America

Contents

Chapter 1

Religion and International Political Economy—A Case of Mutual Neglect

Sabine Dreher

The new wave of religious activism since the 1970s has forced the social sciences in general and the discipline of International Relations (IR) specifically, to reconsider the role of religion in society, politics, and, to some extent, economics. Previously, religious activists were written off as remnants of traditions soon to be wiped out by the modernization process, and were, therefore, supposed to restrict themselves to the private sphere. However, beginning in the 1970s, religious activism emerged into the public sphere, often under dramatic or violent circumstances. Prominent examples of "public religion" (Casanova 1994) are the Islamic revolution in Iran in 1979, the Solidarity movement in Poland in the 1980s supported by the Catholic Church, Protestant fundamentalism in American politics and its role in the Republican Party, the fatwa against Salman Rushdie, and the emergence of a new form of global Islamic Jihadism with the 9/11 attacks against the United States. Somewhat overlooked in lists such as these is liberation theology in Latin America, but it shows that the demands of religious activists ranged from more progressive to more reactionary responses to modern life, though, it has to be said, reactionary responses are more prominent in the debate.

The reemergence of religion into the public sphere took many observers by surprise since secularization—the process by which religious institutions are subordinated to and separated from politics, economics, and society—was supposed to have relegated religion to the private sphere. In addition to the separation of religion from other spheres, social scientists also assumed that religion would simply disappear; yet, religious movements are now among the key oppositional movements in the twenty-first century according to Tuğal (2002, 85). Moreover, Rinehart (2004, 271) points out that religious doctrines have emerged as real alternatives to communism, socialism, and liberalism.

1

In IR, this led to a debate on how to interpret the role of religion. On the one hand, there have been those who interpret the emergence of religious activism as a successful and dangerous challenge to the secular and territorial Westphalian system of sovereign states that needs to be contained. On the other hand, others have argued that religious activism is a reflection of the need for greater pluralism and authenticity in the international system, signaling the need for deeper structural and democratic reforms in global institutional arrangements.

According to this second perspective, the Westphalian state-centered system characterized by anarchy, hierarchy, and territoriality has been complemented (but not supplanted) by global governance and a global civil society (McGrew 2013; Kaldor 2003). The disaggregation of the state in the "post-Westphalian" system has created space for other identities that were suppressed: new social movements around women's rights; civil rights; peace and environment; movements around sexual identities; and right-wing, regional, and ethnic movements, to name just a few (Eisenstadt 2000; Badie and Smouts 1992). It is in this context of the emergence of identity politics against the modernizing, nationalist secular state that scholars in IR have discussed the "resurgence" of religion since the early 1990s (Huntington 1993; Thomas 2000; Hurd 2007; Rinehart 2004).

The problem with this scholarship on religion in IR is, however, according to Bellin (2008), that it did not integrate itself into a larger field of inquiry such as culture and IR or international political economy (IPE) but largely studied religion in isolation. One further and more important difficulty is its focus on the political aspect of the new religious activism while largely ignoring economic questions. Even within IPE, which unites students interested in the economic side of world politics, researchers have not studied the religious resurgence to a significant degree (Dreher 2012).[1]

There is little research on whether the new religious activism has had any impact on the neoliberal globalization project that not even the 2008 economic crisis was able to derail. On the contrary, the main theme coming out of the crisis has been that there is a need for more, and not less, of the same (Centeno and Cohen 2012). Neoliberalism is defined here as a project of global market making (McMichael 2000) with the goal to abolish all state regulations that are seen as impediments to economic growth (or the freedom of maneuver for business, whether nationally or globally), while the surveillance and regulatory capacity of the state are strengthened to better implement these reforms. This combination of a free economy and a strong state is the hallmark of the neoliberal revolution according to Gamble (1994). But it is startling to see that the crisis of 2007–2008, the biggest crisis since the Great Depression of the 1930s, has not completely delegitimized neoliberal ideas, and that we are, instead, pondering the "strange non-death of neoliberalism" (Crouch 2011).

This persistence of neoliberal thinking is unexpected since it has not been a resounding success in economic terms. While neoliberal policies have increased profit rates for firms and lowered inflation, they have also reduced overall growth rates of the economy, increased global economic instability through recurrent financial crises, amplified global and national economic inequality, facilitated corporate corruption in the absence of state regulation, increased rent-seeking by firms, and boosted public and private debt (Piketty 2014; Rodrik 2007; Stuckler and Basu 2014; Wilkinson and Pickett 2010; Crouch 2011). This persistence of neoliberalism, despite its many negative effects, and an increasing movement of resistance (see below), begs the question of how to explain the staying power of neoliberal ideas and policies. Of course, as Crouch (2011) points out, corporate power is one key factor, but it cannot account for the popularity of neoliberal policies in elections.

The argument presented in this volume is that there is a form of religiosity that promotes neoliberalism. This volume thus complements research in IPE with regard to neoliberal globalization. It shows that IPE scholars will have to pay more attention to the study of religion if they want to understand both the continuity and the ever-increasing fissures within the neoliberal project. Indeed, as this volume highlights, one of the more interesting ideas on how to resist neoliberal globalization (*buen vivir*) is coming from religious social movements. At the same time, the volume showcases forms of religiosity within each religious tradition that are highly compatible with the neoliberal globalization project and its post-Fordist insistence on flexibility and adaptability (Harvey 1989).

The purpose of this introduction is to outline the debate on religion in IR and its three limits: the absence of economic questions, the Westphalian presumption, and the approach to the analysis of religion. This discussion will lay the groundwork for the introduction of a constructivist social movement approach to the study of religion. The proposed typology ("promote," "reform," and "resist") is derived from a discussion of neoliberal globalization and its contestation by global civil society. The various case studies presented in this volume show that religious activism has promoted, reformed, or resisted neoliberal globalization. Religious activism is, therefore, an explanatory factor in the staying power of the neoliberal project but, at the same time, also a significant challenger to its predominance.

THE DEBATE ON RELIGION IN IR AND ITS LIMITS

The debate on religion and its role in world politics has largely been shaped by the 9/11 attacks, even though there had been a number of prior studies (Huntington 1993; Juergensmeyer 1993). It was Samuel Huntington's argument (1993)—that the future of world politics would be characterized by a clash of civilizations—that dominated the debate in IR about culture, identity, and religion after the end of the Cold War and specifically after 9/11. Huntington and others (Winfield 2007; Lewis 2002; Juergensmeyer 2008) portrayed religion, especially the Islamic religion, as a violent attack on the secular values of the free world. In the eyes of these authors, the "free" and now "secular" world appears as the key unit that needs to be defended in a new global conflict, and each new terror attack strengthens this argument.

The prominence of violent religious actors resulted in scholarly research largely focused on religious violence. Juergensmeyer's (1993; 2008) documentation of current events and movements seemed to confirm Huntington's prediction of a clash. Juergensmeyer clarified this debate substantially by pointing out that religious nationalism will lead to a new form of global confrontation between secular and religious forces as the two are diametrically opposed and fight over the same terrain. In his view, accommodation of secularism to religion or of religion to secularism is unlikely and difficult to bring about. For Juergensmeyer (2008, 17), it is a question of either secular or religious nationalism as both are ideologies of order.

Secularism in this specific pattern of argumentation has taken on the appearance of an immutable force that has specific features—one of which is supposed to be a strict separation of politics from religious interference and where any expression of religiosity, even the simple wearing of a headscarf, is seen as an assault on this secular order. The "secularist" camp (Winfield 2007; Philpot 2002; Lewis 2002) claims that a secular order is a precondition for democracy and prosperity since religious ideas and practices are often undemocratic and irrational, and impede economic development (Kuran 2011). For the secularist, the Westphalian peace treaty of 1648 marked the end of the intrusion of religion in public affairs by cementing the separation between politics and religion. It turned religion into a private affair centered on the individual but strictly separated from politics, and left international politics to the more rational calculations of states (Philpott 2002). According to Thomas (2000), this "Westphalian presumption" even *requires* the relegation of religion to the private sphere in order to pacify international politics.

It is this rational, peaceful, and secular order that is under attack by irrational and violent religious forces. In the eyes of the secularist, they question key values of the free world with their different interpretation of the organization of public space and, specifically, women's comportment (see Schyff and Overbeeke 2011; Cote-Boucher and Hadj-Moussa 2008; Falkenhayner 2010 for critical analysis). Philpot (2002) even argues that the 9/11 attacks ended the Westphalian sovereign state system because they highlighted the existence of a nonstate religious authority that was able to assault a sovereign state. Some authors have concluded from this debate that secularization as such has come to an end and is being reversed (Berger 1999), and that we need to speak about post-secularism.

Predictably, the argument that religion undermines the political order has been countered by its opposite: religion may represent a corrective to such an order, which can be as violent and irrational as the religious order. For example, the Catholic Church supported the resistance against Communist regimes in the 1980s; the Jubilee Debt campaign changed the nature of the debate on global debt by declaring high debt burdens as morally wrong and in need of cancellation or at least reduction (Shawki 2010); liberation theology in Latin America contributed to a critique of modern capitalism (Löwy 1996). These examples showcase that religious activists are not only a problem for modernity and democracy but also present important interventions into specific modern problems. From this perspective, some religious activists can be integrated into the public sphere as one voice among many and their integration will not necessarily mean an end to secularization or the state system (see chapter 2).

Another group of authors concludes that the real problem is not religion but specific secularist assumptions about religion. Following Talal Asad (1993), they focus on the idea of secularism itself and its various forms. Their main contribution is to distinguish between a passive secularism that accepts some forms of religious expressions whereas more authoritarian secularism perceives any religious activism immediately as a threat (Kuru 2007). Hurd has even argued that there is not really a resurgence of religion but an increase in authoritarian secularism (Hurd 2007) and, for her, the debate is better conceptualized as a struggle over authoritarian definitions of religious and secular spheres. Hurd's and Kuru's works point to the fact that there are a variety of secular regimes—for example, some allow for a surprising degree of expression of religiosity while others restrict all or some religious expression—and that the emphasis on a singular secular Westphalian state system may be problematic (see chapter 2). From this perspective, the emergence of religious activists signals a need for a more plural order that is more accommodating than the existing Western-dominated order. Modernity in this view is not unilinear but there are multiple ways to be modern (Eisenstadt 2000). For Thomas (2000), the reemergence of religion indicates a return of authenticity that had been undermined by modernization processes. Theoretically, this second set of authors encourages us to see religious activists in a more positive light and to accept that they are making valid contributions to debates in the world polity about an international order characterized by great power imbalances and inequality of life chances, though this second camp is not discussing these economic questions either.

By focusing on the political aspects, the debate in IR ignores one key insight from research on secularization: the importance, but also the intensity, of religion diminishes with increased prosperity according to Norris and Inglehart (2010); conversely, religious fervor increases in times of existential insecurity. Given that the neoliberal globalization project and the support for repressive regimes have dramatically increased existential insecurity during decades of failed structural adjustment programs, we should not be surprised by the recent resurgence and increase in extremist forms of religion. Except that the connections are not drawn; problems of economic insecurity created by neoliberal globalization are not systematically seen as an explanatory factor for the religious resurgence. While the "Westphalian presumption" will be problematized in more detail in chapter 2, the next section will introduce a constructivist perspective on religion—here defined as the study of religious movements and their frames—as the key unit of analysis. This is necessary as both sides in the debate in IR rely on an essentialist understanding of religion stemming from their origin in "world religion" thinking.

A CONSTRUCTIVIST PERSPECTIVE ON RELIGION

A largely overlooked aspect of the debate in IR is its problematic understanding of religion. Both sides rely on an essentialist understanding of religion assuming that religion has an irreducible component that can be identified by the researcher. Both Thomas (2000) and Juergensmeyer (2008), for example, present religious activism as the expression of a community. Juergensmeyer's argument about religion as an ideology of order in direct opposition to secular nationalism has already been outlined, but Thomas (2000) who comes from the opposite camp expresses a similar idea when he postulates that religion needs to be defined in a "social" way, as a "community of believers" (Thomas 2000, 820; Bosco 2009, 94). In other words, both camps share the idea that there is an essence to religious activism that necessarily also shapes actors' preferences and choices. However, there are two problems with this approach.

First of all, feminist and postcolonial analysts have criticized the description of religious activism as the authentic expression of a community. For feminists, the authentic expression of a community usually ends up being one specific male voice of this community that ignores some of the female perspectives that may have a different view on polygamy, wife beating, child marriage, or divorce (Okin 1999; Moghadam 2007) even while accepting the religious viewpoint as such. Postcolonial authors, in contrast, emphasize the social construction of religion in a geopolitical context influenced by imperialism and colonialism. Bosco (2009) therefore pushes for a more refined definition of religion in the discipline of IR that avoids orientalism and essentialism.

Secondly, the essentialist approach in IR has its origin in the notion of "world religion" developed in religious studies—the idea that there exists a clearly describable set of "world religions." This idea has its origin in missionaries in the nineteenth century who used it to summarize other belief systems in order to better proselytize (Fitzgerald 1990). What emerged from this enterprise are textbooks on the world's religions where each religion is accorded a chapter. The list of what classifies as a world religion varies, but generally there is Buddhism, Hinduism, Islam, Judaism, and Christianity according to Kurtz (2007), but his third edition includes a new chapter on indigenous traditions. This approach to religious studies stems from Durkheim's definition of a religion as a "unified system of beliefs and practices relative to sacred things, that is to say, things set apart and forbidden—beliefs and practices which unite into one single moral community called a Church, all those who adhere to them" (Durkheim cited in Kurtz 2007, 11). From this perspective, it is possible to present each of the world's religions as a unified system of beliefs and practices and as a representative expression of its community. It is obvious that Durkheim's original definition only applies to the Catholic Church. Yet, this way of defining religion is generally used to develop a comparative presentation of the world's religions in textbooks, and informs public discourse (Fitzgerald 1990, 104).

The key problem is that the idea of a "world religion" ignores the differences within religions that can be nearly as enormous as the differences between religions. Fitzgerald (1990) developed this insight by studying the critique of Hinduism by Ambedkar, an activist fighting for the Untouchables (Dalits). According to Fitzgerald, Ambedkar's activism highlights that textbook chapters on Hinduism present only the Brahamanical interpretation of Hinduism. They do not discuss Ambedkar's argument that Hinduism is merely an ideology to justify the exploitation of the Dalits by the higher castes (Fitzgerald 2011, 52). The question thus arises of whose interpretation of Hinduism one is to follow. For the Islamic tradition we have a similar problem. As Soroush (quoted in Yavuz 2013) has argued, "There is no such thing as a 'pure' Islam that is outside the process of historical development. The actual lived experience of Islam has always been culturally and historically specific, and bound by the immediate circumstances of its location in time and space" (3).

For this reason, Fitzgerald (2011) and others (Owen 2011) propose that religious studies need to integrate the societal basis of religion into their research. To put it differently, all religious traditions are characterized by a struggle about what their religion is supposed to be and this struggle takes place not only within the religious tradition itself but also with respect to outsiders. From a critical religion perspective (Fitzgerald 2011), the study of religion therefore needs to focus on this struggle and integrate it into its research design. Yavuz employs the term constructivism for this approach because it starts from the idea that "any society is a human construction and subject to multiple interpretations and influences" (Yavuz 2003, 20). According to Yavuz (2003), we need to take this into consideration when we study religion. The advantage of a constructivist approach is that it does not attribute actor quality to a reified Islam or any other "world religion," but, instead, studies concrete interpretations of religious traditions in their specific local context while taking beliefs as a serious object of study (21).

The constructivist approach allows us to move away from the study of religion as "world religion" and to focus on religious movements and their specific practices (see also Lynch 2009). This approach allows us to see more clearly that a religious tradition is a contested discourse. A religious tradition such as Hinduism or Christianity should therefore be set in plural (Riesebrodt 2014, 6) with a focus on the study of its concrete expressions: pietistic movements, outward-oriented movements, political movements, social movements, violent movements, peaceful movements, reformist or traditionalist movements, to name just a few of the typologies in the field (Yavuz 2003). In short, and to paraphrase Wendt (1992), "religion" is what religious actors and their counterparts have made of it. Each social movement studied in the respective chapters of this volume is thus part of an internal contestation within its faith tradition and is by no means representative of the religious tradition as a whole.

One important category in this context is the notion of "frames" from social movement theory. Framing processes occur when social movement actors develop interpretations of their individual and collective experiences and articulate them in the public sphere. Ayres (2004) describes it as "meaning work": "An active and contentious process where actors are engaged in producing and disseminating meanings that differ from and may in fact challenge existing socio-political conditions" (13). Frames are meant to mobilize adherents and to develop a conceptual guide to understand the reality. Using the notion of frames allows us to take religiosity seriously, and also to use social science methods in their study.

Taking a social movement approach to the question of religious activists is contested, as there are misgivings when comparing religious activists to other actors in civil society because of the hierarchical nature of many religious organizations and because membership in religious movements is often decided at birth, and not a conscious choice of the adherent (Kennedy 2012). According to Kennedy, religious organizations have even refused to see themselves on par with other civil society actors because they perceive themselves as concerned with the salvation of humankind or questions of the sacred and the spiritual, as opposed to more mundane matters that are of concern to social movements (293–94). Yet, once they enter the public sphere—making claims in the name of their religious ideas—religious movements will have to accept that they will be measured by the same standard as any other civil society actor in the context of their respective setting. In consequence, religious actors speaking out in the public sphere need to be interrogated with regard to their rationality, purpose, and method just like any other actor that engages in the public sphere, and cannot claim preferential treatment on the grounds of sacredness.

This section has presented the argument that studies of religion are better undertaken at the level of specific religious movements and their frames. While it may be helpful to retain a definition of religion as the "ultimate ground of existence" (Philpott 2002) to reflect the interests of the individual believer, such an essentialist understanding of religion needs to be complemented by the focus on specific religious social movements and their larger context. The concluding section will now explain the neoliberal globalization project and integrate the study of religious movements into the discussion on globalization and resistance. It shows that the inclusion of religious movements adds an important dimension to this research agenda.

FRAMING NEOLIBERAL GLOBALIZATION FROM A RELIGIOUS PERSPECTIVE

Neoliberal globalization is understood as a project by a multitude of social forces located at the level of government and private business that seek to restructure the welfare and regulatory state through austerity politics, privatization, deregulation, and integration into the global economy, while strengthening its surveillance function (Harvey 2007; Gamble 1994). The objective is to shift economic power away from the state to market actors as these are seen as more efficient at the provision of goods than the state (Strange 1996). Phillips-Fein (2010) has shown in her masterful study how this project was engineered in the United States by economic elites opposed to social democracy and the idea of human security for a large majority from the very beginning of the New Deal in the 1930s. They used the crisis of Keynesian economics in the 1970s as a lever to push through their program and have largely succeeded (Harvey 2007) by relying increasingly on more repressive policies and surveillance techniques.

By now the impact of neoliberal policies are clear: the welfare state has been pruned, state entities have been privatized, inflation has been reduced, profit rates are up and the competitiveness of firms has increased, key impediments to growth (from the perspective of neoliberal ideology) such as labor unions have been defeated, and the one percent have restored their share of wealth to levels not seen since the 1930s. However, the promised restoration of economic growth has not taken place; on the contrary, economy after economy has been shaken by financial crises while economic growth is lower than before; it would be even lower had debt levels not increased everywhere, even among the poor (Rodrick 2007; Soederberg 2014). At the same time, neoliberal policies have amplified economic concentration while the free market has largely been replaced by strategic alliances and corporate negotiations (Cowling and Tomlinson 2005). Evidence has emerged regarding how neoliberal policies have had a devastating impact on communities in terms of public health (Stuckler and Basu 2014). The upsurge in inequality (traced back to changing state policies by Piketty 2014) is associated with a decline of community life, an increase in mental health problems and drug use, lower physical health and lower life expectancy, an increase in obesity, lower educational performance, more teenage births, an increase in violence, higher levels of imprisonment and lower social mobility, as the research by Wilkinson and Picket (2010) has pointed out.

Social movement and globalization research has documented the resistance to this project of global market making from its outset in the early 1980s worldwide (Smith 2008; Evans 2008). The increasing number of demonstrations against neoliberal governance that started with the so-called IMF riots in the 1980s continued with the uprising of the Zapatistas in Mexico in 1994. During this period, religious activists also developed fair trade as an alternative to free trade (Robinson 2011). There were some major success stories in the 1990s with the prevention of the Multilateral Agreement on Investment in 1998, the disruption of the meeting of the World Trade Organization in Seattle in 1999, and the successful Jubilee debt campaign (Shawki 2010). It seems that having clear ethics that allow actors to frame something as "wrong" made for a more effective impact (Shawki 2010). This process culminated in the creation of a global set of meetings with the World Social Forum (see Smythe and Smith, this volume). In the process, the global social justice movement established a clear alternative narrative to challenge neoliberal hegemony. The activists claimed that globalization is a race to the bottom initiated by an anti-democratic form of global governance dominated by a handful of countries and multinational corporations. They demanded a de-ratification of major "free trade" treaties, reform of existing treaties, redistribution from rich to poor (debt cancellation, Tobin Tax), rules to rein in multinational corporations, a reform of the international economic institutions, and an end to environmental destruction (Ayres 2004).

The problem with social movement research is that it posits a simple dichotomy between the neoliberal globalization project, on the one hand, and resistance to it, on the other hand, focusing largely on the latter and overlooking that there are also more moderate voices in the debate. In order to understand the role of religious activists, however, we need to take into account the whole complexity of possible approaches to neoliberal globalization. For this reason, the chapters in this volume will differentiate between the promotion of neoliberal globalization, reforming neoliberal globalization, and creating an alternative form of living.[2]

In this, the chapters are supported by a new dataset, the Religious Characteristics of States (RCS), developed by Davis Brown and Patrick James (see chapter 3). RCS provides annual estimates for populations and percentages of adherents of religions. It does so by differentiating the various subgroups within religious traditions. For Protestantism, the dataset includes the demographic development over time for approximately ten subgroups. Brown's chapter therefore supplements the qualitative in-depth case studies provided here. It shows how religious adherence has changed over time in the countries under discussion and in this way provides historical context for the discussion in the chapters.

Promoting Neoliberalism

Neoliberalism as a political project cannot stand on its own and needs ideologies to support it (Overbeek and van der Pijl 1993) and a strong state to survive (Gamble 1994). It is precisely at this intersection that religious social movements and their frames have made a surprising comeback over the last twenty years. Starting with evangelical activism in the United States (Hackworth 2012), we now have an increasing number of governments and movements relying on religious rhetoric to justify significant neoliberal restructuring and integration into the global economy. Hindutva in India (Gopalakrishnan 2009), Australia under Howard (Maddox 2005), and Turkey under the Justice and Development Party (AKP), whose religious underpinning has become increasingly prominent (see Bozkurt in this volume), are some of the key examples of this trend. Religious authoritarian neoliberal populism is an emerging trend as a part of the more general tendency toward illiberal democracies.

A second aspect of how religious social movements facilitate neoliberalism can be studied at the level of the individual. Neoliberalism's concern with privatization and deregulation means that a host of tasks are now downshifted to the individual or the family and are no longer available from the state. It is here that religious social movements have stepped into the breach either by providing welfare services or by providing spiritual guidance in a world turned upside down. To some extent they are creating their own "state" within a state: Hezbollah in Lebanon is spearheading reforms aimed at consolidating the political and politico-economic gains of the country's Shiite community, as described by Fouad Marei in this volume. In doing so, religiosity, piety, and entrepreneurship are invoked and infused with neoliberal practices. Another example are the gurus in India who guide individuals from the professional middle classes that work in the new flexible economy (Upadhyay, this volume). This seems to be similar to what Rudnyckyj (2009) describes for a specific Islamic activism in Indonesia where several spiritual reform movements have combined Western business management principles with Muslim practice to develop a capitalist ethics based on Islam. This type of market Islam (Haenni 2005; Atia 2012) is geared toward self-improvement and increasing the competitiveness of individuals in the marketplace (see also Gauthier and Martikainen 2013). More extreme is prosperity religion described for Nigeria by Ukah and its globalization by Wilkinson in this volume. Here, pastors bestow economic blessing and faith healing and focus on personal success—a believer's faith can be measured in terms of health and wealth outcomes. One interesting side aspect of prosperity religion is that it is accompanied by a focus on business development in the form of megachurches, television ministries, publishing houses, and conference networks to market the faith and to increase the income of the pastor.

Reforming Neoliberalism—Social Democratic Religion

Social democracy is the compromise between the free market and the state. Its key starting point is that businesses should enjoy the freedom to develop new products, but labor markets should be supported by strong citizenship rights in order to mitigate some of the insecurities created by the boom and bust cycles of capitalism (Marshall 1950).

Closer to reforming neoliberalism is the Gülen or Hizmet movement (Dreher, in this volume) with its emphasis on business people giving back to the community, but its classification falls somewhere in between social democracy and outright neoliberalism. Likewise, Webb's chapter on Ennahda in Tunisia highlights the complexity of a country in transition and an Islamist party trying to adjust to the new reality. It also shows that neoliberalism itself has changed over time—indicating a need to apply the social constructivist approach to neoliberalism itself, an argument that is also developed in the chapters by Marei and MacLeod.

The chapter on Tanzania by Kwayu is closer to the original idea of social democracy. It highlights a form of religious social democracy where a coalition of Christian and Muslim activists is pushing for higher taxes on mining corporations—joining a global movement to hold transnational corporations (TNCs) to account and to reduce their ability to repatriate profits out of the country. The insistence on more corporate social responsibility by activist religious investors needs to be counted in this category as well, as is highlighted in the chapter by MacLeod. Besides the local context, at the global level also, religious activists in this category are active. The fair trade movement is one key early example of a global approach to reform (Reynolds 2013; Robinson 2011). The success of the Jubilee debt campaign has already been mentioned.

Resisting Neoliberalism—Rebuilding Society through Progressive Movements

Some activists, however, are pointing out that in the face of global climate change, more radical reforms are needed because an economy based on growth is incompatible with limited resources. Even *The Economist* in its October 2012 issue called for more progressive forms of policies, so we should give serious consideration to more radical ideas.

In the context of research on religion, "radical" usually refers to violent movements—such as the Islamic state (or Hezbollah in Lebanon; see the chapter by Marei in this volume). But a careful look at "radical Islam" shows that this specific interpretation of the Islamic tradition actually facilitates further neoliberal globalization because it creates an atmosphere of "us" versus "them" that is willingly taken up by conservatives and more right-wing populist forces. As a result, the discourse that emerges from the war on terror now prevents any serious criticism of the functioning of the global economy. This is because expression of such criticism implies that one is with "them" and not with "us." Thus, by impeding critical questioning of the functioning of the global economy, terrorism ends up in further extending neoliberal globalization. In other words, terrorism indirectly strengthens and reinforces the very system that is, according to Moghadam (2002), one of the root causes of terrorism in the first place.

This insight leads to the need to define resistance positively and not just negatively as in opposition to neoliberal globalization. Resistance here refers to the abolition of systems of oppression and the end of exploitative social and economic arrangements. It should lead to the creation of alternative modes of existence suited to the local context that will end (neoliberal) global capitalism and put in place an economic system guaranteeing survival for everybody. This means that while some religious movements are in violent opposition to Western forms of power, their propositions for governance are far from democratic in the political as well as in the economic sense and are excluded from the category of progressive resistance to neoliberal capitalism.

Following Polanyi (1957), resistance to capitalism implies putting an end to markets for labor, capital, and land and to allow for democratic community control over resources (Lacher 1999). In other words, what is needed is to end the market as a primary distribution mechanism for life chances (Marois and Pradella 2015). Given that for a large number of people the market does not deliver stable incomes, social protection, health care, adequate housing, water, food, medical drugs, and basic infrastructure, it may be time to reflect on whether state or community involvement in the production of basic goods and services might be a more plausible alternative. It will take committed religious activists to develop plausible arguments around this claim given the resurgence of the "morality of capitalism" argumentation on the right (Palmer 2011).

Within environmental movements, the need for more radical change has been recognized in the face of finite resources on planet Earth and impending climate change. Some of the Christian churches in the United States have come to accept that serious changes in lifestyle are needed if our planet is to have a chance at survival, as Nicinska describes in her chapter. Alternative ideas for the global economy have also been developed by religious activists in the World Social Forum and in the Occupy Movement, as presented in the chapter by Smith and Smythe. The most radical of these proposals is the idea of an economy that is based on "living well," complementarity, and community, as proposed by the indigenous movement from Latin America, detailed in the chapter by Scauso. In both Bolivia and Ecuador, nature has received legal standing. Indigenous communities in Bolivia remind us that the good life depends on many things, one of which is a friendly community that allows for better forms of living in a sustainable way.

CONCLUSION

This introduction has shown that the debate on religion in IR is narrowly focused on politics, ignores economic questions, and has a problematic understanding of religion. This has been countered with an invitation to focus on the study of specific religious movements and their frames for which the introduction has provided a three-fold typology: promoting, reforming, and resisting neoliberal globalization. The good news is, as Smith will point out in his conclusion, that the most radical idea of *buen vivir* is no longer limited to Latin America but is increasingly globalized. There is then hope that the religious resurgence sweeping through the planet may also support a necessary fundamental transformation of an economy that has taken on god-like features and whose criticism is often presented as blasphemous by the defenders of the free market and private property rights (Fitzgerald 2011, 10). Admittedly, the evidence from our volume points toward the opposite as it was easier to find religious movements in support of neoliberalism. Nevertheless, the case studies collected here demonstrate that the question of the religious contestation of the global economy is an important question for students of the global economy in the twenty-first century, and requires more research and discussion.

NOTES

1. For an introduction to International Political Economy, see O'Brian and Williams (2010) and Balaam and Dillman (2014).

2. This typology has been inspired by Polanyi's (1957) idea of a double movement, by Kaldor's (2003: 588–89) classification of civil society actors into social movement, neoliberal, and postmodern activists, by Munck's (2006) discussion of the contestation of globalization by various progressive and regressive forces, by Rupert's (2000) exposition of ideologies of globalization, by Moghadam's (2009) overview of social movements in global contestation, and by the author's own work in a research group at the University of Bremen (Walter, Beisheim and Dreher 2005; Dreher 2005 and 2007).

REFERENCES

Asad, Talal. 1993. *Genealogies of Religion: Discipline and Reasons of Power in Christianity and Islam*. Baltimore: John Hopkins University Press.

Atia, Mona. 2012. "A Way to Paradise? Pious Neoliberalism, Islam, and Faith-Based Development." *Annals of the Association of American Geographers* 102 (4): 808–27.

Ayres, Jeffrey M. 2004. "Framing Collective Action Against Neoliberalism: The Case of the 'Anti-globalization' Movement." *Journal of World-systems Research* 10 (1): 11–34.

Badie, Bertrand and Marie-Claude Smouts. 1992. *Le Retournement du Monde: Sociologie de la Scène Internationale*. Presses de la Fondation Nationale des Sciences Politiques.

Balaam, David M. and Bradford Dillman. 2014. *Introduction to International Political Economy*. Boston: Pearson Education Inc.

Bellin, Eva. 2008. "Faith in Politics. New Trends in the Study of Religion and Politics." *World Politics* 60 (2): 315–47.

Berger, Peter L. 1999. "The Desecularization of the World: A Global Overview." In *The Desecularization of the World: Resurgent Religion and World Politics*, edited by Peter L. Berger, 1–18. Washington, DC: Ethics and Public Policy Center and W.B. Eerdmans Pub. Co.

Bosco, Robert M. 2007. "Persistent Orientalisms: The Concept of Religion in International Relations." *Journal of International Relations and Development* 12 (1): 90–111.

Casanova, José. 1994. *Public Religions in the Modern World*. Chicago: University of Chicago Press.

Centeno, Miguel A. and Joseph N. Cohen. 2012. "The Arc of Neoliberalism." *Annual Review of Sociology* 38: 317–40. doi: 10.1146/annurev-soc-081309-150235.

Cote-Boucher, Karine and Ratiba Hadj-Moussa. 2008. "Malaise identitaire: islam, laicité et logique preventive en France et au Quebec." *Cahiers de Recherche Sociologique* 46: 61–77.

Cowling, Keith and Philip R. Tomlinson. "Globalisation and Corporate Power." *Contributions to Political Economy* 24 (1): 33–54.

Crouch, Colin. 2011. *The Strange Non-death of Neo-liberalism*. Cambridge: Polity.

Dreher, Sabine. 2005. "Citizenship and Migration in Germany and the United States," in *Globalizing Interests. Pressure Groups and Denationalization*, edited by Michael Zürn, with the assistance of Gregor Walter, 125–86. Albany: State University of New York Press.

Dreher, Sabine. 2007. *Neoliberalism and Migration: An Inquiry into the Politics of Globalization*. Münster: Lit Verlag.

Dreher, Sabine. 2012. "International Political Economy and the Religious Resurgence." Paper presented at the Annual Conference of the *International Studies Association*, San Diego, April 1–4.

Eisenstadt, Shmuel Noah. 2000. "Multiple Modernities." *Daedalus:* 1–29.

Evans, Peter. 2008. "Is an Alternative Globalization Possible?" *Politics and Society* 36 (2): 271–305.

Falkenhayner, Nicole. 2010. "The Other Rupture of 1989: The Rushdie Affair as the Inaugural Event of Representations of Post-secular Conflict." *Global Society* 24 (1): 111–32.

Fitzgerald, Timothy. 1990. "Hinduism and the 'World Religion' Fallacy." *Religion* 20 (2): 101–18.

Fitzgerald, Timothy. 2011. *Religion and Politics in International Relations: The Modern Myth*. London: Black.

Gamble, Andrew. 1994. *The Free Economy and the Strong State. The Politics of Thatcherism*. 2nd edn. London: MacMillan.

Gauthier, François and Tuomas Martikainen, eds. 2013. *Religion in the Neoliberal Age: Political Economy and Modes of Governance*. Farnham: Ashgate Publishing.

Gopalakrishnan, Shankar. 2006. "Defining, Constructing and Policing a 'New India': Relationship between Neoliberalism and Hindutva." *Economic and Political Weekly* 41 (26): 2803–13.

Hackworth, Jason. 2012. *Faith Based: Religious Neoliberalism and the Politics of Welfare in the United States*. Athens: University of Georgia Press.

Haenni, Patrick. 2005. *L'Islam de marché: L'autre révolution conservatrice*. Paris: Seuil.

Harvey, David. 1989. *The Condition of Postmodernity: An Enquiry into the Origins of Cultural Change*. Oxford, UK: Blackwell.

Harvey, David. 2007. "Neoliberalism as Creative Destruction." *The Annals of the American Academy of Political and Social Science* 610 (1): 21–44.

Huntington, Samuel P. 1993. "The Clash of Civilizations." *Foreign Affairs* 72 (3): 22–49.

Hurd, Elizabeth Shakman. 2007. "Theorizing Religious Resurgence." *International Politics* 44 (6): 647–65.

Juergensmeyer, Mark. 2008. *Global Rebellion: Religious Challenges to the Secular State, from Christian Militias to Al Qaeda*. Berkeley: University of California Press.

Juergensmeyer, Mark. 1993. *The New Cold War? Religious Nationalism Confronts the Secular State*. Oakland: University of California Press.

Kaldor, Mary. 2003. "The Idea of Global Civil Society." *International Affairs* 79 (3): 583–93.

Kennedy, James. 2012. "Protestant Ecclesiastical International," in *Religious Internationals in the Modern World: Globalization and Faith Communities since 1750*, edited by Abigail Green and Vincent Viaene, 292–319. Palgrave: Macmillan.

Kuran, Timur. 2011. *The Long Divergence. How Islamic Law Held Back the Middle East*. Princeton: Princeton University Press.

Kurtz, Lester R. 2007. *Gods in the Global Village: The World's Religions in Sociological Perspective*. 2nd edn. Thousand Oaks: Sage Publications.

Kuru, Ahmet. 2007. "Passive and Assertive Secularism: Historical Conditions, Ideological Struggle, and States' Policies Towards Religion." *World Politics* 59 (4): 568–94.

Lacher, Hannes. 1999. "The Politics of the Market: Re-reading Karl Polanyi." *Global Society* 13 (3): 313–26.

Lewis, Bernard. 2002. *What Went Wrong?* New York: Oxford University Press.

Löwy, Michael. 1996. *The War of Gods: Religion and Politics in Latin America*. New York: Verso.

Lynch, Celia. 2009. "A Neo-Weberian Approach to Religion in International Politics." *International Theory* 1 (3), 381–408.

Maddox, Marion. 2005. *God under Howard: The Rise of the Religious Right in Australia*. Allen and Unwin: Sydney.

Marois, Thomas and Lucia Pradella, eds. 2015. *Polarising Development—Introducing Alternatives to Neoliberalism and the Crisis*. London: Pluto Press.

Marshall, T. H. 1950. *Citizenship and Social Class*. Cambridge: Cambridge University Press.

McGrew, Anthony. 2013. "Globalization and Global Politics." In *The Globalization of World Politics: An Introduction to International Relations*, edited by Smith Steve and Patricia Owens, 15–34. Oxford: Oxford University Press.

McMichael, Philip. 2000. "Globalisation. Trend or Project?" In *Global Political Economy: Contemporary Perspectives*, edited by Ronen Palan, 100–113. London: Routledge.

Moghadam, Valentine M. 2002. "Violence, Terrorism and Fundamentalism: Some Feminist Observations." *Global Dialogue* 4 (2): 66–76.

Moghadam, Valentine M. 2007. "Book Review: Foucault and the Iranian Revolution: Gender and the Seductions of Islamism. By Janet Afary and Kevin B. Anderson. Chicago: University of Chicago Press, 2005." *Perspectives on Politics* 5 (1): 141–42.

Moghadam, Valentine M. 2009. *Globalization and Social Movements: Islamism, Feminism, and the Global Justice Movement*. Lanham, MD: Rowman & Littlefield.

Munck, Ronaldo. 2006. *Globalization and Contestation: The New Great Counter-Movement*. London: Routledge.

Norris, Pippa and Ronald Inglehart. 2010. "Are High Levels of Existential Security Conducive to Secularization?" Paper for Mid-West Political Science Association Annual Meeting, Chicago, April 22.

O'Brien, Robert and Marc Williams. 2010. *Global Political Economy: Evolution and Dynamics*. 3rd edn. Basingstoke: Palgrave Macmillan.

Okin, Susan Moller. 1999. *Is Multiculturalism Bad for Women?* Princeton University Press.

Overbeek, Henk and Kees Van der Pijl. 1993. "Restructuring Capital and Restructuring Hegemony: Neo-Liberalism and the Unmaking of the Post-War Order." In *Restructuring Hegemony in the Global Political Economy*, edited by Henk Overbeek, 1–27. London and New York: Routledge.

Owen, Suzanne. 2011. "The World Religions Paradigm: Time for a Change." *Arts and Humanities in Higher Education* 10 (3): 253–68.

Palmer, Tom G., ed. 2011. *The Morality of Capitalism: What Your Professors Won't Tell You*. Ottawa, IL: Jameson Books, Inc.

Phillips-Fein, Kim. 2010. *Invisible Hands: The Businessmen's Crusade Against the New Deal*. New York: W.W. Norton and Company.

Philpott, Daniel. 2002. "The Challenge of September 11 to Secularism in International Relations." *World Politics* 55 (1): 66–95.

Piketty, Thomas. 2014. *Capital in the 21st Century*. Cambridge: Harvard University Press.

Polanyi, Karl. 1957. *The Great Transformation*. Boston: Beacon Press.

Reynolds, Amy. 2013. "Networks, Ethics, and Economic Values: Faith-Based Business and the Coffee Trade in Central America." *Latin American Research Review* 48 (1): 112–32.

Riesebrodt, Martin. 2014. "Religion in the Modern World: Between Secularization and Resurgence." Max Weber Lecture Series. European University Institute, MWP-2014/01.

Rinehart, James F. 2004. "Religion in World Politics: Why the Resurgence?" *International Studies Review* 6 (2): 271–74.

Robinson, Phyllis. 2011. "To Tell the Truth: Who Owns Fair Trade?" *Fair World Project*. Accessed October 2, 2014. http://fairworldproject.org/voices-of-fair-trade/to-tell-the-truth-who-owns-fair-trade/.

Rodrik, Dani. 2007. "How to Save Globalization from its Cheerleaders." *Journal of International Trade and Diplomacy* 1 (2): 1–33.

Rudnyckyj, Daromir. 2009. "Spiritual Economies: Islam and Neoliberalism in Contemporary Indonesia." *Cultural Anthropology* 24 (1): 104–41.

Rupert, Mark. 2000. *Ideologies of Globalization: Contending Vision of a New World Order*. London: Routledge.

Schyff, Gerhard van der and Adriaan Overbeeke. 2011. "Exercising Religious Freedom in the Public Space." *European Constitutional Law Review* 7: 424–25.

Shawki, Noha. 2010. "Issue Frames and the Political Outcomes of Transnational Campaigns: A Comparison of the Jubilee 2000 Movement and the Currency Transaction Tax Campaign." *Global Society* 24 (2): 203–30.

Smith, Jackie. 2008. *Social Movements for Global Democracy*. Baltimore: John Hopkins University Press.

Soederberg, Susanne. 2014. *Debtfare States and the Poverty Industry: Money, Discipline and the Surplus Population*. London: Routledge.

Strange, Susan. 1996. *The Retreat of the State: The Diffusion of Power in the World Economy*. Cambridge: Cambridge University Press.

Stuckler, David and Sanjay Basu. 2014. *Quand l'austerité tue. Epidémies, depressions, suicides: l'économie inhumaine*. Paris: Autrement.

Thomas, Scott M. 2000. "Taking Religious and Cultural Pluralism Seriously: The Global Resurgence of Religion and the Transformation of International Society." *Millennium* 29 (3): 815–41.

Tuğal, Cihan. 2002. "Islamism in Turkey: Beyond Instrument and Meaning." *Economy and Society* 31 (1): 85–111.

Walter, Gregor, Marianne Beisheim, and Sabine Dreher. 2005. "Conceptual Considerations: Analytical Framework, Design and Methodology." In *Globalizing Interests. Pressure Groups and Denationalization*, edited by Michael Zürn with assistance of Gregor Walter, 39–64. New York: Suny Press.

Wendt, Alexander. 1992. "Anarchy Is what States Make of It: The Social Construction of Power Politics." *International Organization* 46 (2): 391–426.

Winfield, Richard Dien. 2007. *Modernity, Religion, and the War on Terror*. Aldershot, Hampshire, England: Ashgate.

Wilkinson, Richard and Kate Pickett. 2010. *The Spirit Level: Why Equality is Better for Everyone*. London: Penguin.

Yavuz, M. Hakan. 2003. *Islamic Political Identity in Turkey*. Oxford: Oxford University Press.

Yavuz, M. Hakan. 2013. *Towards an Islamic Enlightenment: The Gülen Movement*. Oxford: Oxford University Press.

Chapter 2

Historical and Theoretical Perspectives on Religion and Capitalism

Sabine Dreher, Peter J. Smith, and Edward Webb

This chapter will discuss the questions of sovereignty, secularization, and capitalism from a historical and theoretical perspective to complement the introduction that was more focused on the current debate in international relations (IR). Here we want to locate the IR debate within research in international political economy (IPE) and historical sociology as well as new research on secularization. In doing so, the chapter challenges the Eurocentric bias of much contemporary social science research. Too often it has been assumed that what was perceived to have happened in Europe could be universalized as a general process of human development. To understand modernity, state formation, the rise of capitalism, and the decline of religion from a European perspective was to know it everywhere. Yet, as this chapter argues, too often social scientists got it wrong, misled by the same "propaganda of the victors" as can be seen at work in the history of nineteenth-century Europe, where "the victors appeared to be rationalism, political economy, utilitarianism, science, liberalism" (Thompson 1993, xiv). Today it is increasingly clear that Europe was not the harbinger of things to come, but, rather, the exception (Casanova 2012).

In the first section, we highlight the limitations of the "Westphalian presumption" that is the usual starting point for the debate on religion in IR. In the second section, we argue that the "return" of "religion" can be more fruitfully understood by developing a differentiated understanding of secularization that gives room for religious activists and also provides a framework for their role in the public sphere. Lastly, the chapter calls for another look at both Weber's Eurocentric interpretations of the origin and development of capitalism and Marx's understanding of religion as a "theory of this world." The goal of the chapter is to highlight that the uncritical acceptance of traditional interpretations in the debate on religion has impoverished our understanding of the possible role of religious movements in IR and IPE. The chapter is an invitation to a debate. We hope it will, along with the chapters that follow, provide a good starting point for further reflection and conversation.

BECOMING MODERN: RELIGION, STATES, AND CAPITALISM

Institutional differentiation is seen as a hallmark of modernity, a process by which separate secular spheres—state, economy, and science—are freed from religious institutions, norms, and control. A key starting point in the analysis of this process is within the discipline of IR in its analysis of the secular Westphalian system centered on the modern state that emerged from the seventeenth century onward against the Catholic Church that also claimed sovereignty over territories and people. As the introduction has already shown, the dominant account in IR portrays "religion" as an intruder into this Westphalian secular system: "On September 11 the synthesis was shaken by . . . a figure whose identity is public religion—religion that is not privatized within the cocoon of the individual or the family but that dares to refashion secular politics and culture" (Philpott 2002, 67). But the conventional account of the history of the modern state system centered on the Treaty of Westphalia has been called into question by research in IPE, IR, and historical sociology.

According to the conventional account, the Treaty of Westphalia of 1648 ended thirty years of religious conflict in Europe and provided for the rise of the modern international system of sovereign states by ejecting religion from international affairs and confining it to the sphere of domestic politics. Philpott (1995) defines sovereignty as "supreme legitimate authority within a territory" (357). Internally, this authority implies complete sovereignty over all inhabitants and externally, independence from an outside authority, be it another country or church. No longer, for example, should there be interference in the religious preferences of other states. Bellin's (2008) overview of the literature summarizes the prevailing understanding well: "The historical experience of Westphalia indelibly associated the removal of religion with the establishment of international order and planted an enduring suspicion of injecting religion into international affairs" (318). Likewise, Thomas sees the idea that "religious and cultural pluralism cannot be accommodated in international society, but must be privatized, marginalized, or even overcome" as the key aspect of what he calls the "Westphalian presumption" in IR (Thomas 2000, 815). In this view, religion represents discord and violence, whereas sovereignty is associated with peace and reason. Peaceful coexistence of religion within a secular public sphere cannot be imagined.

There are several problems with this "Westphalian presumption." The first one has already been pointed out in the introduction: the assumption that religion equals violence whereas state sovereignty equals peace is simply wrong in the light of the history of secular repressive states such as Nazi Germany or the Communist regimes in Eastern Europe. Secular regimes or ideologies can be equally violent, as Cavanaugh (2009) points out. Here we are concerned with three further problems: 1648 as a marker for modernity is problematic; Westphalian states did not privatize religion to the extent claimed by scholars; and the sovereignty of the modern state was always significantly limited by the economic system. In modernity, the market makes sovereignty a myth.

The Nonmodernity of Westphalia

To begin with, the notion that the Peace of Westphalia in 1648 is the starting point for the modern state system defined by its sovereignty has been called into question (De Carvalho Leira and Hobson 2011, 738; Teschke 2006). "The notion of a golden age of sovereignty . . . in which states exerted full control over societies neatly delimited by territorial boundaries, is a myth," according to Lacher (2006, 8).

In fact, a state in the Westphalian sense of the term that has internal and external sovereignty emerged much earlier, according to Fukuyama (2011). Fukuyama's history singles out China because it had developed a state in the Weberian sense—establishing a monopoly on the legitimate use of force over a given territory—by 200 B.C. Europe was a latecomer in terms of state building. Indeed, for much of the history of agrarian civilizations, Europe was at the periphery and only belatedly accepted many innovations coming from elsewhere. It was only with the onset of industrial society in the late eighteenth century that it became the center of the world economy and global state system (Hodgson 1963). Any history of the international system that starts with the Westphalian assumption contributes to the general disregard for the developments of civilization that occurred before the onset of European hegemony and overlooks the slow development and accumulation of technical knowledge in preceding civilizations (such as writing, compass, gunpowder, numbers, money, and banking system) that made industrialization possible (Hodgson 1963). It is for this reason that Fukuyama (2011) changed the definition of the modern state to include not only sovereignty with its origin in China but also the rule of law with its initial beginning in Hinduism and accountability with its origin in Europe, thus distributing the slow development of the state over various regions of the world.

The second reason why 1648 is problematic as a marker for a modern sovereign state system is colonialism. The idea of a sovereign Westphalian state system overlooks the fact that most of the states in the system were not sovereign (Schmidt 1998, 123ff; Lawson and Shilliam 2009, 662). European powers colonized much of the planet and created a hierarchical relationship between themselves and the colonies. This process was essential to industrialization, as the commodities grown in the plantations of the tropical periphery fed the factories and workers of the core states (Mintz 1986). In other words, the sovereign state system only existed in the center and did not apply to the periphery (De Carvalho, Leira and Hobson 2011, 742). The Westphalian assumption leaves out the hierarchy institutionalized by colonial empires (that, incidentally, also assisted in, or even promoted deliberately, the spread of Christianity to other lands—see next section). From a "peripheral" point of view, the development of the modern state system is better described as integration into a system of exploitation. Such a starting point would also make it obvious why there are so many critical voices when it comes to the purported advantages of modernity.

Only if one understands that the majority of the planet was forcibly integrated into a world system can the many voices critical of this system be understood (Smith 2004). Such a vision of "sovereignty" also helps us to pay attention to the other organizational forms calling into question the sovereign nation-state norm such as the Islamic *umma*, pan-racial movements, regional formations such as the Bandung movement, transnational diaspora communities, transnational social movements, indigenous groupings, and cosmopolitanism. Indeed, the United Nations itself embodies this contradictory approach to sovereignty by, on the one hand, legitimizing the "Westphalian" state system and, on the other hand, developing a universal system of human rights that sets limits to the sovereign right of states (Lawson and Shilliam 2009, 664).

The Nonprivatization of Religion

Contrary to mainstream argumentation (Bellin 2008), Westphalia did not push religion into the private sphere, nor did it secularize international politics. Indeed, the Peace of Westphalia and the concept of sovereignty associated with it were shaped by religious thinking, aligning states with specific sectarian identities (Wilson 2011). Reformation theology, most notably articulated by Martin Luther, had argued for the separation of two realms, the spiritual and the temporal. In challenging the power of the Church, Reformation theology contributed to the development of the notion of sovereignty in IR. Moshe Halbertal (2012) has pointed to the parallel emergence of the seeds of modern nationalism (via divine right) in the shift of the locus of sacrifice from God to the state: in modern nation-states, a secular and political sacrifice for the nation as embodied in the state is generally considered legitimate. In other words, the secular is religious or is a form of religion, and we therefore need a better understanding of what, precisely, counts as religion

(Cavanaugh 2009). The latter raises the interesting question whether research on religion encompasses all the correct objects. If secular institutions such as the state and the market behave like gods (e.g., in demands for sacrifice in the name of nationalism or efficiency), then much of the focus of research on religion may overlook some important "real religions" in a society.

A closer look at some so-called secular states shows that they have, in fact, instrumentalized religion for their nation-state building project. A model example in this context is Turkey, which is often portrayed as successful because of its secularism. But Turkey, in fact, did not abolish official religion as such. Ataturk's reforms sought to suppress independent civil forms of Islam, but they also established a religious directorate (later ministry) that appoints Imams to mosques and to this day writes their sermons. Ataturk created a form of state Islam and outlawed folk Islam. Webb therefore has classified this not as a secular regime but as a form of religious Jacobinism where religion serves to build the nation in a specific image (Webb 2007). Kuru (2009) classified the Turkish model as assertive secularism, like that of France, but also noted the difference in the details of the two countries' institutional control of religion. His useful classificatory scheme that distinguishes between assertive and passive secularism highlights that many European states, far from being secular or antireligious, have, in fact, established churches, where religion remains part of the governing order. In other words, the notion that the Westphalian system systematically privatized religion and abolished public forms of religion needs to be relativized in the light of the fact that even in very modern states such as Britain, the head of the state is also the head of the Church.

"Religion" was also very much a key ingredient in international politics after Westphalia. The missionary activity of the colonizing states has already been mentioned above—it largely accounts for Catholicism's dominance in Latin America today (though it is challenged by Pentecostalism) and the global dominance of Christianity in general. Another example is the Ottoman Empire that had to suffer frequent interference by foreign powers with regard to its Christian subjects under the system of capitulations. These were primarily economic treaties with provisions through which minorities in the Ottoman Empire came under foreign protectorship. Stipulations such as these allowed, for example, Britain to insist on greater religious freedom in the Ottoman Empire than existed at home (Berkes 1964, 151). It also had consequences for the ability of the Ottoman state to protect itself against foreign competition (Ahmad 2000, 5) as it created a class of citizens not under state control. The capitulations can be studied as an example of how religion was instrumentalized by all Western states in the exercise of foreign policy. France consistently maintained its role as protector of Catholics in the Middle East, appointed as such by the Pope, despite its own transitions through many regime types following the revolution of 1789. This even survived the law of 1905 separating Church and State, and helped drive French actions in post-Ottoman Lebanon and Syria in the inter-War years.

Capitalism and Westphalian System

Some interpretations of the concept of sovereignty in historical sociology decouple it from Westphalian sysytem and see its development in terms of its relationship to technological developments and the growth of an industrial capitalist economy in the nineteenth and twentieth centuries. Osiander (2001), for example, argues that the concept of sovereignty was refined much later, in the nineteenth and twentieth centuries. Rosenberg (1994) is another advocate for a later starting date for modernity, pointing to the violent nature of the creation of what he calls the "empire of civil society" (160). He sees the nineteenth century as the true origin of today's modern world system, as it finalized and completed the colonization of the globe by European powers and created a hierarchical world economy (163). Furthermore, the process of the creation of "sovereign" states in Europe was gradual, preceded by technological processes (e.g., transportation and communication), which provided greater powers to central administrations over their territories. In particular, it was the rise of more densely integrated economic circuits of production and exchange that funded the central administration and expression of sovereign control. In other words, we need to understand, according to Lacher (2006, 10–11), that capitalism has been from the start a "transnational form of economy and society. Even during the age of imperialism and protectionism, or at the height of the welfare state in the postwar period, the nation-state never 'contained' the economy and society to the degree implied by the proponents of the globalization thesis and defenders of classical state-centrism alike."

Today, however, capitalism has morphed into a dysfunctional system. Soros—the investor who forced Great Britain to leave the European Exchange rate mechanism in 1992—even proclaimed that "the main enemy of open society . . . is no longer the communist but the capitalist threat" (1997). Similarly, for Walzer (1984, 322), unlimited economic power threatens the democratic process and the political system. However, the way in which capitalism can undermine democracy does not receive even a small fraction of the attention in the Western academy given to the religious challenge to the modern state. This seems misguided, since some researchers even link the roots of the threat from religious extremism to the dysfunctional system that global capitalism has become (e.g., Rogers 2000; Ayoob 2007). Reforming global capitalism, then, could lead to a reduction in political and religious extremism.

Taking up the idea developed in the previous section about the conceptual confusion surrounding religion, it may be time to study capitalism as a religious phenomenon, where we observe that in the name of structural adjustment, human lives and living standards are sacrificed to satisfy international financial institutions and banks (see introduction). This is why Agamben takes up Walter Benjamin's fragment on *Capitalism as Religion* (Benjamin 1991) to conclude that capitalism is

> the most fierce, implacable and irrational religion that has ever existed because it recognizes neither truces nor redemption. A permanent worship is celebrated in its name, a worship whose liturgy is labor and its object, money. God did not die; he was transformed into money. (Agamben 2012)[1]

This section has shown that the Westphalian assumption needs to be questioned. It does not capture the process of state formation. It does not reflect the role of religion in modern states and international politics. And it overlooks the fact that economic actors have challenged and manipulated the "sovereign" state from the very beginning—there are significant economic limits on sovereignty in modern societies created by "the economy." On the other hand, complicating the Westphalian myth of a secular international order composed of sovereign nation-states does not mean abandoning all notions of secularization or all attempts to differentiate between religious and nonreligious economic orders. Irrespective of the idea of post-secularity (see below), it should have become clear from the introduction that the contemporary global economic system has not dramatically been influenced by religious ideas of moral justice. Nor have political systems reverted *en masse* to religious forms (the Iranian revolution is still an exception). One must be cautious in speaking of a return of religion globally—the religious and secular coexist in economics and politics alike.

SECULARIZATION—TOWARD A DIFFERENTIATED APPROACH

The simplified theory of secularization held that religion would disappear in the process of modernization as the progress of rationalization and reason would make the reliance on magical thinking and belief unnecessary. This would affect both individuals and society (Berger 1999, 2–3). Many intellectuals in the nineteenth century were convinced that this would happen. Auguste Comte developed positivism with the argument that human society would outgrow theology and replace it with a science of sociology to make moral judgments (Stark 1999, 250). Berger, a prominent sociologist, wrote in

1968: "By the 21st century, religious believers are likely to be found only in small sects, huddled together to resist a worldwide secular culture" (quoted in Stark 1999, 25). In contrast, in 1999, Berger concluded that the secularization theory needed to be revised because the world today "is as furiously religious as it ever was, and in some places more so than ever" (2). This observation has led some observers to claim that we now live in an age of post-secularism (Mavelli and Petito 2012). But the idea of post-secularism is the secularization thesis merely in reverse, and suffers from the original's flaws of overgeneralization from Western experience and of unnuanced determinism. What is needed is a differentiated understanding of secularization.

As the previous section has already highlighted, there have been many varieties of secularization processes that resulted in many different forms of secularism. In some states, an established church where the head of state acts also as head of church, such as in England, remained while in others, such as in France, the Catholic Church was pushed out of public life more or less completely. The idea of religion receding and being pushed to the private sphere was therefore too simple-minded an interpretation of secularization to begin with. It is considerations like this that led Casanova (1994) to propose a disaggregation of the theory of secularization into three components (see also Dobbelaere 2002).

The first component concerns *institutional separation or differentiation*. Should religious authorities and norms have authority over the state, over the economy, over the sciences? Secularization here refers to the question whether religious teachings should apply to economic, political, and many cultural affairs. This component of sphere differentiation is generally left in place by most religious activists. The discussion of post-secularism is therefore premature. The second component is concerned with *individual religiosity*. It asks how many individuals in a given society consider themselves as religious. It also questions to what extent religiosity has changed and taken on new forms or changed in doctrine (Dobbelaere 2002, 21). Secularization would mean that more and more individuals do not identify themselves as religious. The third component deals with the relationship of religious movements and their *involvement in politics*. Should religion be a private affair or do believers have a right to participate in the public debate and if so in what way? It is this last question that has become especially contested in Western societies over the last thirty years, and where Casanova (1994) proposes a three-fold distinction of public religion (see below). Secularization then is composed of three dimensions that are independent from each other: institutional separation of spheres, degree of individual religiosity, and involvement in politics (public sphere). We may have secularization in one of these spheres but not in others in a given society.

Casanova (2012) argues that "such an analytical distinction enables testing each of the three subtheses separately as different empirically falsifiable propositions" (25). This allows, for example, to recognize that in the United States there was secularization through differentiation but not necessarily a decline of individual religiosity, nor did religion retreat into the private sphere. It allows for a comparison of the institutional differentiation across time and space and to develop research questions with regard to regime type and religious beliefs (e.g., Kuru 2009). It also shows that institutional separation is not a prerequisite for democracy. There are states with an established religion that are democratic (e.g., Great Britain) whereas others are not (e.g., Saudi Arabia and Iran). The relationship between religion and democracy is therefore open-ended (Casanova 2012, 30–31).

In other words, this disaggregation of secularization allows us to see that religious social movements by being simply religious do not necessarily undermine modernity, democracy, or secularism, in contrast to what some secularists claim. Instead, following Casanova, we need to differentiate the process of secularization into different aspects and be more nuanced in our discussion as to what role religious social movements can play in a modern society.

In this context, Casanova made a second proposition arguing for a dissolution of the simple dichotomy of public versus private in favor of an understanding with more and finer distinctions. He argued that there are three different possible ways for a religion to enter the public sphere, to become a public religion. It could be an *established religion* such as a state church and therefore be a part of the state and thus impose its vision as mandatory (or in a state defined as secular, it could remain separate). Second, religious movements could be working at the level of *political society* and trying to influence the political process through lobbying, social movement activity, or even within political parties. Lastly, public religions could remain at the level of *civil society* and participate in public discussions or offer services. Of course, in reality, these categories would often be mixed but, overall, they show that religious activists can enter the public sphere in manifold ways (Casanova 2012, 27).

Neoconservatives and many feminists are rightly concerned with the entry of religion into the public sphere as there are, indeed, in all religions (see Juergensmeyer 2008), movements that are extremist and that seek to justify limits on women's or lesbian, gay, bisexual, and transgender (LGBT) rights. There is in this limited sense a clash between some specific forms of religious convictions and liberal feminism and LGBT activism, and there are, indeed, religious movements that deny the legitimacy of the liberal order. These movements may be fruitfully studied in the context of other illiberal movements and how modern democracies have dealt with them. Thus, even if there is no automatic link between religion and authoritarianism, individual religious social groups may be assessed as dangerous to the public order, much as extremist political groups are assessed as threats to public order. Such an approach allows for the open discussion of the terms of participation of religious actors in a pluralistic public sphere. Religious freedom has to be strong enough to allow individuals to renounce or accept a specific religious conviction. There must be rules for missionary activities in a given context to avoid the imposition of religious beliefs on others. Religious activists will have to accept the idea of "free exercise" of all religions within a public sphere (Casanova 2012, 30) and cannot demand exemptions in all areas with the claim to "religious rights." Overall, Casanova's framework allows us to move away from simple dichotomies and to develop a more differentiated approach.

Unfortunately, Casanova does not discuss economics. His typology of public religion only includes "political" activism. There is no discussion of how religious groups have interacted with the economic order, even though there is a long history of the interaction between religion and the free market. Initially this developed in opposition. As Tawney's (1938) study showed, in the European context, religious control of the economy stood in the way of unimpeded profit making in free markets since it allowed the Catholic Church to maintain its wealth (68); this included a complete acceptance of feudal serfdom by the Church (69). To move from feudalism to a capitalist society thus required a complete change in society and its mentality for some religions, especially Catholicism. Religious actors and institutions have responded to economic change in a variety of ways. Following Casanova's model, we may suggest a similar three-fold typology (civil society, economic national society, and state) of the economic activism that seems to be undertaken by religious social movements.

Religious movements may create firms and economic organizations that are shaped by their religious beliefs. These may even be profit-oriented and may serve the purpose of financing the activities of the group. The Hizmet community is one such example wherein interfaith activities are financed through entrance fees or other charges associated with the activities in the organization. In a similar vein, the sale of "salvation wares" (see Upadhyay) serves to finance the religious activities of the religious group or movement—while Wilkinson and Asonzeh also highlight that the prosperity gospel has allowed individual pastors to prosper through the sale of properties, media, and seminars. But not all religious entrepreneurship necessarily supports neoliberal capitalism. The Catholic Church provides examples of economic institutions in support of local economies as opposed to the interest of faraway corporations. This has led to the creation and support of cooperative enterprises such as Mondragon in Spain, which was founded by a priest. Cooperatives are enterprises, to quote Pope Francis, "where capital does not have command over men, but men over capital" (Schneider 2015).

Religious movements may create institutional mechanisms to support the market participation of their adherents. They may create economic associations that start influencing economic policies, or they may lobby for better economic policies as a religious movement. And they may even replace the market with a religious form of economy, which would be an abandonment of the institutional separation of spheres and, indeed, pose a challenge to secular, economic modernity. Such a merger of spheres may seem necessary from many First Nations perspectives, for instance, where nature is seen as spiritual and where the exercise of private property rights desacralizes nature—this conflict between these two different views of nature is at the core of the fight against pipelines in Canada (see also the Scauso chapter for the Bolivian debate).

At the level of the national or global economy, religious movements may also use religious arguments in order to maintain power in their pursuit of specific policies, as in the case of the Justice and Development Party (AKP) in Turkey. But this also means that religious movements have a right to voice their objection to particular interpretations and aspects of capitalist development, with which they disagree. The Jubilee Debt Cancellation campaign made it clear to everybody that the debt burden of many countries was unbearable and that this needed to be changed (see introduction). This is not a threat to a secular economy and a demand for a retreat to a premodern economy, but a contribution on the governance process of the existing neoliberal world economy.

Neoliberalism is challenging and transforming religions today. While Casanova acknowledges that globalization greatly affects world religions, he does not address a key aspect of globalization: the challenge posed by neoliberal global capitalism, and religions' response to it. While this typology is by no means complete, it could serve as a starting point for further studies in the way religious movements are active at different levels. The last section returns to the fundamental paradox of religious activity in global capitalism: there are religious groups who actively promote further neoliberal globalization while there are also groups who are opposed to it. How do we account for this Janus-faced aspect of religion in today's world?

RELIGION IN SOCIOLOGICAL THEORY: MARX AND WEBER

Karl Marx and Max Weber are two theorists whose approaches to religion have been interpreted in a very specific way that has given rise to more misunderstandings than clarity. Weber's argument on the origin of capitalism has been used to dismiss whole societies as incapable of development. Marx is famous for the idea that religion is opium for the people and for the subsequent summary dismissal of religious activists as deluded and in need of reeducation (e.g., under Communist regimes). The perspectives of these two thinkers are still influential in our understanding of religion today (see also Wilkinsoon and Upadhyay, this volume). But, as this section highlights, there is a serious need for reconsideration.

Max Weber famously posited that development depends on ideas. Up until 1800 there was a rough equality in economic terms in the global economy. But at the end of the century, Britain, the United States, Australia, Canada, and Argentina "had per capita incomes 10 times those in Asia and India. By the mid-1900s, on a per capita basis, the developed countries were about 20 times richer than the non-oil exporting Third World" (Schwartz 2000, 43). The modern capitalist world economy does not produce convergence, but "divergence, big time" as Pritchett has pointed out (1997). The question posed by Weber is how to understand and explain the development of the economic system that made this divergence possible. His answer—that it is due to Calvinism—has been misleading scholars ever since, at least those who have never really read the original where he clearly points out that he in no way should be interpreted as having posited a direct causal connection between Calvinism and capitalism (Weber 2001, 49).

In his descriptions of other religions, however, there is a tendency to overplay the impediments in Catholicism, Hinduism, Buddhism, Confucianism, and Islam toward the development of free markets and downplay them with regard to Calvinism or Protestantism (Parkin 1982, 63–64; see also Novak 1993). Some of the chapters in this book highlight that religious traditions contain teachings that support rational behavior in favor of the free market (Upadhyay, Webb, Dreher, Marei; see also Parkin 1982, 64). It is for this reason that this book has moved away from an understanding of religion as "world religion" to propose a constructivist social movement approach to the study of religion (see introduction). Such an approach allows scholars to bypass orientalist and Eurocentric assumptions and focus more on the concrete and everyday experiences and practices of religiosity.

Lastly, by putting the emphasis on internal factors such as religion, by *de facto* blaming poor countries for their poverty, today's Weberians ignore the existence of a global economic system into which all societies are integrated and whose rules are set by the most powerful actors in the system—advanced industrialized states, international financial institutions, and banks—and whose path has been laid by colonization (Waltz 2000, 14–18). Wade (2003) has demonstrated the degree to which the current rules of the system impede national policies that promote economic development, but in general, the organization of the global economy centered on a hegemonic country makes development more difficult or has even led to underdevelopment itself (Schwartz 2000). Even Huntington in his 1993 article understood that global governance and economic processes disfavor the Global South, and at the end of his article he called for a deeper study of such alternative understandings. In other words, countries find themselves in a global economy whose rules they did not write, where they have no say in the global governance but are required to conform; national policies therefore often do not have much of a room for maneuver. To ascribe the blame for underdevelopment to religion is therefore extremely problematic. Instead, it is time to study religious activism more systematically as one possible expression of resistance to Western domination of the global system (Ayoob 2007), as a "general theory of this world," to quote Karl Marx, that does not necessarily lead to emancipation in the critical theory sense but may end up producing different forms of domination and exploitation.

For Marx, the withering away of religion was an inevitable consequence of socialist consciousness as he wrote in the *Economic and Philosophic Manuscripts of 1844* because religion led to resignation, whereas the spread of socialism would lead to activism and social change (Tucker, Marx, and Engels 1978, 92–3). In contrast, some of his twentieth-century intellectual descendants, like Max Horkheimer, struggled with the problem of a possible moral void at the heart of Enlightenment thought and the instrumental reason it had spawned, the very genius that had given birth to scientific and economic progress, but also to mass extermination. In a powerful essay written late in his life, "Theism and Atheism" (1963), Horkheimer saw in "honest theism" the possibility of resistance to "totalitarian rule of whatever denomination" and noted that "theism is again becoming an actual force in the period of its decline." Having despaired of instrumental reason, he saw "hope that, in the period of world history which is now beginning, the period of docile masses governed by clocks, some men can still be found to offer resistance, like the victims of the past and, among them, the founder of Christianity" (Horkheimer [1963]1994, 49; for a critique, see Habermas 2002).

There is then a dual understanding of religion within Marxism: religion has both an incitement and a resignation dimension (Achcar 2009, 58). Unfortunately, Marx and Marxism have focused mostly on the role of religion as justifying prevailing exploitative political and economic orders where religion is used to make misery palatable to present hope for salvation after death. It is for this reason that Marx condemned religious thought. He was convinced that a good life can be created on earth and that religious activists stand in the way of movement for change. This is behind his famous introduction to the *Critique of Hegel's Philosophy of Right*, where he writes: "Religion is the sigh of the oppressed creature, the heart of a heartless world, and the soul of soulless conditions. It is the opium of the people" (Tucker, Marx, and Engels 1978, 54). This quote is usually used to make the claim that Marxism supposedly ignores the role of ideas. This, however, only holds true if one ignores the context of this citation. The context is that for Marx, religion is also "the general theory of this world." This citation actually is an invitation to seriously study religion in order to understand how the world works. Why are so many people accepting the idea that the world is a miserable place and that salvation will come after death? It is this question that led to the criticism of religion as fundamental to the criticism of politics and society for Marx. After all, his frustration with philosophy was that it analyzed social conditions without changing them. For Marx, analysis must move to action, to praxis. What he unfortunately overlooked is that many religious people took this step with him and developed serious criticism of the functioning of their societies, taking initiatives to change conditions, before and since. It is not necessary to go through a criticism of religion to arrive at a criticism of society. On the contrary, many religious activists criticize society and the economy on the basis of religious texts (Bryant 1996).

Marx's severe criticism of religion also stems from the fact that the Protestant Reformation in Germany consolidated the authority and power of the princes over peasants when Martin Luther, the most prominent German instigator of the Reformation, sided with the aristocracy during the Peasant War. As Marx writes in the introduction to the *Critique of Hegel's Philosophy of Right*, while Luther represents an important step toward individualism, his siding with the aristocracy during the Peasant War meant that a real individualism for peasants to be free from feudal exploitation became impossible (Tucker, Marx and Engels 1978, 61). It is here that we find "religion" firmly on the side of authority with Luther's condemnation of the peasant revolt (Luther 1525). From a Marxist perspective, the Protestant Revolution prevented a more profound economic and social revolution in Germany that would also extend freedom to peasants. Unfortunately, Marx's criticism of religion was then taken to extremes under Communist regimes. It is therefore ironic that the oppressive Communist regimes were brought down also in part by the courage of religious people supporting the resistance (Kazimerz 2006).

CONCLUSION

The goal of this chapter has been to raise questions with regard to religion, secularization, the nature of the Westphalian state system, and capitalism, and to point to the need for a more systematic debate, instead of relying on traditional assumptions. Globalization and the accompanying transformation of politics, economics, and culture have increased the need to be more nuanced as researchers. We therefore hope that this chapter shows where there is debate and a need for reconsiderations.

Specifically, we have pointed toward the need to reconsider the Westphalian assumption that consists of several interrelated propositions: modernity started with 1648 in Europe; religion in modernity was privatized and needs to stay so; and the state is sovereign. Against these assumptions we have argued that the sovereign state was, in fact, already in existence in China in 200 B.C., religion was never privatized and has been used consistently as a tool of foreign policy, and if capitalism is allowed to threaten or overtake politics, then it is open to question who poses the more serious threat to politics—religious activists, or an economy that is out of control.

We also point toward the need to refrain from simple assumptions about the end of secularization and the emergence of a post-secular society. Just because we now have religious activists in the public sphere, this does not imply that secularization has ended. We therefore propose, following Casanova, to differentiate secularization into the institutional, political, and civil or societal dimension and to suggest that today secularization can occur at all levels in different ways. This allows us to take account of the high level of religiosity in a secular state such as the United States and of secular society coexisting with an established religion as found in Great Britain.

Lastly, Max Weber's assumptions about non-Western societies and their assumed inability to develop modern capitalism need to be questioned in the light of the development of modern forms of capitalism in the Islamic world or in India. Instead of pontificating about the incompatibility of "Islam" with "capitalism," it would be better henceforth to be more differentiated in the analysis of both. There are Islamic capitalists and there are various forms of capitalism such as neoliberal capitalism. In the same vein, Marx did not ignore the importance of religious ideas. To the contrary, he took them very seriously, which may explain his vehement rejection of a religion that promises liberation and freedom only after death and his insistence that human beings can have a decent life on earth while they are still alive. As we have shown, there are many religious activists who agree with him, and the insistent secularism that is displayed by many on the left may be in need of reconsideration in the face of religious activists who call for a fundamental transformation of the modern economy.

Ultimately, there is a need to consider some forms of religiosity as an expression of the legacy of colonialism and the need for a deeper decolonization and independence. Religious revival can be a form of a political theory or critique and needs to be taken more seriously as a reflection on the type of world order currently in place. In other words, had there been no colonization, specific Islamic religious activists might have appeared in a very different light or might not even have existed. Muslim-majority societies might have been able to keep their historical balance between the religious and the secular order (Mardin 2000, 103–104, for the Turkish case). This balance was dramatically destroyed by colonization, leaving religion to assume the legacy. Taking colonization and its legacy seriously would allow IR and IPE to move toward a global discipline that no longer perpetuates the violence that lies at their origin (Smith 2004). In conclusion, old certainties about Westphalia and a Western-dominated order, a dysfunctional capitalist system, and secularization in the midst of an economy that has turned into a vengeful god need to be considered in a new light in order to fully appreciate and understand the various roles of religious activists in the current world order. We hope that this chapter serves as a starting point for further reflection.

NOTE

1. There is an interesting quote by Jacques Maritain, writing in 1930 from a Catholic perspective, who came to the same conclusion: "The economic has as its end the acquisition and increase without limit of material riches as such. And all which can promote this end—even an injustice, even oppressive and inhumane conditions of life—is *economically* good." Quoted in Viner 1978, 122. Emphasis in original.

REFERENCES

Achcar, Gilbert. 2009. "Religion and Politics Today from a Marxian Perspective." *Socialist Register*. London: Merlin Press.

Agamben, Giorgio. 2012. "God Didn't Die, He Was Transformed into Money." An Interview with Giorgio Agamben by Peppe Sava, *libcom.org*, accessed July 14, 2015.

Ahmad, Feroz. 2000. "Ottoman Perceptions of the Capitulations 1800–1914." *Journal of Islamic Studies* 11 (1): 1–20.

Ayoob, Mohammed. 2007. "Challenging Hegemony: Political Islam and the North-South Divide." *International Studies Review* 9 (4): 629–43.

Bellin, Eva. 2008. "Faith in Politics." *World Politics* 60 (2): 315–47.

Benjamin, Walter. 1991. "Kapitalismus als Religion [Fragment]." In *Gesammelte Schriften, Hrsg.: Rolf Tiedemann und Hermann Schweppenhäuser*, 7 Bde, Frankfurt am Main: Suhrkamp, 1. Auflage, 1991, Bd. VI, S. 100–102.

Berger, Peter L. 1999. "The Desecularization of the World: A Global Overview." In *The Desecularization of the World: Resurgent Religion and World Politics*, edited by Peter L. Berger, 1–18. Washington, DC: W.B. Eerdmans.

Berkes, Niyazi. 1964. *The Development of Secularism in Turkey*. Montréal: McGill-Queen's Press.

Bryant, Chris. 1996. *Possible Dreams: A Personal History of the British Christian Socialists*. London: Hodder and Stoughton.

Casanova, Jose. 2012. "Rethinking Public Religions." In *Rethinking Religion and World Affairs*, edited by Timothy Samuel Shah, Alfred Stepan and Monica Duffy Toft. doi:10.1093/acprof:oso/9780199827978.003.0003, Oxford Scholarship Online.

Casanova, Jose. 1994. *Public Religions in the Modern World.* Chicago, IL: University of Chicago Press.

Cavanaugh, William T. 2009. *The Myth of Religious Violence: Secular Ideology and the Roots of Modern Conflict.* Oxford: Oxford University Press.

De Carvalho, Benjamin, Halvard Leira, and John M. Hobson. 2011. "The Big Bangs of IR: The Myths That Your Teachers Still Tell You About 1648 and 1919." *Millennium* 39 (3): 735–58.

Dobbelaere, Karel. 2002. *Secularization: An Analysis at Three Levels.* Brussels: Peter Lang.

Fox, Jonathan and Shmuel Sandler. 2004. *Bringing Religion into International Relations.* London: Palgrave Macmillan.

Fukuyama, Francis. 2011. *The Origins of Political Order: From Prehuman Times to the French Revolution.* London: Profile Books.

Habermas, Jürgen. 2002. *Religion and Rationality: Essays on Reason, God, and Modernity.* Cambridge, MA: The MIT Press.

Halbertal, Moshe. 2012. *On Sacrifice.* Princeton, NJ: Princeton University Press.

Hodgson, Marshall G. S. 1963. "The Interrelations of Societies in History." *Comparative Studies in Society and History* 5 (2): 227–50.

Horkheimer, Max. [1963] 1994. "Theism and Atheism," in *Critique of Instrumental Reason.* New York: Continuum, 34–50.

Huntington, Samuel P. 1993. "The Clash of Civilizations?" *Foreign Affairs* 72: 22–49.

Juergensmeyer, Mark. 2008. *Global Rebellion: Religious Challenges to the Secular State. From Christian Militias to Al Qaeda.* Berkeley: University of California Press.

Kazimierz, Sowa. 2006. "Dissent and Civil Society in Poland." *Journal of Interdisciplinary Studies* 18 (1–2): 57–74.

Kuru, Ahmet. 2009. *Secularism and State Policies toward Religion: The United States, France, and Turkey.* Cambridge, UK: Cambridge University Press.

Lacher, Hannes. 2006. *Beyond Globalization: Capitalism, Territoriality and the International Relations of Modernity.* London: Routledge.

Lawson, George and Robbie Shilliam. 2009. "Beyond Hypocrisy? Debating the 'Fact' and 'Value' of Sovereignty in Contemporary World Politics." *International Politics* 46 (6): 657–70.

Luther, Martin. 1525. *Wider die Mordischen und Reubischen Rotten der Bawren (Against the Murderous, Thieving Hordes of Peasants).* Wittemberg.

Mardin, Serif. 2000. *The Genesis of Young Ottoman Thought: A Study in the Modernization of Turkish Political Ideas.* Syracuse, NY: Syracuse University Press.

Marx, Karl and Friedrich Engels. 1848. *Manifesto of the Communist Party.* Online: https://www.marxists.org.

Mavelli, Luca and Fabio Petito. 2012. "The Post-secular in International Relations: An Overview." *Review of International Studies* 38 (5): 931–42.

Mintz, Sidney W. 1986. *Sweetness and Power: The Place of Sugar in Modern History.* New York: Penguin.

Novak, Michael. 1993. *The Catholic Ethic and the Spirit of Capitalism.* New York: The Free Press.

Osiander, Andreas. 2001. "Sovereignty, International Relations, and the Westphalian Myth." *International Organization* 55 (2): 251–87.

Parkin, Frank. 1982. *Max Weber*, revised edition. London: Routledge.

Philpott, Daniel. 2002. "The Challenge of September 11 to Secularism in International Relations." *World Politics* 55 (1): 66–95.

Philpott, Daniel. 1995. "Sovereignty: An Introduction and Brief History." *Journal of International Affairs* 48 (2): 353–68.

Pritchett, Lant. 1997. "Divergence, Big Time." *The Journal of Economic Perspectives* 11 (3): 3–17.

Rogers, Paul. 2000. *Losing Control: Global Security in the Twenty-First Century.* London: Pluto Press.

Rosenberg, Justin. 1994. *The Empire of Civil Society: A Critique of the Realist Theory of International Relations.* London: Verso.

Schmidt, Brian. 1998. *The Political Discourse of Anarchy: A Disciplinary History of International Relations.* New York: Suny Press.

Schneider, Nathan. 2015. "How Pope Francis Is Reviving Radical Catholic Economics." *The Nation*, online edition, September 9, 2015, thenation.com, accessed September 20, 2015.

Schwartz, Herman M. 2000. *States Versus Markets: The Emergence of a Global Economy.* London: Macmillan.

Smith, Steve. 2004. "Singing Our World into Existence: International Relations Theory and September 11." *International Studies Quarterly* 48 (3): 499–515.

Soros, George. 1997. "The Capitalist Threat." *The Atlantic Monthly* 279 (2): 45–58.

Stark, R. 1999. "Secularization, R.I.P." *Sociology of Religion* 60 (3): 249–73.

Tawney, Richard H. 1938. *Religion and the Rise of Capitalism.* London: Peregrine.

Teschke, B. 2006. "Debating 'The Myth of 1648': State Formation, the Interstate System and the Emergence of Capitalism in Europe—A Rejoinder." *International Politics* 43 (5): 531–73.

Thomas, Scott M. 2000. "Taking Religious and Cultural Pluralism Seriously: The Global Resurgence of Religion and the Transformation of International Society." *Millennium* 29 (3): 815–41.

Thompson, Edward P. 1993. *Witness Against the Beast: William Blake and the Moral Law.* New York: The New Press.

Tucker, Robert C., Karl Marx, and Friedrich Engels. 1978. *The Marx-Engels Reader.* New York: Norton.

Viner, Jacob. 1978. "Secularizing Tendencies in Catholic Social Thought from the Renaissance to the Jansenist-Jesuit Controversy." In *Religious Thought and Economic Society: Four Chapters of an Unfinished Work by Jacob Viner*, edited by Jacques Melitz and Donald Winch, 114–52. Durham: Duke University Press.

Wade, Robert H. 2003. "What Strategies Are Viable for Developing Countries Today? The World Trade Organization and the Shrinking of 'Development Space.'" *Review of International Political Economy* 10 (4): 621–44.

Waltz, Kenneth. 2000. "Structural Realism after the Cold War." *International Security* 25 (1): 5–41.

Walzer, Michael. 1984. "Liberalism and the Art of Separation." *Political Theory* 12 (3): 315–30.

Weber, Max. 2001. *The Protestant Ethic and the Spirit of Capitalism.* Translated by Talcott Parsons, with an introduction by Anthony Giddens. London: Routledge.

Webb, Edward. 2007. "Civilizing Religion: Jacobin Projects of Secularization in Turkey, France, Tunisia, and Syria." PhD diss., University of Pennsylvania.

Wilson, Erin K. 2011. *After Secularism: Rethinking Religion in Global Politics.* London: Palgrave Macmillan.

Chapter 3

Religious Demographic Trends

Patterns of Growth and Decline, 1950–2010

Davis Brown

Religion has been one of, if not, the most understudied and undertheorized phenomena in the social sciences including political science. This could be due to the *prima facie* incompatibility of the rational processes of social scientific inquiry with the seeming irrationality of belief in the transcendental or supernatural. Particularly in the field of international relations, scholars have neglected the role of religion in generating political preferences and outcomes while focusing on more materially quantifiable factors such as military spending, industrial output, regime type, proximity, and time. Indeed, Douglas Johnston and Cynthia Sampson (1994) labeled religion as the "missing dimension of statecraft" in the title of their book. Only in the last twenty years has the field begun to recognize (1) the superficiality of the treatment of religion as irrational, and (2) that religion's effects on political preferences are real and observable, independent of the rationality and observability of religion itself. Hence, religion has experienced a "resurgence" of attention in the field (Thomas 2005; Snyder 2011; Toft, Philpott and Shah 2011).

Despite the field's new attention to religion, mid-level theorizing and empirical inquiry has been hampered severely by a lack of usable data to determine empirically whether religion influences political preferences and thus shapes foreign policy. Ironically, existing data on religious demographics and other state-level religious characteristics are reasonably ample. However, until recently the existing datasets on religion had proved inadequate for the task of making large-N empirical measurements. Specifically, there have been two obstacles.

The first one has been how to operationalize religion. Most data sources are limited to the religious identity of populations (percent Christian, Muslim, Buddhist, etc.). Religious demographics has the benefit of being one of the most objective indicators for measuring religion in terms of the number of people belonging to a specific religious tradition (whether so classified by states' governments or not). However, I readily concede that demographics alone cannot account for other religious factors that may affect political preferences more directly. One such factor is religiosity, that is, degree of faith (see World Values Survey Association 2009). If the population is particularly devout and the governmental officials are a microcosm of the population, then we should expect governmental policy to reflect the values of the most devoutly followed religion. Another is Government Involvement in Religion (GIR; Fox 2008, 2009), measuring the extent to which religion and the state are intertwined. This feature may take the form of either religious influence on government policy, or government influence on the policies of religious organizations or even suppression of them. A third factor is Government Religious Preference (GRP; Brown 2015a), measuring the degree to which a government is favorably disposed toward a religion by conferring on it official status, supporting religious education, providing financial support and lightening its regulatory burdens, and/or suppressing nonfavored religions. This measurement of the favoring of a religion serves as a natural proxy for measuring the extent of that religion's influence on the government's preferences, policies, and decisions.

This chapter is agnostic as to whether religious demographics are reflections of any of the other religious factors enumerated above. It does not follow that changes in demographics indicate changes in religiosity. It is certainly a possibility, most likely in the case of the rapid growth of a newly introduced religion. However, countries' religious demographics also change through migration patterns and birth rates. For example, the decline of Judaism in Morocco and the concurrent growth of Islam is primarily the result of Jews emigrating to Israel and that population not being replaced; therefore, it does not necessarily follow that Morocco's remaining Jews are less fervent and the majority Muslim population more fervent. Nevertheless, this chapter helps us understand the changes or the continuity in the adherence of a particular religious tradition over time. The best operationalization of religion available to the field now that is also conducive to large-N statistical measurements across space and time is the populations and percentages of adherents of selected religions.

The second obstacle to large-N empirical measurements of religion has been that no single dataset has provided coverage that is broad, deep, and consistent. Datasets need breadth in their coverage of many major world religions. They also need depth in their coverage of many religious branches, sub-branches, and denominations. Datasets that report only on major world religions, for example Christianity, Islam, and Buddhism, permit only essentialist accounts of the effects of religious tradition (see also the introduction to this volume). However, to measure only Christianity, Islam, and Buddhism is to overlook the rich diversity within them. The Religious Characteristics of States dataset (RCS) reports demographics on these three major world religions as a whole, and also 33 branches, sub-branches, and denominations within Christianity, 17 branches and sub-branches or schools within Islam, and 4 branches of Buddhism. RCS affords researchers the opportunity to test theories and effects that are far more nuanced than the large-scale demographic trends commented on in this chapter.

The field also needs a dataset that reaches far back in time; the Correlates of War and Polity datasets' coverage begins in 1816 and 1800, respectively; an ideal dataset for International Relations researchers should match that temporal coverage and the RCS is the only one that does so. Furthermore, to be usable by social scientists, a dataset's coverage must be consistent: all religions must be covered for every observation, and the dataset must employ the state-year as its primary unit of observation (the standard for the field). Other data sources of religious demographics do not possess all three of these necessary traits (e.g., Central Intelligence Agency 1981–2013; Brierley 1997; Barrett, Kurian, and Johnson 2001; Johnson and Grim 2013; Maoz and Henderson 2013; and the many reports from the Pew Research Center for Religion and Public Life, www.pewforum.org).

In response to these shortcomings, RCS was constructed by pooling data from, and incorporating the most valuable features of, several dozen sources. Phase 1 of the dataset covers religious demographics of 202 countries and 22 selected sub-state entities from 1800 to 2010. Although other measurements of states' religious characteristics exist (see above), demographics was selected as the most operationalizable for the project's initial phase. RCS covers 87 religious denominations for 32,629 state-years, and contains over 6.7 million data points. The dataset is posted on the Association of Religion Data Archives (www.thearda.com) and is available to the field for general use.

RCS provides *annual* estimates of populations and percentages of adherents of religions, which no other demographics dataset does. In addition, RCS reports as much detail as possible on the subdivisions and denominations within major world religions. Within Christianity, RCS reports on Catholics, Protestants, Quasi-Protestants (Anglicans and Pentecostals), Orthodox, and "Liminal Christians" (a composite category of denominations that self-identify as Christians but are not widely regarded as mainstream by the other major branches). Within Catholicism, RCS reports on Roman Catholics Latin Rites, Roman Catholics Eastern Rites, and Other Catholics. Within Protestantism, RCS estimates Lutherans, Reformed (including Presbyterian and Congregational separately), Baptist, Adventist, Wesleyan (including Methodist), multi-denominational churches such as the United Church of Canada and Lutheran-Reformed state churches in Germany, and a composite category labeled Anabaptist-Brethren-Pietist. Within Orthodox Christianity, RCS reports on Oriental Orthodox (Armenian et al.) and Eastern Orthodox (Greek, Russian, et al.). Liminal Christianity is divided into Extra-Canonical (including Mormons) and Non-Trinitarian (including Jehovah's Witnesses). Within Islam, RCS estimates Sunnis, Shias, Khariji Muslims (of which only the Ibadi denomination remains), and Liminal Muslims (Druze and Ahmadi). Where data is available, RCS reports on the four major legal schools within Sunni Islam and the major branches of Shia Islam (Twelver, Ismaili or Sevener, and Zaydi). One other important composite category must be mentioned: Buddhist Complex, which is an amalgamation of Buddhism, Confucianism, Taoism, and Shinto (each of which is also reported separately). For a detailed account of all denominations covered, sources of direct observations and methods for selecting them, methods of interpolations and extrapolations, and explanations of the composite categories including their rationales, see the online Codebook that is available for download with the dataset (Brown 2015b).

The purpose of this chapter is to describe the religious demographics of each country covered in this volume from 1950 to 2010, using RCS as the data source, and presented in the order in which these countries are examined in the volume. For each country, a graph shows the percentage of the population of selected religious categories year by year, in a format that enables visualization of trends.[1] The chapter will end with an estimate of global trends.

CANADA

Figure 3.1 shows the change in Canada's religious demographics from 1950 to 2010. With the settling of immigrants primarily from Western Europe, especially Great Britain and France, Canada historically has been predominantly "Western Christian," with nearly 95% of the population divided roughly evenly between Catholics and a mix of Anglicans and Protestants. The category "Western Christianity" is a composite of all Catholics (except Eastern Rites), Protestants and Quasi-Protestants, and Liminal Christians.[2]

Five overall trends are observable. The first is that until about 2000, the percentage of Catholics in Canada did not change much. Since that time, however, the percentage of Catholics has diminished moderately but steadily, from 43% to 38%. The second trend is the rise in proportions of Christians that are not Catholic, Protestant, or Anglican. This rise is consistent with the growth of Pentecostal, Mormon, and Jehovah's Witness churches in many other countries.

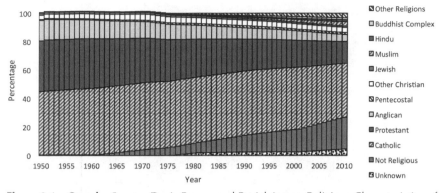

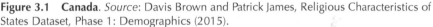

Figure 3.1   Canada. *Source*: Davis Brown and Patrick James, Religious Characteristics of States Dataset, Phase 1: Demographics (2015).

The third trend is the rise in proportions of non-Christian religions, from a negligible amount to about 10% of the total population today. The fastest growing religion in Canada is Islam, which had only 1,708 adherents in 1950 but nearly 1.014 million in 2010 (an increase of 59,300%). The percentage of Muslims in Canada rose in that period from 0.01% to 2.97%. Until 1964, when Ahmadi Islam was introduced, all of that population was Sunni. Shia Islam was introduced in Canada in 1968 and in 2010, about one-tenth of the Muslim population comprised Shia Muslims.

The fourth trend is a sharp increase in the Not Religious category (Atheism, Agnosticism, etc.), from 0.4% in 1950 to 22.3% in 2010.[3] This is consistent with the increase in Non Religion that has been observed in most Western democracies. The fifth trend is the sharp decline of Protestantism-Anglicanism from 50.3% in 1950 to 20.3% in 2010.

UNITED STATES

As seen in Figure 3.2, estimations of religious demographics in the United States are hampered somewhat by a lack of reliable data (the number of unknown is relatively high). Whereas the percentage of Catholics in Canada has begun to wane, it has remained relatively steady in the United States since the 1960s (dipping only a bit since its 1970 peak of 23%). Protestantism, in contrast, has waned significantly, halving from 48% in 1950 to 24.5% in 2010. The small percentage of Anglicans (Episcopal) also halved in this period. Analogously, Judaism, once the most prevalent non-Christian religion, steadily declined from 3.2% in 1950 to 1.68% in 2010. In contrast, the percentages of Pentecostals and Other Christians (including Orthodox, Mormons, and Jehovah's Witnesses) have both nearly doubled

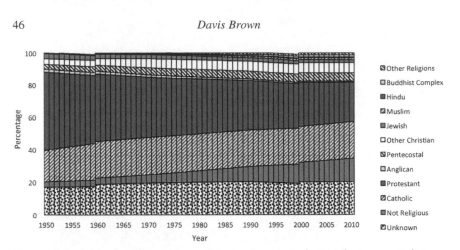

Figure 3.2 United States. *Source*: Davis Brown and Patrick James, Religious Characteristics of States Dataset, Phase 1: Demographics (2015).

since 1950, and the Not Religious category grew from 3% in 1950 to over 14% in 2010.

The fastest growth in the United States, other than Non Religion, has been by non-Western religions: from under 0.5% in 1950 to 4.35% in 2010. Islam, estimated at 0.13% in 1950, had grown to 1.32% in 2010, though its *rate* of growth had actually slowed. Shia Islam has grown from just under one-fifth of Muslims in 1950 to just under one-fourth in 2010. However, if the growth and decline rates of Islam and Judaism continue at their 2010 rate, then Islam is estimated to displace Judaism as the largest non-Christian religion in the United States in 2021.

NIGERIA

Nigeria's religious demographics are shown in Figure 3.3. This table reflects Nigeria's place on a Huntingtonian fault line (the boundary between two major world civilizations; Huntington 1993), with the population about evenly divided between (Sunni) Muslim and non-Muslim. In 1950, prior to Nigeria's independence, adherents of Indigenous religions outnumbered Christians by about four to one. However, all Christian denominations have experienced a steady but significant growth, culminating in a population that is 53.8% Christian in 2010. As is the trend in much of sub-Saharan Africa, Pentecostalism has experienced the fastest growth and Catholicism the slowest (though even the Catholic percentage increased 2½ times during that period). As with Tanzania, and consistent with the overall African trend, Indigenous religions declined significantly and the Not Religious category has grown very slowly.

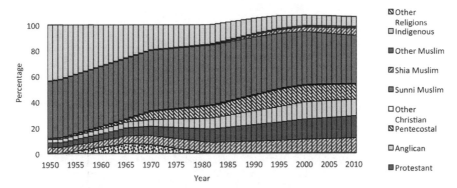

Figure 3.3 Nigeria. *Source*: Davis Brown and Patrick James, Religious Characteristics of States Dataset, Phase 1: Demographics (2015).

The interesting story for Nigeria is that of Islam. Sunni Islam peaked in 1968 at 46.75% and since then actually declined to 37.37% in 2010. The Shia and Other Muslim categories, negligible in 1950, have grown to a combined 6.86% in 2010. The growth in Ahmadi Islam has been slow and steady since 1950; Shia Islam is estimated to have been introduced in 1981 and in 2010 accounted for one-eighth of the Muslim population in Nigeria.

INDIA

Figure 3.4 shows the religious demographics of India. The biggest story here is that of the slow decline of Hinduism from 84.68% in 1950 to 78.49% in 2010. In the same period, Islam has grown from just under 10% in 1950 to 13.86% in 2010; both Sunni and Shia Islam have grown about 40% from their 1950 levels. Sikhism, at 1.74% in 1950, experienced a much slower growth, peaking at 1.97% in 1981, but then declined to 1.86% in 2004, and has held steady since then. Some small minorities in 2010 experienced a quite rapid growth, namely Not Religious (from 0.23% to 1.32%) and the Buddhist Complex (from 0.05% to 0.8%). Indeed, Buddhism (individually, not within the Complex) has been the fastest growing religion in India.

An interesting and unusual trend is the relative stability of Christianity during this period; in many other countries Christianity has experienced either a significant growth or a significant decline. Christians accounted for 2.23% of the population in 1950 and 2.35% in 2010. However, within Christianity, Catholicism has declined from 1.39% to 0.77%, while other branches

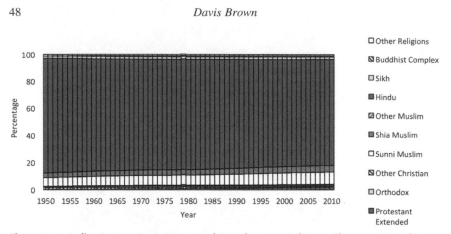

Figure 3.4   India. *Source*: Davis Brown and Patrick James, Religious Characteristics of States Dataset, Phase 1: Demographics (2015).

have grown: Protestants, Anglicans, and Pentecostals combined from 0.62% to 1.11%, Other Christians (i.e., Mormons, Jehovah's Witnesses, and other unclassified denominations) from 0.03% to 0.27% (a growth of 900%). Orthodox Christianity peaked from 0.19% in 1950 to 0.25% in 1972, but has since declined nearly to 1950 levels.

TURKEY

The demographics of Turkey are depicted in Figure 3.5. Of all the countries examined in this volume, Turkey has seen the least change in its religious demographics. Estimates within branches of Turkish Islam vary; RCS estimates about 84% Sunni Muslim and that estimate has remained relatively stable (84.21% in 1950, peaking to 84.62% in 1965, and declining to 83.79% in 2010). Shia Islam is estimated at 14.47% in 1950 and that estimate has fluctuated only slightly, to 14.51% in 2010.

The strongest growth has been in Not Religious, growing from 0.02% in 1950 to 1.11% in 2010. For a predominantly Muslim country in the Middle East, this trend is unusual; few other Muslim countries in the region have a significant Not Religious population. The Buddhist Complex, while still negligible in 2010 (0.05%), has grown from nil in 1950.

Christianity, which accounted for only 0.95% in 1950, has steadily declined to 0.33% in 2010. The strongest decline has been in Orthodox Christianity, which during this period shrank from 0.73% to 0.16%. The percentage of Catholics also halved during this period (from 0.1% to 0.05%). Protestantism Extended (Protestants plus Anglicans and Pentecostals) experienced a brief surge from 0.055% in 1950 to 0.085% in 1965. This surge was likely

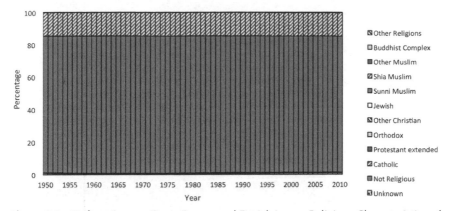

Figure 3.5 Turkey. *Source*: Davis Brown and Patrick James, Religious Characteristics of States Dataset, Phase 1: Demographics (2015).

not indigenous; the sources used by RCS attribute this growth mainly to the deployment of US military forces during the Cold War. Since that time, the percentage has declined very slowly, to 0.074% in 2010.

TUNISIA

As shown in Figure 3.6, the very large majority of the population of Tunisia has been Sunni Muslim since before the country's independence. Since independence, that majority has grown to overwhelming proportions: from 89% in 1952 to 98.64% in 1982. Shia Islam was introduced about 1980 but its presence has remained negligible. Ibadi Islam (classified in RCS as Khariji) has long maintained a small presence and its percentage has increased three-fold (to just under 1.9%) since it began growing in 1982.

Prior to independence, the largest religious minority was Roman Catholic, reflecting Tunisia's status as a French colony. The Catholic percentage peaked at 7.64% in 1954 but declined sharply after independence in 1956. Catholicism's decline slowed in 1970 but has continued; less than 0.2% of the country is Catholic today—and that percentage represents the large majority of all Christians.

Judaism, a small but significant minority prior to independence, peaked at 2.7% in 1955, halved in eight years, and dropped to 0.21% by 1968. Like that of Catholicism, Judaism's decline then slowed but has continued; today Jews account for only 0.02% of the population. These patterns (of the decline of Christianity and Judaism and the rise of Sunni Islam) are consistent with the trends in other Arab countries of North Africa.

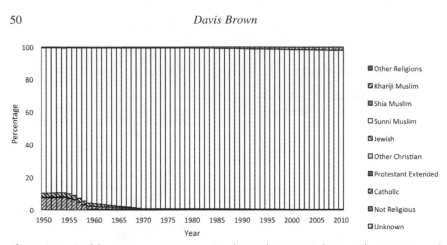

Figure 3.6   Tunisia. *Source*: Davis Brown and Patrick James, Religious Characteristics of States Dataset, Phase 1: Demographics (2015).

LEBANON

The demographics of religion of Lebanon, shown in Figure 3.7, are as complex as the country's politics of religion.[4] Five major religious categories dominate in Lebanon: Catholic, Orthodox Christian, Sunni Muslim, Shia Muslim, and Druze. Historically, Catholics were the largest denomination, and such was the case in 1950. However, after peaking at 43% in 1970, Catholicism has steadily declined to 29.5% in 2010. Orthodox Christianity has also steadily declined, with the decline accelerating beginning in 1970. At 8.1% in 2010, its percentage has nearly halved since 1950 (15.79%). In the same period, Lebanon's percentage of Protestants has also halved and Anglicans dwindled to nil, but the percentage of other Christian denominations, including Pentecostal, has nearly doubled (though still under 0.5%). Judaism experienced its most significant decline from 1956 to 1967 (0.63% to 0.13%) and also dwindled to nil in the late 1980s.

Consonant with Christianity's peak in 1970, Islam's trough was in the same year. However, Islam has grown since then and it displaced Christianity as the majority religion in 1997.[5] In 2010, 57.92% of the population is Muslim, with Sunnis and Shias comprising 46 and 45% of the Muslim population, respectively (i.e., Muslims were about evenly divided between Sunnis and Shias, with the remainder being predominantly Druze). The proportion of Sunnis to Shias has fluctuated a little, but since 1950 neither branch has outnumbered the other by more than a few percentage points. Druzes have declined from 6.34% in 1950 to 5.0% in 2010.

An interesting and unexpected pattern is the growth of the Buddhist Complex (Buddhism, Confucianism, Taoism, and Shinto combined), from nil in 1950 to 2% in 2002 and slowly rising.

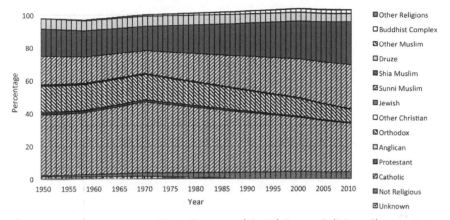

Figure 3.7 Lebanon. *Source*: Davis Brown and Patrick James, Religious Characteristics of States Dataset, Phase 1: Demographics (2015).

TANZANIA

As seen in Figure 3.8, the religious demographics of Tanzania are more diverse than in many other countries, with no one major religion holding a majority until 1994. Other than this feature, the demographic trends in Tanzania have been similar to those in many other sub-Saharan African countries. In 1950 (before its independence), just under half of the population practiced Indigenous religion (down from 95% in 1900). The largest minority was Islam. Christianity was the second largest minority, with most Christians being Catholic.[6]

In 2010, however, Christianity has a majority (55%). Catholicism has grown only slightly since 1970, but other denominations (nearly all Western Christian) have grown from 6.85% in 1950 to 32.56% in 2010. Another trend, common in Africa, is the growth of Pentecostalism and Other Christianity (especially Liminal Christianity) at a higher rate than in most Christian-majority countries. Islam, which peaked at 31.9% in 1957, has declined only slightly to 29.9% in 2010, whereas Indigenous religions have declined very sharply in the same period (from 49.9% in 1950 to 11.84% in 2010). In 1950, Muslims in Tanzania were predominantly Sunni, but Shia and Ahmadi Islam have both grown significantly since 1970. From 1950 to 1979, only 1% of all Muslims in the country were Shiite. Shia Islam is believed to have grown significantly in Africa after 1979, and today 20% of all Muslims in Tanzania are Shiite. Ahmadi Muslims comprised less than one-half percentage of the Tanzanian population in 1970 but their population has grown to 4.5% in 2010.

Other religions, on the other hand, have grown only slowly. Hinduism grew by about 800% from 1980 to 1990, but has grown very slowly since then

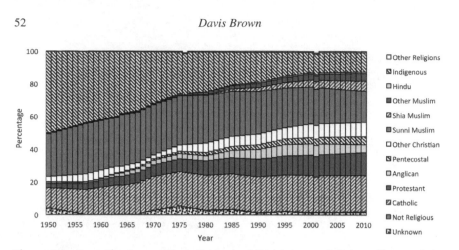

Figure 3.8   Tanzania. *Source*: Davis Brown and Patrick James, Religious Characteristics of States Dataset, Phase 1: Demographics (2015).

(to 0.87% in 2010). Non Religion has also grown very slowly, in contrast to the trend of the Global North, but its growth is consistent with the overall trend observed in many other African countries.

BOLIVIA

As shown in Figure 3.9, the prime story on Bolivian demographics has been the decline of the majority religion, Catholicism, which is consistent with that in much of the rest of Latin America. Catholics constituted 94% of the population in 1950 but only 75% in 2010, with the decline accelerating after 2001. However, unlike in a number of other Latin American countries, Catholicism lost adherents not primarily to Non Religion, but to Protestantism and Pentecostalism. Therein lies another interesting development: Protestantism grew from 1.8% in 1950 to 10% in 2001, and since then has nearly halved, declining to 5.28% in 2010. This is likely due to conversions to Pentecostalism, which surged from 6.1% in 2001 to 11.5% in 2010. The Other Christian and Non Religion categories, while fewer in number, have experienced the greatest growth: Other Christian from 0.02% in 1950 to 3.07% in 2010, and Non Religion from 0.22% to 2.68% (peaking and troughing along the way).

The majority of the population still being indigenous in race and ethnicity, for example Aymara and Quechua, Indigenous religion is still practiced among some communities. Indigenous religion had been declining steadily, from 3.69% in 1950 to 1.66% in 1970, but it then grew again, peaked at 3.56% in 2000, and has declined again to 3.15% in 2010. The Buddhist Complex, whose presence has always been relatively negligible, also peaked in 1970

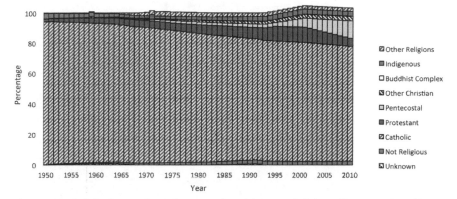

Figure 3.9 Bolivia. *Source*: Davis Brown and Patrick James, Religious Characteristics of States Dataset, Phase 1: Demographics (2015).

(at 0.1%), and has slowly declined to 0.07% in 2010. The slow growth of other religions accelerated in 1964, growing five times in less than a decade (2.99% in 1973), and has fluctuated since (to 2.25% in 2010).

THE WORLD

We now situate the religious demographics of the individual countries mentioned above within the trends of the entire world. RCS is not yet constructed in a way that facilitates its use as a data source for the entire world combined (it does not yet include micro-states or dependencies and the individual country-year observations are not easily summed); therefore these estimates are drawn from the Correlates of War World Religion Project (Maoz and Henderson 2013). This dataset reports estimates only for every five years (from 1945 to 2010) and at the level of individual countries, it contains a significant amount of missing data (which it reports as zero adherents, creating a host of other problems). Therefore, its data on individual states is provided with significantly less confidence and constructing a graph similar to the others above was not possible. However, it is the only dataset that reports worldwide religious demographics at regular intervals.

The first noteworthy trend is the rise and decline of Non Religion: from 8.68% of the world's population in 1950 to its peak of 17.16% in 1975, then back down to 12.27% in 2010. This finding is consistent with the observation among many scholars that religion has experienced a resurgence since the late 1970s (Kepel 1994; Snyder 2011; Toft, Philpott and Shah 2011). The second trend is the steady growth of Islam, from 13.19% of the total world population in 1950 to 22.33% in 2010.[7] In contrast, the population of

Indigenous religions (mostly African, mislabeled by Maoz and Henderson as "Syncretic") declined sharply from 19.15% in 1950 to 10.94% in 1960, then more slowly to 7.91% in 2010.

The percentages of several other major world religions have remained relatively stable. One such religion is Hinduism, which accounted for 13.51% of the world's population in 1950, troughed at 12.08% in 1975, and peaked again at 13.38% in 2005. Buddhism has followed a similar pattern: from 7.13% in 1950 to 6.26% in 1970, then peaking again at 7.27% in 2005.[8]

Christianity has also remained relatively stable, accounting for just under a third of the world's populations, but the fluctuation pattern is different. From 31.65% in 1950, Christianity grew to 33.11% in 1960, declined to 31.75% in 1985, and has fluctuated since then (32.0% in 2010). Not reflected in Maoz and Henderson global estimates, but reflected in RCS, is the overall trend of Christianity declining in much of the Global North, especially Europe, but growing significantly in sub-Saharan Africa, South Korea, China, and Taiwan. Catholicism remained stable, between 18% and 19%, from 1950 to 1985, but has since declined to 16.8% in 2010. Protestantism fluctuated significantly between 6% and 8%, rising from a low of 6.18% in 1950 to 7.53% in 2010. In contrast, Orthodox Christianity steadily declined from 4.78% in 1950 to 2.63% in 2010 (though with a slight rise from 1990 to 1995). Of particular interest is Maoz and Henderson's reporting of "Other Christians," which doubled from 0.78% in 1950 to 1.53% in 1960, and then doubled again to 3.84% in 2010. Maoz and Henderson provide no definition of this category; Mormons and Jehovah's Witness are very likely included in it (and both have experienced a significant growth worldwide since 1950). However, it is not known whether Pentecostals, who also have experienced a significant growth, are classified in by Maoz and Henderson as "Other Christians" or Protestants.

CONCLUSION

As this chapter has shown, religious demographics of countries are seldom fixed. They may often change slowly, sometimes over generations, but they do change. Indeed, in our post-world war environment characterized by uneven population booms, mass migrations, and large-scale conversions (including conversions away from religion), religious demographics of countries appear more fluid today than ever before in our lifetimes. We would therefore expect that as the religious identities of whole populations change, these changes find reflections in governmental preferences and decisions. To better appreciate these changes, which may occur only over generations, researchers must be equipped with more refined tools such as RCS.

Furthermore, the effects of religions cannot be truly understood without disaggregating their many diversities. Assumptions that major world religions are monolithic undermine the nuance and precision of causal analysis that political scientists always endeavor to achieve. In offering estimates of many denominations, branches, and sects within some of the larger religions, RCS enables researchers to begin the process of shedding those assumptions.

NOTES

1. Due to the methodology of the dataset's construction for handling double-affiliates, a few of the total demographic estimates contained herein exceed one hundred percent. The dataset corrects for this using an "unspecified" category within each major religious category, which does not appear in these tables.

2. This category was constructed to facilitate the testing of effects theorized to be common to Catholicism, Extended Protestantism, and Liminal Christianity, for example, the effects of the just war tradition. For further detail and rationale, see the RCS Codebook (Brown 2015b).

3. New Age Religion and revived spiritist and spiritualist religions are not classified as Not Religious, but as New Age and Other Indigenous, respectively.

4. One characteristic complicating the reliability of religious demographics estimates in Lebanon is the widespread belief that the Lebanese census itself has become politicized, especially after 1970. This complication makes it more difficult than for other countries to assess whether the changes in percentages described herein are due genuinely to demographic shifts or to the new "politics of census." The frequent use of sources other than official government figures (for all countries, not only Lebanon) can mitigate this problem to some degree, but as acknowledged in the RCS Codebook, no source is completely devoid of bias. The sources selected for direct observations of Lebanese demographics are, of course, those that this author considers the most authoritative; however, the caveat that every estimate is subject to uncertainty applies here more than for other countries covered in this volume.

5. RCS classifies Druzes as Liminal Muslims, hence they are included in estimates for Islam overall.

6. Although reports by the Pew Forum and others claim that many African churches have incorporated elements of African traditional religions, RCS draws from sources that generally do not account for that phenomenon and has refrained from second-guessing those churches' self-identification with their respective denominations.

7. The Maoz and Henderson dataset contains too much missing data on the Sunni and Shia branches to provide reliable estimates of their percentages individually.

8. Because of excessive missing data, deriving the Buddhist Complex composite reliably from the Maoz and Henderson dataset is not possible.

REFERENCES

Barrett, David B., George Thomas Kurian, and Todd M. Johnson. 2001. *World Christian Encyclopedia: A Comparative Survey of Churches and Religion in the Modern World.* 2nd edn. Vol. 1: *The World by Countries: Religionists, Churches, Ministries.* Oxford: Oxford University Press.

Brierley, Peter W. 1997. *World Churches Handbook.* London: Christian Research.

Brown, Davis. 2015a. "The Permissive Nature of the Islamic War Ethic." *Journal of Religion and Violence* 2 (3): 460–83.

Brown, Davis. 2015b. The Religious Characteristics of States Dataset (RCS), Phase 1, Version 1.0: Demographics Code Book. Available online at www.thearda.com/ Archive/Files/Description/BROWN.asp. Accessed May 31, 2015.

Central Intelligence Agency. 1981–2013. *The World Factbook.* Washington, DC: Central Intelligence Agency.

Fox, Jonathan. 2008. *A World Survey of Religion and the State.* Cambridge: Cambridge University Press.

Fox, Jonathan. 2009. "Quantifying Religion and State: Round Two of the Religion and State Project." *Politics and Religion* 2 (3): 444–52.

Huntington, Samuel P. 1993. "The Clash of Civilizations?" *Foreign Affairs* 72 (3): 22–49.

Johnson, Todd and Brian Grim. 2013. World Religion Database, Research Version. Boston: Brill (accessed November 2013). Available online at http://www.worldreligiondatabase.org/wrd_default.asp. By subscription only. I thank Todd Johnson for making this data available to me.

Johnston, Douglas and Cynthia Sampson, eds. 1994. *Religion, the Missing Dimension of Statecraft.* New York: Oxford University Press.

Kepel, Gilles. 1994. *The Revenge of God: The Resurgence of Islam, Christianity and Judaism in the Modern World.* Trans. Alan Braley. University Park, PA: Pennsylvania State University Press.

Maoz, Zeev and Errol A. Henderson. 2013. The World Religion Dataset, 1945–2010: Logic, Estimates, and Trends. *International Interactions* 39 (3): 265–91.

Snyder, Jack, ed. 2011. *Religion and International Relations Theory.* New York: Columbia University Press.

Thomas, Scott M. 2005. *The Global Resurgence of Religion and the Transformation of International Relations.* New York: Palgrave Macmillan.

Toft, Monica Duffy, Daniel Philpott, and Timothy Samuel Shah. 2011. *God's Century: Resurgent Religion and Global Politics.* New York: W.W. Norton.

World Values Survey Association. 2009. *World Values Survey 1981–2008 Official Aggregate v. 20090901.* Madrid: ASEP/JDS. Available at http://www.wvsevsdb. com/wvs/WVSData.jsp?Idioma=I. Accessed October 4, 2014.

Chapter 4

The Prosperity Gospel and the Globalization of American Capitalism

Michael Wilkinson

Throughout the twentieth century, a religious transformation occurred, with the vast majority of the world's Christians shifting from Europe and North America to Africa, Asia, and Latin America. The relocation of the center of Christianity from the so-called Global North to the Global South is not just a shift in demographics. It is accurate that the number of Christians has grown in the Global South, as has the overall percentage of the world's share of Christians. But another important transformation has to do with the way in which Christianity itself has changed. Christianity is increasingly taking on the character of what scholars refer to as renewalist Christianity or what is traditionally referred to as Pentecostal and Charismatic Christianity (Hefner, 2013; Miller, Sargeant, and Flory, 2013; Wilkinson, 2015). With the numbers reaching well over 600 million, this type of Christianity is monolithic and yet not homogenous. There is a family resemblance suggesting sameness but there is also great variation in this global type as it adapts to local contexts. Furthermore, one important variation that appears to appeal to the masses shares certain qualities with its American variant: the prosperity gospel that emphasizes a theological vision of blessing in economic terms. The prosperity gospel is not limited to economic blessing and also includes related and overlapping themes of health and victory or personal success. The economic aspects of religious blessing and prosperity, however, point to an interesting case study of the close relationship between economic expansion and religious action. Furthermore, the prosperity gospel illustrates an important religious transformation with one option being the modeling of religion after the economic sphere.

This chapter explores the influence of the American prosperity gospel and its role in shaping the economic behavior of Christians throughout the world. The prosperity gospel is characterized by themes of abundance, blessing,

health, wealth, and victory. These cultural values have translated into specific economic action in the United States and throughout the world among
millions of Christians. The globalization of the prosperity gospel is facilitated
largely by multimedia evangelists like Creflo Dollar and Joel Osteen in the
United States and also increasingly by non-Americans like Joseph Prince in
Singapore. The message of blessing and its economic implications illustrates
one way in which people embrace religion and free market capitalism. This
chapter thus shows how prosperity religion supports the further spread of
neoliberal globalization while the religion itself also transforms as it is modeled after the economic sphere.

There are several strands that make up this chapter. First, it offers an
overview of the social-historical development of the prosperity gospel in
the United States, including key ideas and individuals that have shaped
this movement. Second, it examines the role of congregations, especially
megachurches, as important mediators of the culture of prosperity. Third,
it discusses the relationship between religion, economics, and globalization
showing how religion is a globalizing economic force.

SOCIAL HISTORICAL BACKGROUND

Pentecostalism refers to a movement within Christianity that is characterized
by an emphasis on personal and subjective experiential religion with specific
qualities such as speaking in tongues, healing, dreams and visions, and, along
with evangelical Protestants, the importance of evangelism and missionary
work. The experiential dynamic of Pentecostalism is described as highly
emotional, with rituals encouraging energetic bodily participation of its members: "exuberant worship; an emphasis on subjective religious experience and
spiritual gifts; claims of supernatural miracles, signs and wonders—including
a language of experiential spirituality, rather than a theology; and a mystical
'life in the Spirit' by which [its members] daily live out the will of God"
(Burgess and Van der Maas 2002, 5). The energetic and emotive quality of
Pentecostalism illustrates the embodied and affective dimensions of religion
(see Riis and Woodhead 2010).

Pentecostalism emerged in the early twentieth century and grew to become
one of the most important changes in Christianity, with 628 million Pentecostals around the world in 2010, representing approximately 26% of all Christians (Wilkinson 2015, 98). The globalization of Pentecostalism includes
issues about its emergence, development, growth, and ongoing transformation. Furthermore, Pentecostalism is not simply an American religion, if
it ever was one. Rather, Pentecostalism is diverse and found throughout
the world. One particular variant of Pentecostalism is represented by the

"prosperity gospel," which is the focus of this chapter (for details on Nigeria, see the chapter by Ukah in this volume).

The prosperity gospel is one of a number of terms that is used to characterize this movement within Christianity. In some cases it is referred to as the "health and wealth" gospel or "word of faith" or, more pejoratively, the "name it and claim it" gospel by its critics (see Attanasi and Yong 2012; McClymond 2014). Historically, the prosperity gospel is aligned with the Pentecostal revivals that began in the early twentieth century in various places around the world, most notably the Azusa Street Revival in Los Angeles from 1906 to 1909. The early movement is often referred to as Classical Pentecostalism and is represented by denominations such as the Assemblies of God. Following the first wave, some scholars see the charismatic renewal that occurred in the mainline Protestant Churches and the Roman Catholic Church in the middle of the twentieth century as the second wave of Pentecostalism. More recently, the term neo-Pentecostalism has come to designate the various types of Pentecostalism that some prosperity gospel leaders and megachurches would characterize as the third wave. While this three-wave metaphor appears to make sense in the United States, generalizing this analysis as a universal or global pattern is severely critiqued by historians like Allan Anderson (2004, 2013).

Allan Anderson argues that there are a number of sites in which Pentecostalism emerged, showing its polygenesis nature. For example, in India, Wales, and Canada, there is evidence that Pentecostalism developed prior to some of the key events in the United States, namely, the Azusa Street Revival in 1906. In Canada, for example, Adam Stewart discusses the important contribution of Ellen Hebden and her faith mission as the birthplace of Pentecostalism in Canada (2010, 17–38). Hebden was clearly shaped by revivalist trends in the United Kingdom and not the United States. Furthermore, her account of how Pentecostalism began in Canada was not directly linked with the Azusa Revival. India offers another important example of how Pentecostalism emerged prior to the American revival with the events surrounding the Mukti Mission in 1905 when Pandita Ramabai claimed the Holy Spirit was being poured out on India for the development of a new type of Christianity (see Anderson 2013, 25–33). The main contribution of Anderson's work is the finding that significant antecedents in the nineteenth century were already globalizing, including radical evangelicalism, apocalypticism, revivalism, and the missionary movement. Likewise, there are other strands in this period, according to Bowler (2013, 12–14), that are incorporated into early Pentecostalism that especially have an influence on the prosperity gospel, including nineteenth-century metaphysical philosophy with an emphasis on ideas about the unity of God and humanity, the reality of a spiritual world, and the idea that like God, humans shared a creative capacity associated with positive thinking. In some cases, positive thinking was associated with healing.

The prosperity gospel, according to Kate Bowler (2013) mixes metaphysical philosophy with Christianity and the American ethic of optimism, which became rooted among some early Pentecostals like E. W. Kenyon, a revivalist who preached for over fifty years until his death in 1948. It then takes off in the middle of the twentieth century when the hope of postwar capitalism was embraced with religious fervor. A coalition of healing revivals, newfound wealth, economic success, and optimism coalesced to strike a message that was embraced by those already inclined to the Pentecostal message of holiness and personal victory. Bowler (2013, 7) writes extensively about four themes that characterize the movement:

> *Faith, wealth, health,* and *victory.* (1) It conceives of *faith* as an activator, a power that unleashes spiritual forces and turns the spoken word into reality. (2) The movement depicts faith as palpably demonstrated in *wealth* and (3) *health.* It can be measured in both the wallet (one's personal wealth) and in the body (one's personal health), making material reality the measure of the success of immaterial faith. (4) The movement expects faith to be marked by *victory.* Believers trust that culture holds no political, social, economic impediment to faith, and no circumstance can stop believers from living in total victory here on earth.

Bowler offers a broad-ranging historical analysis of a great number of individuals and cases for understanding the development and impact of the prosperity gospel that cannot be covered here. Furthermore, while recognizing the important relationship between these four themes (e.g., that faith is causally related to wealth), the theme of wealth will be the focus in this chapter.

Two of the most prominent American pastors who developed the theology of wealth are Kenneth Hagin (1917–2003) and Kenneth Copeland (1936–present). Each operated expansive ministries based in Texas that included media operations. Hagin and Copeland were also well connected with other preachers within Pentecostalism and networked with key American evangelists like Oral Roberts, T. L. Osborne, and a host of other charismatic preachers with a significant number of followers. Hagin and Copeland shared similar views about prosperity that included the idea that Christians were blessed according to their faith. If you were in need for some kind of miracle, whether financial or physical, but lacked faith, you would not receive your blessing from God. If on the other hand, you had a great amount of faith and demonstrated that trust in God by giving money to a ministry, then God would bless you in return for blessing another. Your answer to prayer would be received. This was referred to as a principle of sowing and reaping. Often, followers were exhorted to demonstrate their faith by giving large amounts. They were told not to rob God of his tithes and offerings. Rather, as followers, you were to give generously to God. Often, illness and poverty were associated with some type of sin in the person's life or evidence that someone was not giving financially to the church. Andrew Chesnut (2003) shows how this tension between illness, poverty, and the prosperity gospel operates in a way that transforms people who are economically poor into consumers. Paradoxically, while giving money to the church appears counterintuitive, the conversion of the poor is related to a social transformation whereby the convert adopts a new economic ethic of work, savings, and investment. According to Chesnut (2003, 143), the conversion process impacts the family unit and reorients the spending patterns of families from activities such as gambling and drinking to attending church, family, and work, activities conservative Christians often refer to as moral issues.

The churches of these American prosperity preachers were often mega-churches with massive budgets, a large staff, media departments, marketing teams, and social influence (Chaves 2006; Ellingson 2010). Megachurches are a type of congregation that have come to characterize and symbolize the wealth associated with the prosperity gospel. These large facilities or campuses are similar to large corporations and in some cases look like the international offices of a multinational organization. They do not share the architecture of the traditional nineteenth-century church with a spire that was the highest point in a village, illustrating its centrality in the life of its citizens. Rather, the corporate office with its president, vice presidents, and managers is the form these large congregations take, modeled after the dominant economic institution of capitalism.

Wealth, according to Bowler, is a far-reaching, radical claim among prosperity preachers. Wealth and, more specifically, the idea that Christians can obtain wealth is often one of the more demonstrable assertions of the movement. It is often the most controversial, and easily a target of its critics. One of the most flamboyant, highly visible, and regularly watched television preachers of prosperity in the 1980s was Jim Bakker and his wife Tammy Faye Bakker. The Bakkers operated a major television show called *Praise the Lord* (PTL) and in 1981 just over a million viewers regularly tuned in to the show. With funds from viewers, the Bakkers built a 2,200-acre Christian resort and theme park in South Carolina called Heritage USA, which at one time was the third most-visited theme park in the United States. "It was a Christian playground for believers, who, flushed with their own successes, caught the vision of the charismatic couple who made the abundant life seem possible" (Bowler 213, 77).

The Bakkers' version of the prosperity gospel translated into a billion-dollar televangelism ministry for the Assemblies of God and represented the height of what Bowler refers to as the "hard prosperity" version where direct results were guaranteed in relation to one's faith. The "hard prosperity" kind of the Bakkers was rooted in the teachings of prosperity preachers like Kenneth Copeland and Kenneth Hagin. Both preachers built megachurches, television ministries, publishing houses, and conference networks, along with copious amounts of marketing exhorting the faithful to give to God and watch God bless them with success in the form of the American capitalist dream. Prosperity preachers claimed that whatever you gave to God you would receive back according to your faith. The return could be tenfold or even a hundredfold if you had faith. Believing that God did not want his children to be poor, these preachers developed all kinds of theological schemes that rewarded faithful givers. If you gave a dollar to the ministry, said Gloria Copeland, then God would give you a hundred dollars in return. If you gave a thousand dollars, then one hundred thousand dollars would be yours (Bowler 2013, 99). These promises were regularly supported with testimonies from followers and the preachers themselves in programs like infomercials where people claimed they needed a job and after giving to the ministry they got the job or someone needed money to pay off credit card bills and after giving to the church, God provided for him or her the money to get out of debt and buy a new car or start a new business. Americans flocked to hear these preachers. "For many, faith in supernatural hundredfold returns appeared a reasonable economic strategy. It was a movement that treasured the God of checks and balances, whose financial formulas and principles ensured that, when all was tallied, God was more than fair" (Bowler 2013, 100).

By the end of the 1980s, Jim Bakker was charged and jailed for fraud. The ministry eventually shut down and the faithful were less inclined toward the hard version of prosperity. In the United States, the prosperity gospel did not close its doors, however. Rather, it shifted to a softer version, argues Bowler (2013, 125) that fit more with the therapeutic culture of the 1990s. The softer version moved slightly away from the direct cause and effect relations to one that was more about relationships between followers and God, prosperity and psychological health, the benefits of being generous, and giving to God and others not just your money but also your time and service. Spiritual health was key to personal life including family and work. Therapeutic language was embraced in a more holistic fashion and signified a move away from the ostentatious life of Wall Street and Church Street in the 1980s. This softer version was found in people like Joyce Meyer, T. D. Jakes, Creflo Dollar, and Joel Osteen.

Joel Osteen is the senior pastor of Lakewood Church, Houston, Texas, that seats 16,000 people, and with multiple services, is home to 45,000 weekly worshipers. His Sunday worship service is broadcast on many different stations and has an estimated seven million weekly viewers. Like prosperity preachers of the past, Osteen sells books including *Every Day a Friday: How to Be Happier 7 Days a Week* that was on the New York Times best seller list in 2011. According to Katja Rostow (2015, 216), "Joel Osteen may be the perfect embodiment of a 'pastorpreneur' in today's consumer society. Consumerism, backed by an increasingly globalized mediascape and the growing influence of neoliberalism, has become the dominant sociocultural and economic order in the years following World War II."

"Pastorpreneur" refers to the qualities of the preacher coupled with many of the same characteristics as the entrepreneur (see also the chapter by Upadhyay). Mixing American capitalism with religion allows Osteen to market his particular product of religion to a growing global audience that not only purchases what he is selling through new technological means and social networking, but also sells it to others. In turn, not only are followers learning about religion, but they are also being socialized into the culture of neoliberal economics through these religious preachers who model success in the way they dress, the books they sell, the sermons they share, the homes they live in, and, generally, what the American dream may look like. One of the most important representatives outside of America with direct relation to Osteen is Joseph Prince, a prosperity preacher based in Singapore who has preached in Osteen's church. Prince has adopted Osteen's message of hope and prosperity with his own mix of grace that is marketed in a way that is appealing to the local and the global audiences that observe his media presentations (Yip and Ainsworth 2013). Prince's message has found a home in America where it is regularly televised. He has also launched a church site in the United States known as "Grace Revolution Church" (www.gracerev.org). The contextualization of prosperity from the United States in Singapore is what Roland Robertson (1992) refers to as "glocalization" where the local and the global can be observed. Furthermore, the globalization of American prosperity is not simply about its diffusion from the United States to the rest of the world. It is also about a global return where its themes of success are repackaged and sold in new ways to religious consumers in the United States.

AMERICAN PROSPERITY AND THE INSTITUTIONAL ROLE OF CONGREGATIONS

The study of congregations by sociologists offers particular insight into the various roles they play in society (see Ammerman 1997; Chaves, 2004). More specifically, prosperity-type congregations offer important insight into how the subculture is organized, produced, and distributed. While the themes of faith, wealth, health, and victory characterize the subculture, the megachurches and their institutionally related ministries are the locus of subcultural interaction. The churches are the building blocks of the culture of prosperity. And by churches are meant all of the related ways in which the product of prosperity is packaged and marketed throughout the world. Very clearly, prosperity churches are organized around clear statements of mission and vision, programs, leaders, financial budgets, and networks with the broader culture of prosperity. While the prosperity gospel represents a subculture of evangelicalism, each congregation or megachurch is the metasite where mentors who network with other congregations in the larger global marketplace of religion manage the subculture. Institutionally, prosperity churches play an integral role in producing and exporting the subculture. One such example is Oasis Christian Center in Hollywood, California.

Oasis Christian Center is a neo-Pentecostal congregation that preaches a soft version of the prosperity gospel. It began in the 1990s and quickly grew to a megachurch of about 2000 people. The congregation has a higher than average number of people who are either employed in or aspire to be in the entertainment industry. Gerardo Marti's (2008, 2010, 2012) rich sociological research shows how the congregation serves to provide those interested in working in the industry not only the religious means to do so, but also the important social and cultural links for finding economic success.

In his book *Hollywood Faith*, Marti shows how the church's growth and success revolves around the revitalization of the old Destiny Theater and the ambiguous alliance between the Hollywood entertainment industry and Christianity. However, Oasis negotiates this relationship by sanctifying the perception of the industry among those Christians seeking employment in Hollywood. The church manages through its prosperity teachings to find pathways for accommodating itself to Hollywood by redefining success in the industry and, ultimately, employment. One particular way is to redefine Hollywood as a mission field that needs Christians to be there to exert influence from the inside. Hollywood, however, also influences Oasis where the adoption of the entertainment industry culture shapes the performance and presentation of Christianity. According to Marti:

> As a church, Oasis intentionally strives for relevance to those in the entertainment industry, where success is measured in fame and profit. When Hollywood workers start attending Oasis, they view the industry as an arena of opportunity for the accumulation of wealth and fame. But the common experience of disenchantment with pursuing fame provokes them to embrace broader ideals. Their motivations undergo a transformation (104).

Oasis is an example of what sociologists describe as religious innovation whereby religious institutions negotiate social and economic change through adaptation. In this case, the congregation adopts the language of prosperity and facilitates an economic transition for the creative class seeking employment in Hollywood. In turn, the congregation also adapts to the local economic situation. However, the congregation also needs to reorient itself in such a way that it still looks like a Christian congregation. In other words, religious innovation has limits. In turn, those who come to attend Oasis seeking a passageway into Hollywood find not only economic success but also religious affirmation for their new employment. Oasis praises success and achievement in the workplace while forming a new economic identity for its followers. This new identity facilitates the followers' transition into the new post-Fordist economy where individuals are required to be self-promoters, flexible workers, able to demonstrate high levels of specialization, while working on short-term contracts, and low-paying jobs (see Waters 2001, 214–15).

One final example illustrates how congregations are globalizers of religion and, in this case, not only of a religious message but also of an economic mode of action. Simon Coleman's work on the Word of Life church in Sweden is an ethnographic study of religion, globalization, and the prosperity gospel (2000). Its charismatic leader, Ulf Ekman, who was influenced by the prosperity gospel teachings of Kenneth Hagin, founded the Word of Life church in the 1980s. Ekman attended Hagin's Rhema Bible Training Institute and returned to Sweden to start his own prosperity church. Based in the suburbs of Uppsala, the church quickly grew to 2,000 members and included extensive programs for families, a media center with radio and television broadcasting facilities, a bible school which later became a university, and a vast network of transnational relations with other independent prosperity churches throughout the world. Through its ministries, Word of Life planted churches and bible training centers in Europe. Regular conferences attracted key prosperity speakers from the United States, which served to mutually reinforce the subculture and its growing global presence. The Scandinavian-American network, however, quickly grew to include other nodes in the United Kingdom, Europe, Africa, and Asia.

Coleman's study of the Word of Life church serves as an important example of how congregations mediate the culture of prosperity. Congregations are agents of socialization whereby its members not only learn about the values and beliefs of prosperity, but they also find ways to practice and reproduce this way of life. Structurally, congregations are infused with cultural practices supported by rituals that support the various ways in which the prosperity gospel is understood and practiced. The embodiment of the prosperity gospel through ritual implies that participants carry with them the experiences of prosperity from places of worship to the workplace. In other words, the prosperity gospel narrative is internalized and externalized (Coleman 127–33). Increasingly, the economy is less constrained by time and space, and so is religion as work and faith flow across the globe (Wilkinson 2007). As a religion "made to travel" (see Cox 1995) and "the world their parish" (see Martin 2002), the prosperity gospel message is globalized.

Globalization and the Gospel of Neoliberal Economic Prosperity

How then should we explain the relationship between religion and economics and, more specifically, between neoliberal capitalism and the prosperity gospel? Does religion shape economic behavior? Is religion an economic globalizer? Or do religions respond and adapt to new global economic factors? There are several explanations that will be discussed in this section. Beginning with Max Weber, there is a long tradition in sociology of analyses explaining the relationship between economics and religion. In his most recognized book, *The Protestant Ethic and the Spirit of Capitalism* (1958[1976]), Weber sought to show how Calvinist beliefs shaped economic behavior. Weber's work focused on the idea of rationalization as a process associated with modernity where traditional ways of life were increasingly replaced by rational values and means-ends thinking. The rationalization of social life was the main focus of his work and *The Protestant Ethic* illustrates his ideas about religion and economics (for another assessment on this discussion, see the chapter by Upadhyay in this volume).

In *The Protestant Ethic and the Spirit of Capitalism*, Weber showed how religious beliefs shaped the economic behavior of Calvinists. Specifically, he highlighted how Calvinist views of calling, vocation, and work contributed to a work ethic that had the unintended consequences of increased capital. Unsure about what to do with the profits, Calvinists did not want to give them away. Appearing to be selfish by hoarding it was not an option. However, one could reinvest the capital into factories, which in turn acted as a catalyst for the development of capitalism. Weber is clear that Protestants did not cause capitalism although there is an important relationship between religious beliefs and economic behavior. The inevitability of the rationalization process, however, is that capitalism comes to operate with its own rationale devoid of its Calvinist beliefs. The rationalization and institutionalization of the economic system operates in the modern world according to a new set of values. Weber was pessimistic about this process and believed the new economic system would become an iron cage in the modern world.

The issue about the relationship between Pentecostalism and capitalism has also been raised with considerable debate about whether or not there is a Pentecostal ethic that informs a new spirit of global capitalism. To what extent do Pentecostalism and, more specifically, the prosperity gospel shape economic behavior? Does the prosperity gospel propel consumers into the global economy in a way other religions do not? David Martin explored this idea initially in his book *Tongues of Fire* (1990) to see whether or not there was a new Pentecostal ethic developing in Latin America. Martin, following Weber, attempted to assess the extent to which one could see a direct relation between Pentecostals and the transformation of Latin American economies. Were Pentecostals leading the way in the adoption of neoliberal economics? Were they doing so at a more successful rate than the Roman Catholics? Does economic success and the culture of prosperity religion account for the growth of Pentecostalism? Were Roman Catholics leaving the Church to join the Pentecostals for economic reasons? The decline of Catholicism in Latin America along with the growth of Pentecostalism has important implications for the region including political and economic changes (see Stoll 1990; Chesnut 2003). Martin does not argue for a cause and effect relation but he did observe that there was something going on between the expansion of new economies and Pentecostalism. However, he did not want to reduce the appeal of Pentecostalism simply to the material. Pentecostalism offered more than economic blessing and a fast track to the new global economy.

Bernice Martin (1995), however, developed David Martin's work and argued that there was "a partial consonance between the 'inner-worldly asceticism' of the fast-growing Protestant movement in Latin America and the economic imperatives of the global capitalism into which Latin America has been progressively incorporated since the 1960s" (101). Drawing upon face-to-face interviews with participants from Pentecostal churches in Latin America, Bernice Martin examined the symbiosis between the beliefs and practices of Pentecostals and the implications for economic behaviors, arguing that economic success was related to Pentecostal values of strict living whereby converts reoriented their economic behavior, for example, from wastefulness on things such as gambling to hard work for supporting the family unit and the local church. For Bernice Martin, the Pentecostal ethic in Latin America represents a mutation of Weber's Protestant ethic that was observed among Calvinists. Bernice Martin makes it clear that she is not arguing for a universal pattern that is observable in all societies across all cultures. And yet, the comparison with Max Weber and David Martin could be understood as an argument observing how a specific interpretation of a religious tradition shapes and legitimizes economic behavior that is not simply limited to segments of a society but has an overall impact on the economics of a nation-state, if not a region of the world.

David Martin expanded his analysis in another important book, *Pentecostalism: The World their Parish* (2002), where he extended his Latin American analysis globally. Martin explores the development of Pentecostalism in Africa and South Asia where he also examines the cultural, political, and economic factors of Pentecostal expansion in relation to the modern and globalized world. Further, Martin sees similarities not only between Calvinism and economic behavior but also an important historical link with the role of Methodism during the nineteenth century in England. In Weberian fashion, Martin sees Pentecostalism as a catalyst for the expansion of a new global economy. The new Protestantism, represented by Pentecostalism, enables people to become modern global actors who are successful agents in the new global economy. He acknowledges that while Pentecostals in the Global South are still quite poor as compared to their Northern counterparts, they are disciplined and world affirming, yet also pragmatic and entrepreneurial, which supports a new Pentecostal economic ethic.

One important critic of the Pentecostal ethic argument is Birgit Meyer (2010) who attempts to show how her work is different from that of scholars who simply want to see Pentecostalism through the eyes of Max Weber's *Protestant Ethic* thesis. Meyer's analysis focuses on the relationship between globalization and Pentecostalism while employing a cultural frame of analysis. While rejecting an economic analysis where religion is a shaper of economic action, she does employ Weber's methodological approach of *verstehen,* which for Weber meant an interpretive approach aimed at understanding the subjective reasons for social action. This has implications for Meyer's approach and also for assessing the relationship between the preachers of the prosperity gospel and neoliberal economics.

Meyer offers an interpretive analysis of Pentecostal self-understanding as it relates to action in the world drawing upon her fieldwork in Ghana. Her approach is to examine the ways in which Pentecostals engage in globalizing activities. In doing so, she discusses four ways in which Pentecostal discourse is globalizing and constructing Pentecostalism as a global religion (2010, 116–122). First, Pentecostalism is globalizing through what she calls a *Pentecostal imaginary of the world.* By this she refers to how Pentecostals imagine the world as a single place. This represents an important approach found in the work of Roland Robertson (1992). Robertson views globalization as an increased awareness of the world as a single place and the role of religious responses to the world as a globalizing force. In this case, Meyer describes Pentecostal views of the world as dualistic or as a set of binaries as illustrated by spiritual warfare. For Meyer, Pentecostalism constructs the world as a place of cosmic warfare filled with spirits. Engaging the economic among Pentecostals in Africa is akin to spiritual warfare where the spirit of capitalism is one of many spirits engaged with the Holy Spirit. Second, she discusses the role of Pentecostal mission activities and how they engage the world, often in a dualistic fashion where one is in the world but not of the world. Third, she shows how mission activity revolves around conversion narratives of being born again that contrast with the stories that propose a rupture with the past. In this sense, Pentecostal engagement with the world is more like what anthropologists call a cargo cult (the observation among some non-Western societies that the practice of certain rituals will lead to economic benefits). The prosperity gospel, therefore, is embraced as a means to an economic end but ultimately as a competing spirit where there are winners and losers.

Peter Beyer offers another perspective with his analysis of the globalization of religion (2012, 2013a, 2013b). Beyer's sociological work has focused on how the entire world has become structured as a global society with the development of worldwide institutional systems such as economics, politics, education, law, and religion. His primary focus is on the way religion has developed as a system in relation to other institutions. Beyer argues that a process of differentiation characterizes world society with each sphere emerging and organizing as an independent entity with its own functional qualities. However, all institutions, whether they be economics or politics or religion, are interdependent upon one another. One of the main ways this has occurred historically is with the distinction between the sacred and profane or the secular and religious.

Beyer spends considerable time developing his argument with an overview of the historical process in Europe and the development of independent nation-states following the Peace of Westphalia in 1648. Each sovereign region was given authority to develop as a political entity, which also included the establishment of an official religion. States were granted authority over citizens and churches required the devotion of believers. Of importance here is the argument that Beyer makes demonstrating how the religious sphere was constructed or modeled after the political. The state church had authority and was organized hierarchically; it was bureaucratic, with official offices each with specific roles and legal authority, and was thoroughly enmeshed with the culture. This model, according to Beyer, is the most dominant form in the modern world.

However, the forces of globalization, says Beyer, are once again pointing to further social change as religious forms are pluralizing. While the modeling of religion in relation to politics was for several centuries a dominant, but not sole model, there is no historical or sociological reason to assume that any modeling from the past will be the form in the future. What the world is witnessing is a pluralization of the forms of religion in a post-Westphalian context whereby the various religions of the world have the option of modeling themselves after other institutions including, for the purposes of this chapter, the economic. This is where the prosperity gospel as a type of Christianity fits into this analysis. The prosperity gospel illustrates one way in which religion is modeled not after the political but the economic system and how religion reinforces the economic system by providing adherents with concrete ways and means to be successful in the global economy, even if they are only claims. The issue about whether or not Pentecostalism actually works and leads to economic success is beyond the scope of this chapter. However, as the chapter by Ukah (this volume) shows, the success is limited. This is in line with the general observation in the literature. While some followers appear to be quite successful, it is theoretically possible that many are not, and just as the global economic system is networked in an asymmetrical way (see Castells 2000), so, too, is the prosperity gospel network, with its potential for winners and losers. Still, the prosperity gospel appears to take its cues from the economic sphere of society so that economic language characterizes the structure and culture of prosperity churches. More specifically, the prosperity gospel is not simply a way for believers to embrace a global economic system; it is also the means by which religion itself is modeled to reflect the structure of the economic system. The prosperity gospel transforms its practitioners from loyal citizens into consumers of religious markets replete with presidents, chief executive officers, managers, consumers, and products that are produced, distributed, and consumed.

CONCLUSION

The prosperity gospel emerged in the early twentieth century as a variant of Christianity. It is characterized by a religious subculture revolving around American Pentecostalism and its values of faith, health, wealth, and victory. Together, these characteristics combine in a unique theological system located within the modernization and economic growth of the United States in the middle of the twentieth century. The cultural pattern of religious prosperity is situated in the social institutions of Pentecostalism, especially the megachurches. The structural context of prosperity highlights the way the subculture is institutionalized, and its members are socialized, and through technology, globalized. However, the subculture is also innovative and adapts to the global social context and contemporary neoliberal values of production, distribution, and consumption. Religious culture shapes global economic activity, but is also shaped by it. Megachurches operated by prosperity gospel preachers function much like any other corporation. Weber's analysis of the relationship between religion and economic behavior continues to offer an optic through which to evaluate religion and economics, even when modified and adopted to new global realities. However, through the work of Beyer, we see how religion in global society is changing as some religions are modeled after the economic system. Religions such as Pentecostalism adapt and adopt new patterns that are modeled after other spheres of society such as the economic, which has the effect of transforming believers into consumers.

REFERENCES

Ammerman, N. T. 1997. *Congregation and Community*. New Brunswick, NJ: Rutgers University Press.
Anderson, Allan. 2004. *An Introduction to Pentecostalism*. Cambridge: Cambridge University Press.

Anderson, Allan. 2013. *To the Ends of the Earth: Pentecostalism and the Transformation of World Christianity*. New York: Oxford University Press.

Attanasi, Katherine and Amos Yong, eds. 2012. *Pentecostalism and Prosperity: The Socio-Economics of the Global Charismatic Movement*. New York: Palgrave Macmillan.

Beyer, Peter. 2012. "Socially Engaged Religion in a Post-Westphalian Global Context: Remodelling the Secular/Religious Distinction." *Sociology of Religion* 73 (2): 109–29.

Beyer, Peter. 2013a. *Religion in the Context of Globalization: Essays on Concept, Form, and Political Implication*. New York: Routledge.

Beyer, Peter. 2013b. "Questioning the Secular/Religious Divide in a Post-Westphalian World." *International Sociology* 28 (6): 663–79.

Bowler, Kate. 2013. *Blessed: A History of the American Prosperity Gospel*. New York: Oxford University Press.

Burgess, Stanley M. and Eduard M. Van Der Maas, eds. 2002. *The New International Dictionary of Pentecostal and Charismatic Movements*. Grand Rapids, MI: Zondervan.

Castells, Manuel. 2000. *The Rise of the Network Society*, Second Edition. Oxford: Blackwell Publishers.

Chaves, Mark. 2004. *Congregations in America*. Cambridge, MA: Harvard University Press.

Chaves, Mark. 2006. "All Creatures Great and Small: Megachurches in Context." *Review of Religious Research* 47 (4): 329–46.

Chesnut, R. Andrew. 2003. *Competitive Spirits: Latin America's New Religious Economy*. Oxford: Oxford University Press.

Coleman, Simon. 2000. *The Globalization of Charismatic Christianity: Spreading the Gospel of Prosperity*. Cambridge, UK: Cambridge University Press.

Cox, Harvey. 1995. *Fire from Heaven: The Rise of Pentecostal Spirituality and the Reshaping of Religion in the Twenty-first Century*. Reading, MA: Addison-Wesley.

Ellingson, Stephen. 2010. "New Research on Megachurches: Non-denominationalism and Sectarianism." In *The New Blackwell Companion to the Sociology of Religion*, edited by Bryan S. Turner, 247–66. Oxford: Blackwell.

Hefner, Robert W., ed. 2013. *Global Pentecostalism in the 21st Century*. Bloomington, IN: Indiana University Press.

Marti, Gerardo. 2008. *Hollywood Faith: Holiness, Prosperity, and Ambition in a Los Angeles Church*. New Brunswick, NJ: Rutgers University Press.

Marti, Gerardo. 2010. "Ego-affirming Evangelicalism: How a Hollywood Church Appropriates Religion for Workers in the Creative Class." *Sociology of Religion* 71 (1): 52–75.

Marti, Gerardo. 2012. "'I Determine My Harvest': Risky Careers and Spirit-Guided Prosperity." In *Pentecostalism and Prosperity: The Socio-Economics of the Global Charismatic Movement*, edited by A. Yong and K. Attansasi, 131–50. New York: Palgrave Macmillan.

Martin, Bernice. 1995. "New Mutations of the Protestant Ethic among Latin American Pentecostals. *Religion* 25: 101–17.

Martin, David. 1990. *Tongues of Fire: The Explosion of Protestantism in Latin America*. Oxford: Blackwell.

Martin, David. 2002. *Pentecostalism: The World their Parish*. Oxford: Blackwell.

McClymond, Michael. 2014. "Charismatic Renewal and Neo-Pentecostalism: From North American Origins to Global Permutations." In *The Cambridge Companion to Pentecostalism*, edited by Cecil M. Robeck, Jr. and Amos Yong, 31–51. Cambridge: Cambridge University Press.

Meyer, Birgit. 2010. "Pentecostalism and Globalization." In *Studying Global Pentecostalism: Theories and Methods*, edited by Allan Anderson, Michael Bergunder, André Droogers, and Cornelis van der Laan, 113–32. Berkeley, CA: University of California Press.

Miller, Donald E., Kimon H. Sargeant, and Richard Flory, eds. 2013. *Spirit and Power: The Growth and Global Impact of Pentecostalism*. New York: Oxford University Press.

Rakow, Katja. 2015. "Religious Branding and the Quest to Meet Consumer Needs: Joel Osteen's 'Message of Hope.'" In *Religion and the Marketplace in the United States*, edited by Jan Stievermann, Philip Goff, and Detlef Junker, 215–39. New York: Oxford University Press.

Riis, Ole and Linda Woodhead. 2010. *A Sociology of Religious Emotion*. Oxford: Oxford University Press.

Robertson, Roland. 1992. *Globalization: Social Theory and Global Culture*. London: Sage.

Stewart, Adam. 2010. "A Canadian Azusa? The Implications of the Hebden Mission for Pentecostal Historiography." In *Winds from the North: Canadian Contributions to the Pentecostal Movement*, edited by Michael Wilkinson and Peter Althouse, 17–38. Leiden, Netherlands: Brill.

Stoll, David. 1990. *Is Latin America Turing Protestant? The Politics of Evangelical Growth*. Berkeley, CA: University of California Press.

Waters, Malcolm. 2001. *Globalization*. Second Edition. New York: Routledge.

Weber, Max. 1958[1976]. *The Protestant Ethic and the Spirit of Capitalism*. Translated by Talcott Parsons, with an introduction by Anthony Giddens. London: Routledge.

Wilkinson, Michael. 2007. "Religion and Global Flows." In *Globalization, Religion and Culture*, edited by Peter Beyer and Lori Beaman, 375–89. Leiden, Netherlands: Brill.

Wilkinson, Michael. 2015. "The Emergence, Development, and Pluralisation of Global Pentecostalism." In *The Handbook of Global Contemporary Christianity*, edited by Stephen Hunt, 93–112. Leiden, Netherlands: Brill.

Yip, Jeaney and Susan Ainsworth. 2013. "'We Aim to Provide Excellent Service to Everyone who comes to Church!': Marketing Megachurches in Singapore." *Social Compass* 60 (4): 503–16.

Chapter 5

God, Wealth, and the Spirit of Investment

Prosperity Pentecostalism in Africa

Asonzeh Ukah

Apart from the colonial imposition of political boundaries, and the foisting of new governance structures and the tethering of colonial African states to the Western neoliberal capitalist system, the greatest, most pervasive, and far-reaching socio-cultural transformation in Africa in the last century was religious in nature.* In sub-Saharan Africa, the practice of indigenous religions declined from a high of 76% in 1900 to a low of 13% in 2010; at the same time, Christianity increased from a low of less than 10% to a high of 56%. Islam further gained ground from 14% to 29% during the same period. Africa accounts for well over 21% of Christians worldwide (Pew Forum on Religion and Public Life, 2010; see also the chapter by Brown this volume). This is more than a seventyfold increase from 1900. It follows that religious conversion from indigenous religions to Christianity (and to a lesser extent, Islam) has transformed the social ecology of Africa. The fastest strand of Christianity in Africa is Pentecostal-Charismatic Christianity (PCC), whose popularity and social force are partly attributed to its dynamic engagement with the neoliberal market (for a general overview, see the chapter by Wilkinson in this volume). More than 80% of Pentecostal Christians in Africa subscribe to the gospel of prosperity (Ukah 2013, 77). Prosperity Pentecostalism as practiced in Africa is pro-market, with many individuals advocating that it is a way of addressing poverty and hunger. However, empirical evidence indicates that this type of religion rarely interrogates or reforms the structures of poverty as it concentrates wealth in the hands of a few individuals in its support for neoliberal principles and practices.

*Part of the research for this study was carried out under the Nagel Institute for the Study of World Christianity project on "Religious Innovation and Competition: The Impact in contemporary Africa" (sub-project: "Miracle Cities: The Economy of Prayer Camps and the Entrepreneurial Spirit of Religion in Africa" [ID 2016-SS350], headed by the author), with funding from The John Templeton Foundation.

All over sub-Saharan Africa, PCC has gained immense popularity and acceptance with adherents now constituting close to a quarter of the overall population of Christians. In countries such as Nigeria, Cameroon, Zimbabwe, Kenya, and South Africa, the popularity and social force of Pentecostal Christianity is such that scholars of the phenomenon characterize it as a "revolution" (Ojo, 2006; Helgesson 2006; Burgess 2008; Marshall 2009; Gifford 2009; Drønen 2013). Because of a combination of diverse factors, the spread of PCC in Africa has far surpassed that of other branches of Christianity, or even Islam (see Cox 2001, 245; Hanciles 2008, 121). While some scholars have expressed optimism that PCC will continue to grow in Africa, it is clear that numerical expansion has plateaued and what may be occurring in the decades ahead is consolidation and internal fragmentation (McCain 2013).

Many of the megachurches associated with the PCC that have achieved social visibility were founded in the last four decades and are still under the firm (authoritarian) control of their first charismatic founder-owners (see Wilkinson, this volume, for a discussion of megachurches). Leadership transition and the resultant routinization of charisma are a veritable litmus test of institutional stability. With a few exceptions, history indicates that rather than expanding further after the demise of their founder-owners, many Pentecostal churches fragmented and shrank, focusing more on control of property and investment, particularly by members of the family of the late founder. In the second decade of the twenty-first century, however, many of the mega Pentecostal churches have become socially, economically, and politically powerful, playing significant roles in the lives of millions of their members as well as in the social context in which they exist. A significant factor in the popular appeal and widespread enthusiasm with which Pentecostal Christians embrace their faith is the interface between Pentecostalism and economic practice and doctrines. Some scholars are of the opinion that because there is a discernible "Pentecostal ethic and the spirit of development" (Freeman 2012) akin to Weber's "Protestant ethic" (see the chapters by Wilkinson and Upadhyay), Pentecostal practices in Africa have the impulse and impetus to transform the continent (economically and developmentally) by infusing its developmental agenda with a certain degree of spiritual urgency and energy (Wariboko 2012). Èmile Durkheim (2008 [1915], 416) writes that "the believer who has communicated with his god is not merely a man who sees new truth of which the unbeliever is ignorant; he is a man who is *stronger*. . . . It is as though he were raised above his condition as a mere man; he believes that he is saved from evil, under whatever form he may conceive this evil" (emphasis in original). Religion, therefore, may be an impetus that helps a believer deal with, and overcome, existential necessities; how Pentecostal Christianity accomplishes this in Africa is a question of ongoing research and debate and a concern for this chapter.

Because Pentecostalism is a protean movement that adapts and appropriates different elements within its immediate environment in order to produce a lively hybrid of doctrines, rituals, ideas, and institutions, its impact or influence is not uniform all over Africa. Generally, however, there seems to be a negative correlation between increased Pentecostal penetration and expansion and economic well-being in Africa. In the last four decades, which have witnessed the "Pentecostal revolution," more Africans have fallen into the poverty trap than previously. Subsequently, after more than four decades of Pentecostal expansion and the preaching of faith in God as a condition for return on investment, Africa remains the world's poorest and most under-developed continent with a continental GDP that accounts for just 2.4% of global GDP. In the context of massive economic disruptions and prolonged *dedevelopment*,[1] Prosperity Pentecostalism has caught on like wildfire in a savannah field in different parts of sub-Saharan Africa (see World Bank 2014, 1–14). With more than 240 million Africans undernourished, Prosperity Pentecostalism has become a magnet for a new Pentecostal elite that believes religion is a gateway to economic investment and wealth transfer (Ashimolowo 2006).

Under the conditions of social, political, and economic underperformance and uncertainty, Prosperity Pentecostalism has flourished, often promising to deliver wealth and well-being (which the postcolonial African states have failed to deliver to their citizenry) to adherents. However, such a promise has hardly translated into reality. This chapter addresses how a particular Pente-costal organization interfaces with global neoliberal capitalism. Examples are drawn from Nigeria; however, in many instances, what obtains in Nigeria, *mutatis mutandis*, may be transposed to another sub-Saharan African country. While Nigeria is the most populous African country, it is also home to the largest Pentecostal population on the continent. Furthermore, the wealthiest and largest Pentecostal church is found in Nigeria, making the country a spe-cial site to examine how Pentecostal ecclesiality accommodates neoliberal globalization (Wariboko 2014b, 54f). The socioeconomic force of Nigerian Pentecostalism is modeled after neoliberal economic practices revolving around profit making and investment opportunities. This is evident in the case study of this chapter, which focuses on how a popular Pentecostal organiza-tion accommodates neoliberal practices through its engagement with the real estate market in Nigeria. Before this can be explained, a brief overview of the economic theology and practices of Pentecostal churches in Nigeria provides the general context.

PROSPERITY PENTECOSTALISM AND THE OPTION FOR THE RICH

Pentecostalism represents an internally variegated set of doctrines, rituals, ideas, and practices that transcend the metaphysical domain of how humans relate to superhuman entities. Sometimes called "wealth and health gospel," Prosperity Pentecostalism is now a global movement. It is one leg of the tripod on which African Pentecostalism is built; the other two legs are healing and deliverance. In their book, *God Is Back*, John Micklethwait and Adrian Woodridge (2009) write, "The success of Pentecostalism [in Africa] is a strange mixture of unflinching belief and pragmatism, raw emotion and self-improvement, improvisation and organization: it is as if somebody had distilled American-style religion down to its basic elements and then set about marketing it globally" (218). In accounting for the success of African Pentecostalism in the twenty-first century, its affinity to global incarnations of neoliberal economic thinking and practices cannot be ignored. In other words, a major strength of African Pentecostalism is its mixture of spiritual energy, competitive and entrepreneurial spirit, accumulation, and conspicuous consumption.

The political economy of Pentecostalism in sub-Saharan Africa shows that as the postcolonial state underwent liberalization, deregulation, and subsequent downsizing in the late 1970s and 1980s, Pentecostalism and similar "strong religions" stepped into the spaces and functions previously occupied and performed by the state (on the concept of strong religion, see Almond, Appleby, and Sivan 2003). The shrinking of the state correlated positively with the expansion and consolidation of Pentecostal formations. From June 1986, under the military regime of Ibrahim Babangida, the Nigerian state started rolling back state functions such as the provision of subsidy for essential commodities, the provision of subsidized healthcare, as well as important social services under a Structural Adjustment Program (SAP). The national currency, the naira, was also devalued in line with the directives of the International Monetary Fund and the World Bank. According to Falola and Heaton (2008, 219), "devaluation of the currency brought with it rapid inflation and a decrease in the purchasing power of the average Nigerian. The naria, which stood at N1 = [US] $1 in 1985, fell to N 4.21 to the dollar in 1988, N7.48 in 1989, and N22 by 1994. The inflation rate stood at between 40% and 70% from about 1988 to 1995, and per capita income declined from an estimated $778 in 1985 to just $105 in 1989." The unfulfilled promises (such as health for all, wealth, prosperity, employment, security, adequate housing or accommodation, and improved well-being) of the postcolonial state became the self-advertising slogan of Pentecostal structures. The popularity of Pentecostalism is, therefore, closely tied to its promises of miracles (quick, instant solutions) in solving human challenges. Under the context of economic liberalization—which means the breakdown of government monopoly in providing social goods, the privatization of public enterprises—the emergent Pentecostalism assimilated the ideas and practices of neoliberal economics, such as private property, laissez-faire, consumerism, commodification, and the supremacy of profit (Dairo 2010, 191–192). The religious leader or pastor became a spiritual entrepreneur, producer, and chief executive officer, his church became his firm; congregants became spiritual consumers; religious services, spiritual knowledge, and rituals became commodities exchangeable for money (see also Wilkinson, this volume). More than three decades on, the Pentecostal formations of the 1980s have come to maturation.

Some scholars argue that the prosperity doctrine "draws deeply from the philosophical springs that inform neo-classical economics" (Wariboko 2014a, 87). However, African practitioners of prosperity gospel rarely follow any harmonized doctrine or practice; religious leaders bring to bear their own interpretations and understanding of both the scriptures and economic philosophy. Of the three major doctrinal emphases in African Pentecostalism, prosperity gospel permeates virtually all aspects of thinking and preaching and practices of major Pentecostal churches in Africa. Practitioners of prosperity gospel justify their actions by reference to the Bible: "Beloved, I pray that all may go well with you and that you may be in good health, just as it is well with your soul" (3 John 1:2 NRSV). "That all may go well with you" is translated in the King James Version of the Bible—which is the preferred translation for most Pentecostal Christians—as "that you may prosper." The theology of "that all may go well with you" is comprehensive and totalizing in conception; practitioners describe prosperity as material advancement, success, and promotion in worldly affairs.

Material uplift is a consequence of a covenantal outcome of believing right and acting accordingly. The born-again Christian who believes in correct doctrine as expounded and taught by "a wo/man of God" has "legal rights" enforceable through the merits of the death of Jesus Christ on the Cross. The born-again Christian's "legal rights" are such that are not bestowed by the state but by the law of the covenant. According to David Oyedepo (1997, 30–31), who is a Nigerian prosperity gospel entrepreneur, "the economy of your nation has no bearing on our covenant walk. They are two separate laws. The law of the spirit of life (under which we operate) is always able to cheaply handle the law of sin and death." According to this exegesis, a born-again Christian cannot be sick or poor because Christ was wounded and was poor in order that his followers are healed and become rich. To be rich, and to be publicly perceived as such, is a demonstration, a material testimony, of being in the right with God, manifesting divine justification and glory. Christians are to be prosperous so that they may invest in Kingdom business: "The ultimate goal of biblical prosperity should be to let your money work for you so you can work for God" (Ukpabio 2010, 47). Irrespective of the details, anecdotes, and other narratives with which prosperity theology is couched and explicated, the fundamental element that ties together a large number of Pentecostal entrepreneurs is the "calculated and calculating mentality" and disposition that links faith in God and investment returns (Wariboko 2014a, 88). For these preachers, to genuinely believe in God means putting into practice scriptural principles (as discerned and described by a particular man or woman of God), and the inevitable investment returns that it yields.

Although Pentecostalism is a religion that emerged as a demonstration of the power of the spirit over matter, such as speaking in tongues, seeing visions, and practicing prophecy, dealing with economic and practice concerns is also an important engagement. At the core of Pentecostal economics is tithing and donations, usually to the ministry of a wo/man of God. Some prominent African proponents of prosperity preaching have even dispensed with faith or belief in God altogether, insisting, instead, that the epicenter of prosperity architecture is giving to God through a recognized wo/man of God. According to Isaac Giwa (2005, 11–12), a Nigerian prosperity preacher and author, "sixteen out of Jesus' thirty-eight parables were concerned with how to handle money and possessions. The Bible includes five hundred verses on prayer, less than five hundred verses on faith, but more than two thousand verses on money and possession." Many African prosperity preachers are inclined to believe and act on this type of biblical analysis, inferring, therefore, that "money and possession" are the cornerstones of biblical Christianity: "God wants you healthy, wealthy and prosperous above every other thing in life" (Giwa 2005, 11). It is, therefore, the duty of every Christian to "learn how to make enough money for the future as well as today," which will involve cultivating the "attributes, qualities and skills to become wealthy" (Ukpabio 2010, 48).

Because there is no "authorised standard version" of the prosperity message in Africa, different preachers have been free to quote Bible verses to bolster their subjective interpretations. Some have also attempted to put into practice the central theme of investment in the kingdom principles in order to reap a hundredfold reward. Almost every Pentecostal pastor of means and resources has turned into an author of "best seller" books and pamphlets that are privately published, principally to evade paying taxes. An important source of revenue and spiritual capital is the production of devotionals (see also Upadhyay, this volume). The devotionals are daily spiritual or biblical readings, reflections, and prayers by a popular pastor. They attempt to contextualize Pentecostal spirituality according to their authors' perspective and understanding.

Most devotionals produced by African Pentecostal leaders follow the oldest format of devotionals known in the continent, which is "Our Daily Bread," produced and distributed free of charge since 1956 in more than fifty-five languages by Radio Bible Class Ministries and targeted at a wide audience of Christians and non-Christians alike. Some of the popular devotionals from Africa include "Our Daily Manna" produced by Chris E. Kwakpovwe of Voice of Liberty Ministries, "Quite A Time" by controversial female pastor Helen Ukpabio of Liberty Gospel Church, and "Bread and Wine" by Simeon Afolabi of First Love Assembly. By far the two most popular devotionals coming from Africa are "Open Heavens" by Enoch Adeboye of the Redeemed Christian Church of God (RCCG) and "Rhapsody of Realities" by Chris Oyakhilome of LoveWorld Ministries, Inc. (A.K.A. Christ Embassy). Published in a single yearly volume format, "Open Heavens" faithfully follows the format of "Our Daily Bread" (with a memory verse, "the Bible in one year" section, and a short commentary, and concluding with a prayer point). Published as a monthly booklet in 552 languages and available in 242 countries, Christ Embassy authorities describe "Rhapsody of Realities" as "the no. 1 Daily Devotional in the world" on their website (Rhapsodyofrealities.org).

The way in which these devotionals are distributed illustrates one significant, yet often ignored, pattern of Pentecostal engagement in neoliberal practice. There are noticeable differences between "Our Daily Bread" and African-produced devotionals. The most important difference is the entrepreneurial spirit that informs and undergirds the economy of devotionals produced in Africa by Pentecostal leaders. African Pentecostal devotionals are for sale. They are a huge source of income for the different individuals and organizations responsible for their distribution. For the devotionals produced by African Pentecostal leaders that are electronically available on the internet, or have mobile apps, such as "Rhapsody" and "Open Heavens," financial subscription is necessary to access them. Pentecostal media production (DVDs, books, devotionals, mobile apps) improves and extends a leader's authority and standing among his or her followers and the larger Pentecostal public. These productions are organized as "commodities of the spirit" and are underpinned by a neoliberal mentality and logic informed by profit making. The subscription system, for example, is driven by the principle of profit and the market, that is, competition for resources such as clients and revenue.

To illustrate the profit-making logic that drives African Pentecostal practices and rituals, Christ Embassy has institutionalized since 2010 a gate-taking procedure during its most popular annual event, the New Year's Eve service. During this "Crossover Service," the church charges a fee of a thousand Nigerian naira (about US $6) from participants; ushers and other security personnel in the church turn away those who are unable to make this payment. Christ Embassy justifies this practice as a crowd control mechanism. Nevertheless, with a sitting capacity of more than 20,000, each service brings into the church's coffers huge revenues for which the church pays no taxes to the state. Taxation laws in Nigeria exempt ecclesiastical activities from taxes on profit if they are not involved in "trade" but fail to define what accounts as "trade." The worth of a pastor is judged by his net worth in financial terms.

The value of his services is measured by what it costs his followers to access them. The Pentecostal publishing industry (as well as the broader electronic media domain) in Nigeria (and by extension, Africa) embraces and accommodates neoliberal global practices rather than challenging or resisting them or even introducing countermeasures to them. The Pentecostal publishing industry is erected on the celebrity system of the book industry where authors of bestselling books are celebrities recognized for their books' ability to rake in revenues.

Another facet of practices within the Nigerian Pentecostal field that has so far gone unnoticed is the different ways major Pentecostal actors insert themselves within the neoliberal economy by providing services and goods clearly driven by the principle and logic of the market. Pentecostal organizations are strongly represented in the educational and healthcare sectors where they operate private secondary schools, universities, hospitals, maternities, and clinics. Unlike the mission churches, which provide subsidized social services as an important aspect of their missionary activities, the Pentecostal organizations charge the highest fees and tuitions for their services, which target the very rich segment of the population. The three most expensive universities in Nigeria in terms of tuition are owned by Pentecostal churches. The real estate market, explained below, offers yet another opportunity for Pentecostal participation in the market, and the most prominent Pentecostal actor in this arena is the RCCG.

THE REDEEMED CHRISTIAN CHURCH
OF GOD: THE MASTER BUILDER

In contemporary times, successful religious organizations have demonstrated an uncanny ability in mobilizing and effectively managing three significant resources: manpower, money, and media outreach. These factors reinforce and build upon one another, enlarging and consolidating the presence and power of the organization to further recruit more resources. The RCCG exemplifies the patterns of productive entrepreneurial religion in the neoliberal age. In the last four decades, the RCCG has been one of the most important religious and cultural players to emerge from Africa with global ambitions. The RCCG is arguably the largest Pentecostal franchise in Nigeria with nearly 60,000 branches in the country and a self-reported membership of five million, and over 15,000 branches in 188 countries. To demonstrate its growing popularity, the church announced during its National Convention in August 2015 that between 2012 and 2014, it had converted and enrolled 840,272 new members into its fold, according to the *Nigerian Tribune* online edition (August 9, 2015). In Nigeria, the RCCG also has the reputation of being the wealthiest religious organization and the single largest private property owner.

Until 1988, the RCCG was a little-known religious group in the country; it was then a poor storefront church with few educated members in its folds. When the founder, Josiah Akindayomi, died in 1980, the reins of power fell on a young, educated university lecturer, Enoch Adeboye, who laboriously undertook the task of restructuring the group by changing its doctrines from a holiness, world-avoiding organization to a world-accommodating one. He did this by introducing prosperity doctrines appropriated through his association with the annual convention organized by Kenneth Hagins (Sr.) (1917–2003) in Tulsa, Oklahoma. Born in 1942 into an Anglican family, Adeboye converted to the RCCG in 1973 (the same year as his wife, Folu Adeboye, who was instrumental in her husband's conversion) and earned a doctorate in mathematics from the University of Lagos in 1975. He taught at two different universities for some time before resigning his appointment to head the church in 1981. As an enlightened leader, Adeboye traversed the world in search of ways to grow his church at home; he gleaned significant ideas and practices from the United States and Canada as well as from South Korea. Expanding the church meant inculcating economic rationality into religious organization and practices: Adeboye recruited marketers and companies who aggressively sponsored his evangelistic activities and provided organizational infrastructure, media equipment, electricity-generating plants, and buildings. The profit model, which informs commercial business, soon became imbibed as a pattern of growing the RCCG.

The taste of success and wealth meant that the RCCG did not limit its activities to the purely spiritual sphere; from the 1990s, it became a prominent market player. First, the church set up numerous business schools where students were educated on how to utilize Christian principles in shaping and capturing market segments. Second, the church started establishing its own businesses and firms mainly in the financial sector. Apart from hospitals, and primary and secondary schools (run mainly for profit and charging relatively high fees), the church also established more than six separate banks, insurance companies, used-car dealerships, satellite and cable television stations, and mortgage institutions (see also the chapter by Dreher on business and religion). In 2005, the church invested three billion naira (about US $15 million) in the Dove Media Group, which is a conglomerate that involves satellite and cable television, radio and internet broadcasting, and audio, video, and print media that produce programs with core Christian and moral values.

The company is also into the promotion of Christian artists and ministries. According to the managers of Dove Media, the company wants to claim the airwaves and cyberspace for God (personal interview with P. A., managing director of Dove Television, Redemption Camp, Mowe, Ogun State,

Nigeria, 08.10.12). The Church promoted Dove Media as an outfit that will promote evangelism and the gospel for all Bible-believing churches all over the world. In 2005, the church raised the sum of US $3.5 million through an Initial Public Offer in Lagos. The chief executive officer of Dove Media explains the attractiveness of the business angle of the company thus: "We want investors to plough their money into Dove Media just the same way they invest in shares of banks and cement companies. They have an added advantage because they are not only investing for profit, their investment shall be used to promote the gospel and evangelism all over the world"—cited on the news website Proshare in May 2005. The combination of evangelism and profit-making ventures means the integration of neoliberal rationality into religious culture. Considering the economic stagnation being experienced in Nigeria at the time, this proposition met with positive outcomes (interview with P.A. 08.10.12). For the Church, there is no contradiction in serving the spirit of evangelism and profit making; one reinforces, sustains, and promotes the other. More than 3 million Nigerians access Dove Television through a dedicated decoder; outside Nigeria, the number of viewers may be more than 3 million, most of them members of the church.

Having dominated the religious media market in Nigeria, the RCCG scoured the local economic landscape in search of new opportunities for investment. The search for investment opportunity paid off in 2008 when the Nigerian stock market collapsed. Because of economic and financial reforms undertaken by the Nigerian government starting in 2003, the capital market experienced a boom between 2004 and 2007 with the value of some stocks quadrupling during the period. A combination of factors such as the effects of the global financial market crisis of 2008, corruption, and undue government interference in the market led to a "free-for-all downward movement" in the stock market with investors losing as much as 70% of the value of their stock (Nwude 2012, 105; Adamu, 2010). Additionally, the country's currency, the naira, depreciated considerably against the US dollar.

These factors resulted in panic, contagion, and fiscal flight (Zubair 2013). Financial and stock market volatility created a need to secure investment. Furthermore, during the same period, it was becoming increasingly difficult to move funds abroad because of the global searchlight on the money-laundering activities of Nigerian politicians, some of whom were experiencing legal challenges with European and American governments. The entrepreneurial spirit of the RCCG quickly dictated a new sphere of investment atmosphere, promising investors a secure rate of returns in a secure, sacred environment immune from market shocks, volatility, and publicity. A persistent teaching of the leader of the church is that "it is prayer that can solve the problem of lack," that is, the problem of poverty and maladministration in the country can only be solved through prayers and the intensification of piety

(Adeboye 2015). A prayerful spirit of investment led the church to move into the real estate industry.

In 2008, the RCCG delved into real estate development on a large expanse of land measuring 1,540 hectares called "The Redemption Camp," situated on the outskirts of Lagos, about forty-two kilometres from the city. From its inception in 1983, this site has actively been advertised as a "miracle city," a hybrid space where heaven and earth meet and where God answers prayers and performs miracles of healing and prosperity. Further, the leader of the church, Enoch Adeboye, through popular legend and well-orchestrated church advertising and publicity narratives, became a miracle brand, a miracle maker whose charismata are spectacular in resolving existential problems of all types. In an interview, a senior church official attributes the success in the expansion and the wealth of the church to what he calls "the Adeboye brand": "We have a brand; Daddy Adeboye is our brand and he sells our products more than any other brand in the market today. He is a brand of God" (personal interview with Pastor U. P., Redemption Camp, 08.10.2012). For church members, the Camp became a holy city where a new sacred vision was incarnated in material form. According to a senior church official, the Camp "has every infrastructure that makes life sweet and smooth in a city"; it is a place where "prayers and songs of praise pervade the air all day"; it has become the "spiritual capital of Nigeria" where "God is always on duty . . . solving all manners of life's problems" (Olubiyi 2006, 25).

At its present 2012 size, the Redemption Camp is "the largest private estate in Nigeria" and arguably the "largest Christian estate in the world" (Bible-Davids 2009, 146–47). One of the reasons for this runaway acquisition of land is that the RCCG discovered a new investment strategy for the surplus sacred space within the Camp. Only 25% of the landmass of the Redemption Camp is dedicated to the construction of religious facilities: of the 2,335 physical buildings in the Camp, only fifteen are places of worship; forty-three are academic buildings and 184 are for offices and commercial activities, such as shops and mini-supermarkets. A total of 1,855 buildings are residential: 956 bungalows, 562 duplexes, and 336 chalets, hostels, and dormitories for low-level workers or low-income church members. The spatial configuration of the Camp shows that it is split into 22 zones; more than eleven of these are dedicated to real estate (personal interview with the Chief Town Planning Office of the Camp, Mowe, Ogun State, 08.10.2012).

There are two types of real estate on the Camp. The first is an owner-built type of estate where members of the church who demonstrate their financial means of building their own houses are allocated a plot of land after the payment of a certain sum of money. Individuals are supposed to complete the building of their homes within six months according to strict specifications approved by the building committee of the church. A furnished, self-contained room is given over to the church to do as it pleases (mainly in accommodating church guests). Such owner-constructed homes are not transferable to a second party, not even to owners' descendants. While a church member may own the house, he or she does not own the land upon which it is built; it remains the church's property in perpetuity. In this sense, all owner-built homes will, at some point in future, revert to the property of the RCCG at the death of their original owners. The second type of residential estates in the Camp are prebuilt homes developed by the church's real estate planners and Investment companies. The names ascribed to the estates point to the philosophy behind the investment: Next Level Estate; Tree of Life; Haggai Estates I–VIII; Glory Court.

Each of the nine estates contains between forty and hundred units of one-bedroom apartments and three-bedroom duplexes. Premium property prices within the Camp range from four million naira (US $20,500) to 19.5 million naira (US $95,000). Located just close to the Holy Ghost Arena, which is the area where the third and largest auditorium is built, Glory Court Estate, for example, comprises forty units of one-bedroom terrace apartments for sale at three million naira (US $15,500) per unit (interview with A.T., sales agent, Haggai Estate, Mowe, Ogun state, 07.10.2012). At this price, this is the cheapest, prebuilt residential unit on the Camp. Similar to the conditions governing property ownership for owner-built houses, buyers of prebuilt flats own only the property and not the land on which it is located. The property is nontransferable; owners who wish to sell their units can only do so to the church's mortgage firms. Also, prospective buyers may either pay in cash or arrange mortgages only through the church's mortgage company. For both types of estates, the final outcomes are the same; they ultimately belong to the RCCG because the land is a private property of the Church.

What is new and innovative in RCCG's incursion into the real estate industry is the establishment of commercial developers and mortgage and finance corporations to efficiently utilize the surplus sacred spaces within the Camp. The church owns about four different real estate and property firms that are responsible for the development of the commercial real estate within the Camp and elsewhere in Nigeria. City Planners Property and Investment Limited developed Glory Court Housing Project in the Camp. Opheav Developers and Jubilee Life are two other real estate developers owned fully by the RCCG that are active in real estate development in the Camp. However, the flagship of the church's real estate investment is Haggai Mortgage Bank Limited (HMBL). Formerly known as Haggai Community Bank Limited, HMBL was established by the RCCG in the early 1990s. The RCCG claimed to have "a God-given mission to finance God-given dreams/visions of individuals and corporate institutions. We are resolute in our determination to bring them to manifestation to the glory of God" (cited in Ukah 2008, 161). It is arguably the most successful mortgage bank in Nigeria with a profit before tax of 228.3 million naira (about US $1.14m) in 2012 and 412.98 million naira (about US $2.04m) in 2013, according to its website.

While the banking sector in Nigeria is generally experiencing turbulence and difficulties in recent years in light of the reforms, consolidation, and capitalization demanded by the Nigerian Central Bank, HMBL is flourishing because it has a strong market niche. To demonstrate its global reach, Haggai developers source the architectural designs of its homes from South Africa, unarguably the most economically developed and most globally connected economy in Africa. It belongs to the wealthiest religious organization in Nigeria within whose ranks are the politically and economically powerful in the country (Ukah 2011, 2014; Bible-Davids 2009, 145–148; Marshall 2009, 75).

The Nigerian stock market crash provided an investment opportunity for the RCCG to study and exploit the real estate and property market in Nigeria. In order to justify its incursion into an economic sphere driven by the neo-liberal ideology of the tyranny of profit, the church generated a theology that presents it as "the Master Builder." In 1 Corinthian 3: 10–15, Paul uses the metaphor of a "master builder" to describe his work in relation to the Christian community in Corinth. The RCCG presents itself through its real estate developers as building apartments in the tradition of Paul, the "skilled master builder." According to this narrative, the RCCG builds houses to accommodate homeless or inadequately housed members of the Christian community in Nigeria. The developers and the mortgage institutions owned by the RCCG present their objectives as the provision of "affordable homes for low- and medium-class house[s] (yet in a conducive and attractive environment)" according to their website. Indeed, a high-density city such as Lagos with nearly twenty-five million inhabitants is in dire need of housing for its teeming low-income earners. According to Audu Liberty Oseni, "Lagos State alone needs more than 250,000 housing units yearly for the next 20 years for it to reduce the housing deficit it faces at the moment" (Audu 2012).

Generally, therefore, the "master builder" narrative of the RCCG positions the church as a socially responsible organization that is contributing to the alleviation of the critical housing deficit in Nigeria. Contrary to this rhetoric, however, three important factors deflect from this self-representation of the RCCG. The first is that the housing units in the Redemption Camp are restricted to the church's members. They are not openly available to any willing and financially able citizen to purchase. The second factor is that, considering that the monthly minimum wage in Nigeria is 18,000 naira (ca. US $100) and that more than 76% of Nigerians live on less than US $1.25 (N180) per day, less than 1% of the church's membership is able to afford the houses put on sale by the church. The type of houses the church provides (bungalows and duplexes) are not what more than 90% of Lagos dwellers who are facing dire housing deficits need or can afford. The RCCG builds for the top end of the real estate market. The third factor is that, even when nearly all the prebuilt housing units have been bought and paid for, the entire estates in the Camp are virtually unoccupied. The situation of many properties remaining unoccupied by their owners after they have been bought poses a real security risk for the managers of the Camp who fear that hoodlums and homeless persons could sneak into them and cause breaches of the peace within the Camp (interview with the chief security officer, redemption Camp, Mowe, Ogun State, 23.10.12).

In effect, the housing developments are not in any way reducing or targeting the acute shortage of shelter in Lagos or in any of the nearby cities. According to one of the developers, to own one of the housing units, one must have a home elsewhere, particularly in Lagos. The housing units in the Camp are second or third homes for buyers. Homeowners in the Camp use their property to warehouse excess funds as an investment that will appreciate over time. In view of the fact that houses are sold to church members only, and according to the terms and conditions of sale, are not transferable, house owners cannot put them on rent or on lease in order to recoup part of their investment; only a few individuals are able to set aside the high cost of the houses. Politically and economically powerful persons—often with dubious sources of wealth—who are in search of a highly secure environment to invest in are the primary market for such housing projects. Individuals of this stature seek security, privacy, and nondisclosure. The RCCG provides these secure services at a profit. Overall, investors in the housing project profit from the scheme because the Camp provides a secure space to warehouse excess funds outside the prying eyes of the state (they cannot be seized or taxed by the state because the Camp is a private, tax-free property) or the public. Furthermore, the funds invested in the housing schemes are secure and not exposed to the volatility of the stock market.

CONCLUSION

The Nigerian real estate market is a vibrant sector of the Nigerian economy. In 2011, according to the National Bureau of Statistics in Abuja, Nigeria, the real estate market contributed 1.64% to the gross domestic product in the first quarter of 2011; similarly, the building and construction subsector contributed 1.99% to the GDP in the fourth quarter of the same year (Audu 2012). The real estate market in Nigeria is a profitable investment and strategic economic arena where rapid and ongoing urbanization processes are escalating demands that continually outstrip supply. However, the RCCG's real estate projects get their inspiration not only from the "skilled master builder" narrative but also from neoliberal globalization and the liberal political economy that unchains religious organizations from regulation as charity corporations to fully participate as primary economic players spreading global liberal ideas and practices. RCCG real estate development projects in the Redemption Camp are examples of gated leisure communities with expensive and exclusive real estates designed for the rich who must now be accommodated within the surplus sacred space sourced from a diversity of relatively poor families and individuals.

RCCG's investment in the real estate market is both a reaction to and participation in global neoliberal practices. The church appropriates economic liberalization ideas and domesticates them within biblical texts that give impetus to its reinterpretation. Jesus did not have a home (while birds of the air had trees and foxes had holes, Luke 9:53), so his true followers will have decent homes to live in. Furthermore, it is by effectively multitasking or serving two masters at the same time that the church demonstrates its skills and ability to be faithful in the management of "dishonest wealth" in order to prove its preparedness to manage true spiritual wealth (Luke 16:11, Gateway Bible). The material success and wide appeal of religious organizations such as the RCCG are to be found in their creativity in relating their religious messages to the rapidly changing socioeconomic and political contexts in which their members live. RCCG is emulated in Nigeria as well as in many other countries as a church that has transgressed boundaries and has innovated in the practice of religion, and also in the adaptation of religious narratives in political and economic practices. The RCCG is a clear example of the inexorable expansion of economic globalization in different spheres of life in far-flung corners of the earth. However, although the prosperity message of the RCCG anchors its relevance on economic practices, it concentrates a disproportionate amount of wealth in the hands of a few rather than spreading the profit of economic globalization across religious consumers.

RCCG's practices within the Camp as described in this chapter clearly illustrate in concrete form its perspective on neoliberal globalization. It does not resist neoliberal globalization; rather, it accommodates, adapts, and expands its logic of practice undergirded by the profit motive. The history of the organization from its founding in 1952 to the death of its founder in 1980 indicates that the organization resisted neoliberal global economic practices as antithetical to the spiritual purity necessary for salvation as preached by Jesus Christ. The attitude of the RCCG to the world changed from 1981 onward when the group began shedding its sectarian behavior, started recruiting educated, upwardly mobile members of the elite, and repositioned itself as a mainstream, world-affirming organization. In contemporary times, the church actively and aggressively promotes neoliberal globalization, which its real estate investment practices unambiguously demonstrate. The RCCG firmly anchors its economy in the financial services industry; hence, it is not involved in agro-allied businesses, and farming and the keeping of livestock are prohibited in the Camp.

RCCG models its global religioeconomic power and expansion after the Coca-Cola Company; this company is one of the most successful global conglomerates of the modern era (Premack 2014). The RCCG claims that in the decades to come, just as Coca-Cola promises to have at least one member of every family on earth drink its products, so also one member of every family on earth will belong to the church (Ukah 2008, 269). Successful companies whose practices have shaped global neoliberal policy and practice provide the RCCG with a blueprint for expansion and wealth creation. For the RCCG, the neoliberal global political economy is evangelism-friendly and compliant because it promotes profit making and generates funds that are in theory—and according to the justification of church leaders—ploughed into the spreading of the Kingdom of God. Furthermore, defenders of the church's practices point to the magnificence of the camp as a spectacular demonstration of the power of God that inheres in a charismatic oracle, in this case, in the person of Enoch Adeboye, who, in August 2015, claimed to be richer than Bill Gates of America because he owns property in 188 countries where the RCCG has branches, as reported in the Vanguard in August 2015 by Femi Aribisala. Like global neoliberal practices everywhere, which benefit a percentage of individuals, the RCCG's practices benefit only a few persons while a large majority of church members remain poor and destitute and unable to access even the houses and services (houses, schools, health care) that the church provides because these services and goods address the concerns of the very wealthy in the society.

NOTE

1. The concept of "dedevelopment" is used to emphasize the fact that Africa is poorer in 2010 than it was in 1970; it is a case of economic stagnation and a shrinking of economic performance and well-being for the majority of Africans.

REFERENCES

Adamu, Abdul. 2010. "Global Financial Crisis and Nigerian Stock Market Volatility," paper presented at the conference on "Managing the Challenges of Global Financial Crisis in Developing Economies," Nasarawa State University, Keffi, Nasarawa State, Nigeria.

Adeboye, Enoch. 2015. *Open Heavens*, Vol. 15. Mowe, Ogun State: Open Heavens Media Limited.

Audu, Liberty Oseni. 2012. "Mortgage Financing Option for Mass Housing." *West Africa Insight* 3 (11): 3–5.

Almond, Gabriel A., R. Scott Appleby, and Emmanuel Sivan. 2003. *Strong Religion: The Rise of Fundamentalism around the World*. Chicago: Chicago University Press.

Ashimolowo, Matthew. 2006. *The Coming Wealth Transfer: Believing the Prophecy, Applying the Principle, Preparing to be a Millionaire for God*. London: Mattyson Media.

Bible-Davids, Rebecca. 2009. *Enoch Adeboye: Father of Nations*. London: Biblos Publishers.

Burgess, Richard. 2009. *Nigeria's Christian Revolution: The Civil Revival and its Pentecostal Progeny (1967–2006)*. Cumbria: Paternoster Press.

Cox, Harvey. 2001. *Fire from Heaven: The Rise of Pentecostal Spirituality and the Reshaping of Religion in the Twenty-First Century*. Cambridge: Da Capo Press.

Dairo, Olalekan A. 2010. "Privatization and Commercialization of Christian Message." In *Creativity and Change in Nigerian Christianity*, edited by David O. Ogungbile and Akintunde E. Akinade, 193–97. Lagos: Malthouse Press Limited.

Drønen, Tomas Sundnes. 2013. *Pentecostalism, Globalisation, and Islam in Northern Cameroon: Megachurches in the Making?* Leiden: Brill.

Durkheim, Èmile. 2008 [1915]. *The Elementary Forms of the Religious Life*. Translated by Joseph Ward Swain. New York: Dover Publications.

Falola, Toyin and Matthew M. Heaton. 2008. *A History of Nigeria*. Cambridge: Cambridge University Press.

Freeman, Dena, ed. 2012. *Pentecostalism and Development: Churches, NGOs and Social Change in Africa*. New York: Palgrave Macmillan.

Gifford, Paul. 2009. *Christianity, Politics and Public Life in Kenya*. London: Hurst.

Giwa, Isaac. 2005. *Get Ready: Money Cometh*. Lagos: Isgibson Services.

Hanciles, Jehu J. 2008. *Beyond Christendom: Globalisation, African Migration, and the Transformation of the West*. Maryknoll: Orbis Books.

Helgesson, Kristina. 2006. *"Walking in the Spirit": Complexity of Belonging in Two Pentecostal Churches in Durban, South Africa*. Uppsala: DICA.

Marshall, Ruth. 2009. *Political Spiritualties: The Pentecostal Revolution in Nigeria*. Chicago: University of Chicago Press.

McCain, Danny. 2013. "The Metamorphosis of Nigerian Pentecostalism: From Signs and Wonders in the Church to Service and Influence in Society." In *Spirit and Power: The Growth and Global Impact of Pentecostalism*, edited by Donald E. Miller, Kimon H. Sargent, and Richard Flory, 160–83. Oxford: Oxford University Press.

Micklethwait, John and Adrian Wooldridge. 2009. *God Is Back: How the Global Revival of Faith is Changing the World*. New York: Penguin Press.

Nwude, Chuke E. 2012. "The Crash of the Nigerian Stock Market: What Went Wrong, the Consequences and the Panacea." *Developing Country Studies* 2 (9): 105–17.

Ojo, Matthews A. 2006. *The End-time Army: Charismatic Movements in Modern Nigeria*. Trenton: Africa World Press.

Olubiyi, Olaitan. 2005. "Redemption Camp . . . Playing a Role in Nigeria's Destiny." *Redemption Light* 8 (7): 25–26.

Oyedepo, David. 1997. *Understanding Financial Prosperity*. Lagos: Dominion Publishing House.

Pew Forum on Religion and Public Life. 2010. *Tolerance and Tension; Islam and Christianity in Sub-Saharan Africa*. Washington, DC.

Premack, Laura. 2014. "The Coca-Cola of Churches Arrives: Nigeria's Redeemed Christian Church of God in Brazil." In *The Public Face of African New Religious Movements in Diaspora*, edited by Afe Adogame, 215–31. Surrey: Ashgate Publishers.

The World Bank. 2014. *Youth Employment in Sub-Saharan Africa*. Washington, DC: International Bank of Reconstruction and Development/The World Bank.

Ukah, Asonzeh. 2008. *A New Paradigm of Pentecostal Power: The Redeemed Christian Church of God in Nigeria*. New Jersey and Asmara: Africa World Press.

Ukah, Asonzeh. 2011. "Die Welt erobern, um das Himmelreich zu errichten. Pfingstkirchen, Prayer Camps und Stadtentwicklung in Lagos." In *Urban Prayers. Die weltweite Renaissance religiöser Bewegungen in den Metropolen*, edited by MetroZone, 109–27. Berlin: Assoziation A und metroZone.

Ukah, Asonzeh. 2013. "Prosperity Theology." In *Na God: Aesthetics of African Charismatic Power*, edited by Annalisa Butticci, 77–79. Padova: Fondazione.

Ukah, Asonzeh. 2014. "Redeeming Urban Spaces: The Ambivalence of Building a Pentecostal City in Lagos." In *Global Prayers: Contemporary Manifestations of the Religious in the City*, edited by Jochen Becker, Katrin Klingan, Stephan Lanz, Kathrin Wildner, 178–97. Zurich: Lars Müller Publishers.

Ukpabio, Helen. 2010. *God's Prosperity Methods*. Calabar: Kings View Publishing House.

Wariboko, Nimi. 2012. "Pentecostal Paradigms of National Economic Prosperity in Africa." In *Pentecostalism and Prosperity: The Socio-Economics of the Global Charismatic Movement*, edited by Ketherine Attanasi and Amos Yong, 35–59. New York: Palgrave Macmillan.

Wariboko, Nimi. 2014a. *Economics in Spirit and Truth: A Moral Philosophy of Finance*. New York: Palgrave Macmillan.

Wariboko, Nimi. 20154b. *Nigerian Pentecostalism*. Rochester: The University of Rochester Press.

Zubair, Abdulrasheed. "Causal Relationship between Stock Market Index and Exchange Rate: Evidence from Nigeria." *CBN Journal of Applied Statistics* 4 (2): 87–109.

Chapter 6

Neoliberal Capitalism and the Emergence of Corporate Hinduism in Urban India

Surya Prakash Upadhyay

In the early 1990s, a new type of spiritual *gurus* (religious teacher) emerged in Hinduism differing markedly from more traditional forms of Hinduism and spiritual leadership traditions. These gurus have become popular figures as a result of their regular appearance on satellite and cable television channels. Their use of modern media has made their appeal much more widespread but also different from that of more traditional Hinduism. The spirituality they offer is presented as a tool to combat uncertainties created by global capitalism and the changing role of the welfare state. Specifically, these new gurus deliver leadership and personality-building lectures at corporate houses and create special spiritual programs for the employees of multinational corporations. Blending various texts, scriptures, and contents of Hindu eschatology with management knowledge, the gurus produce a corporate form of Hinduism. This "Corporate Hinduism" addresses various personal issues of people working in the neoliberal economic enclaves that have developed in India; these include time management, health, happiness, and wealth issues that need to be addressed in order to survive in a very competitive domestic as well as global market. Followers claim that the spiritual practices and methods are beneficial, scientific, and rational.

In addition to the spiritual advice and guidance that they offer, there is a definitive economic aspect associated with these gurus as they develop products, here referred to as "salvation wares," to be sold in the market and promoted through television channels and other forms of media. Some of these are labeled as *swadeshi* (locally produced goods). This is done in an effort to traditionalize and to imbricate their efforts in Indian history; the *Swadeshi Movement* was an integral part of the struggle for independence from British colonialism. Its key plank is its insistence on homegrown goods and products claimed to be herbal, natural, *ayurvedic* (based on traditional Indian medicine), and free from chemicals. By linking to the independence struggle and its historical insistence on locally produced goods, the gurus secure their own market share domestically while at the same time, paradoxically, supporting the further integration into global capitalism of the individuals seeking their guidance.

The chapter argues that the emergence of these gurus is a sign of how structural changes bring about changes in religiosity and, in turn, how these changes in religiosity serve economic and political interests. The emergence of these gurus shows, in contrast to Max Weber's positing Hinduism as a barrier to economic development, that religions are adaptable and can change in response to demand. This also highlights the degree to which the affinity between religion and capitalism is a two-way street. After outlining the Weberian thesis on the "spirit of capitalism," the chapter shows how spiritual gurus produce similar ideas to those that Weber found in Calvinism. In the light of this finding, Weber's argument should not be restricted to the historical understanding of the development of capitalism. As this chapter shows, various recent processes—political, economic, technological, cultural—have brought transformations in social structures in India that have led to changes in the underlying value system of a society; the spirituality of the gurus plays a major part in this process.

Several social structural changes in India responsible for the emergence of these new forms of religion will be detailed in the following sections: first, the liberalization of television and the privatization of the entertainment sector in the 1990s created an increased need for content and provided space for the diffusion of religious ideas; second, the emergence of the right-wing nationalist-populist *Hindutva* movement in politics made Hinduism fashionable and brought it back into the public sphere and consciousness as different than before and provided the space for the more open and aggressive expression of religion; third, the integration of India into the neoliberal global economy in the 1990s and the parallel expansion of the middle class created market opportunities for the new spiritual gurus.

It is to the middle classes working in neoliberal enclaves in the cities, often for multinational corporations, that these gurus direct their "salvation wares" (products and spiritual advice) to help them succeed in an uncertain and competitive market place. This class emerged as a result of the political, cultural, and economic transformation of India under neoliberal globalization. The latter brought about a gradual rollback of the welfare state, increased the challenges of living in cities and working in the market, and raised the aspirations to excel in everyday life. At the same time, existing traditional religious establishments were unable to address the needs of this new middle class and they, therefore, were receptive to the appeal of these new spiritual gurus. Their basic "salvation ware" is to provide ontological security in a life characterized by increased uncertainty and the many pressures on individuals to succeed.

The question of whether these gurus promote, reform, or resist neoliberal globalization cannot be answered in a simple way. On one hand, they oppose multinational firms and because they see them as competitors for their products, they align somewhat with the more assertive and somewhat anti-Western political project of Hindutva. On the other hand, the gurus promote neoliberalism by selling religious wares in the market place. Furthermore, through their spirituality workshops, management advice, and teachings, they engage in grooming self-disciplined and motivated employees suitable for the neoliberal market.

WEBER AND CAPITALIST DEVELOPMENT IN INDIA

In examining the cultural attributes of capitalism, one turns inevitably to the work of the German sociologist Max Weber (1864–1920). Weber (2001) argued that, with the exception of Calvinism, other world religions lacked the "spirit" that would lead them to modern economic development. Weber had identified specific characteristics of Calvinism such as the spirit of asceticism, disciplined absenteeism from worldly affairs, a particular type of attitude toward work, and a business orientation emphasizing profit, honesty, and thrift (see also Wilkinson, this volume). For Weber, Calvinism encourages individual enterprise not only in the management of capital, knowledge, and skill but also by a sustained commitment toward work, responsibility, and willingness to engage in profit-generating businesses.

With respect to Hinduism, Weber (1958) in his book, *Religion of India*, argued that such an entrepreneurial spirit did not exist in Hinduism. He claimed that because of its theodicy and social system, Hinduism does not offer enough scope for the genesis and growth of capitalism. Weber's claim has an element of truth. Historically, textual and scriptural emphasis on the doctrines of *karma* (fate), *dharma* (duty), *moksha* (salvation), and *punarjanma* (rebirth), the ritual values assigned to the caste system, and the other-worldly motivations of Hinduism did not orient Hindus toward profit-making activities. The Hindu eschatology generates a different set of concerns for the individual, at least as far as texts and scriptures describe it. The ideas of karma, dharma, moksha, and punarjanma do not restrict an individual from performing his or her duties in this world. However, these ideas have sufficient scope for putting moral restrictions on involvement in profit making and economic action beyond one's requirements. According to this view, the emphasis on satiation restricts the cultivation of an entrepreneurial spirit.

Weberians in India concur with this argument and have presented Hinduism as an impediment to economic progress and modernization. The slow economic growth rates after independence in 1947 were attributed to these

characteristic features of Hinduism. In fact, in the initial years after independence, scholars devised the phrase "Hindu rate of growth" to describe
the economic growth of India. Scholars like William Kapp (1963), Gunnar
Mrydal (1968), David Mandelbaum (1970), and Surajit Sinha (1974)
acknowledged "India's backwardness by citing the attitudes inculcated by
Hinduism" (Gellner 1982, 528). Similarly, Sinha agrees with Weber's thesis,
arguing that Hinduism is a major "stumbling block for modernization" in
India (Sinha 1974 as quoted in Gellner 1982, 528).

However, Max Weber's argument is, in fact, contested. The English histo-
rian Trevor-Roper argued that it is not religion that shaped modern capitalism
but that modern capitalism created a new form of religion. In other words,
according to Trevor-Roper (1967), "it was not Calvinism [that] created a
new type of man, who in turn created capitalism; it was rather that the old
economic elites of Europe were driven into heresy because of the attitude
of mind which had been theirs for generations" (27). According to Singer
(1966, 497), it is this insight that has led Robert Bellah (1963) to conclude
that "it is not mere presence or absence of this or that component of motivations, institutional arrangements, or entrepreneurial group that constitutes a
proper analogy to the Protestant ethic in Asia. The analogy must be looked
for . . . in the transformation of basic structure of a society and its underlying
value-system" (as paraphrased in Singer 1966, 497). In other words, Singer
argues that we need to see religion as integral to the complete structural and
ideological transformation of states and societies.

As this chapter will show in the following section, there have been
enormous transformations in India under neoliberal globalization leading
to changing approaches to the work ethic, personhood, imaginations and
images about work, the evolution of a new middle class, the liberalization of
television, and the emergence of political Hinduism (Hindutva). Together,
these changes have produced a new form of spiritualism. Some of the gurus
discussed later in the chapter have optimized and reinforced, but also transformed, these changes. This chapter thus shows that structural changes have
consequences for religiosity and that religions are adaptable, but that religiosity serves to secure larger-scale structural change. Hinduism as a religious
tradition is thus not the stumbling block to economic development—if it
ever was. In adapting and integrating themselves within the larger structural
change, the forms of Hinduism discussed in this chapter follow the same pattern as has been shown for Islam in Indonesia (Rudnyckji 2012) and in other
countries, as the chapters in this volume demonstrate (see Wilkinson, Ukah,
and Dreher). It is therefore possible to postulate that changes in religiosity
may be an important aspect of neoliberalism as a project, especially at the
level of the individual. As a result, our understanding of neoliberalism is also
in need of refinement, a task to which the chapter now turns.

NEOLIBERALISM, RELIGION, AND CULTURE— THE LEVEL OF THE INDIVIDUAL

Since the early 1990s, India has opened up its market to foreign investment, trade, and business. With economic restructuring, the role of the state undergoes changes, and so do notions of citizenship and individual subjectivity. This has led scholars to conclude that there is a specific Indian version of neoliberalism (Münster and Strümpell 2014; Oza 2006; Patnaik 2007) in which the market as well as the state imagines a particular kind of subject and citizen (Gooptu 2009). Indeed, in order for neoliberal transformation to take hold, individuals as well as their habits and behavior need to be transformed. Specifically, the subjects in the neoliberal imagination are self-driven, responsible, self-governed, and prepared to take responsibility for their well-being and for managing risks and vulnerability (O'Malley 1996 quoted in Gooptu 2009, 45). In a consumer society, the risks are portrayed as personal and a good citizen is one who is self-dependent and autonomous, and acts as an entrepreneurial agent in the neoliberal economy (Voyce 2006). Therefore, neoliberalism is not only about the expansion of market forces and changes in governance patterns. It is also related to how the state, its citizens, and its subjects are imagined.

Neoliberal globalization is thus more than about politics and the economy because it also brings changes in notions of citizenship and individual subjectivity. It directs everyday discourse on economic, social, political, and cultural relations (Köse, Senses, and Yeldan 2007). For the purpose of this chapter, the starting point for the analysis of neoliberalism is inspired by Hart and Hann's idea (2009) that irrespective of the universal logic of capital accumulation, the "actual modalities of surplus extraction have always been socially and culturally embedded" (Hann and Hart 2009 quoted in Münster and Strümpell 2014, 4).

This chapter therefore argues that in order to understand the neoliberal age, a more culturally sensitive approach needs to be taken that allows for a closer focus on the individual. It follows Springer's (2012) call for a "cultural turn" in both international political economy and economic geography to better conceptualize neoliberalism. Springer (2012) argues that "a culturally informed critical political economy has a major role to play in developing politically enabling understandings of the entanglements of power in an increasingly interdependent neoliberal world" (134). How the economic and political aspects of neoliberalism are translated, justified, and legitimized at the societal and, especially, at the individual level needs to be studied as neoliberalism also changes the ways in which people refashion themselves.

This necessitates studying neoliberalism as discourse (Springer 2012). This has the potential to incorporate the "cultural turn of international political economy and economic geography" (133). By looking at neoliberalism as a discourse, it becomes easier to understand the various ideas, practices, and agencies that produce neoliberal citizens and subjects like the new spiritual gurus. The chapter therefore shows that the spiritual gurus should be seen as a key aspect of the neoliberal discourse and project in India in the way they support some of its aspects such as the flexibility of the labor market and the need of the individual or company to be competitive. By providing spiritual guidance, they help people to survive in a very uncertain and competitive market place. In this way they transform the subjectivity of the self and adjust it to the neoliberal age while at the same time providing reassurance because of their enmeshment in local traditions. In the following section, the chapter highlights the structural changes brought about by neoliberal globalization in India, how they implicate the individual, and how they in turn relate to the growth of the new gurus.

STRUCTURAL CHANGES IN INDIA
AND THE RISE OF THE GURUS

Neoliberal globalization in India might have started with the opening up of its market for foreign trade, investment, and business in the early 1990s, but alongside it several other events and processes took place that now define the character of India. Oza (2006) identifies at least three developments: neoliberal economic reforms; the work of the *Sangh Parivar* in the rise of the *Hindutva* movement; and the manner in which both the economic power structure and the Hindu Right bolstered the consolidation of middle-class identity and power (Oza 2006, 2). In particular, neoliberal economic policies led to the growth of private satellite and cable networks. All these factors together enabled the growth of the new corporate Hinduism centered on the spiritual gurus. This in turn helped enable the cultural turn in India discussed in the previous section.

Hinduvta and the Media

With economic liberalization and the privatization of the entertainment sector, foreign channels started appearing on the Indian landscape. New television channels such as Star TV, MTV, and many others came into being. The emergence of these new channels and their need to fill airtime allowed many spiritual gurus to appear on television and increased the face-to-face encounter of individuals with gurus, at least in a virtual sense. Whereas before, individuals had to undertake pilgrimages, or at least leave the house, in order to encounter their gurus, now the gurus came into the privacy of the home. Even before the arrival of new religious and spiritual channels, *Doordarshan*, India's national television channel, and All India Radio, occasionally used to relay the spiritual discussions of a few gurus. Later, from the early 1990s, television channels such as ATN (Asia Television Network), Zee TV, and Sony TV began to telecast spiritual discourses of gurus. Furthermore, various full-fledged spiritual television channels, such as *Astha* and *Sanskara*, started telecasting spiritual/religious programs of various gurus. Now, with the expansion of spiritual television channels, there is regular spiritual instruction and people tune in to their favorite gurus and have *darshan* (visual encounters) with the guru for the whole day.

In a sense, the new age was heralded already by *Doordarshan*'s broadcast of the Hindu epic *Ramayana* in the late 1980s (later to be remade by a private channel in 2008). "The broadcast of the Ramayana in a serial form across the country suddenly made Hindu gods, symbols and values and beliefs available, accessible and legitimate" (Upadhyay and Robinson 2011, 161). The symbols and images portrayed in the serial supplied content that popularized Hindu nationalism and intensified the political mobilization of Hindus by the *Sangh Parivar*. Sangh Parivar is a collective term used to refer to the Hindu Right. It consists of the political party, the *Bharatiya Janata Party* (BJP), the *Vishva Hindu Parishad* (VHP), a nationalist civil society organization oriented toward the protection of the Hindu identity, and the *Rashtriya Swayamsevak Sangh* (RSS), a volunteer organization that has been involved in charitable work, but also in many controversies, and is for many associated with political violence. Together, these organizations have radically changed how many Indian citizens understand themselves and their role in world politics (White 2006; Gopalakrishnan 2006).

This movement laid the groundwork for the gurus in that it made religious ideas popular again but gave them a completely different connotation. As Hansen (1999) notes: "After the new economic policy, including liberalization, deregulation and privatization of the public sector, had been proclaimed by the government, the RSS embarked on a campaign for a swadeshi approach to economic development" (Hansen 1999, 170–71). Hansen further writes that the Sangh Parivar prepared a list of 326 consumer products manufactured by multinationals and mentioned an Indian-produced alternative to each product. The Sangh Parivar argued that foreign products should be banned in India as these products potentially contaminate Indian culture and urged Indians to buy local products. For the Sangh Parivar, the idea of swadeshi has its location in economic nationalism. More importantly, an emphasis on swadeshi would "save" India from cultural contamination. Alternative products were sought and the Hindu Right urged the government to protect local industries from a second wave of what they described as global imperialism. The ideas such as cow protection, vegetarianism, India as a Hindu nation, *swadeshi*, and so on are the products of the works of the Sangh Parivar and its Hindu nationalist movement now legitimized by the spiritual gurus.

The spiritual gurus took up these Hindutva ideas because they allowed them to establish a market for their *ashram* (monastery or religious compound)-made products. The idea of *swadeshi* (local) in opposition to *videshi* (foreign) production and the fear of cultural contamination, the impure and chemically treated products of multinationals, that was diffused by the Hindutva movement became a base for the gurus to attract consumers for their products. It is important to note, however, that the gurus do not share the same understanding as the Hindu Right, and even within the Hindu Right there are differences.

Unlike the RSS that focused on the negative consequences of economic liberalization, the BJP as a party found no contradiction between the idea of swadeshi and liberalization. The idea of swadeshi that seems to be followed by spiritual gurus is entangled in between the ideas of both the RSS and the BJP. The gurus oppose multinationals along the lines followed by the RSS whereas they enter into business and compete in the market at par with multinationals within the logics of globalization and liberalization by selling their projects. It is here that we can see clearly how neoliberal market making is entwined with a local nationalist project that, paradoxically, is built on using the market.

The Professional Middle Classes

The liberalization of the Indian market and the expansion in the service sector, in particular in the information technology and management sectors, created new forms of employment and contributed to the growth of a middle class with more disposable income. This new class is the direct product of the policies of economic liberalization that were pursued from the early 1990s onward (Fernandes 2004, 2006). This new middle class is often compared to the new rich in contemporary Asia that are the prime beneficiaries of contemporary globalization (Beng-Huat 2000). Apart from the policies of liberalization and greater participation in the market economy, by virtue of which the new middle class is expanding, there were specific government policies that could be said to have brought more people and communities into the middle class: the affirmative action policies such as reservations in education and jobs for erstwhile *Other Backward Classes*[1] and the ratification of the recommendations of a government commission that revised salaries and perks for government sector employees in 2006. These two policies diffused more wealth in the population and contributed to the increase in the middle class. However, despite the entry of lower caste Hindus into the middle-class category, it is basically upper caste Hindus who are participating in the organizations and seminars of corporate Hinduism.

In a historical sense, the middle class in India can be categorized as old and new. The old middle class emerged during the colonial times. This is the English-speaking occupational class working in the administration of British India. The middle class of colonial times was considered an important agent to bring in progressive changes in indigenous cultures in India. However, the new middle class of today is an outcome of economic liberalization and it consists of those who are integrated in the global market economy and who work in different capacities in neoliberal economic enclaves that have emerged as one key form of neoliberal development policies (see Sampat 2010). The new middle class is considered a potential agent that can help in the establishment of neoliberal global capitalism in India. It would be an overgeneralization to argue that the middle class is a uniform actor whose subjectivity is aligned in one direction. There are various elements that need to be distinguished in the new middle class. There is an elite and a nonelite middle class, for example, but economic, caste, regional, linguistic, and religious distinctions also play a role in differentiating the middle class within itself (Donner 2011). Deshpande (2003) rightly says that the term middle class is more of a social connotation and self-location. One factor that plays a role in specifying the middle class is the distinction from upper classes, on the one hand, and from people who hardly own resources, social or economic, on the other hand. It is the recognition that they do not have enough resources to be included in the upper class, but at the same time knowing that they are better off than people living in slums and working as servants in offices, driving autorickshaws, or owning a *pan* (betel) and cigarette shop or grocery store that leads many individuals to feel part of the middle class in India.

Different groups within the middle class are seen following different types of spiritual leaders. A few may be seen in the organization of transnational gurus such as Sri Sri Ravishankar, who speaks in English and caters to the needs of people working at the higher echelons in the global market. The followers often are upper caste, though there are a few low caste Hindus as well, while a few others follow gurus like Asaram Bapu, who attracts followers from specific regional, caste, and linguistic groups and also many low caste Hindus. However, it would be wrong to put a strict segregation of followers along caste and class lines. Many times, one person follows several gurus. S/he may like the products of Baba Ramdev but may prefer the spiritual instructions of Sri Sri Ravishankar. While upper caste Hindus are more dominant in these organizations, it needs to be noted that the gurus themselves avoid the issue of caste. This shows how the general project of the Hindutva is able to unite people from different economic backgrounds by proposing a new form of discourse based on a new form of Hinduism—whether this is the more right-wing nationalist discourse of the Hindu Right or the more spiritual discourse of the gurus discussed. Thus, caste questions do not become a point of discussion in the discourses of the gurus. Rather, their central type of inquiry rotates around the idea of a "healthy, happy, and prosperous life." Therefore, while they speak to different audiences, a common denominator that connects various gurus is that they emerged after economic liberalization and the advent of private television channels, and are popular among the various segments of the middle classes.

The approach toward spirituality in these guru organizations is on a similar plane as presented by Mara Einstein in her study (2008). She argues that marketing and branding have become integral elements in the religious marketplace. In fact, to a large extent the gurus have modified the approach toward religion and consumerism wherein spiritual development and material gain go hand in hand. In the guru organizations, there is no contradiction between spiritualism and materialism. It is a Hinduism very different from the one portrayed by Max Weber in his book *Religion of India*.

The gradual rollback of the welfare state, the expansion of market economy, and the emergence of an imagination of citizens and subjects as self-responsible and self-dependent have led people to follow spiritual gurus. The neoliberal economy desires efficient people in the market, influenced by the social Darwinian principle of survival of the fittest. People often say that though they have attained formal education and a job, it is the pressures from the market that lead them to look at gurus who not only instruct them spiritually but also help them regenerate interest in culture (personal observation). The followers of the gurus claim that they assist them in realizing their potential by helping them excel in their employment and everyday life. As Turner (2011) argues, in modern society religion has been "commodified" as well as "commercialized," which has attracted the attention of an upwardly mobile middle class. In India, too, one can see that under the aegis of spiritual gurus, Hinduism is developing as a business model (Beyer 2012) suitable for the neoliberal age and economy.

THE NEW SPIRITUAL BARONS AND THE CORPORATIZATION OF HINDUISM

The inheritance of political ideas of the Hindu Right such as safeguarding local industries from foreign economic encroachment and the protection of Hindu and, thereby, Indian culture from cultural contamination and the "impure" products of multinationals (MNC) created a particular mood among the individuals that buy and consume products prepared in guru ashrams. The opposition to MNCs and international products by the Hindu Right made it possible for many gurus to start up their own businesses and for these businesses to be profitable. The opposition to foreign products as spiritually impure, bodily harmful, chemically treated, culturally contaminating, economically exploitative, and representing a second colonialization of India provided the ground for selling ashram-made products in the market. The spiritual gurus claim to offer products that are chemical-free, natural, organic, homemade, and herbal, unlike foreign products. The gurus claim that these products are not only economical and natural but also keep money in India. With this they take up the idea of swadeshi, locally produced goods that the independence movement had promoted.

As conceived during the Indian freedom struggle, swadeshi was against the economic policies of British Indian government. The swadeshi of colonial times revolved around the idea of indigenous manufacture and consumption. This idea was then extended by the Hindu Right to include the idea of integral India in the 1990s. As Hansen (1999) notes, the Hindu Right conceived swadeshi as a platform to create harmony, cultural-national values, and discipline, among other things. The Hindu Right conceived of developing an indigenous economic planning different from capitalism and communism (Hansen 1999, 92).

It is instructive to note that swadeshi in guru organizations is erected on similar principles of cultural ethos, harmony, and discipline but differs from colonial times in that it distinctly embodies a neoliberal market logic and is thus not part of a dichotomy between global and local. This can be seen, for example, in the way the guru organizations advertise their products, which is similar to that of MNCs. While ashram-made products are not advertised on television to the same degree as products by MNCs, the logic of using advertisements to sell their "salvation wares" is similar. Lately, many MNCs have also started claiming that their products are chemical-free, made of natural products, herbal, harmless for the body, and largely beneficial. In fact, the extent of claims to the naturalness of products by guru ashrams is even higher. In the following sections, the operations of three gurus—or spiritual barons—Baba Ramdev, Asaram Bapu, and Sri Sri Ravishankar and their organizations and mode of operation will be explained in more detail.

Like many of the spiritual gurus, Baba Ramdev, Asaram Bapu, and Sri Sri Ravishankar deal in specific types of consumer goods. These are items used in prayers and rituals, ayurvedic products, and medicines made of homemade products, booklets, CDs, and DVDs, to name just a few examples. Baba Ramdev is now a globally recognized Yoga Guru; Sri Sri Ravishankar and his foundation, "The Art of Living," are also known globally; they sell books, apparel, and beauty products (among other things), while Ashram Bapu is mainly popular within India for his spiritual discourse. Each of the gurus owns several franchise outlets for his ashram-made products.

In 2014, *Patanjali Ayurveda Limited* owned by Baba Ramdev grossed more than Rs. 1,200 crore (approximately US \$185 million) in sales, which is expected to reach Rs. 2,000 crore (around US \$300 million) in the fiscal year of 2015. "In five years, I will take swadeshi products of Patanjali to such great heights that foreign companies will dwarf in front of them," declared Ramdev in a news report written by Rajiv Singh on the website of the Economic Times in 2015. The article makes some more interesting observations. For example, Baba Ramdev hires employees who previously worked with multinationals for marketing purposes. Furthermore, there is no advertising for Baba Ramdev's products. Instead, advertising is done through word of mouth, especially during his yoga classes. Similarly, Asaram Bapu offers distributorships to his followers to sell his ashram products. Many of the products are manufactured in companies owned by his followers, but marketed by Asaram Bapu's ashram. The consumers of these products are usually the respective followers but nonfollowers also buy and consume guru ashram products, which, according to them, offer quality and economy. For example, corn flakes sold by Baba Ramdev cost around Rs. 80 (i.e., around US \$1) while Kellogg's sells corn flakes at around Rs. 90. The prices for these guru ashram products are lower compared to those of multinationals because they do not spend much on advertising. Also, the labor cost is reduced because followers often contribute in factories as *seva* (service) for the guru. The guru ashrams produce a large range of products from bath soap and shampoo, spices, everyday products, and homemade medicines. The products are claimed to be natural with no harmful effects to the body compared to the products of multinationals. In fact, these products are said to enhance one's spiritual level. It is declared that such products do not create impediments in spiritual growth as mind and body are kept healthy by the regular use of swadeshi. There is an integral business model developed by guru ashrams and their products are presented as bringing benefits for the integrated spiritual development of the followers.

In addition, the gurus also profit from their association with corporations. Corporate houses organize meditation-based self-management leadership programs for their executives. Using themes and ideas from Hindu texts and scriptures and blending them with management knowledge, the gurus attract employees working in the IT sector and management firms. The gurus have designed specific spiritual programs for employees working in the neoliberal market economy. Sri Sri Ravishankar's spiritual program, "Sudarshan Kriya," was developed into a course by the organization he founded. The course was named "Achieve Personal Excellence" (APEX) and it was aimed at business professionals. His website explains that APEX "is a simple, practical, and effective training program that empowers managers and employees, and promotes calmness and focus in the midst of any challenge or responsibility."

Sri Sri Ravishankar claims that the course improves concentration, enhances creativity, increases efficiency, and builds a sense of work and achievement. It is different from other management courses according to followers as the course is not based on quick-fix solutions but, rather, provides practical lessons that offer tangible and direct results (personal observation). Taking this as an inspiration, other gurus have also developed such programs designed for people working in neoliberal market enclaves. Swami Sukhbodanand's "Life program" and Jaggi Vesudev's "Inner Engineering" are two examples of guru programs that enjoy huge success in the corporate world.

In addition to selling products and delivering programs and workshops, these gurus also give leadership lectures and personality-building workshops. Swami Sukhbodhanand, referred to as the "Corporate Guru," has lectured at corporate houses such as Asian Paints, ICICI, Raymond, TERI, and Infosys, to name just a few. Swami Sukhbodhanand argues that he offers personality-building skills based on what is written in the *Bhagavad Gita* (a Hindu scripture). He synergises Hindu philosophy with Western management thought. He offers holistic empowerment workshops and packed spirituality as "3A—Arise, Awake and Accomplish," and "3S—Steps to Success and Satisfaction."[2] The spiritual contents of these workshops are often taken from the language of management studies (e.g., relationships are described as personnel management) but associated with religious traditions. Jaggi Vasudev speaks in English, and has delivered lectures at the World Economic Forum, Davos (a meeting place for the global economic elite, see the chapter by Dreher in this volume) for several years; he has discussed themes such as inclusive economics and inner engineering, postulating that a spiritual transformation may also lead to social justice. He declares, in an article in the Huffington Post on May 2010 that "the spiritual process need not be taught as a philosophy or a belief system; what we refer to as spirituality is just a technology for inner well-being—it can be imparted as simple methods which will naturally lead to a more inclusive way of experiencing life" (see also his website).

Usually, in these lectures, the gurus concentrate on how to remain spiritual while working in the corporate world. They have come up with shortcuts for many yogic and meditative exercises that allow corporate employees to rejuvenate their energy levels in a few minutes. In an interesting discussion, Asaram Bapu says that one does not have to sit in a yogic posture to re-create one's energy. Rather, one can simply stretch oneself on an office chair and achieve energy rejuvenation. The spirituality of these guru organizations is projected as a tool for creating energy and potential, not just bodily but also mentally. The gurus claim that suggestions offered by them are helpful in everyday life and the workplace. The yoga, dietary suggestions, and so on, as claimed by gurus, help people work efficiently in their everyday life. The techniques for stress management restrain tension, reduce strain, and keep the body and mind healthy, according to the gurus. In this way, the discourses of the gurus seek to enmesh the everyday with the spiritual and we can see the intertwining of the ritualistic, the philosophical, the meditative, and the introspective aspects of religion with the everyday life of individuals in a neoliberal enclave. The works of spiritual gurus and the spiritual practices offered by them demonstrate how certain Hindu concepts are modified in the wake of neoliberalism that emphasizes individual self-restraint, self-disciplined, productive capacities, and the pursuit of excellence as human goals.

CONCLUSION

The gurus introduced in the chapter and the new cultural logic of capitalism and corporate Hinduism that they support have their roots in larger transformations that took place in India during the late 1980s and early 1990s. Each transformation offered some unique tool or logic that made the works of gurus acceptable. If media provided an instrument for transmission and a greater spread of the appeal of gurus, then ideas, moods, and motivations created by the Hindutva movement provided sufficient material and space as well as logic for gurus to be accepted among the people. The persona, charisma, and methods of approaching religion and guiding people spiritually were repackaged or rather reimagined in such a way that economic aspects of religion and, thereby, the marketing of religion was made possible.

The chapter has argued that there is a greater commercialization as well as commodification of religion. We have seen that gurus give lectures in enterprises, have their own businesses, advertise products, offer franchises, establish networks for the sale of products, and target consumers. All these activities are done within the logic and method of modern business enterprise. One can say that the marketing of such products is possible because of the logics created by the gurus and by the neoliberal transformation. The gurus are always seen speaking about benefits, be it spiritual lessons, spiritual exercises, or the use of spiritual products. It is this idea of benefit that is at the center of their activities. Neoliberal ideology claims that it is about progress and for such progress one has to be competitive in the marketplace. Many of the more traditional religious institutions do not offer specific services that directly contribute to the capability of individuals to survive in this new logic of organizing society and, therefore, people approach these gurus. The emergence of gurus and their works are very much a part of a changing situation, partly innovations in the job market and other institutions.

Hindutva offered a space for the gurus to expand their activities. In fact, the alignment of the gurus with the Hindu Right may not be very apparent but they definitely extend the ideas of Hindutva. The idea of vegetarianism and cultural purity, and attempts to restrain cultural contamination by avoiding Western products and lifestyles are a few areas where gurus come very close to the ideologies of Hindutva. If one looks at the products of guru ashrams, one can easily see the appeal of swadeshi, to both the gurus and Hindutva. The stories of a *Rama*, a *Krishna*, or a *Shiva* (various Hindu gods) and the practical use of lessons are done publicly. The Hindutva political campaigns not only created identity politics but they also pronounced the cultural logic of such politics in which gurus have inserted themselves beautifully. In this sense, the gurus are one element in the cultural and spiritual underpinning of neoliberalism in India, of which the Hindutva movement is one key aspect today.

As the chapter has demonstrated, Weber's idea about Hinduism and capitalism must be altered to understand certain capitalist developments that are taking place in India and that are spearheading a transformation of Hinduism from within by developing new forms and expressions of Hinduism. The works of spiritual gurus and the spiritual practices offered by them demonstrate how certain Hindu concepts are modified in the wake of neoliberalism that emphasizes self-restraint, self-discipline, productive capacities, and the pursuit of excellence as human goals. This also shows that Hinduism is far from a monolithic tradition of thought but needs to be conceptualized in a more differentiated way (White 2006, see also the introduction on religion as a social construct).

The conclusion from this study is that Weber's question of the interrelationship between religion and capitalism needs to be studied in an open-ended manner. Traver-Roper has shown that Calvinism was created by the new economic elites; similarly, Bellah argues that we need to look at the transformation of societies and the changes this produces in their value systems. The chapter has shown that neoliberalism in India has created a new middle class, one with a much greater emphasis on the individual. This middle class is characterized in part by a need for spirituality, but also feelings of economic insecurity, a hallmark of the neoliberal restructuring process. As a result, different types of religious expressions have emerged: on the one hand, various spiritual gurus have emerged who engage in business and offer salvation wares to those who are more economically insecure. On the other hand, an ethics of self-development has developed among the people who are exposed to the high work demand of the neoliberal market in which people seek self-assurance in yoga and meditation. In both cases, religion has been transformed into a consumer product to be bought and sold.

NOTES

1. Other Backward Classes: The Government of India uses the term to collectively refer to low caste Hindus who are also socially and economically marginalized in contemporary times.

2. The 3-A program is a workshop devised by Pujya Swami Sukhabodhananda, conducted by trained pracharaks. The modalities of the workshop include an audio presentation of unfolding each mantra and based on them, introject their values for ones well-being through meditation, processes, and chanting (www.swamisukhabodhananda.net).

REFERENCES

Beyer, Peter. 2012. "Socially Engaged Religion in a Post-Westphalian Global Context: Remodeling the Secular/Religious Distinction." *Sociology of Religion* 73 (2): 109–29.

Bellah, Robert. 1963. "Reflections on Protestant Ethic Analogy in Asia." *Journal of Social Issues* 19 (1): 52–60.

Beng-Huat, Chua. 2000. *Consumption in Asia: Lifestyles and Identities*. New York: Routledge.

Deshpande, Satish. 2003. *Contemporary India: A Sociological View*. New Delhi: Penguin.

Donner, Henrike. 2011. *Being Middle Class in India: A Way of Life*. London: Routledge.

Einstein, Mara. 2008. *Brands of Faith: Marketing Religion in a Commercial Age*. London: Routledge.

Fernandes, Leela. 2004. "Politics of Forgetting: Class Politics, State Power and the Restructuring of Urban Space in India." *Urban Studies* 42 (12): 2415–30.

Fernandes, Leela. 2006. *India's New Middle Class: Democratic Politics in an Era of Economic Reform*. Minneapolis: University of Minnesota Press.

Gellner, David. 1982. "Max Weber, Capitalism and the Religion of India." *Sociology* 16 (4): 526–43.

Gooptu, Nandini. 2009. "Neoliberal Subjectivity, Enterprise Culture and New Workplaces: Organized Retail and Shopping Malls in India." *Economic and Political Weekly* 44 (22): 45–54.

Gopalakrishnan, Shankar. 2006. "Defining, Constructing and Policing a 'New India': Relationship between Neoliberalism and Hindutva." *Economic and Political Weekly* 41 (26): 2803–13.

Hann, Chris and Keith Hart. 2009. "Introduction: Learning from Polanyi." In *Market and Society: The Great Transformation Today*, edited by Chris Hann and Keith Hart, 1–16. Cambridge: Cambridge University Press.

Hansen, Thomas Blom. 1999. *The Saffron Wave: Democracy and Hindu Nationalism in Modern India*. Princeton, NJ: Princeton University Press.

Kapp, William. 1963. *Hindu Culture, Economic Development and Economic Planning in India*. New York: Asia Publishing House.

Köse, Ahmet H., Fikret Şenses, and Erinc Yeldan. 2007. *Neoliberal Globalization as New Imperialism: Case Studies on Reconstruction of the Periphery.* New York: Nova Science Publishers.

Mandelbaum, David. 1970. *Society in India Vol. 1 and 2.* Bombay: Popular Prakasham.

Münster, Daniel and Christian Strümpell. 2014. "The Anthropology of Neoliberal India." *Contributions to Indian Sociology* 44 (1): 1–16.

Mrydal, Gunnar. 1968. *Asian Drama: An Inquiry Into the Poverty of Nations.* New York: Pantheon.

O'Malley, Pat. 1996. "Risks and Responsibility." In *Foucault and Political Reason: Liberalism, Neo-liberalism and Rationalities of Government,* edited by Andrew Barry, Thomas Osborne, and Nikolas Rose, 141–64. Chicago: University of Chicago Press.

Ong, Aihwa. 2006. *Neoliberalism as Exception: Mutations in Citizenship and Sovereignty.* Durham, NC: Duke University Press.

Oza, Rupal. 2006. *The Making of Neoliberal India: Nationalism, Gender and the Paradoxes of Globalization.* New York: Routledge.

Patnaik, Utsa. 2007. "Neoliberalism and Rural Poverty in India." *Economic and Political Weekly* 42 (32): 3132–50.

Rudner, David West. 1994. *Caste and Capitalism in Colonial India: The Nattukottai Chettiars.* Delhi: Munshiram Manoharlal Publishers.

Rudnyckji, Daromir. 2012. *Spiritual Economies: Islam, Globalization and the Afterlife of Development.* Ithaca: Cornell University Press.

Sampat, Preeti. 2010. "Special Economic Zones in India: Reconfiguring Displacement in a Neoliberal Order." *City and Society* 22 (2): 166–92.

Singer, Milton. 1966. "Religion and Social Change in India: The Max Weber Thesis, Phase Three." *Economic Development and Cultural Change* 14 (4): 497–505.

Sinha, Surajit. 1974. "The Sociology of Religion." In *A Survey of Research in Sociology and Social Anthropology,* Vol. II, chap. 9, edited by Indian Council of Social Science Research. Bombay: Popular Prakashan.

Springer, Simon. 2012. "Neoliberalism as Discourse: Between Foucauldian Political Economy and Marxian Poststructuralism." *Critical Discourse Studies* 9 (2): 133–47.

Subrahmanyam, Sanjay. 1990. *The Political Economy of Commerce.* Cambridge: Cambridge University Press.

Tawney, Richard Henry. [1926] (2012). *Religion and the Rise of Capitalism.* New Delhi: Aakar Books.

Traver-Roper, Hugh R. 1967. *Religion, Reformation and Social Change and Other Essays.* London: Macmillan.

Turner, Bryan S. 2011. *Religion and Modern Society: Citizenship, Secularisation and the State.* Cambridge: Cambridge University Press.

Upadhyay, Surya Prakash, and Rowena Robinson. 2011. "Globalization, Mass Media and Proliferating Gurus: The Changing Texture of Religion in Contemporary India." In *The Globalization Turbulence: Social Tensions in India,* edited by Prashant Kumar Trivedi, 159–79. New Delhi: Rawat Publications.

Voyce, Malcolm. 2006. "Shopping Malls in Australia: The End of Public Space and The Rise of 'Consumerist Citizenship'?" *Journal of Sociology* 42 (3): 269–86.

Weber, Max. 1958. *Religion of India*. Garth and Martindale (trans.). New York: Macmillan.

Weber, Max. 2001 [1930]. *The Protestant Ethic and the Spirit of Capitalism*. Trans. by Talcott Parsons with an introduction by Anthony Giddens. London: Routledge.

White, David Gordon. 2006. "Digging Wells While Houses Burn? Writing Histories of Hinduism in a Time of Identity Politics." *History and Theory* 45 (4): 104–31.

Chapter 7

The Globalization Project of the Hizmet Movement

Sabine Dreher

The Gülen or *Hizmet* movement is a transnational religious movement from Turkey inspired by the teachings of Fethullah Gülen (1941–). It is now present in over hundred and sixty countries with an estimated 2,000 schools and businesses (Hansen 2014); its goal is the revitalization of Islam (Gülen 2005). It is part of the Nursi movements in Turkey that take their inspiration from the writings of Said Nursi (1877–1960), a Turkish Islamic activist who sought to combine religion and modernity. Gülen built on Nursi's ideas (Ergil 2012, 274; Gülay 2007, 47) and gradually created his own movement referred to as *Hizmet*—the Turkish word for "service." Whereas Nursi's focus was on the individual, Hizmet places more emphasis on serving society in three areas as summarized by Gülen: "Let us spread the education so that the ignorance can come to an end; do trade so that the country can get rich; let us show tolerance to everyone so that oppositions and divisiveness can be lifted" (quoted in Ergil 2012, 274). This quote shows that Gülen is following the ideas of Nursi who had identified the three enemies of humankind as poverty, ignorance, and disunity (Mardin 1989, 86). Gülen believes that these can be conquered through education, business, and dialogue (Interview, August 2012).[1]

For its adherents, Hizmet is an example of what Casanova has termed public religion at the level of civil society (see chapter 2). Gülen's Islamic civil society activism attracted followers in the seventies because he saw secular education as a means to economic and spiritual development and called for the construction of schools, tutoring centers, and dormitories in lieu of mosques (Sevindi 2008, 70, 74). At the time, the pious population in Turkey was excluded from decision making in the center; to the people, Gülen's activism promised upward mobility for them and their children, and it is this focus on education that explains a large part of the movement's success. Today, adherents serve the movement by working in its organizations, by volunteering (service), and through donations. There are two sides to the movement: the inner, religious core that is organized similar to a "sect," and the outer, secular layer in the public sphere with educational businesses (schools, tutoring centers, and universities), general businesses (organized in a business association called *TUSKON*), a charity (*Kim Se Yok Mu*), and Dialogue and Research Institutes (Ergil 2012, 183).

The outstanding aspect of the movement is its global orientation and the explicit creation of secular civil society organizations only loosely tied to the faith community. After establishing itself across Turkey in the 1980s, the community moved into the former Turkic republics and the Balkans and further expanded into Africa, Asia, and Latin America to grow into what is now classified as a significant transnational actor (Ebaugh 2014). One key purpose of the movement was to bring the world to Turkey, for example, through study trips organized by all the centers, and to bring Turkey to the world (through investment, and dialogue activities) in an effort of education and persuasion in a global atmosphere characterized by prejudices against the Islamic faith.

Notwithstanding Hizmet's own understanding of civil society activism (Çetin 2009), most see the movement as negatively implicated in Turkish politics, as it occupied key positions in the judiciary and the police force, and therefore was a part of the increasingly repressive Turkish state. Most observers perceive a power struggle between the movement and the Justice and Development Party (AKP) and its leader Erdoğan over the direction of Turkish politics that was won by the AKP. Even sympathetic observers such as Akyol (2015) question Hizmet's democratic, apolitical, and civil society credentials. The current AKP government, in power since November 1, 2015, is employing various methods, including illegal ones, to suppress the movement in its quest for absolute control over the Turkish state (see Bozkurt, this volume). The future of the movement therefore rests upon further transnationalization and a retreat from its focus on Turkey.

But what exactly is the transnationalization process and what are its goals? Owing to the prominence of violent radical Islam, research on the political economy of Islamic activism is largely absent. While this chapter will address the politics of the movement to some extent, the key objective is to evaluate the Hizmet approach to neoliberal globalization.[2] The main concept to be applied is that of a "globalizing elite." The latter is one of the key carriers of neoliberal globalization, according to neo-Gramscian authors.[3] The chapter will investigate Hizmet as a non-Western expression of this globalizing elite, having created its own "globalization project" based on two pillars: an ideology based on dialogue, interfaith, and intercultural activities, on the one hand, and community-oriented businesses in the free market promoting a "Hizmet development model," on the other hand. The perspective in this chapter is therefore not on the power struggle in Turkey but on the Hizmet movement as a transnationalizing actor.

POLITICS: HIZMET AS AN EXPRESSION OF CIVIL ISLAM?

Islamophobia—hatred directed toward Muslims—is increasingly prevalent in Western countries. It has placed many Muslims in a defensive position because it is often combined with secularist assumptions: the idea that religious activists have no place in the public sphere (see introduction). This combination has created a double standard with regard to Islamic activism, as any nonviolent Islamic movement is often automatically labeled as liberal, modern, and democratic. Wiktorowicz (2004) defines Islamic activism as the "mobilization of contention to support Muslim causes" (2). Contention is a broad term that includes terrorist groups, political groups, and inward-oriented movements. While Hizmet would object to the term "contention" (Çetin 2009), it is nevertheless a movement that promotes a specific form of Islamic activism at the level of civil society (Yavuz 2003, 30). However, there are different forms of nonviolent Islamic activism: conservative and oriented toward civil society (Hizmet), more political and conservative (see Bozkurt and Webb, this volume), liberal (Kurzman 1998) and progressive (Moghadam 2014).

The Islamic tradition in Turkey consists of three different strands (Akyol 2011, 214): the various Nursi movements such as the Hizmet, official state Islam, and the Sufi orders, the largest of which are the Naqshbandi; they are all conservative in the sense that they emphasize law and order, the nation, family (values), and property rights (Yavuz 2003). In theory, the Nursi movements also belong to the Sufi orders within the Naqshbandi tradition (BPC 2015, 24). However, they never accepted the more political Islam promoted by the Naqshbandi under their leader Erbakan since the seventies. Erbakan was dismissive of the Nursi approach. He labeled it the "Islam of flowers and bugs," and chided it for its Western orientation (Akyol 2011, 216). The AKP is a successor party within this tradition of Islamic activism in Turkey, which was very much anti-Western and state interventionist up until 1997. The military coup in the same year led this group of activists to temporarily support integration into the European Union as well as neoliberal policies in order to reduce the power of the military and secular establishment. To this end, a strategic alliance among all Islamic activists and liberals was formed, which led to the election of the AKP in 2002. By 2008, the AKP succeeded in conquering the state through the trials of high-ranking military personnel and by 2010, it had consolidated its power. Initially, it was hoped that this would imply a democratic consolidation in

Turkey (Akyol 2011), but since 2010 there has been an increasing effort on the part of the AKP and the current president of the Turkish Republic, Recep Tayyip Erdoğan, to centralize power (Savran 2015). As a result, the global policy community is now assessing Turkish Islam and its relationship to democracy more negatively (Akyol 2015; BPC 2015; Idiz 2015; Seufert 2015). The transformation of the AKP shows that Yavuz's (2003, 6) assessment of Islamic movements as Janus-faced (both modern and authoritarian) is still valid.

The changing alliances in Turkish politics have led to a reversal of fortune for the Hizmet movement: while initially a part of the anti-Kemalist coalition together with the AKP, today it is classified as a menace by the AKP. For most observers, the movement was a part of both the state and the AKP, and is largely seen as instrumental in the victory over the military because of its widespread presence in the judiciary and on the police force (Seufert 2014). The latter also meant that many saw it as a part of the repressive state apparatus in Turkey. Indeed, during the interviews in Turkey conducted in August 2012, adherents admitted that Hizmet had become too involved with the AKP government. Most observers are convinced that an intense power struggle took place over the control of the state and the judiciary from 2011 onward. Critics argue that the movement resented President Erdoğan's bid for the centralization of power and was engaged in its own bid for power, while Hizmet adherents argue that they defend democracy against AKP authoritarianism. Critics are convinced that both sides have resorted to less than democratic and transparent means in order to dislodge the other side (Akyol 2015; Hansen 2014; Savran 2015; Seufert 2014).

The size of the movement and the uncertainty over who belongs to it lead to speculation. The problem is the "strategic ambiguity" of the movement (Hendrick 2013, 207). It refers to the fact that many institutions and members do not display their affiliation to Gülen openly. This was a difficult thing to do under the repressive Kemalist state before the arrival of the AKP government in 2002. However, even today it creates difficulties in understanding the reach or the influence of the movement.[4] With the creation of another AKP majority government on November 1, 2015, it is clear that the AKP has consolidated its power and that the Hizmet movement will see its activities curtailed as the government now considers the movement as a terrorist organization. Hizmet businesses are taken over by the state; a similar fate is likely for its schools and universities, or their activities will be impeded through arbitrary regulations; adherents have been purged from the police and the judiciary; and many are serving prison sentences or facing prosecution.

Hizmet strictly separates its public, secular manifestation from its religious identity. The religious aspect is both hierarchical, as it is organized like a business with different managerial levels (Tittensor 2014, 161ff; Bruinessen

2013), and patriarchal, with a majority of executive roles occupied by men (Turam 2007, 117). Its adherents regularly meet up for discussions on ethics in so-called *sohbet* (talks on religious matters that often include a discussion of specific projects). There is no compulsion with regard to membership, but to leave would result in the loss of access to a network that serves as a means of socialization and that provides business and employment opportunities (Hendrick 2013). From a global perspective, the goal of the "sect" is to reach out to Muslims and to restore their faith—whereas to non-Muslims, the movement seeks to explain its version of Islam (Tittensor 2014, 132–33; 114–15), but also to generate revenue. It would be important at some point to evaluate the transnational aspect in its relevance for the Turkish power struggle, but this is a separate investigation.

Within Turkey, it is one of the few Islamic activist groups that is critical of the increasing authoritarianism; however, it does not seem to have much support. This may be due to its elite orientation, its strategic ambiguity, and the general perception of its having instrumentalized the state apparatus for its own benefit, as well as not seizing the opportunity to further Turkish democracy when it could have done so (Akyol 2015; Jenkins 2009; Seufert 2015). Outside Turkey, the movement is a transnational civil society movement that promotes dialogue, develops businesses, and educates students and the public on the idea of a civil Islam (Tittensor 2014, 75). The next section will discuss the economics of the movement and introduce the notion of a "globalizing elite."

ECONOMICS: SOCIAL BUSINESS, MARKET ISLAM, OR GLOBALIZING ELITE?

The economics of the movement have been described in a contradictory manner: Is it, as Çetin (2009, 244) argues, a part of the third sector, in between the market and the state, or is it even a social business (Tittensor 2014), or do we have to see it as a form of Islam in favor of the free market and neoliberalism akin to prosperity religion? (See Wilkinson and Ukah in this volume.) Given that a large number of followers are businessmen, that most of the activities are profit oriented, that the movement is in the process of establishing female entrepreneur associations (Dreher 2015), and that it has its own business association (TUSKON), there are many reasons why Hendrick (2013) and Haenni (2005) have classified Hizmet as a form of market Islam.

For Hendrick (2013, 7–8), market Islam refers to the marketization and rationalization of Islamic activism through a focus on business and education with an emphasis on the sciences and mathematics. Hizmet legitimizes neoliberal economics because its financing occurs through the success of its business members in the marketplace (24). Hendrick concluded that the establishment of preparatory schools played an integral role in the success of the movement as such schools are in high demand in a globally competitive economy (142–43). Market Islam also implies that businessmen benefit from the market while donating to the community to "purify" the profits (236). There is thus a contradiction in the movement in Hendrick's view (238–39): on the one hand, it promotes modesty, Sufism, spiritual frugality, peace, and dialogue but on the other, it is a very powerful economic actor in its own right.

Hendrick, however, overlooks the community-oriented nature of the businesses that willingly pay substantial "taxes" to the movement to further its purposes, and they see this in religious terms—difficult to capture with rational choice argumentation. In contrast stands Tittensor's (2014, 156) classification of the movement as a "social business." A social business is characterized by its environmental or social goals instead of being solely profit oriented. While many of the community-funded projects are, indeed, social businesses, this omits the profit-oriented businessmen (and women) that produce goods and services in the free market, and support the movement through donations and volunteer work. Hizmet is therefore both: social business and free-market oriented.

As Ebaugh (2014) highlights, the transnational aspect of the movement, and its global orientation and reach imply that it belongs to a specific set of religious movements that are a part of the general global civil society formation underway since the seventies. However, civil society here refers to the original seventeenth-century definition: a society of property owners supported by volunteers and employees. Therefore, given that neither market Islam nor social business adequately describe the movement, the chapter will assess Hizmet as a non-Western expression of the "globalizing elite" and set it in relation to the latter's "globalization project."

The globalizing elite is the international expression of anti-new deal activism in the United States dating back to the thirties that had successfully replaced social democracy by the eighties with a market-oriented approach, strengthening the power of private property owners (see introduction). At the international level, its key goal is to reduce state intervention and increase the reliance on market mechanisms. The globalizing elites are located in multinational corporations and transnational banks and they have developed what Overbeek and van der Pijl (1993) have called "concepts of control" (similar to "frames" in social movement analysis, see Nicinska, this volume). These contain three themes: foreign policy, power relations in domestic society, and prescriptions for the role of the state (5). A concept of control comprises not only economic questions but situates the capitalist elite in a specific context.

Gill (1994) defines "globalizing elites" as intellectual and practical apparatuses within transnational capitalism "whose goal is to maintain and expand global capitalism" (169). He argues that because of globalizing elites, the world economy has become more integrated since the crisis in the 1970s, instead of sliding back into protectionism. Others speak of the transnational capitalist class (Robinson and Harris 2000), a social movement for global capitalism (Sklair 1997) or an expression of modern corporate power (Carroll et al. 2010).

Over the last thirty years, this globalizing elite has successfully promulgated the idea of "free trade"—or global economic integration—as the only rational policy, and they are now able to sanction deviant states through capital strikes and significant tax evasion (Gill and Law 1993; Deneault 2007; Kwayu in this volume), thus depriving, as Keynes predicted, the welfare state of significant resources to provide human security in phases of economic downturn or periods of structural change in the economy (Kirshner 1999). The result of neoliberal capitalism is severe economic concentration: one percent of the world's corporations are responsible for fifty percent of all foreign direct investment while the share of world GDP controlled by transnational corporations (TNC) is increasing and stood at 33% in 1995 (up from 17% in 1965; McMichael 2000, 112). Vitali, Glattfelder, and Battiston (2011) showed that 147 of the 43,060 TNCs in their study controlled forty percent of the total sample. It is, therefore, not surprising that global inequality has increased to dramatic proportions: eighty-five people possess as much wealth as do 3.5 billion people on this planet according to Oxfam (Wearden 2014). Given that economic inequality ultimately leads to political instability for reasons already explained by Aristotle (who argued that political stability depends on a large middle class), it should not be surprising that world politics is characterized by an increase in extremist politics—as the poor need to resort to civil disobedience or even violence to obtain resources, and the rich need a strong state to defend themselves against the poor (Aristotle IV.11.1296a, 7–9, in Barker 1958, 179). Even prominent capitalists such as George Soros write about the "Capitalist Threat" (in the journal *Atlantic* in 1997).

Past research on the globalizing elites has heavily focused on industrialized countries. In contrast, this chapter shows that there is also a globalizing elite from the "periphery." Hizmet contradicts the description of Islamic activists in the literature as being in direct opposition to the West or the free market (Butko 2004; Moghadam 2009, 121). On the contrary, neoliberal policies and the idea of a free market allowed Hizmet to prosper and to develop its own version of neoliberalism with an Islamic twist—a form of Islamic capitalism. The next sections will show that Hizmet has developed its own globalization project based on education, business, and dialogue.

EDUCATION IN A GLOBAL MARKETPLACE

Tutoring for school and university achievement is the key to success for the movement in Turkey and abroad. As middle-class parents are willing to pay substantial fees to ensure the future of their children in a globally competitive environment, Hizmet schools have been able to capture a large segment of the tutoring market where its students are quite successful in the competitive entrance exams for universities in Turkey (Hendrick 2013). This success in education has ensured the legitimacy of the movement in the eyes of the public. Typically, exceptional students receive a scholarship to attract them to the tutoring center and their accomplishment in university admission is advertised widely. This success allows the schools to charge substantial fees and to become self-financing, a pattern repeated abroad (Balçi 2003). In the United States, the charter school system allows private educational businesses to open schools financed by the state. Hizmet has used this openness to provide workplaces for its teachers through the temporary visa program and as they—like all movement members—donate to the movement, there was financing available to support the further expansion of the movement in the United States. As a result, it has become one of the largest providers of charter schools, but is now also under investigation for financial improprieties (Hendrick 2013).

The initial goal of the educational efforts in Turkey was to create an elite that would be able to withstand Western competition while maintaining its Islamic tradition (Seufert 2014, 9). While the schools themselves are secular, the students in the dormitories are under close surveillance by movement members who motivate them to study hard, invite them to *sohbet* (discussion about ethics), and to pray. As a result, forty to fifty percent of the students in the schools in Turkey join the movement (Tittensor 2014, 168). The teachers in the schools are, therefore, at the heart of the movement as they increase the number of supporters by inspiring students through their behavior (*temsil*), providing significant academic support, and a working environment that encourages study (Tittensor 2014, 119–21). More important, however, is that teachers seek to become mentors for their students and to advise them not only in academic matters but also with regard to their general attitude toward life (Tittensor 2014, 112–13). This then often leads to conversations about morals and religion that allow the teacher, after having gained the trust of the student, to introduce Gülen's ideas, and to invite him or her to join the religious movement. The current struggle with the government will thus significantly limit the expansion of the movement in Turkey if the schools and businesses are forced to shut down.

One of the expression of the global success of the schools is the Turkish Olympiad. In order to motivate students at the schools abroad to study

Turkish, teachers started to organize a festival in Turkey between 2003 and 2013 under the name "Turkish Olympiad." National competitions were held to send a delegation to the festival in Turkey. There were competitions in different categories (e.g., song and poem recitation) but it also included a Turkish language test (Interview August 2012). In 2013, 250,000 people attended the final event showcasing the winners from among 2,000 students from 140 countries that had come to Turkey for the 16-day event (Üzüm 2013). The festival is a clear indicator of the growing globalization of the movement. The number of countries represented by students at the Olympiad increased from 17 in 2003 to 140 in 2012. These students came from all world regions. In addition, since the first schools were established outside Turkey, approximately 300,000 people have taken Turkish language classes (TÜRKÇEDER 2012, 14). Before the fallout, Erdoğan and other ministers attended its ceremonies and supported the festival. In other words, Hizmet has contributed to the globalization of the Turkish language and culture but at the same time brought globalization to Turkey.

From 2014 onward, the festival had to move abroad as Erdoğan clamped down on its Turkish operation. This led to the organization of festivals in different countries with 2500 students from 150 nations participating in 2015 (Zeynalov 2015). The move abroad has altered the overall theme of the festival. Whereas the focus was mostly on Turkish culture, now it also integrates elements from the host culture. In Germany, for example, it is now language and culture exchange in both German and Turkish (Südwest Presse 2015).

BUSINESS, DEVELOPMENT, AND NEOLIBERAL ISLAMIC FEMINISM

The Turkish economy moved from an average GDP per capita of less than 2,000 US Dollar in 1960 to about 10,000 US Dollar in 2005 (Subaşat 2014), making it the eighteenth largest market economy in the world. This is often attributed to the success of export-led growth and the emergence of Islamic capitalism from the provinces, the so-called Anatolian Tigers (Demir, Acar and Toprak 2004; Moudouros, 2014), supported more intensively than ever before by official government policy from 2002 onward (Bugra and Savaskan 2014, 12). Islamic capitalism is based on small and medium-sized firms characterized by a close cooperation between managers and workers and the rejection of trade unions, but infused with an Islamic ethic with regard to donations and volunteer work (Moudoros 2014, 851). While the dependence on foreign investment may soon destabilize this success story (Subaşat 2014), a new economic model based on integration in world markets emerged (Bugra and Savaskan 2014, 2).

Islamic capitalists, including those from Hizmet (Interviews August 2012; Cetin 2009), tell a story of exclusion under the Istanbul bourgeoisie before the arrival of the AKP in power. In their view, the Istanbul elite has dominated the Turkish economy and has centralized access to capital, making economic success for the pious entrepreneurs difficult. This situation has led to an innovative approach of Islamic activism in Turkey: instead of focusing only on capturing the state, they also concentrate on gaining economic power (Yavuz 2003). As a result, some Islamic companies have now made it to the Turkish 500 list (Tanyilmaz 2015).

While there is a charitable element in the way the movement operates (e.g., the scholarships to students, the support for student housing, many of the health services undertaking development work abroad), the actual charity, *Kimse Yok Mu*, is a latecomer; it was established in 2004 and it has international sister organizations and is now undertaking projects in 113 countries according to its website. It is also registered with the UN Social and Economic Council.

The history of the Confederation of Businessmen and Industrialists of Turkey (TUSKON), founded by Hizmet businessmen, can serve as an indicator for the creation of a globalizing Islamic capitalist elite. TUSKON is an umbrella organization for seven regional federations that include 202 business associations and over 50,000 members in Turkey. Its main activity is to organize export fairs, "Trade Bridges," for members to expand their international business ventures. These were quite successful, with 130 countries represented in 2015 by 1,300 international and 1,750 Turkish participants (tuskonwtb.com). Since 2006, when they were first organized, the Trade Bridges have brought in $30 billion of investment with trade agreements that are now promoting Turkish brands through franchise agreements (Soy 2014). TUSKON has offices in Washington, Brussels, Beijing, Moscow, and Addis Ababa and partner organizations in 140 countries (tuskonwtb.com). Until 2013, it also used to accompany government ministers and presidents on their trips abroad. Often, the creation of business contacts and the establishment of schools preceded the opening of a Turkish embassy in a country, an indicator of the degree to which business interests used to go hand in hand with Turkish foreign policy.

A more recent development in TUSKON is its adoption of neoliberal feminism (Dreher 2015). Neoliberal feminism refers to the idea that empowerment of women is beneficial in economic terms as it will increase economic growth. It is an effort by international financial organizations and the globalizing elite to legitimize neoliberalism, especially after the financial crisis of 2008, and to gain another set of supporters through feminism (Roberts 2014). TUSKON's adoption of neoliberal feminism is an indicator of its parallel development with the neoliberal globalization project and also of its global orientation.

Hizmet Development Model

It is difficult to separate the development of the business side from the education side as they form a part of a general "Hizmet development model." This is characterized by the close interconnection between business and schools and resembles the "Third Italy model" (Bianchi 1998). The latter refers to the combination of small-scale firms in the North of Italy organized along family lines and more or less nonunionized that had been heralded as an alternative to mass production with more flexibility in product design (Piore and Sabel 1989). This led to economic growth in these regions and to the linking of several of such growth regions across the European Union. The strong interrelation between education, business and dialogue, seems to create similar synergies for Hizmet but on a global scale. The schools are important for the movement not only because they increased the number of adherents but also because they provided a secure market for the businesses associated with the movement. Suppliers had a protected market to develop more expertise (e.g., publishing) and then expanded into the global economy (see Hendrick 2013, 159). What we can see here is an example of "industrial policy" on a community level. The strong market orientation of Hizmet permitted the circumvention of the "protectionist elite," and ultimately undermined the developmentalist Kemalist regime to create more opportunities for Islamic capitalists (to the dismay of the Istanbul elite Savran 2015; Cetin 2009). Today, the economic activities of Hizmet are spread across all economic sectors of the Turkish economy. Most prominent examples are Bank *Asya*, the newspaper *Zaman*, the various tutoring schools and universities, and the TV station *Samanyolu*. Both the newspaper and the television station have counterparts abroad.

The schools also provide Turkish-speaking students work experience in the trade fairs organized by TUSKON as translators or as contacts in their home countries. As Meral, president of TUSKON, indicated during a graduation ceremony for foreign students in Istanbul: "We have come here from the World Trade and Investment Bridge. Nearly 500 international students assisted us there. They helped us establish business contacts. . . . You are not only the bridge of trade but also the strong steel ropes for bridges of the soul" (Zaman 2014). This is one instance where social capital in the form of personal relationships, language skills, and familiarity with culture builds economic capital.

There are now over 2,000 schools in over 160 countries worldwide and most of these schools are networks of supporters made up of volunteers and businesspeople. The "Hizmet development model" from schools to business to trade and development, and also dialogue and intercultural exchange is in full force. In Bosnia where the Hizmet is active since the mid-nineties (even during the war), graduates from the Hizmet-founded university have already established a business association that has organized the construction of a student-dormitory and is a regular participant in the Trade bridges organized by TUSKON. The first Bosnians are already working in the Hizmet schools, and soon the Turkish administrators will leave (interview August 2012). Similar successful economic development processes are reported for other locations and countries (see Agai 2004, 316 for Albania, and 345 for Macedonia; Balçi 2003 for the Turkic Republics; Bruinessen 2013 for the Netherlands; Hendrick 2013 for the United States).

However, all the institutions and businesses in Turkey are now under attack from the government (Bank Asya is under government management, the editor of Zaman is on trial, and the same is true for Samanyolu. The charity Kim Se Yok Mu has also run into difficulties). Graduates of Hizmet-affiliated schools and universities are blacklisted and face difficulties finding employment as its businesses are closed down. The future of the Hizmet economic base in Turkey is therefore much in question, and it may depend on "Global Hizmet" for survival.

Hizmet has realized economic prosperity for its members through the creation of businesses and schools and uses these resources to charitable ends as well. TUSKON's trade fairs were important to support the international integration of the Turkish economy not just with Europe or the Middle East but also at a global level (whereas other Turkish business associations are more regionally oriented). There seems to be a "Hizmet development model" in which businessmen and, increasingly, women have access to a secure market in the schools in a form of localized industrial policy—an important innovation given that the World Trade Organisation (WTO) has reduced the space for national industrial policies (Wade 2003). While there are limits to such an ethno- or community-centered approach (as it is difficult for outsiders to join), Hizmet capitalists have, nevertheless, captured a miniscule share of the global market from the globalizing elite and have built a transnational Hizmet space and a globalization project (or concept of control) that consists of business, education, and dialogue (Dreher 2013). Key in the diffusion of this project in industrialized countries are the dialogue initiatives that provide the movement with entry points to local elites and valuable allies in their fight with the Turkish government.

GLOBAL INTERCULTURAL AND INTERFAITH DIALOGUE AND TURKISH NATIONALISM

Dialogue activities form the third part of Hizmet's globalization project. They are anchored in "Dialogue Centers" that have different names across the globe. Their activities include the organization of trips to Turkey, courses

on Turkish culture (language, cooking, Ebru painting), academic conferences and books on the "Gülen" movement, lecture series, and a journal of
Dialogue Studies (dialoguesociety.org). The Dialogue Society in London has
published a book on Dialogue Theories with contributions by David Bohm
(quantum physicist), Jürgen Habermas (philosopher), and Fethullah Gülen,
among others.

The most important initiative for dialogue within Turkey has been the
Abant Platform initiated by the Journalists and Writers Foundation in the
nineties. At the time it was an important platform through which scholars,
intellectuals, and policymakers met to discuss various divisive issues confronting Turkish society such as "Islam and secularism," or "religion and the
state" (see Yavuz 2013, 143). These meetings are now taking place annually
as Abant Platform meetings not only in Turkey but also in the United States,
Europe, and other countries.

The Canadian Intercultural and Dialogue Center has a host of programs
that promote dialogue and intercultural exchange. There are essay contests
for students centering on themes such as "Who is my neighbor?"; support
for the Third World Canada tour (an event designed to highlight first nation
problems in Canada); prizes for public sector workers (firefighters, police-
men, emergency services) who have shown a dedication to altruism and
multiculturalism; luncheon programs on various aspects relevant to Toronto
(e.g., racism, the discussion of secularism in Quebec); Ramadan dinners; and
the yearly friendship dinners, which are directed at the political and economic
Canadian elite (even Prime Minister Harper sent greetings, personal observation). The friendship dinners have now morphed into a prize ceremony for
"Peace and Dialogue Awards" with tickets selling for CAN $125.

An important activity of all these centers worldwide are trips to Turkey
partially sponsored by Hizmet (for Australia see http://www.intercultural.org.
au/, for Germany see www.fidev.org). Today, owing to the fallout with the
government, the trips to Turkey are supplemented by trips to other countries
where Hizmet institutions are present. From Toronto, participants can visit
Thailand or Azerbaijan. Overall, these events and programs offer a meeting
point for many religious and secular activists seeking a more fruitful engagement with "Islam," which is subject to many misinterpretations in Western
societies (see Yavuz 2013 for a critical discussion of the dialogue activities),
but they also allow for the establishment of useful contacts for the businessmen (and women) and facilitate their entry into the Canadian market and
integration into society.

Globalization has changed the emphasis on nationalism within Hizmet. The
focus on Turkey has been important for the movement and also for Gülen's
discourse. Gülen sees the Turkish nation as in decline since the advent of
modernity; his key goal was to reverse this and to reestablish the greatness

of the Turkish nation through the establishment of a "golden generation" of activists firmly grounded in the modern sciences while maintaining their religious devotion. This nationalist discourse was more prominent in the seventies and eighties, but with the end of the Cold War and with Gülen's move to the United States, it has become less pronounced, giving way to a more globalized discourse and interfaith dialogue, according to Agai (2004); The terrorist attacks against the United States in 2001 strengthened the emphasis on interfaith and intercultural activities, and the need for the reconciliation of different faith traditions worldwide (209–24).

CONCLUSION

The globalization project of Hizmet has three aspects: it centers on economic development in free markets through the promotion of *businesses*, especially in education, but also in many other sectors, on teachers in the *schools* providing individual guidance and mentoring inside and also outside of classrooms to help students succeed in school and in life, and on *dialogue* outreach activities that help in their settlement and integration into host societies at the elite level, provide information about Islam, and also deliver useful contacts for the businesses. It has created a transnational Hizmet space that allows adherents to move across the globe in search of opportunities and to utilize their skills in new places. Hizmet profits from neoliberal globalization because it has enhanced opportunities for business; many former state activities such as education are now privatized and allow Hizmet to expand into new areas with the skills and expertise gained elsewhere. It is therefore reasonable to conclude that Hizmet represents a version of the neoliberal globalizing elite and strengthens neoliberal globalization.

At the same time, by providing alternatives within neoliberal globalization, it has created its own niche. Using social capital centered on the teachings of Fethullah Gülen, adherents have created a global social Hizmet space that gives them security within a free market and allows them to compete successfully. The community compensates for market failures through social capital, the networks, and access to financial capital. Businesses support the movement through significant donations that allow for its further expansion. Unlike neoliberalism that promotes the idea that business does not have any social responsibility other than to be profitable, the Hizmet model is based on social responsibility to the community first. It is this integration that then guarantees profits.

In comparison with the other case studies in this volume, the Hizmet approach is very close to facilitating neoliberal globalization. Community-based businesses are better than the neoliberal alternative, but people not within the community who are unemployed or cannot afford education are excluded from the Hizmet development model. By strengthening neoliberal globalization, Hizmet—much like the general neoliberal globalization process—undermines state capacity as the increasing disparities in wealth create more insecurity (Rogers 2000). Private action is no replacement for state capacity, it is at best a useful complement. Today, there is an urgent need to evaluate the morality of capitalism more critically from a religious perspective. It may even be time, as many of the chapters in this volume highlight, to reconsider key aspects of the economic model. None of these questions with regard to global economic structures are currently on the radar screen of the Hizmet movement; however, until its survival has been ensured, there will be no opportunity to even begin interrogating the economic system more systematically.

Most people are insignificant on their own. It is only by joining together that they can gain a sense of purpose and power through collective action. Hizmet is one example of collective action where a religious group created a global project in defiance of the authoritarian Turkish context and the secular, profit-oriented globalizing Western elite. While there are many problems with the Hizmet approach—its strategic ambiguity and secrecy, some of its religious teachings, its vision for women, its hierarchical internal organization, its ethnic basis, and its focus on classical conservative values such as economic growth or the family—the movement has allowed a different set of elite to gain access on its own terms to neoliberal globalization. While it strengthens neoliberal globalization, it also offers a limited alternative from within.

NOTES

1. The chapter represents the outcome of a three-year research project in Toronto, Canada, and a research trip to Turkey and Sarajevo (financed by the Glendon Faculty Council, CUPE 3903, and logistically supported by Hizmet) in 2012. Since the current government persecutes the movement, I prefer not to identify individuals. When using information from the research trip I indicate Interview August 2012.

2. The literature on the movement is extensive. It consists of academic studies (Agai 2004; Balçi 2003; Bruinessen 2013; Gülay 2007; Hendrick 2013; Tittensor 2014; Turam 2007; Yavuz 2003, 2013), and studies published by adherents or sympathizers. In this chapter, these are Çetin (2009); Ebaugh (2014); Ergil (2012); Sevindi (2008); and any newspaper article from Zaman. Seufert (2015), Jenkins (2009), and BPC (2015) are policy papers with bias in terms of financing or geopolitical positioning; the writings of this author have been characterized as "whitewashing" of the movement and as too critical (reviewers for Dreher 2013 article). Since the question in this chapter is about Hizmet in the context of neoliberal globalization, the usual debate about the *politics* of Islamic movements is tangential.

3. The neo-Gramscian perspective is an approach within IPE (see introduction); for an overview, see Overbeek (2000). Using this approach in the Turkish context is problematic because the AKP is charging the Hizmet for being aligned with Western powers. This shows that the power struggle between the Hizmet and the AKP is not just about internal issues but also about the geopolitical orientation of Turkey (Dreher 2015).

4. In Canada, the Intercultural Dialogue Centers openly discuss the ideas of Fethullah Gülen in all of their events (personal observations). But according to the Australian journalist Margaret Coffey on ABC's Encounter Program on September 4, 2013, many members of parliament or other officials were surprised to hear that events they had supported were organized by Hizmet (see Dreher 2013 for similar problems in Germany).

REFERENCES

Agai, Bekim. 2004. *Zwischen Netzwerk und Diskurs. Das Bildungsnetzwerk um Fethullah Gülen (geb. 1938): Die flexible Umsetzung modernen islamischen Gedankenguts.* Hamburg: ebv.

Akyol, Mustafa. (2011). *Islam without Extremes: A Muslim Case for Liberty.* New York: W.W. Norton.

Akyol, Mustafa. 2015. "Turkey's War Within the Judiciary Deepens." *Al-Monitor.* Accessed August 21, 2015, http://www.al-monitor.com/pulse/originals/2015/04/turkeys-war-within-the-judiciary-deepens.html.

Balci, Bayram. 2003. *Missionnaires de l'Islam en Asie centrale, les écoles turques de Fethullah Gülen.* Paris: Maisonneuve and Larose.

Barker, Ernest. 1958. *The Politics of Aristotle.* London: Oxford University Press.

Bianchi, Giuliano. 1998. "Requiem for the Third Italy? Rise and Fall of a Too Successful Concept." *Entrepreneurship & Regional Development* 10 (2): 93–116.

BPC (Bipartisan Policy Center). 2015. *Turkey Transformed: The Origins and Evolution of Authoritarianism and Islamization under the AKP.* Washington, DC.

Bruinessen, Martin van. 2013. "The Netherlands and the Gülen Movement." *Sociology of Islam* 1 (3–4): 165–87.

Buğra, Ayşe and Osman Savaşkan. 2014. *New Capitalism in Turkey: The Relationship between Politics, Religion and Business.* Cheltenham, UK: Edward Elgar.

Butko, Thomas. 2004. "Revelation or Revolution: A Gramscian Approach to the Rise of Political Islam." *British Journal of Middle Eastern Studies* 31 (1): 41–62.

Carroll, William, Meindert Fennema, Eelke Heemskerk, and John P. Sapinski. 2010. *The Making of a Transnational Capitalist Class.* London: Zed Books.

Çetin, Muhammed. 2009. *The Gülen Movement. Civic Service Without Borders.* New York: Blue Dome Press.

Demir, Ömer, Mustafa Acar, and Metin Toprak. 2004. "Anatolian Tigers or Islamic Capital: Prospects and Challenges." *Middle Eastern Studies* 40 (6): 166–88.

Deneault, Alain. 2007. "Tax Havens and Criminology." *Global Crime* 8 (3): 260–70.

Dreher, Sabine. 2013. "What is the Hizmet Movement? Contending Approaches to the Analysis of Religious Activists In World Politics." *Sociology of Islam* 1 (3–4): 257–75.

Dreher, Sabine. 2015. "The Geopolitical Implications of Neoliberal Feminism in Turkey." International Studies Association. Annual Conference, New Orleans.

Ebaugh, Helen Rose. 2014. "The Gülen Movement: Sunni Islam." In *Global Religious Movements Across Borders*, edited by Stephen Cherry and Helen Rose Ebaugh, 61–78. Farnham: Ashgate.

Ergil, Dogu. 2012. *Fethullah Gülen and the Gülen Movement in 100 Questions*. New York, NY: Blue Dome Press.

Gill, Stephen and David Law. 1993. "Global Hegemony and the Structural Power of Capital." In *Gramsci, Historical Materialism and International Relations*, edited by Stephen Gill, 93–126. Cambridge, UK: Cambridge University Press.

Gill, Stephen. 1994. "Structural Change and Global Political Economy: Globalizing Elites and the Emerging World Order." In *Global Transformation: Challenges to the State System*, edited by Yoshikazu Sakamoto, 169–99. Tokyo: United Nations University Press.

Gülay, Erol N. 2007. "The Gülen Phenomenon: A Neo-Sufi challenge to Turkey's Rival Elite?" *Critique: Critical Middle Eastern Studies* 16 (1): 37–61.

Gülen, Fethullah. 2005. *The Statue of Our Souls: Revival in Islamic Thought and Activism*. Somerset, NJ: The Light.

Haenni, Patrick. 2005. *L'Islam de Marche: l'autre révolution conservatrice*. Paris: Seuil.

Hansen, Suzy. 2015. "Whose Turkey Is It?" *The New York Times*. Accessed August 14, 2015. http://www.nytimes.com/2014/02/09/magazine/whose-turkey-is-it?

Hendrick, Joshua. 2013. *Gülen: The Ambiguous Politics of Market Islam in Turkey and the World*. New York: New York University Press.

Idiz, Semih. 2015. "Will G-20 Summit Improve Erdogan's International Image? *Al-Monitor: The Pulse of the Middle East*. Accessed November 20, 2015. http://www.al-monitor.com/pulse/originals/2015/11/turkey-g20-summit-improve-erdogan-international-standing.html.

Jenkins, Gareth. 2009. *Between Fact and Fantasy: Turkey's Ergenekon Investigation*. *Silk Road Paper*. Washington, DC: Central Asia-Caucasus Institute.

Kirshner, Jonathan. 1999. "Keynes, Capital Mobility and the Crisis of Embedded Liberalism." *Review of International Political Economy* 6 (3): 313–37.

Kurzman, Charles. 1998. *Liberal Islam: A Sourcebook*. New York: Oxford University Press.

Mardin, Şerif. 1989. *Religion and Social Change in Modern Turkey: The Case of Bediüzzaman Said Nursi*. Albany: State University of New York Press.

McMichael, Philip. 2000. "Globalisation: Trend or Project?" In *Global Political Economy: Contemporary Perspectives*, edited by Ronen Palan, 100–113. London: Routledge.

Moghadam, Valentine M. 2009. *Globalization and Collective Action*. Lanham: Rowman & Littlefield.

Moghadam, Valentine M. 2014. "Islamic Feminism and its Discontents: Toward a Resolution of the Debate." *Signs* 40 (1): 1135–71.

Moudouros, Nikos. 2014. "The 'Harmonization' of Islam with the Neoliberal Transformation: The Case of Turkey." *Globalizations* 11 (6): 843–57.

Overbeek, Henk and Kees Van der Pijl. 1993. "Restructuring Capital and Restructuring Hegemony: Neo-Liberalism and the Unmaking of the Post-War Order."

In *Restructuring Hegemony in the Global Political Economy*, edited by Henk Overbeek, 1–27. London and New York: Routledge.

Overbeek, Henk. 2000. "Transnational Historical Materialism: Theories of Transnational Class Formation and World Order." In *Global Political Economy: Contemporary Perspectives*, edited by Ronen Palan, 168–83. London: Routledge.

Piore, Michael J. and Charles F. Sabel. 1989. *Das Ende der Massenproduktion.* Translated by Jürgen Behrens. Frankfurt: Fischer.

Roberts, Adrienne. 2014. "The Political Economy of 'Transnational Business Feminism.'" *International Feminist Journal of Politics.* doi:10.1080/14616742. 2013.849968.

Robinson, William I. and Jeffrey Harris. 2000. "Towards a Global Ruling Class? Globalization and the Transnational Capitalist Class." *Science and Society* 64 (1): 11–54.

Rogers, Paul. 2000. *Losing Control: Global Security in the Twenty-first Century.* London: Pluto Press.

Savran, Sungur. 2015. "Class, State and Religion in Turkey." In *The Neoliberal Landscape and the Rise of Islamist Capital in Turkey*, edited by Neşecan Balkan, Erol Balkan, and Ahmet Öncü, 41–88. New York and Oxford: Berghan.

Seufert, Günter. 2015. "Is the Fethullah Gülen Movement Overstretching Itself?" SWP Research Paper 2014/RP 02, Berlin.

Sevindi, Nevval. 2008. *Contemporary Islamic Conversations: M. Fethullah Gülen on Turkey, Islam, and the West.* Edited by Ibrahim M. Abu-Rabi'. Translated by Abdullah T. Antepli. Albany, NY: State University of New York Press.

Sklair, Leslie. 1997. "Social Movements for Global Capitalism: The Transnational Capitalist Class in Action." *Review of International Political Economy* 4 (3): 514–38.

Soy, Nesibe Hicret. 2015. "Unaffected by Tension, TUSKON Promotes Turkish Economy." *Today's Zaman.* http://www.todayszaman.com/business_unaffected-by-tension-tuskon-promotes-turkish-economy_337590.html.

Subaşat, Turan. 2014. "The Political Economy of Turkey's Economic Miracle." *Journal of Balkan and Near Eastern Studies* 16 (2): 137–60.

Südwestpresse. 2015. "Wo Kultur Brücken Bauen Soll—Und Es Auch Kann." *Swp.de.* http://www.swp.de/ulm/lokales/ulm_neu_ulm/Wo-Kultur-Bruecken-bauen-soll-und-es-auch-kann.

Tanyilmaz, Turktar. 2015. "The Islamist Big Bourgeoisie in Turkey." In *The Neoliberal Landscape and the Rise of Islamist Capital In Turkey*, edited by Neşecan Balkan, Erol Balkan, and Ahmet Öncü, 41–88. New York and Oxford: Berghan.

Tittensor, David. 2014. *The House of Service: The Gülen Movement and Islam's Third Way.* New York: Oxford University Press.

Turam, Berna. 2007. *Between Islam and the State. The Politics of Engagement.* Stanford: Stanford University Press.

TÜRKÇEDER. 2012. 20 yılda 300 bin kişi Türkçe öğrendi. Türkçe Olimpiatları 10. Yıl, Mayis- Haziran 2012, Istanbul: Uluslararası Türkçe Öğretimi Derneği.

Üzüm, Ipek. 2015. "Students Give International Turkish Olympiad a Moving Sendoff." *Today's Zaman*, http://www.todayszaman.com/national_students-give-international-turkish-olympiad-a-moving-sendoff_318550.html.

Vitali, Stefania, James B. Glattfelder, and Stefano Battiston. 2011. "The Network of Global Corporate Control." *PLoS ONE* 6 (10): e25995.

Wade, Robert H. 2003. "What Strategies Are Viable for Developing Countries Today? The World Trade Organization and the Shrinking of 'Development Space'." *Review of International Political Economy* 10 (4): 621–44.

Wearden, Graeme. 2014. "Oxfam: 85 Richest People as Wealthy as Poorest Half of the World." *The Guardian*, http://www.theguardian.com/business/2014/20/oxfam-85-richest-people-half-of-the-world.

Wiktorowicz, Quintan. 2004. "Introduction: Islamic Activism and Social Movement Theory." In *Islamic Activism. A Social Movement Theory Approach*, edited by Quintan Wiktorowicz, 1–36. Bloomington: Indiana University Press.

Yavuz, Hakan. 2003. *Islamic Political Identity in Turkey*. Oxford: Oxford University Press.

Yavuz, M. Hakan. 2013. *Toward an Islamic Enlightenment: The Gülen Movement*. Oxford: Oxford University Press.

Zaman. 2015. "Students from 70 Countries Celebrate Graduation in Turkey." *TodaysZaman*. http://www.todayszaman.com/anasayfa_students-from-70-countries-celebrate-graduation-in-turkey_350826.html.

Zeynalov, Mahir. 2015. "White House Courts Int'l Students as Language Festival Concludes in DC." *TodaysZaman*. http://www.todayszaman.com/anasayfa_white-house-courts-intl-students-as-language-festival-concludes-in-dc_379997.html.

Chapter 8

Islamic Social Democracy? Ennahda's Approach to Economic Development in Tunisia

Edward Webb

The constructivist approach to religion developed in the introduction to this volume points out that each faith tradition contains various groups struggling over the definition and interpretation of the belief and practices associated with the tradition. This struggle has been highly politicized in many Muslim-majority societies, particularly those of the postcolonial Arab world, including Tunisia. Both the French colonial state and its postindependence, secular successor—Tunisia became independent in 1956—engaged in struggles with various actors in society, organized or not, over the proper nature and role of religion—principally Islam—in public life and politics.

This chapter discusses Tunisia's democratic Islamist Renaissance Party—Ennahda—which moved from a suppressed opposition movement of the late twentieth century to one of the prime movers participating in and helping to oversee the democratic transition after the uprising of late 2010 and early 2011. Tunisia is where the so-called "Arab Spring" began, and where demonstrations led to the flight of President Ben Ali and a transitional government overseeing elections for a Constituent Assembly to write a new constitution. Ennahda had the largest representation in that Assembly and in the three-party government that governed for the next two years, until political violence led to their agreeing to hand over the reins to a technocratic government for the last few months of the constitution-drafting process and the free and fair elections that followed.

In the one case, so far, of a pluralistic democratic system emerging from the uprisings sweeping much of the Arab world at that time, how did the leading religious movement frame its response to the economic demands that were so significant in driving protestors to the streets? In the framework of possible responses to neoliberal globalization that we envisage for religious social movements—promote, reform, or resist—I argue that Ennahda's history and ideology mostly puts it in the *reformist* camp. But I will also argue that it has both inherited a difficult legacy (political, institutional, and economic) and lived a difficult history that make it above all pragmatic and prone to compromises for the overall success of the transition, such that it seems now to be closer to promoting neoliberal globalization.

ISLAMISM, DEMOCRACY, AND CAPITALISM: ENNAHDA'S HISTORICAL TRAJECTORY IN BRIEF

In much of the existing scholarly and journalistic discussion of Ennahda, the main focus is on the compatibility of the party's interpretation of political Islam with pluralistic democracy. Ennahda most often compared itself to Turkey's Justice and Development Party (AKP) that was—until its more recent authoritarian turn—a moderate Islamist-leaning party operating within a secular political framework and competing in multiparty elections. However, Ennahda's opponents and some observers compared it with Egypt's Muslim Brotherhood, geographically closer and coming to power at around the same time. Secularist opponents looking at both the Brotherhood-led government in Egypt and the Ennahda-led coalition in Tunisia are unconvinced about these movements' commitment to democracy and pluralism. They express concerns about the possibility of either an Islamic revolution on the Iranian model of 1979, or a collapse into civil war as occurred in Algeria after the electoral success of the Islamist Islamic Salvation Front (FIS) was countered by fierce military reaction (with Western approval) at the start of the 1990s. Indeed, the Brotherhood has fallen to military reaction, although full-scale civil war has not quite broken out—rather, parts of the country face insurgency, most prominently the North Sinai. Likewise, the AKP's rule in Turkey has taken an authoritarian turn (see Bozkurt, this volume).

In these circumstances, it is understandable that some of Ennahda's secularist foes voice suspicions that consistent professions of commitment to constitutional democracy hide ambitions to roll back secularism and impose conservative Islamic single-party rule on society, accusing them of dissembling, or, in French, "*double discours.*" But Ennahda diverged from the Brotherhood in many aspects of its thought and organization long before the uprisings of 2010–11, including its relationship to democracy. At the leadership level, at least, it became an organization willing to work within a pluralist framework and make political compromises, rather than one prioritizing *sharia* (law based on Islamic principles) (Tamimi 2001).

Less explored in the literature is the party's approach to economic questions. Just as there is no single approach among Islamist parties and movements to political or social questions, although there are some broad areas of overlap, so, too, is there no single approach to the economy. During the Cold War and the heyday of the Non-Aligned Movement and "Third-Worldism," some looked to Islamic economics as offering a potential third way between capitalism and state socialism, just as Islamism could be an ingredient in political liberation, particularly after the 1979 revolution in Iran (Ayoob 2007). The ideas of the Iranian "Islamo-socialist" Ali Shariati, aiming at "negotiating a third way between top-down and Eurocentric secularization on the one hand, and reactionary and essentialist Islamism on the other" (Saffari 2015, 8), influenced a wide audience in the 1960s and 1970s, including some who went on to be leaders of Ennahda.

In the post–Cold War era, when neoliberal globalization seems hegemonic, one can note the rapid development of Islamic banking by major global banking corporations and the full embrace of the global economic order by Muslim-majority countries such as the Gulf Cooperation Council (GCC) states, Malaysia, and Turkey. But one can also observe the challenge to that global order by transnational terror networks with their parallel financial systems and desire to strike at global capital's infrastructure, functioning, and symbols.

Ennahda's rhetoric and ideology on the economy is certainly a long way from that of Islamist terror. But it is not a full embrace of the unfettered market, either. As I have written elsewhere (Webb 2014), Ennahda's approach to improving economic conditions hinges on improving human beings as economic *actors*, with economic structures a secondary concern. Markets will function better if those within them are virtuous: this seems to be the logic. Good Muslims will make better workers and better managers of resources and each other. I have called this concept *homo islamicus*, replacing the self-interested *homo oeconomicus* of classical liberal economic theory. Variants of this kind of thinking can be found in the economic thinking of Turkey's Islamist business associations and elsewhere (Webb 2014). But one can also trace it back to Shariati who argued that structural determinants can be overcome by human action.

> Modernity, according to Shariati, had enhanced the condition for overcoming structural limitations and 'manipulating' the forces of historical and material determinism. In his view, initiating a normative and cultural reorientation, and giving recognition to individual agency and autonomy, could help Muslim societies overcome the structural causes of their stagnation and underdevelopment. (Saffari 2015, 11)

The implications of Shariati's project for Iran and other societies and, hence, for Tunisia, if Ennahda's leaders accepted the logic, would be an emphasis on empowerment of individuals as a tool of structural transformation, rather than vice versa.

This is not to say that in building what Ennahda leader Rached El Ghannouchi has referred to as "a system of free social economy: the same system of the market but within the framework of justice and humanity, not the system of brutal markets" (cited in Webb 2014, 4), they are uninterested in structural issues. But it means that they steer a pragmatic course between positions that one might associate more usually with the social democratic left—such as their two coalition partners in the transitional governments, 2011–14—and between more market-friendly, neoliberal policies. The next sections will show Ennahda's pragmatic triangulation between social democratic and neoliberal positions in the transitional period when it was part of the government; in its role in shaping the new constitution; and in its election program in 2014, the first election under the new constitution.

MANAGING TUNISIA'S ECONOMY THROUGH THE POLITICAL TRANSITION

Unlike some Arab states of North Africa, such as Nasser's Egypt, Tunisia did not see large-scale nationalizations after independence, tending to follow a mixed developmental model where state companies and investment banks worked alongside the private sector. The country's second president, Zein El-Abedine Ben Ali, who came to power in a bloodless coup in 1987, appeared in some respects and in certain periods of his rule to be a reformer, although his prisons came to be as full of political prisoners as his predecessor's. During the 1990s and, particularly, after 2000, Ben Ali perfected a deceptive form of crony capitalism masked by false accounting that drew accolades from the international financial institutions (IFIs): while he concentrated control of the most lucrative sectors of the economy in the hands of an inner circle of family members and trusted advisors, he brought the country into a closer relationship with the European Union and appeared to be setting Tunisia on a course of macroeconomic and developmental rectitude, at least in terms of liberal globalization orthodoxy. In fact, by allowing the quality of education to founder—Tunisia's education system had been the envy of the Arab world in its first few decades of independence—youth unemployment to rise, environmental degradation to run unchecked in parts of the country, and the inland and southern parts of the country to be developmentally neglected, he was putting in place conditions for worker unrest in 2008 and ultimately the uprising that overthrew him in 2010–11 (King 2003; World Bank 2014a). The Ben Ali years left a toxic legacy in the levels of cronyism and pervasive corruption in certain sectors.

Any government seeking to answer the demands of the revolution faced a daunting task. The World Bank's review of Tunisia's economy under Ben

Ali makes clear the massive deception that had taken place. What had been held up in some ways as an exemplar for development was a mirage. Instead, we find, according to the World Bank (2014a), a lack of competition because of excessive regulation, an overregulated and therefore inefficient financial sector, labor market rules that led to job insecurity, and distortion-inducing public policies for industry and agriculture. Together, these circumstances deepened Tunisia's regional disparities.

> These policies accompanied what had been a tightly controlled social and political space, in which public support for the ruling party was highly beneficial, if not an outright requirement for social inclusion, whether it be hiring in the public sector, access to finance, or engagement in social action, such as the limited space allowed for civil society. (World Bank 2014a, 16)

In the light of these conditions, the transition government had a difficult task, but it succeeded in starting reforms, restored economic growth, and reduced unemployment (Ennahda 2014).

> The government managed to mobilize the country's needs from external resources to finance development and government programs in collaboration with international economic partners, attracted more foreign investments which grew by 80% in 2012 and 15% in 2013 after a decline of about 30% in 2011, and made the necessary efforts to control prices and ensure market supply. (Ennahda 2014, 8–9)

Nevertheless, Paciello's (2013) verdict is quite damning on what the governments led by Ennahda Prime Ministers Jebali and Larayedh were able to achieve, given the care Ennahda took to be in control of almost all the economic portfolios. They did not introduce "any real change in the direction of economic policies with respect to the previous interim governments and Ben Ali's regime," although she notes the resistance and interference they encountered inside state institutions and outside. Agreements with the main international donors also "essentially commit Tunisia to implementing the same neo-liberal agenda and macro-stabilization measures pursued under Ben Ali's regime" (18). A specific criticism she levies is that the governments did little to reform the regressive subsidy system, which weighs heavily on the state budget while reaching only twelve percent of poor households. Even after the Jebali government restrained fuel subsidies somewhat, they still made up sixty percent of total subsidies, for instance.

There were minor wage increases. But as for the major priority, job creation, "results have been very modest" (Paciello 2013, 22). There was little innovation and generally policies were characterized by continuity with the

Ben Ali era, so that in civil service hiring, for instance, despite some minor reforms, "clientelism and nepotism are still pervasive" (24). The World Bank (2014a) notes that opportunities for rent offered by heavily regulated market access continue more or less unabated: "an environment, still largely in place three years after the revolution, where cronyism and rents extraction (rather than competition and performance) drive economic success" (16).

Effective policy *implementation* seems to have been a pervasive problem, even if policies were well conceived. Privatizations, including those of confiscated properties, generated criticism when not handled transparently. Development projects aimed at neglected areas of the south and central-western parts of the country were launched but delivered little, leading to continuing protests by young unemployed and underemployed. The World Bank (2014a, 18) notes that Tunisia's food security policy shifts production away from labor-intensive crops produced in the interior, hindering development in that region, and away from crops in which Tunisia has a natural comparative advantage toward those benefiting a few large landowners.

Paciello's (2013) conclusion on Tunisia, as on Egypt, is that the Islamist parties coming to power after the revolutions "failed to transform their promises of social justice into a coherent long-term strategy for improving people's living standards and employment prospects for youth" (28). This was in part due to their inability to exert full control over state institutions or find alternatives to borrowing from IFIs, and also due to their exclusion of important social and political forces from economic debate, reducing the chance of arriving at a consensus on a new economic model.

Guazzone (2013) also recognizes the weaknesses of Ennahda's performance, particularly in the crucial fields of security and economy, based in part simply on the general inexperience of *all* political actors after fifty-four years of authoritarian rule—"the action of the Ennahda-led governments after the first free election . . . can on the whole be considered mostly reactive, relatively inefficient and lacking a generally innovative program" (36)—and in part on the resistance of actors within the state apparatus and outside it mentioned by Paciello. But she also assesses the party's overall contributions in terms of moderation and pragmatism as critical to the success of the political transition. Their performance may have been middling in these critical areas, but if they had made worse choices, the transition might have foundered altogether.

That broader context matters greatly in assessing what the Ennahda-led governments did or didn't do in the transitional period, and what we can infer from them about the party's priorities. It was a period of exception, of more or less continuous crisis, particularly as political violence led to the decision to move to a technocratic government and the population struggled to maintain its patience with a Constituent Assembly process that greatly exceeded its initial estimate of how long it would take to produce a new constitution. Particularly in light of the collapse of the political transition in Egypt into renewed authoritarianism, we can understand that Ennahda and its partners in the so-called Troika—the governing partnership with two center-left parties—viewed a successful outcome of the constitutional process and moving to elections without collapse of public order as the highest priorities. We should not be too surprised if economic achievements in this period were limited and ambitions muted, even if the effects of that may have been problematic in terms of popular satisfaction.[1] As Monica Marks (2014) has shown, Ennahda's commitment to functioning as a broad-tent political party rather than as an ideologically pure movement and to being a productive player in the constitutional process led to much internal as well as external compromises. An echo of Shariati's spiritual rather than scripturalist approach (Saffari 2015) may perhaps be discerned in how party elites managed these competing pressures in the most sensitive areas of the negotiations over the new constitution:

> On the place of sharia in the constitution, for example, the party ultimately opted not to include the word. While Ennahda members do look to sharia as an ideal ethical framework, most members accept a more abstract, ethical definition of Islamic law (focusing on social justice, equality, and good governance). Key members of the Shura Council were persuaded that this was the appropriate course of action for the party, keeping itself a relevant and viable political player. (Marks 2014, 1)

There are good electoral reasons, beyond the relative success of the party's collaboration with the secular left in the transition period, to predict that Ennahda would seek to broaden its appeal beyond religiously motivated voters and to have a reasonable chance of doing so. They could not take their base for granted. As Roháč (2013) argues (based on admittedly limited data from around the Middle East and North Africa region and beyond): In "Muslim majority countries, the documented links between personal religiosity and political and voting behavior are not very reliable. This is at odds with the evidence from Europe where Catholicism is a strong predictor of voting for Christian Democratic parties" (264). Moreover, part of Ennahda's transformation toward a political party willing to compete in a pluralist democratic system involved finding ways to articulate the grievances of those dispossessed by the authoritarian regimes of Bourguiba and Ben Ali: this is a far broader constituency than those narrowly committed to Islamic revivalist politics. As Cavatorta and Merone (2013) discuss, in building Ennahda out of the earlier Islamic Tendency, Ghannouchi, Abdelfattah Mourou, and others drew inspiration from Shariati, whose ideas helped them "make the connection between the promotion of the material interests of the disenfranchized and religious principles, proposing the establishment of an economic model that would eliminate the shortcomings—read profound inequalities—of the capitalist system" (862). It was not Khomeini's concept of a theocratic state that they imported from Iran, as some of their critics allege, but Shariati's class analysis: "the conflict between the *mustadaafeen* (the disenfranchized) and *mustaqhbareen* (the arrogant)" (868) became useful ways to articulate a critique of the Bourguibist state in ways that were more palatable to Tunisian society than either the hitherto dominant Marxist left opposition or the harder-line Brotherhood-inspired or Salafist Islamist alternatives.

On the other hand, the party may have left that phase of broad-tent social democracy behind. Cavatorta and Merone (2013) argue that while Ennahda "maintains in some ways that this third way is still potentially pursuable, it is quite evident that it has moved significantly towards the acceptance of a market economy integrated into the global neoliberal system as the only way for Tunisia to develop" noting that the "constituency of reference" is mainly business people rather than the fully disenfranchized or marginalized (862).

Having laid out the historical, institutional, and international context under which Ennahda had to operate, I will now focus on the 2014 election campaign. This campaign came after Ennahda had already been the dominant power in the Troika government and had contributed to the caretaker technocratic government. It provides an opportunity to evaluate how Ennahda defended its economic record in the transition period and what aspirations it held out to the Tunisian people, seeking to appeal beyond its core constituency of pious conservatives. To what extent does their election program support a reading of Ennahda as being reconciled with neoliberal globalization?

THE 2014 ELECTION MANIFESTO—
LIVING WITH NEOLIBERALISM

It should be clear by now that Ennahda is a democratic party, as Marks (2014) emphasizes. While they continue to arouse suspicions among secularists, they have cooperated with other parties, helped oversee the writing of a democratic constitution, during which they made many compromises, and have conceded defeat in an election and handed over power to conservative secular opponents, including some remnants of the old regime. It is reasonable to apply the label of "Muslim Democrats" to them provisionally, as Islamists who have adapted to working within democratic political systems and accepted pluralism and liberal rights, much like their Christian Democratic counterparts in continental Europe.[2] As Guazzone (2013) notes, Ennahda has "worked out its own model for combining Islam and democracy in a modern state, a model that is different from that of the Egyptian Muslim Brotherhood (because it puts less emphasis on the centrality of sharia), and from that of the Turkish Islamist party, AKP (because it rejects any causal link between secularism and democracy)" (45).

The party's 2014 program locates them somewhere between facilitators of neoliberal globalization and reformers of it. There are many areas of apparent convergence between Ennahda's prescription of what Tunisia needs and that of the World Bank. As with democracy, part of their role in that regard may be to localize and translate globalizing capitalism for their pious, conservative constituency. On the other hand, the "free social economy" or social democratic tendency continues in certain respects, suggesting a will to tame or mitigate aspects of globalization, so perhaps we can still discern a little of Shariati's influence.

Ennahda entered the 2014 electoral campaign with a problem of widespread disappointment at their performance in government. But they had the advantage of being a seasoned political party, in contrast to the surprise, underdog winners they had been in the first post-Ben Ali elections for the Constituent Assembly. They had branches throughout the country, a solid ground game, a polished media operation, and an electoral program designed to address what the polls and the streets showed to be the highest concerns: Tunisia's underperforming economy and persistent insecurity. The economy is very clearly the priority. In the English translation of the document, which runs to sixty pages (it was published in French, Arabic, and English), the section explicitly addressing security runs from pages 44–47, while pages 48–60 cover matters related to the proper functioning of the democratic state, culture, youth, women, and sport. In contrast, the section entitled "Social and Economic Fields: Economic Reforms to Create Wealth and Generate Social Mobility" runs from pages 17–39, and is followed by four pages on "Basic Services: Providing the Basis for a Dignified Life and Reducing Inequalities between Regions and Social Groups." Even the discussion of international relations stresses that "priority will be given to the economic and financial dimensions in our foreign relations" (Ennahda 2014, 15). The introduction concludes thus: "We believe that the number one priority for the coming term is a successful economic transition that consolidates our successful democratic transition by achieving prosperity and growth and protecting the future of coming generations" (Ennahda 2014, 16). This is *overwhelmingly* an economic manifesto. To what extent, then, is it an Islamist, neoliberal, or other kind of economic program?

I analyze the electoral program in light of insights gleaned from earlier Ennahda statements on economics (Webb 2014) and broadly through the lens of sociological discourse analysis or, more specifically, critical discourse analysis, an approach that pays close attention to the ways in which "discourse is involved in dominance, namely through the enactment of dominance in text and talk in specific contexts" (Van Dijk 1993, 279). In what follows, I move through the main elements that address the economy, analyzing how it mediates between a developing Tunisia and the global economy, and how it seeks to establish Ennahda as a credible guardian for Tunisians' interests.

The introduction to Ennahda's election program suggests that this will be largely a neoliberal document of a type familiar by analogy to that of Christian Democrat parties as they emerged after the Second World War in Continental Europe, where "the social market economy as an extension of neo-liberal thought was deliberately not a defined economic order but an adjustable holistic conception pursuing a complete humanistic societal order as a synthesis of seemingly conflicting objectives, namely economic freedom and social security" (Glossner 2010, 12). In the beginning, the Muslim Democrats of the AKP of Turkey, which has been in some respects a model for Ennahda (Webb 2014), had spoken a similar language—before the authoritarian turn documented by Bozkurt in this volume—building their winning coalition on the basis of small and medium enterprises (SMEs) in Anatolia as well as key urban strongholds.

> The Tunisian model, which nears the completion of its transition phase, will now focus its efforts on stimulating the economy and encouraging private initiative, entrepreneurship and investment in order to create jobs and improve the living conditions of the daughters and sons of Tunisia. (Ennahda 2014, 5)

The economic section of the electoral program—the bulk of it—begins by emphasizing the party's experience in government since the uprising, what it has thereby learned about the state of the economy, the obstacles to effective development, the legacy of the Ben Ali years in bureaucracy and corruption, and what it deems the ineffectiveness of past development models. It accordingly wishes to present "an alternative development model" to address obstacles including "value systems that discourage work and respect of laws, the spread of corruption, the absence of good governance, the weakness of social cohesion and the deterioration of the state's role in developing human capital in general, and in particular through education and health care" (Ennahda 2014, 17–18). The obstacles cited are hard to parse in terms that slot neatly into ideological categories familiar among Western political parties. But there is also not much here that is incompatible with the Washington Consensus and the kind of medicine recommended by the IFI or international donors over recent decades: improving good governance, including transparency and the rule of law, and reducing corruption; and investing in human capital—although in the heyday of the

Consensus, spending on education and health care was often reduced as part of structural adjustment, we are now living in the world of the Human Development Index and the Millennium Development Goals where a more holistic approach is generally preferred. Indeed, the World Bank specifically argues for strengthening the social protection system in Tunisia in its book-length report, reflecting the criticism that had been leveled at the institution since the 1980s (World Bank 2014a, 20). The particular emphases on value systems and social cohesion are less typical of the discourses of IFIs, perhaps, and that is one of the areas where the distinctiveness of religious hybrid forms of globalizing development shows itself. It also shows that neoliberalism has changed over time as well.

The party describes its alternative development model as an "inclusive development model" based on "social capitalism as a strategic economic choice" (Ennahda 2014, 18). Social capitalism appears to be the new term for what Rached El Ghannouchi referred to in 2011 as "free social economy" (Webb 2014, 4). Its elements are (1) honest and fair competition; (2) social balance; (3) free enterprise; and (4) solidarity—the whole "combining merit and fairness" (Ennahda 2014, 18). Along with social capitalism, the other two main planks of the development model are the following: moving from "a rentier economy to a genuine competitive economy through a definitive break with nepotism, clientelism and instrumentalisation of political relations in the economic field"; and renewing "the role of the state as a catalyst for growth, a regulator of market imbalances, a guarantor of social justice and equal opportunities and a protector of low- and middle income groups" (Ennahda 2014, 18).

How do these three elements situate Ennahda vis-à-vis an evaluation of them as Islamist, neoliberal, or something other? "Social capitalism" seems intended to dilute or mitigate the rigors of the untamed market promoted by neoliberalism. This seems to echo the "third way" of the consensus-building Christian Democracy seen in Germany in the mid-twentieth century. The second point on corruption and rent-seeking is a response to specific local and historic circumstances, as recognized by numerous local and outside observers. Ben Ali and his inner circle created the appearance of liberalizing economic reforms while, in fact, building a pervasive system of crony capitalism with numerous opportunities to extract rent. The transitional period has not done enough to undo that system (World Bank 2014a).[3] The last point on the role of the state is challenging if one wishes to cast this as a purely neoliberal economic vision: this goes beyond the "nightwatchman state" of Adam Smith, and appears to evoke some social democratic ideas of safety nets and market interventions in the interest of social justice. Elsewhere, the document summarizes the concept as a "regulatory role for the state that combines economic effectiveness and social responsibility" (Ennahda 2014, 19).

At first sight, none of this appears distinctively Islamic, or religious in any sense. But a study by Roháč has found that in a number of countries, those who value the presence of Islam in politics tend to believe that elections are the most important feature of democracy, that human rights violations in the name of security and stability are rarely justifiable, and that corruption is the main problem plaguing their respective countries (2013, 266). As an electoral strategy, then, like the emphases elsewhere in this document on consolidating democracy and human rights, the corruption focus makes sense here. Roháč's study suggests that a party of Ennahda's type could have an advantage over its secular counterparts in making commitments on tackling the legacy of authoritarian distortions in the economy: "Unlike patronage-based politics, credible religious parties provide a bundle of public goods and transfers, maximizing the utility of the median voter" (2013, 269). Credible commitments would be based in part on past provision of services (social, educational etc.) by the movement, in part by the presumed piety and high moral character of its candidates and membership.

What is the aim of this developmental strategy? The program mentions five top-level aims (Ennahda 2014, 18):

- A structural transformation of the national economy through high productivity, added-value, and job creation.
- Combating unemployment, particularly among youth and university graduates.
- Addressing the development deficit between regions, social inequalities, and poverty in all its forms.
- Improving the country's fiscal balances.
- Qualitative integration of the national economy into the global economy.

The last two points are unexceptionable from the perspective of neoliberal orthodoxy. The first three, particularly the third, with its suggestion of redistribution, suggest more interventionist policies than one might expect of a neoliberal party. But the details matter.

The discussion of macroeconomic policy, committing to maintaining fiscal balances over the medium to long term, controlling inflation below a target of four percent, and reducing budget deficits reads like neoliberal economic orthodoxy with the exception of the (ambitious) target of developing "public funding through Islamic bonds to reach 50% of fiscal markets" (Ennahda 2014, 20).

On the other hand, the party intends to put in place an active industrial policy, something that is out of fashion in the industrialized world. But in the context of a developing economy, seeking to bring about structural transformation, it is not surprising to find ideas of some elements of planning.

It is notable that the strategy envisaged involves public-private partnerships, tax reform, transparency, export orientation, and "the flexibility and adaptation capabilities of businesses towards high-skilled jobs" (Ennahda 2014, 21). The overall strategy is certainly directed to more export-led growth than something more state-centric, and seems intended to integrate an economy of Tunisia's size into the globalizing world economy with minimal friction. Indeed, a brief section is dedicated to effective engagement with the global economic system, including making full use of partnership with the European Union and other agreements to "move from a demand economy to a supply economy." But it has some interesting caveats:

> We must strengthen its ability to adapt in a way that takes into consideration the higher national interest, most importantly through . . . adoption of temporary protection measures for some emerging sectors in line with the national industrial strategy and international trade agreements.

So I think we must assess the industrial and trade strategies as essentially compatible with a neoliberal, globalizing vision for Tunisia's future. But there is pragmatism at work here, conditioned by the circumstances of the economic legacy of the Ben Ali years and the need to make a transition in the economic domain to match the one undertaken in the political field. The reference to Islamic bonds aside, this is not notably a deviation from neoliberal orthodoxy.

The next section of the document, discussing investment climate, is where we see the core concern with corruption appear more strongly and, specifically, Islamic answers offered most obviously: "We will seek, through developing the investment code and competition code, to rid the investment climate of the traces of corruption that had prevented equal opportunities between citizens" (Ennahda 2014, 23). Many of the measures suggested are for straightforward good governance as might be urged by international donors, such as reinforcing the independence of the central bank or applying international standards in the banking sector, or reducing the scope of activities requiring permits (and thus opportunities for graft). But alongside measures such as developing a genuine market for public bonds are the following:

- Completing the legal framework for Islamic finance and diversifying available banking products through adopting Islamic banking products and making Tunisia an international center for Islamic finance.
- Encouraging public and private banks to use Islamic financial tools.
- Creating a part-private part-public Islamic cooperative fund in order to fund small and medium businesses based on musharaka and mudaraba.
- Encouraging the use of Islamic bonds in the financial market.
- Developing Islamic financing of small loans in the regions. (Ennahda 2014, 25)

While the emphasis on SMEs is straight out of the AKP playbook—the Anatolian entrepreneur class remains the backbone of the Turkish ruling party coalition as well as a driver of Turkey's relative economic success—the appeal to Islamic financing models looks elsewhere for inspiration, to the GCC in particular. While it is distinctively Islamist rather than neoliberal, there is nothing incompatible here with globalization: many of the largest multinational investment banks have Islamic finance divisions, and it is a rapidly growing sector (Khan and Bhatti 2008). Moreover, some have suggested it as a corrective to some of the problems that have afflicted the wilder speculative excesses of the global financial system (Chapra 2009). So this is a logical move for a Muslim Democratic party to make as part of its economic strategy, particularly in a context in which the existing system is (accurately) widely perceived as corrupt.

The remaining proposals in this section on investment climate and growth are not specifically Islamic in character, and most are compatible with a broadly neoliberal approach, with the caveat that some are specific to the needs of a developing rather than developed economy, such as the sections on subsidy reform or incorporating the informal sector into the "organized" sector. But on subsidies, as elsewhere, the language seems to be that of social democracy more than neoliberalism, such as when it speaks of directing "subsidies to those genuinely in need in order to protect the middle-income groups, guarantee the purchasing power of low-income groups, and achieve social justice" (Ennahda 2014, 28). Since the overall project is developmentalist and involves correcting maldistribution, it inevitably will involve some degree of redistribution, hence such appeals to social justice. That it aims to do so through tools such as "rationalisation and reform of the subsidy system" and public-private partnerships, including in the crucial area of human capital development, is what marks this as *more* neoliberal than some of the alternatives. But it is not pure neoliberalism.

The largest signal that Ennahda's program is that of a developmentalist rather than purely neoliberal party, seeing an important (vanguard?) role for the state alongside private actors, comes in the section on major national investment programs, where it promises to increase the public investment budget by ten percent annually to build infrastructure, including telecommunications. It also offers a multisectoral approach to tackling unemployment, particularly youth unemployment, including overhauling education and training to match the needs of the market, tax incentives, training agreements with major employers, unemployment insurance, modernization of job centers, a new body to support small businesses, and so on. The list concludes thus: "Revise employment legislation to support workers' rights and guarantee adequate working conditions, which would positively impact on the productivity of economic institutions and improve their competitiveness"—which might possibly be found in the manifesto of a Christian Democrat party in the heyday of European corporatism, but in general is not the sort of argument one would associate with a contemporary conservative party's job creation platform. The concentration may be on the neoliberal side, with an emphasis on the private sector and the state as facilitator rather than initiator. But it is evident that the party sees a significant role for the state in digging Tunisia out of the demographic and economic crisis in which it finds itself, with high youth unemployment, minimal new job creation, and too many barriers to productive investment and entrepreneurial activity. A later section sums this up in its title as "a regulatory role for the state combining economic effectiveness and social responsibility" (Ennahda 2014, 35).

There is also a general commitment to basic quality of life: "Ennahdha Party believes that among its most important duties is improving the quality of basic services for citizens, such as housing, education, healthcare and a clean environment, so that we move closer to achieving justice between groups and regions" (Ennahda 2014, 40). Among the welfare issues mentioned are "a minimum level of income and health coverage for every citizen" and a "distributive system that guarantees retirement payments and health coverage up to a fixed amount" (Ennahda 2014, 27): the specifics on health care include increasing hospital beds from 21,000 to 26,000 in five years and promoting health tourism. Housing is one area where there is a distinct variation from neoliberal orthodoxy, with both price controls and Islamic financing mentioned as part of a package of measures to ensure affordable and middle-class housing (Ennahda 2014, 42). These dilutions of neoliberalism situate the party to the left of many European conservative parties today, but would have put them in the center-right in the more consensual postWar reconstruction era in which Christian Democracy grew up (Glossner 2010).

There are what seem genuinely innovative ideas about how to integrate Tunisia into the world economy: making use of its potential as an entrepôt between Africa and the European Union; promoting desert tourism as a viable sector (away from the already-developed coastal regions); building free trade zones with neighboring countries; seeking markets in developing countries and pushing existing sectors further up the international value chain; and encouraging Tunisians abroad to invest. All of these bespeak integration into the globalized economy. "Strengthening our position as an advanced partner" with the European Union may not be as specific as the recent World Bank recommendations on pursuing a Deep and Comprehensive Free Trade Agreement, on which talks have opened, where potential gains are estimated to be as much as ten percent in output and twelve percent in household welfare (World Bank 2014b, vii–viii). But it does support the idea that Cavatorta and Merone put forward that they are essentially reconciled to full integration in the global economy.

CREATING THE MORAL ACTOR

The most important religious dimension of the program is the belief in the necessity for a re-moralization of society from the individual level up. The party is convinced that the main instrument of developmental change is not (simply) the profit motive operating in an efficient market, nor is it a benevolent and far-sighted developmentalist state, but, rather, it is *homo islamicus* (Webb 2014) (see the chapter on the Hizmet movement, this volume, for a similar approach). In the introduction to the electoral program, we find a pithy restatement of ideas that have been circulating in earlier Ennahda documents:

> We, Ennahdha, believe in the necessity of activating the noble human values stemming from our religion and from the cultural and civilisational heritage of Tunisian society and its Arab and Muslim identity, such as solidarity, social justice, family cohesion, combating corruption, rationalising consumption, upholding the values of hard work, competence, merit and integrity, and strengthening the sense of patriotism. To achieve democracy and economic prosperity and to strengthen the unity of our society and its capabilities, we need to entrench these values in our educational, cultural and media programmes. (Ennahda 2014, 11)

It is the values dimension that sets apart Muslim Democracy from a pure embrace of neoliberal global capitalism.[4] Recognizable conservative keywords include "heritage," "hard work," "merit," and "patriotism." But there are terms here that one would associate in Western political contexts with parties of the center-left, such as "solidarity," "social justice," or "rationalising consumption," and rarely with conservative parties.

Homo islamicus also appears in the section on education.

> Ennahdha Party believes that the education system is the robust foundation for the development of balanced, talented, well-rounded individuals. Thus we devote absolute priority to education given its importance in building society and achieving its members' aspirations. We believe Tunisia needs an educational policy that stresses the centrality of effective, proactive students, and develops the characteristics of teachers as rooted in Arab-Muslim culture while being open to universal values. (Ennahda 2014, 43)

Although this is not, in the end, too alien from the model of moral education attempted under Bourguiba (Webb 2013), with Tunisian roots being planted in Arab-Muslim soil and cultivated by universal civilization, I nevertheless think we should take this as a substantial part of the Ennahda project. I think it is worth taking seriously that the party has a "conviction that education is a strategic sector for the achievement of comprehensive development and the formation of free, proud dignified citizens" (Ennahda 2014, 43) and, not incidentally, the formation of future Muslim democrats and Ennahda voters.

The specific policies discussed do not include a radical overhaul of the curriculum, although there is mention of Arabic language teaching for children of Tunisians abroad and familiarizing new generations with Tunisian culture. But there is no doubt that educational standards have declined since Bourguiba's time, and if Ennahda were to make the investments of resources they mention in their program, the developmental payoffs would be noteworthy. Would a Ministry of Education run by Ennahda "Islamize" the curriculum? It seems unlikely that Tunisian civil society, or the teaching profession itself, would go along with it. But it is really not clear that this is the project, in any case: moral training can come from mosque and home to complement a more vigorous "national" education provided by the state, so long as the state remains democratic and is not actively persecuting the pious to prevent such training. The program speaks, rather, of updating practices and curriculum in line with up-to-date advances and modern sciences, "improving and diversifying pedagogical methods and reviewing the evaluation system" (Ennahda 2014, 44). Alongside the mosque and the family, the school is the greatest instrument available for the production of moral actors, of "entrenching" the values it espouses. Ennahda is not a pan-Islamic or Salafist party, but a pragmatic Muslim Democrat party hoping to find a niche for Tunisian development within the global economy: its educational policy logically seeks to produce well-trained as well as virtuous Tunisians who can build a more prosperous future for their country.

CONCLUSION

Ennahda is distinctively Tunisian, while being influenced by broader currents of Islamist and other thought. Its experiences under the former dictatorship and since the uprising have not mirrored those of the Muslim Brotherhood, for instance; nor does it resemble Turkey's AKP, for all that it may claim some kinship. There are many Islamisms even within the Mediterranean region, let alone in the wider Muslim world, just as there are many secularisms and modernities and paths to those modernities, as Cavatorta and Merone (2013) have directed us to observe. For the moment, Ennahda finds itself out of power, but involved in power as a significant party of opposition in a pluralist democratic system it helped to build and protect through a difficult period of transition. Its economic vision for the longer term seems to be a pragmatic one, recognizing that Tunisia must find a niche in a globalizing world, and not fighting those forces head-on, while having some interest in mitigating the harsher social consequences of those forces. In many respects, its economic approach resembles the conservative pragmatism of the Christian Democrats in the aftermath of the Second World War, who saw minimum social protections for all stakeholders as essential for the success of market-based economic growth and reconstruction, something largely absent in today's austerity politics. Ennahda's longer-term plans envisage a re-moralized Tunisian economy and polity. This may be a good electoral strategy, but whether it will be enough to counter the crises of unemployment, corruption, and the allure of radical Salafist-jihadism that bedevil Tunisia today is unclear.

NOTES

1. For instance, and it would be hard to demonstrate conclusively the causal connection, Tunisia faced an internal security challenge in this period from radical Salafi-Jihadists and has been one of the largest exporters of such volunteers to the battlefields of Iraq and Syria.

2. In many countries, a usually majority Catholic party of that name is either the main party of the center-right or among the significant conservative parties. It is not clear whether Ennahda consciously models itself on such parties, but their Conservatives and Reformists bloc in the European Parliament has reached out to Ennahda with a summit in Tunis in November 2015, as documented on Al-Jazeera on 12 November.

3. The return to power of many of the economic and political class who did well under Ben Ali as part of the Nidaa Tounes-led government is certainly cause for concern on this front as explained by Omar Belhaj Salah on the website of *Middle East Eye* on 24 August 2015.

4. It is ironic, if unsurprising, that there is some considerable overlap between Ennahda's ambitions to diffuse productive values by means of what Althusser termed the "Ideological State Apparatuses," and similar projects attempted by Bourguiba in the postindependence period (Webb 2013). Two generations later, the language of laïc Enlightenment (see chapter 2 for laicism) has ebbed and Islam has taken a more prominent place. But in other respects, it seems familiar.

REFERENCES

Ayoob, Mohammed. 2007. "Challenging Hegemony: Political Islam and the North-South Divide." *International Studies Review* 9 (4): 629–43.

Cavatorta, Francesco and Fabio Merone. 2013. "Democratization: Moderation through Exclusion? The Journey of the Tunisian Ennahda from Fundamentalist to Conservative Party." *Democratization* 20 (5): 857–75.

Chapra, Muhammad Umer. 2009. "The Global Financial Crisis: Can Islamic Finance Help Minimise the Severity and Frequency of Such a Crisis in the Future?" *Islam and Civilisational Renewal* 1 (2): 226–45.

Ennahda. 2014. *Ennahdha Party Electoral Programme 2015–2020: A Rising Economy. A Secure Country.* http://mhabettounes.org/legislative-2014/our-program/?lang=en.

Glossner, Christian L. 2010. "The Making of the German Post-War Economy." In *60 Years of Social Market Economy: Formation, Development and Perspectives of a Peacemaking Formula*, edited by Christian L. Glossner and David Gregosz. Berlin: Konrad-Adenauer-Stiftung.

Guazzone, Laura. 2013. "Ennahda Islamists and the Test of Government in Tunisia." *The International Spectator: Italian Journal of International Affairs* 48 (4): 30–50.

Khan, M. Mansoor and M. Ishaq Bhatti. 2008. "Islamic Banking and Finance: On its Way to Globalization." *Managerial Finance* 34 (10): 708–25.

King, Stephen J. 2003. *Liberalization Against Democracy: The Local Politics of Economic Reform in Tunisia*. Bloomington, IN: Indiana University Press.

Marks, Monica. 2014. *Convince, Coerce, or Compromise? Ennahda's Approach to Tunisia's Constitution*. Brookings Doha Center Analysis Paper Number 10. Doha: Brookings Doha Center.

Paciello, Maria Cristina. 2013. "Delivering the Revolution? Post-uprising Socio-economics in Tunisia and Egypt." *The International Spectator: Italian Journal of International Affairs* 48 (4): 7–29.

Roháč, Dalibor. 2013. "Religion as a Commitment Device: The Economics of Political Islam." *Kyklos* 66 (2): 256–74.

Saffari, Siavash. 2015. "Rethinking the Islam/Modernity Binary: Ali Shariati and Religiously Mediated Discourse of Sociopolitical Development." *Middle East Critique* 24 (3): 231–50. doi:10.1080/19436149.2015.1046708.

Tamimi, Azzam. 2001. *Rachid Ghannouchi: A Democrat within Islamism*. New York: Oxford University Press.

Van Dijk, Teun A. 1993. "Principles of Critical Discourse Analysis." *Discourse and Society* 4 (2): 249–83.

Webb, Edward. 2013. "The 'Church' of Bourguiba: Nationalizing Islam in Tunisia." *Sociology of Islam* 1 (1–2): 17–40.

———. 2014. "Changing the Player, Not the Game: Ennahda's *Homo Islamicus*." *Air and Space Power Journal Africa and Francophonie* 5 (1): 4–18.

World Bank. 2014a. *Tunisia: Development Policy Review—The Unfinished Revolution: Bringing Opportunity, Good Jobs and Greater Wealth to all Tunisians*. Washington, DC: The World Bank Group.

———. 2014b. *Advancing Tunisia's Global Integration: Reforms options in the context of deeper integration with the EU*. Washington, DC: The World Bank Group.

Chapter 9

Promoting Neoliberalism through Islam? The Case of the AKP in Turkey

Umut Bozkurt

The key aim of this volume is to discuss whether the religious movements under scrutiny seek to promote, reform, or resist neoliberal globalization. This chapter provides an answer to this question by focusing on the case of Turkey and its *Adalet ve Kalkınma Partisi* (Justice and Development Party) (hereafter the AKP) that has ruled the country since 2002. To this end, it will not only explore the AKP's relationship to neoliberalism but will also engage itself with two main issues: How did the AKP manage to stay in power for so long? What are the main challenges to its rule?

As the title reveals, this chapter takes a clear position on the question of the AKP's relationship to neoliberalism. Since it came to power in 2002, the AKP has been a proponent of neoliberalism with a human face. In this process, the AKP has aimed to reward the bourgeoisie, on the one hand, and to increase pressures on organized labor, on the other hand. These neoliberal policies have increased economic growth but have also led to more inequality and employment instability.

The key argument of this chapter is that the AKP has been successful in establishing the hegemony of the bourgeoisie for the first time in the history of the Turkish Republic (Yalman 2014, 46). Following the turbulent 60s and 70s characterized by an intensifying class struggle that ended with a coup d'état in 1980, the bourgeoisie looked for a strategy to overcome the hegemonic crisis it experienced. This strategy aimed to prevent the working class from organizing itself based on class identity and, instead, to direct it to associate itself with other identities primarily based on religion and ethnicity.

The aftermath of the coup d'état in 1980 can be defined as a simultaneous process of political authoritarianism and economic liberalism. Although the bourgeoisie sought to consolidate its hegemony in the course of the 1990s by making use of the ideological state apparatuses, the real turning point came in the early 2000s when the AKP came to power. The success of the AKP depended on its managing to overcome the political crisis by manufacturing a unity between the dominant classes and obtaining the active or passive consent of the subordinate classes (Akça, Bekmen, and Özden 2014, 6). That this strategy succeeded can be seen in the fact that various research and opinion polls show that the party managed to gain the support not only of the organized but also of the marginalized sections of the working class (Bozkurt 2013, 373).

Specifically, this chapter will argue that the AKP established a neoliberal hegemony in Turkey by resorting to "neoliberal populism." Populism is a governance strategy where the leader reaches out to followers in a seemingly direct, quasi-personal manner that bypasses established intermediary organizations, such as parties and interest associations. Even if the leader builds new organizations or revives earlier populist organizations, they remain personal vehicles with low levels of institutionalization (Weyland 1996, 5). Barr (2003) explains populism as a "political phenomenon in which a leader attempts to build personalistic ties to the impoverished masses while pursuing neoliberal economic policies" (1161).

In this chapter, neoliberal populism is understood in Gramscian terms as a hegemonic project whereby political leadership appeals to the masses as the "people" and plays a significant role in constituting the hegemony of the power bloc over the subordinate class, in particular, the informal and disorganized sections of the working class (Yıldırım 2009, 82). "Power bloc" is a concept used by Nicos Poulantzas to define the key feature of capitalist states, which is based on a plurality of dominant class fractions, one of which is hegemonic over the others (Poulantzas 1968). The hegemonic project of the AKP depends on constructing the nation as a homogenous political entity resembling a big family, which shares the same values. Such a construct hides class inequalities in the neoliberal era (Saracoğlu 2011, 42) and thereby serves the bourgeoisie's strategy to end class-based politics.

This chapter is composed of three sections. The first section provides a short background and contextualizes the AKP in the tradition of political Islam in Turkey that dates back to the 1970s. The second section discusses the strategies the party employs in order to achieve neoliberal hegemony. Three of these strategies will be elaborated: (1) an emphasis on developmentalism and economic grandeur, (2) populist policies such as social assistance schemes, and (3) the party's use of the symbolic/ideological sphere to constitute its hegemony. The last section discusses the challenges to the rule of the AKP in Turkey.

CONTEXTUALIZING AKP IN THE POLITICAL ISLAM TRADITION IN TURKEY

The AKP's origins can be found in the *Milli Görüş* (National Outlook) tradition that represents political Islam from the 1970s onward. Parties in this tradition include *Millî Nizam Partisi* (National Order Party) and *Refah Partisi* (Welfare Party). These parties have a variegated history of success, failure, and state suppression until various circumstances consolidated their success with the rise of the AKP to power. Their main unifying element was a focus on social justice, redistribution, and heavy state intervention, and, in some cases, an anti-Western orientation. However, they do not represent "Islam" in Turkey in its entirety; there is also a tradition of a civil Islam in Turkey, which is opposed to a political interpretation of Islam as the chapter by Dreher highlights.

The success of the AKP lies in the fact that it went beyond appealing to the traditional support base of its predecessors. The support base of such parties often consisted of the small-scale commercial and industrial bourgeoisie (Toprak 2005, 180). The AKP, in contrast, represented the "second generation" bourgeoisie that flourished under conditions of globalization. In comparison to the "first generation bourgeoisie" or "Istanbul bourgeoisie" represented by the Turkish Industrialists' and Businessmen's Association TÜSİAD that grew in the 1960s and 1970s during the import substitution industrialization era, the Islamic-oriented Anatolian capital groups emerged in the post-1980 period as latecomers in the process of accumulation, becoming the key support base of the AKP. The second generation bourgeoisie today includes not only small and medium-scale employers. From the 1990s onward, Islamic capital has also grown, taking advantage of the export orientation of the economy and leading to the foundation of some holding companies that have reached the size and economic power of many units of "core" capital (Gülalp 2001, 444).

The second generation bourgeoisie benefited from exporting its products under free market principles; therefore, the economic policies of parties such as *Refah Partisi* (RP) that focused on social justice, redistribution, and heavy state intervention increasingly alienated this group (Gümüşcü and Sert 2010, 963). It was the rise of the second generation bourgeoisie that gave way to the AKP's split from its predecessor RP. Therefore, the neoliberalism of the AKP was a response to the demands of the second generation bourgeoisie that was on its way to becoming a significant economic actor in its own right.

In 1990, the representatives of the second generation bourgeoisie founded the Association of Independent Industrialists and Businessmen (MÜSİAD). MÜSİAD reflected the need of these pious capitalists to declare their interests and organize their business relationships independently from TÜSİAD, the first generation bourgeoisie association and until then the most dominant business representation in the Turkish economy (Doğan and Durak 2014, 220). The 1990s represented a breakthrough for these businessmen. By the end of the 1990s, MÜSİAD, the Confederation of Businessmen and Industrialization of Turkey (TUSKON) and the Anatolian Lions Businessmen's Association (ASKON) were becoming stronger through their growing membership resulting from their effectiveness in both private business and government procurement (for TUSKON see Dreher, this volume). In the second half of the 1990s, some of these emergent Islamist firms, such as Kombassan, YİMPAŞ, and Jet-Pa, enlarged their capital accumulation and investment scales (Doğan and Durak 2014, 22).

The second generation bourgeoisie experienced a political setback in 1997 because a military memorandum was issued against the coalition government headed by the Islamist Party in power (RP). The military establishment accused the government of insisting on policies that would undermine secularist policies in Turkey. Controversial steps such as Erbakan's attempt to engineer a shift in Turkey's relations away from Europe and the West toward the Muslim bloc or granting permission to wear headscarves in offices generated deep resentment on the part of the establishment. As a result, the RP was banned and the pious bourgeoisie was persecuted, with police measures and fiscal operations launched against Islamic companies (Doğan and Durak 2014, 222).

The AKP's rise to power in 2002 as a majority government was a turning point for the second generation bourgeoisie in Turkey. Especially after 2007, it is possible to observe a boost in the membership of bourgeoisie organizations such as MÜSİAD, which enabled them to compete against the first generation TÜSİAD members. It should be underlined that soon after coming to power, AKP managed to get the blessing of the first generation bourgeoisie as well. The party achieved this by becoming proactive on the issue of Turkey's EU membership and by displaying greater commitment to economic and political reforms necessitated by the EU integration process. Furthermore, the widespread perception that the secularist establishment had suppressed religious people in Turkey enabled the AKP government to draw on this sense of victimization (*Today's Zaman*, 2015) and to gain the support of the left-liberal intelligentsia.

To sum up then, the AKP's achievement relied upon the party's success in gaining the support of the first and second generation bourgeoisie, the newly urbanized poor, and important factions of the police, as well as the support of the liberal, left-leaning intelligentsia (Tuğal 2007, 5).

THE DYNAMICS BEHIND NEOLIBERAL HEGEMONY UNDER THE AKP

Since coming to power in 2002, the AKP has progressively increased its votes until the June 2015 parliamentary elections. In the 2002 elections, the party received 34.42% of the votes; in 2007, it received 46.58%; and in 2011, it received 49.95%; but in June 2015, it received only 40.86% of the votes (a fact that will be discussed in the last section). These electoral victories enabled the party to further deepen the hegemony of the dominant class. Yet, what kinds of strategies are employed by the AKP to achieve neoliberal hegemony? This section will outline three strategies. It will show how the emphasis by the AKP on developmentalism and economic grandeur, employing populist policies such as social assistance schemes and its use of religious discourse, enabled it to gain the consent of the different social classes in Turkey.

AKP's Emphasis on "Developmentalism" and Economic Grandeur

The AKP's emphasis on Turkey's economic growth and economic grandeur was achieved through large infrastructure investments that contributed significantly to its widespread support. A poll conducted on the day of the presidential elections in August 2014 by the IPSOS Social Research Institute recorded that 97.25% of those who voted for Erdoğan did so because his party had undertaken "significant public services in Turkey" (Ipsos 2014, 48). The policy of "developmentalism" turned the construction sector into one of the "main pillars" of the government, according to Gürcan and Peker (2014, 73). For example, the year 2005 is considered to be a landmark in the spread of shopping malls, increasing from 106 in 2005 to 263 in 2010 and 447 in 2014. Furthermore, in 2002, 43,430 new construction projects were started, 114,204 in 2006 and 106,659 in 2007 (Moudouros 2014, 187).

The AKP's export-oriented free market strategy and huge inflows of foreign investment also contributed to Turkey's economic growth. Since 2002, GNP has expanded from $230bn to $788bn (Yörük and Yüksel 2014, 107). The emergence of new industrial centers in Anatolia meant that new markets developed and the previously neglected Middle East turned into an attractive market (Altunışık and Martin 2011, 579). MÜSİAD and TUSKON have been actively pursuing international business by organizing foreign conferences, delegations, and exchanges, though TUSKON's activities are much reduced after 2014 (see Dreher, this volume). The efforts of these institutions, coupled with the then foreign minister Ahmet Davutoğlu's foreign policy led to an increase in trade between Turkey and its neighbors in the region. As a result, by 2010, Turkey's exports to the Middle East had doubled from 2005, reaching $21 million. Turkey's trade with the EU countries was even more significant, where exports in 2010 were at $53 million (Altunışık and Martin 2011, 580). The AKP government is also credited with increasing the inflow of Foreign Direct Investment (FDI). Turkey became the 22nd most popular investment destination for investors and it took a share of around 1% from global investment (Hürriyet Daily News, June 24, 2015).

So how does the party's emphasis on economic growth, developmentalism, and economic grandeur serve neoliberal hegemony? First of all, this process is functional for the creation of a new community of conservative-Islamic capitalists who are now organically connected to the AKP government. A concrete example is how the Housing Development Administration of Turkey (TOKI) (directly controlled by the prime minister) organized space. It oversees the construction of new buildings such as shopping malls, multi-national companies' offices, luxurious residential complexes, and mosques. These constructions are carried out either by governmental or private construction companies (Moudouros 2014, 187). TOKI is exempt from taxes and is able to buy land at preferential rates without having to consult the privatization administration (Çavuşoğlu and Strutz 2014, 142). TOKI contributed to the proliferation of AKP-led Islamic capitalists insofar as most TOKI contractors are connected to the AKP's conservative-Islamic circles (Gürcan and Peker 2013, 76). Besides creating a space of accumulation for an organically integrated bourgeoisie, the AKP's construction and housing policies are also an effective strategy to generate consent from its poorer constituency. Offering low-interest loans for housing serves as a cultural-hegemonic tool and portrays the AKP government as the protector of the urban poor (Çavuşoğlu and Strutz 2014, 137).

The Explosion of Social Assistance Programs and Health Care Reform

Another significant factor behind the AKP's hegemony are the populist policies it implemented to mitigate the dire consequences of its neoliberal agenda. Populist policies are not peculiar to the AKP, having existed in Turkey since the 1960s. However, the AKP changed their meaning and direction. Before 1980, populism was essentially put into operation in production relations through wage policies. Yet, after 1980, it was relocated to the social reproduction sphere and the destructive repercussions of neoliberal policies were mitigated through social assistance programs, addressing specific areas such as health and education (Bozkurt 2013, 378). This section will focus on the explosion of social assistance programs, significant for the party to expand its support base.

Since the AKP came to power in 2002, there has been a significant increase in the means-tested social assistance to the poor. Since 1986, social assistance had been distributed via the Sosyal Yardımlaşma ve Dayanışmayı Teşvik Fonu (SYDTF, Fund for the Encouragement of Social Cooperation and Solidarity). Two years after the AKP came to power, the Fund was turned into a directorate in 2004 and the name was changed (Buğra and Candaş 2011, 521). The most remarkable aspect of this institutional transformation was the degree of autonomy the directorate gained. With the exception of transfers to the Ministry of National Education and Ministry of Health, SYDGM and its Board were only accountable to the office of the prime minister (Eder 2010, 174). In this way, the office of the then prime minister Erdoğan was able to establish direct control over the distribution of social assistance in Turkey, as it had also done for TOKI (see above). Between 2003 and 2007, 54% of the resources were spent on social assistance (in-kind assistance such as food, coal, etc.), whereas 23% was spent on conditional cash transfers in the form of monthly payments to poor families to send their children to school (Yıldırım 2009, 98). A poll conducted in 2006 revealed that the AKP received the majority of its votes from housewives, followed by farmers, blue collar workers working in the private sector, and the unemployed (Odak Araştırma 2006). Many analysts see the high support coming from women, especially from poorer households, as an outgrowth of these social assistance schemes (Tremblay 2014).

Symbolic, Religious, and Ideological Sources of the Party's Hegemony

This section focuses on the ideological symbols and religious/cultural codes that the AKP employs in order to establish neoliberal hegemony. According to Antonio Gramsci, in order to win consent, a governing power needs to take on at least some of the values of those it attempts to lead (Jones 2006, 34). Therefore, a key element of any hegemonic strategy is the formation of links with elements of subordinate culture. Gramsci refers to the concept of "common sense," which he believes is a complex formation partly drawn from "official" conceptions of the world circulated by the ruling bloc and partly formed out of people's practical experiences of social life. The organic intellectuals associated with the ruling AKP established the party's hegemony by drawing on this "common sense" in the Turkish society.

As Saracoğlu and Demirkol (2015) underline, the AKP has built a new nationalist project over the last decade that became an integral part of the AKP's political discourse in the course of its struggle to construct and consolidate its ideological hegemony in Turkey (302). Nationalism, when organized as an ideology of state, can manufacture the consent of citizens by configuring the moral and political bonds between citizens and the state (Saracoğlu and Demirkol 2015, 304). This nationalist project includes a homogenous political entity with the members sharing some common characteristics: a common past and a set of common national interests (Saracoğlu and Demirkol 2015, 305). Sunni-Muslim values are one key element in the nationalism of the AKP. These values have become the core element defining what the "nation" is. The centrality of Sunni Islam in the AKP's nationalism project becomes manifest in the way AKP redefines Kurds as a component of this larger nation. "The definition of the nation along the lines of common Muslim cultural values and a shared Ottoman history enables the Kurds, as well as other Muslim ethnic groups in Turkey to be incorporated into the nation" from the perspective of the AKP (Saracoğlu and Demirkol 2015, 309).

The AKP essentially constructs the "nation" as a happy extended family, where everybody lives in harmony with others, respects traditions, and resolves problems within the family (Saracoğlu 2011, 41). This portrayal of the nation as a big family that shares the same values hides class inequalities in the neoliberal era and other social conflicts such as the Kurdish problem (Saracoğlu 2011, 42). The main difference of the AKP from its predecessors is that it downplays anticapitalist and anti-Western discourses and makes its Sunni Islam-flavored nationalism more compatible with the needs of the dominant neoliberal economic vision. In this sense, AKP's nationalist project serves its neoliberal hegemony perfectly.

The new foreign policy orientation of the AKP government is a constitutive component of the AKP's nationalist project. The AKP era is marked by a new-style foreign policy activism. This includes an emphasis on soft power and improved relations with Turkey's neighboring countries as well as a more ambitious role for Turkey as an active regional and global power (Öniş 2011, 50). The second phase of the AKP government revealed the tendency on the part of the foreign policy decision makers to act independently of the Western alliance, especially in relation to major regional and international conflicts (Öniş 2011, 50; Altunışık and Martin 2011, 575). The AKP government developed a comprehensive policy toward the Middle East in which it assigned a central position to Turkey because of its geography and history. As a result, Turkey involved itself in regional conflicts as mediator, developing relations with groups and countries in the region (Altunışık and Martin 2011, 578).

According to Saracoğlu and Demirkol (2015), the AKP's domestic nationalist project is intimately related to its neo-Ottomanist foreign policy at the international level. Neo-Ottomanism is used to display that Turkey has successfully managed a multicultural empire in the past, one in which numerous ethnic and religious groups lived harmoniously. They argue that the AKP's nationalist position has informed and justified its new foreign policy orientation. In return, AKP's foreign policy provided political appeal to the nationalist project of the AKP, enabling its consolidation. The authors note that the future of neo-Ottomanism at the international level depends not only on interstate relations and balances of power in global politics but also on the success or failure of the nationalist project at the domestic level. In other words, Turkey's pursuing a neo-Ottomanist foreign policy is not independent from the efforts to consolidate hegemony domestically (Saracoğlu and Demirkol 2015, 305).

Sunni Islamic values are reproduced on a daily basis through specific institutions and networks. Two of these are worth mentioning: congregation networks and Imam-Hatip schools. In his study on Konya, Durak (2013) observed how locally formed work-based congregation networks play a very significant role in consolidating neoliberal hegemony over the working class. Compatriot, ethnic communities, and even groups of relatives have the power to determine the conditions of the production process by asserting what kind of demands in terms of wages and working conditions are legitimate. These community congregation leaders are gaining legitimacy through providing favors such as finding jobs and houses for people in their community.

The accumulation of symbolic capital by religious communities and ethnic elites takes place in a world of meanings dominated by Sunni-Islamist values. Durak emphasizes the strong influence of "customs" on class relations. It is these traditions and customs drawn from Sunni Islam that make the daily replication of the neoliberal Islamic hegemony possible by determining the boundaries of what is "feasible" (Durak 2013, 27). Durak underlines how common religious values held by the proletariat and the bourgeoisie instill loyalty and discipline on the part of the proletariat. Workers who find jobs through the help of their relatives or compatriot and religious communities are inclined to be grateful for the job, especially if they perceive the enterprise owner as religious (Durak 2013, 42). As Durak underlines, there is no need to monitor the working pace of a worker in this case, because, rather than an employee or an administrator in an enterprise, God performs this job as an "otherworldly Panopticon" (Durak 2013, 43).

A second element in the diffusion of the Sunni-Islamist common sense are the Imam-Hatip schools that provide pro-Islamic public education and contribute to the creation of a Muslim elite in support of the AKP (Alam 2009, 363). The number of these schools increased significantly: in 1951, there were only seven; yet by 2001 Turkey had 604 "middle level" and 558 "higher level" Imam-Hatip schools. Enrollment also increased from 876 ("middle") and 889 ("high") students in 1951 to 219,890 and 134,224, respectively, in 1999 (Alam 2009, 363). Even though they were originally founded with the intention of providing vocational training for preachers, these schools soon turned into an alternative educational system in which pupils attended both religious and secular courses. As their graduates came to occupy important public positions and manage businesses, practice law, enter politics, and fill high- and middle-level posts in national and local government administration, they played a critical role in the Islamicization of Turkish society and the state (Alam 2009, 364).

The military intervention of 28 February that led to the closure of the Refah Partisi in 1997 also had a negative impact on the schools. First, a draconian law was introduced that significantly curtailed the opportunities of Imam-Hatip graduates to attend regular university courses. This meant that they could only be admitted to theology departments of universities. Second, a new bill that extended compulsory education to eight years led to the closure of the junior divisions (middle level) of the schools (Çakmak 2009, 836). As a result of these two measures, only 2000 students applied in 1997, compared with 35,000 in 1995. The number of students decreased from 396,677 in 1998 to 71,583 in 2002 (Alam 2009, 364).

The AKP's coming to power in 2002 in turn led to a steady expansion of Imam-Hatip schools. Under the AKP, Imam-Hatip students are again able to attend university since 2011 (Miller 2014, 24). As a part of its educational reforms, the AKP also permitted women to wear the headscarf in colleges and universities (Alam 2009, 373). In 2012, the AKP government introduced a contentious 12-year compulsory education system with four-year phases of primary, middle, and high school, known in Turkey as the "4+4+4," paving the way for religious middle schools (Letsch 2015). Consequently, after AKP, the number of students attending Imam-Hatip schools increased again by 90% to almost one million children aged between ten and eighteen, or 9% of all students (Miller 2014, 23; Letsch 2015).

Finally, in discussing the symbolic/ideological sources of the neoliberal hegemony established by the AKP, there is a need to mention the "tightening [of political-cultural hegemonic] control over the media and educational appointments" (Lovering and Türkmen 2011, 78). According to a Media Monitoring Report, twenty-three journalists and nine distributors were behind bars as of July of 2015. Thirteen of the jailed journalists and all jailed publishers were affiliated with the Kurdish media (Bia News, July 14, 2015). In the words of Esra Arsan, a journalism professor at İstanbul Bilgi University, "in 12 years, the AK Party has got more and more expert about how to censor the press, how to spread fear amongst the media. Practice is making censorship perfect" (cited in Pamuk and Hogg, 2014). Censorship increased. For example, in 2014, seventeen journalists, two newspapers, thirty websites or news sites, three Facebook accounts, three films, two posters, a painting exhibition, a concert, and a book were censored (Bia News, July 14, 2015).

Eğin notes that the year 2009 marks the beginning of the end of media freedom under Erdoğan. Independent journalism in Turkey became very difficult as a result of the collusion of big business and big government (Eğin 2013, 53). Media ownership patterns have shifted drastically in favor of AKP-friendly corporations, which took over such conglomerates as the Uzan and Ciner groups (Gürcan and Peker 2014, 82). Business magnates critical of the AKP were intimidated. The owner of Turkey's most popular newspapers and TV stations, Aydın Doğan, took a stance that led to his media group openly confronting the then prime minister Erdoğan. In return, he was charged with a three-billion-dollar tax penalty (Aksera and Baybars-Hawks 2012, 310). He eventually had to sell the Milliyet newspaper that was the most critical of his media entities. Later on, Milliyet was bought by the Demirören Holding whose owners had a more amicable relation with the then prime minister (Amani 2013).

CHALLENGES TO THE AKP RULE

This section will assess the challenges to the AKP rule especially after the Gezi uprising of 2013.The Gezi protests had started peacefully in May 2013 with the protestors aiming to contest urban development plans that would demolish Gezi Park in İstanbul to build a new mosque and a shopping center. However, Turkish police resorting to violence against protestors soon transformed a peaceful environmental protest organized to save six hundred trees in the Gezi Park into a nationwide political demonstration against Recep Tayyip Erdoğan and his government.

The AKP was initially successful because it had managed to establish a cross-class alliance. It also managed to gain the support of different groups in the Turkish society. A poll conducted by Anar and Pollmark commissioned by the AKP reveals the profile of the electorate that voted for the AKP in the 2011 elections: 27% define themselves as conservative, 24.4% as Turkish Nationalist, 16.4% as pro-Atatürk Kemalist (*Atatürkçü Kemalist*), 7.2% as social democrat, 5.9% as liberal democrat, 3% as nationalist (*ulusalcı*), and 1.4% as Kurdish nationalist (Bostan 2011). The Gezi protest was a significant turning point because it shattered the positive image that the AKP enjoyed both in and outside of Turkey. As its authoritarianism started becoming more explicit, cracks in the alliance that brought the party to power became more visible.

In this context, the rift between Erdoğan and the influential Gülen movement is worth mentioning. The Gülen movement is a religious and social movement led by the Turkish Islamic scholar Fethullah Gülen (see also the chapter by Dreher in this volume). The Gülen movement had played an instrumental role in Erdoğan's consolidation of power. These two groups had joined forces in breaking the power of a common enemy in Turkish politics: the military. They had been the guiding force behind the Ergenekon and Sledgehammer coup plot trials that effectively dislodged the secularist old guard centered on the military from power (Rodrik 2013, 129). Yet, once the common enemy was defeated, this coalition fell apart. Erdoğan became concerned about the fact that the Gülen movement dominated the police, judiciary, media, and other parts of the government bureaucracy (Rodrik 2013, 129). Meanwhile, Gülenists fretted that Erdoğan was becoming too powerful (Rodrik 2013, 129). The conflict between Erdoğan and Gülen's groups reached a climax after the December 17, 2013 anticorruption operation where top businessmen, bankers, bureaucrats, and politicians considered loyal to the government were arrested on corruption and bribery charges. The Gülenist cadres in the law enforcement units were seen as responsible for this operation. Consequently, since December 2013, the government has engaged in an effort to purge Gülenist cadres from the police, judiciary, and bureaucracy. It is also closing down its businesses and schools (see the chapter by Dreher, this volume). The Gülen movement is one group disillusioned with the AKP in power.

In the post-2013 period, the AKP was not only dealing with the crack in the power bloc but also faced increasing antagonism on the part of different groups in the society. As it became more openly authoritarian and socially conservative after every electoral victory, this produced a radicalized secularist constituency, whose disappointment with the failure of the mainstream opposition drove them toward militant street activism in 2013 (Yörük and Yüksel 2014, 109). The policies of the AKP led to a considerable decline in freedom, civil liberties, and political rights. This decline is a consequence of the lack of an independent judiciary, of censorship and the lack of academic freedom. It is documented that thousands of individuals are kept in pretrial detention in campaigns that many believe to be politically motivated (Freedom House 2001, 2013 cited in Gürcan and Peker 2014, 81–82). The AKP's increasing authoritarianism and conservatism, coupled with its increasingly hawkish position on the Kurdish problem, played an important role in antagonizing left-liberal intellectuals who had attributed a pro-democratic stance to the AKP against the Kemalist establishment in the early 2000s.

Another group that became increasingly disillusioned with the AKP rule was that of women who were disturbed by the government's Islamic conservative practices and discourses and who were at the forefront of the Gezi protests (Saraçoğlu and Demirkol 2015, 317). The AKP government tightened the law on abortion even though abortion was legalized in Turkey since the 1980s. It drafted legislation to limit women's rights. It started informing pregnant women's families about their condition. Since 2002, honor killings of women increased fourteenfold alongside the killings of transgendered people. Violence against women also increased dramatically (T24 2013).

The AKP's popularity largely rests on its keeping the economy running smoothly. Yet, there is trouble on the horizon for the economy. Even though the AKP managed to achieve impressive economic growth, Turkish economy flourished on a vulnerable path in the sense that the economic growth achieved essentially relied on short-term capital inflows rather than long-term investments. In 2003, the total net capital inflow to Turkey was about ten billion dollars, while it was over fifty-five billion dollars in 2010.

Capital inflows loosened the external finance constraint of Turkey, enabling it to sustain its chronic and growing current account deficit (Bahçe and Köse 2013, 7). As a result, Turkey's debt rose alarmingly quickly, with 10-year debt hitting 10.45%, the highest since 2010 (Boyle 2014). One of the significant reasons behind this is the fact that savings rates, which were historically quite low, have followed a negative downward slope over the last decade. This ratio has been around 19% over the last decade, which is well below the average of emerging and developing markets—that is, 27.5% (Öniş and Kutlay 2013, 1415). Since savings fall short of investments, Turkey needs foreign capital to finance its current account deficit. "This overdependence on foreign capital, on the other hand, increases the vulnerability of the country, because it makes the economy increasingly sensitive to external shocks, especially at a time when serious economic recession continues to persist at the very centre of the global system" (Öniş and Kutlay 2013, 1416).

The problem is not limited to the current account deficit and overdependence on foreign capital. AKP's economic policies neither reduced unemployment nor led to an increase in real wages. On the contrary, real wages have declined significantly and the gap between rising manufacturing productivity and wage growth has widened (Yöruk and Yüksel 2014, 108). According to research conducted by the OECD, Turkey is in the category of member countries with the highest income inequality (Üstundağ 2008). An OECD report also shows that the rate of child and adult poverty increased between 2007 and 2010 in Turkey (Bahçe and Köse 2013, 7). Furthermore, Turkey is lagging far behind in the human development index, and ranks 92nd among 187 countries; it is barely in a better position than China and India and lags behind Brazil and Russia (Öniş and Kutlay 2013, 1418).

Another challenge to the AKP regime arose as a result of the failure of Turkey's foreign policy, especially in the Middle East, and the collapse of the Kurdish peace process. The AKP won its third electoral victory in 2011, winning almost 50% of the votes cast. Soon after, AKP's "zero problems" foreign policy "pivoted into a dirty war against the Assad regime, rhetorically backed by Sunni chauvinism" (Yörük and Yüksel 2014, 109). The AKP government has long provided both financial and logistical support for the Sunni extremist challengers to President Bashar al-Assad in Syria. The Al-Qaeda/Salafist movement has become the main beneficiary of Turkey's support and hospitality to the opposition groups and they often note Turkey's assistance (Gürcan and Peker 2014, 84). Many Salafists invoked the government protection they received, refusing to pay for services they got from local businesses, saying: "It is Prime Minister Erdoğan who brought us here: he would be the one to pay the bill," or backing up threats by saying: "Or else we will call Recep" (Gürcan and Peker 2014, 84).

It has been widely reported in the media that the Turkish government provided support to the Islamic State of Iraq and Levant (ISIL). Especially in ISIL's fight against the Syrian Kurds in the northern city of Kobane, Turkey was accused of letting ISIL cross the border to attack Kobane. Turkey initially resisted providing support to the Syrian Kurds in this fight. Yet, it later caved in under US pressure, and said it would allow Iraq's Kurdistan Regional Government peshmerga fighters to reinforce the town (Christie-Miller 2014). Ankara's resisting to Western pressure to allow military aid to Syrian Kurds led to growing fury among Turkey's Kurds, eventually leading to the collapse of the Kurdish peace process. Erdoğan's indifferent comments predicting that "Kobane will soon fall" culminated in the worst rioting the country has seen in more than a decade. In October 2014, at least 37 people died in the southeast Kurdish region in unrest that then sparked violent counter-protests among nationalist Turks. The AKP's position on the Kurdish problem became even more explicit following the June parliamentary elections in 2015. Following the Suruç massacre carried out by ISIL that killed 33 young activists who were on their way to bring aid to Kobane, Turkey used this incident to wage war not against ISIL but against the Kurds (Popp and Reuter 2015).

The government ended the peace process by instigating heavy military action against the Partiya Karkeren Kurdistan (PKK) (Kurdistan Workers' Party). Thus, the pro-Kurdish Halkların Demokratik Partisi (HDP) (People's Democratic Party), which received around six million votes in the recent election and gained 80 of the 550 seats in the Turkish parliament, has become the main target of the AKP on the basis of its close ties with the PKK. The collapse of the Kurdish peace process and the beginning of violence once again led to increasing protests as government ministers attended funerals of Turkish soldiers who were killed by the Kurdish rebel group PKK. "Murderer president, murderer AK Party" shouted mourners at a minister attending the funeral of a soldier killed by the PKK. Similar protests have occurred at the funerals of other soldiers as renewed fighting with the PKK escalates (Jones 2015).

As noted thus far, the challenges to the AKP's rule in Turkey are multiple: a crack in the power bloc with the rift between Erdoğan and the influential Gülen movement, Turkey's economic vulnerability, the AKP's increasing authoritarianism and conservatism that antagonized many among its secular constituency, its failed foreign policy in the Middle East, and the collapse of the Kurdish peace process.

The question is, what does this tell us about the neoliberal hegemony constituted by the AKP? Ultimately, we cannot talk about a crisis of the neoliberal hegemony that the party skillfully established in the course of a decade because the integrity of the coalition of dominant classes is still intact (Yalman 2014, 46). Even though the AKP government has experienced certain challenges to its rule after the Gezi protests, this did not lead to a significant and successful resistance to the power bloc.

CONCLUSION

This chapter aimed to explore whether the AKP government in Turkey promoted, reformed, or resisted neoliberal globalization. Two interrelated issues were also discussed: How did the party manage to stay in power for so long and what are the main challenges to its rule?

The main argument of the chapter was that the AKP has been successful in establishing the hegemony of the bourgeoisie for the first time in the history of the Turkish Republic. The real success of the AKP lies in the fact that it managed to overcome the political crisis experienced earlier by the bourgeoisie by manufacturing a unity between the dominant classes and obtaining the active or passive consent of subordinate classes. Even though the AKP implemented policies that led to more inequality and employment instability and increased pressures on organized labor, it, by and large, received the support of the working class. This chapter analyzed the strategies that the party employed in order to establish neoliberal hegemony. It was underlined that the AKP's Islamism became functional in producing the consent of the working classes. In other words, in Turkey, the AKP government promoted neoliberalism by instrumentalizing religion.

In establishing neoliberal hegemony, AKP essentially used three strategies: it emphasized developmentalism and economic grandeur, implemented populist policies, and used the symbolic/ideological/religious sphere. The AKP's emphasis on economic growth and developmentalism became tangible in the radical transformation of urban spaces and it led to the appreciation of the party's policies, even though millions of people lived in poverty. The AKP also used populist policies such as social assistance programs to expand its support base. It was observed that social assistance (in-kind assistance such as food, coal) as well as conditional cash transfers to poor families skyrocketed during the AKP period. AKP's populist policies also explain the high support coming from women, especially from poorer households.

Finally, the AKP used religion in order to establish neoliberal hegemony. It was underlined that the AKP has built a new Sunni Islam-flavored nationalist project over the last decade that envisages the society as a big family. This project hides class inequalities and other social conflicts such as the Kurdish problem and, by not denouncing the capitalist system, it is compatible with the needs of the dominant neoliberal economic vision. In the meanwhile, media censorship peaked during this period making independent journalism very difficult in an environment defined by the collusion of big business and big government. Furthermore, Sunni Islamic values were reproduced on a daily basis in Imam-Hatip schools and congregation networks.

Despite challenges discussed in the last section, it is hard to argue that a hegemonic crisis of neoliberal hegemony is unfolding in the sense that the integrity of the power bloc has been challenged, with a significant resistance coming from the working classes. The fact that the AKP government received 49.47% of the votes in the November 2015 elections despite these aforementioned challenges highlights the fact that the hegemonic power bloc is largely intact.

REFERENCES

Akça, İsmet, Ahmet Bekmen and Barış Alp Özden. eds. 2014. *Turkey Reframed: Constituting Neoliberal Hegemony.* London: Pluto Press.
Aksera, Murat and Banu Baybars-Hawks. 2012. "Media and Democracy in Turkey: Toward a Model of Neoliberal Media Autocracy." *Middle East Journal of Culture and Communication* 5: 302–21.
Alam, Anwar. 2009. "Islam and Post-Modernism: Locating the Rise of Islamism in Turkey." *Journal of Islamic Studies* 20 (3): 352–75.
Altunışık, Meliha B. and Lenore G. Martin. 2011. "Making Sense of Turkish Foreign Policy in the Middle East under AKP." *Turkish Studies* 12 (4): 569–87.
Amani, Aslan. 2013. "Media Freedom in Turkey: Just How Bad Is It?" *Open Democracy,* April 25. Accessed July 30, 2015, https://www.opendemocracy.net/aslan-amani/media-freedom-in-turkey-just-how-bad-is-it.
Bia News. 2015. "Bia-Apr-May-Jun 2015 Media Monitoring Report News and Journalists Under the "Control" of Erdoğan/AKP are at Risk, July 14, Accessed July 30, 2015, http://bianet.org/english/freedom-of-expression/166031-news-and-journalists-under-the-control-of-erdogan-akp-are-at-risk.
Bostan, Yahya. 2011. "İşte %50nin sırrı" (This is the secret of the 50%), *Sabah,* October 3.
Boyle, Catherine. 2014. "Turkey: What's going on and why you should care." *CNBC,* January 28, Accessed August 5, 2015, http://www.cnbc.com/2014/01/28/turkey-whats-going-on-and-why-you-should-care.html.
Bahçe Serdal and Ahmet Hasim Köse. 2014. "The Effects of the New Welfare System on the Inter- and Intra-Class Distribution of Income in Turkey." Paper presented at Global Labour University, Berlin.
Barr, Robert. 2003. "The Persistence of Neopopulism in Peru? From Fujimori to Toledo." *Third World Quarterly* 24 (6): 1161–78.
Bozkurt, Umut. 2013. "Neoliberalism with a Human Face: Making Sense of the Justice and Development Party's Neoliberal Populism in Turkey." *Science and Society* 77 (3): 372–96.
Buğra, Ayse and Aysen Candaş. 2011. "Change and Continuity under an Eclectic Social Security Regime: The Case of Turkey." *Middle Eastern Studies* 47 (3): 515–28.
Çakmak, Diren. 2009. "Pro-Islamic Public Education in Turkey: The Imam-Hatip Schools." *Middle Eastern Studies* 45 (5): 825–46.
Çavuşoğlu, Erbatur and Julia Strutz. 2014. "Producing Force and Consent: Urban Transformation and Corporatism in Turkey." *City* 18 (2): 134–48.

Christie-Miller, Alexander. 2014. "Kurds Accuse Turkish Government of Supporting ISIS." *Newsweek*, October 22.

Doğan, Ekber and Yasin Durak. 2014. "The Rise of the Islamic Bourgeoisie and the Socialisation of Neoliberalism: Behind the Success Story of Two Pious Cities." In *Turkey Reframed: Constituting Neoliberal Hegemony*, edited by İsmet Akça, Ahmet Bekmen, and Barış Alp Özden, 219–34. London: Pluto Press.

Durak, Yasin. 2013. *Emeğin Tevekkülü Konya'da İşçi-İşveren İlişkileri ve Dindarlık* (Workers resigning themselves to their fate; employer-employee relations in Konya and religiosity). İstanbul: İletişim Yayınevi.

Eğin, Oray. 2013. "The Silence of Surrender: Erdoğan's War on Independent Media." *World Affairs*. November/December: 47–56.

Eder, Mine. 2010. "Retreating State? Political Economy of Welfare Regime Change in Turkey." *Middle East Law and Governance* 2 (2): 152–84.

Gülalp, Haldun. 2001. "Globalization and Political Islam: The Social Bases of Turkey's Welfare Party." *International Journal of Middle East Studies* 33 (3): 443–48.

Gürcan Efe Can and Efe Peker. 2014. "Turkey's Gezi Park Demonstrations of 2013: A Marxian Analysis of the Political Moment." *Socialism and Democracy* 28 (1): 70–89.

Hürriyet Daily News. 2015. "Turkey Ranks 22nd Most Popular Spot for Foreign Direct Investors." *June 24*, Accessed August 6, 2015, http://www.hurriyetdaily-news.com/turkey-ranks-22nd-most-popular-spot-for-foreign-direct-investors-association.aspx?pageID=238&nID=84484&NewsCatID=345.

Ipsos Sosyal Araştırmalar Enstitüsü. 2014. *Cumhurbaşkanlığı Seçimi Sonrası Araştırması* (Opinion Poll after the Presidential Elections), 10 August, available at: http://www.ipsos.com.tr/downloads/pdf/IPSOS_SRI_2014Cumhurbaskanligi_Secimi_Sandik_Sonrasi_ArastirmasiVF.pdf.

Jones, Dorian. 2015. "Soldier Funeral Protests Pose Political Challenge in Turkey." *Voice of America*, August 21, Accessed September 5, 2015, http://www.voanews.com/content/soldier-funerals-pose-political-challenge-in-turkey/2926965.html.

Jones, Steve. 2006. *Antonio Gramsci*. London: Routledge.

Letsch Constanze, 2015. "Turkish Parents Complain of Push towards Religious Schools." *Guardian*, February 12, Accessed July 27, 2015, http://www.theguardian.com/world/2015/feb/12/turkish-parents-steered-religious-schools-secular-imam-hatip.

Lovering, John and Hade Türkmen. 2011. "Bulldozer Neo-Liberalism in Istanbul: The State-Led Construction of Property Markets, and the Displacement of the Urban Poor." *International Planning Studies* 16 (1): 73–96.

Moudouros, Nikos. 2014. "Rethinking Islamic Hegemony in Turkey through Gezi Park." *Journal of Balkan and Near Eastern Studies* 16 (2): 181–95.

Öniş, Ziya. 2011. "Turkish Foreign Policy: Underlying Dynamics and a Critique." *Insight Turkey* 13 (1): 47–65.

Öniş, Ziya and Kutlay Mustafa. 2013. "Rising Powers in a Changing Global Order: The Political Economy of Turkey in the Age of Brics." *Third World Quarterly* 34 (8): 1409–26.

Pamuk, Hümeyra and Jonny Hogg. 2014. "Erdoğan Dominates Turkey's Uneven Presidential Race." Reuters. http://uk.reuters.com/article/uk-turkey-presidency-campaign-idUKKBN0G409P20140804, accessed 14 December 2015.

Popp, Maximilian and Christoph Reuter. 2015. "Erdoğan's Cynical Game: Is Turkey Creeping Toward Civil War?" *Spiegel Online International*, July 3.

Poulantzas, Nicos. 1968. *Political Power and Social Classes*. London: Verso.

Rodrik, Dani. 2013. "The Wrath of Erdoğan." *Juncture* 20 (2): 129–30.

Saracoğlu, Cenk. 2011. "Islamic Conservative Nationalism's Projection of a Nation: Kurdish Policy during JDP's Rule" (in Turkish). *Praksis* 26: 31–54.

Saracoğlu, Cenk and Özhan Demirkol. 2015. "Nationalism and Foreign Policy Discourse in Turkey Under the AKP Rule." *British Journal of Middle Eastern Studies* 42 (3): 301–19.

T24. 2013. "BDP Kadın Meclisleri: Kadın cinayetleri AKP döneminde yüzde 1400 arttı" (BDP Women Parliaments: Women Murders increased 1400% during the AKP period), July 26.

Today's Zaman. 2015. "Erdoğan Says He is Proud to be a 'Black Turk.'" June 24.

Toprak, Binnaz. 2005. "Islam and Democracy in Turkey." *Turkish Studies* 6 (2): 167–86.

Tremblay, Pınar. 2014. "How Erdoğan Won the Women's Vote." *Al Monitor*, August 19.

Tuğal, Cihan. 2007. "NATO's Islamists." *New Left Review* 44 (March–April): 5–34.

Üstundağ, Erhan. 2008. "Türkiye Gelir Eşitsizliğinde OECD Şampiyonlarından" [Turkey is Amongst the OECD Member Countries with the Most Unjust Income Distribution], Bianet, 22 October.

Weyland, Kurt. 1996. "Neopopulism and Neoliberalism in Latin America: Unexpected Affinities." *Studies in Comparative International Development* 31 (3): 3–31.

Yalman, Galip. 2014. "AKP Döneminde Söylem ve Siyaset: Neyin Krizi?" (Discourse and Politics During the AKP Era: The Crisis of What?) *İktidarın Şiddeti AKP'li Yıllar, Neoliberalizm ve İslamcı Politikalar*, 23–46, edited by Simten Coşar and Gamze Yücesan. Özdemir İstanbul: Metis Kitap.

Yıldırım, Deniz. 2009. "JDP and Neoliberal Populism" (in Turkish). In *The JDP book: The Balance Sheet of a Transformation*, edited by İlhan Uzgel and Bülent Duru. Ankara: Phoenix Yayınevi.

Yörük, Erdem and Murat Yüksel. 2014. "Class and Politics in Turkey's Gezi Protests." *New Left Review* 89, September–October: 103–23.

Chapter 10

Preaching Development

Shi'i Piety and Neoliberalism in Beirut

Fouad Gehad Marei[1]

In a popular rally in 1974, Imam Musa As-Sadr, considered the founding father of Shi'i political activism in modern Lebanon, proclaimed that the Shi'a are "matawila no more! We are rejectionists! Avengers! Revolutionaries against injustice!" (quoted in Traboulsi 2007, 197).[2] As-Sadr's words of defiance indicate the uncompromising nature and revolutionary commitments of Shi'i political activism.[3] In a state of perpetual protest and resistance, Shi'i activism in Lebanon exemplifies what Dabashi (2011, 297) calls "the combative contestations between Shi'ism and US-led globalized politics of intervention, occupation and hegemony."

Shi'i activism gains particular significance in Lebanon because of the country's febrile political context. Since its inception, Lebanon has been governed by a political system based on confessional consociationalism and an unrelenting commitment to state minimalism and freewheeling capitalism. Cultivated among the downtrodden, Shi'i political activism professed unequivocal enmity to the country's politico-economic system. By the mid-1980s, Hezbollah emerged as the single most important actor articulating a strategic project aimed at consolidating the political and economic gains of Lebanon's Shi'a. Committed to armed resistance against Israel and self-identifying with the "Axis of Defiance," Hezbollah is often reduced to its anti-Westernism. This leads commentators to mistakenly identify everything associated with the party as in opposition to "the West" and its politico-economic models. A closer look at contemporary articulations of Shi'i activism in Lebanon, however, reveals its transformation from a religiopolitical movement inspired by the radical left to its contemporary neoliberal turn.

In this chapter, I contest the dichotomous understanding of religious activism as either promoting or resisting neoliberal globalization. Instead, I rescale the inquiry into local articulations of neoliberalism and expose spaces of compatibility between religiopolitical activism in resistance to the Western order and neoliberalism. In pursuit of this, I examine contemporary expressions of Shi'i activism highlighting the discursive combination of religion and piety with an economic rationale premised on individual responsibility, volunteerism, and self-help. In so doing, I problematize the totalizing understanding of Hezbollah and the Islamic milieu questioning whether Shi'i political activism constitutes an alternative to the neoliberalism championed by the West and international financial organizations. While acknowledging its professed commitment to a religiously motivated project of perpetual resistance to US-led globalization, I undertake a nuanced reading of Hezbollah's urban revitalization project in Beirut's southern suburbs (Dahiya). In this chapter, I examine the institutional setup of the reconstruction process and its accompanying discourses. As such, I highlight areas of compatibility between the logics of the Resistance project and precepts of neoliberal globalization. I argue that Islamist (and other) actors with a professed enmity toward the United States are neither principally opposed to nor passive subjects of US-led neoliberal globalization. Instead, I demonstrate that they are actively involved in (re)creating and recasting neoliberalism into their own political projects. Anchored in unique cultural referents and technologies of governance, Hezbollah's Resistance project exemplifies a variegated neoliberalism that is homegrown, counterhegemonic, and alternative to mainstream configurations of neoliberalism; yet it does not radically depart from the logics of the Western neoliberal ideology.

DISSECTING NEOLIBERALISM

Neoliberalism has become a major preoccupation for scholars and students of politics. Proponents of the neoliberal ideology propose a teleological understanding, positing it as a universal, coherent, and monolithic project. Accordingly, neoliberal reforms are seen to operate in accordance with a set of immutable laws while empirical evidence suggesting failure or deviation is attributed to local actors' ulterior motives and lack of integrity.

Critical scholars, however, question the problematic indistinction between abstract and actual representations of neoliberalism and call for rescaled empirical inquiries into actually existing neoliberalisms (Brenner and Theodor 2002). Inquiries following this broad mandate problematize the ideology's totalizing metanarratives and question (1) the political and institutional contexts within which the neoliberal transformation occurs, (2) the agency of the actors implicated, and (3) the variations and hybrid articulations of actually existing neoliberalisms (Larner 2000; Peck and Tickel 2002; Heydemann 2004).

This chapter argues that neoliberalism is not a seamless process orchestrated by global powers and international institutions, and imposed from above or from outside. It shares Atia's (2012) concern about producing a new false dichotomy positing "alternatives within neoliberalism" against "alternatives to neoliberalism" (i.e. resisting it). To restrict analysis to this binary opposition concedes forms of interaction and contestation based on appropriating, reworking, and recasting neoliberalism into variegated, even conflicting, political projects (Castree 2006; Leitner, Peck and Sheppard 2007). Before examining the interactions and spaces of compatibility between Hezbollah's Resistance project and neoliberalism, it will be necessary to locate Shi'i political activism in relation to the political history of Lebanon's Shi'a and, more broadly, to the Lebanese quagmire.

LEBANON, THE SHI'A AND HEZBOLLAH: CONTEXTUALIZING THE INQUIRY

Annexed to Lebanon in the 1920s, Shi'i populations of South Lebanon and the Bekaa Valley were unfavorably incorporated in Beirut's Eurocentric political economy. This peripherality was consolidated by a postcolonial political system that restricted Shi'i political representation to the feudal elite. Shi'i migration to Beirut accelerated, exacerbated by economic inopportunity and war in the ancestral homelands. Lacking the necessary social and cultural capital to contend for dwindling economic opportunities, the Shi'a constituted the bulk of the subaltern masses inhabiting Beirut's sprawling poverty belts.

While the first waves of Shi'i migration to Beirut produced a generation of Shi'i petty moneymakers, the second generation made an acute leap into the middle class because of education and the accumulation of wealth through emigration. The oil boom of the 1970s accelerated this as repatriated wealth underpinned a Shi'i parvenu bourgeoisie (Shanahan 2005). Between migrants the war displaced and the parvenu bourgeoisie, the amorphous Shi'i community proved to be fertile ground for mobilization against the politico-economic system; so much so that Shi'i and Shyu'i (communist) became synonymous in Lebanese political jargon in the 1970s (Norton 1987).

PREACHERS, COMMUNITY LEADERS, AND SHI'I POLITICAL ACTIVISM

Progressives were not alone in articulating opposition and championing the cause of the downtrodden Shi'a. Solidarity networks forged to address the needs of Beirut's Shi'i newcomers turned into hotbeds for dissent, and the community centers—the ḥusayniyya—developed into a communitarian public sphere. Together, they integrated Shi'i newcomers into the city's social fabric and helped forge ties between Shi'i entrepreneurs and middlemen-turned-patrons.

Crucially, the ḥusayniyya introduced Shi'i preachers (sheikh/s) as community leaders voicing the grievances of the community. Hailing from petty moneymaking migrant households, sheikhs benefited from subsidized education in the seminaries of Iraq and Iran. Upon their return to Lebanon, employment in Ja'afari (Shi'i) courts allowed them to emerge as important actors articulating Shi'i grievances and mobilizing the community. Consequently, Shi'i political activism acquired a religious intonation and a clerical leadership. The emergence of dissident sheikhs coincided with militant and revolutionary fervor in Shi'i seminaries in the mid-twentieth century. As transnational Shi'i revisionism gained momentum in the 1970s, Moussa As-Sadr emerged as the foremost Shi'i revolutionary in Lebanon. As-Sadr embarked not only on mobilizing the Shi'a but also on redefining the functions of the clergy. Inspired by revisionist reinterpretations of Shi'i ontology, As-Sadr viewed the sheikh as the imam (leader) of his community whose role was not only to disseminate religious scholarship but also to serve the community, protect its interests, and undergo martyrdom on its behalf. The imam was to represent the Shi'a in the public sphere and the political arena.[4]

As imam of Lebanon's Shi'a, As-Sadr established the Movement of the Dispossessed (ḥarakat al-maḥrūmīn) in 1974, laying the foundations of a discourse that stressed a Shi'i cultural citizenship (Shaery-Eisenlohr 2008). With the outbreak of the Civil War in 1975, the movement acquired its military wing. Together, they formed the Lebanese Resistance Regiments whose name, when abbreviated, spells out the acronym Amal, or hope. Appealing to an amorphous Shi'i constituency, Amal promised to *"start a new chapter in Lebanese history"* promising to *"pursue the rights of the dispossessed."*[5] Combining religious and Marxist rhetoric, Amal's charter declares the Lebanese political system, the Yazid-made-incarnate, responsible for "injustice and exploitation."[6]

A misconception, however, is that Amal voiced the concerns of a Shi'i lumpenproletariat in Lebanon's geographic and socioeconomic peripheries. In reality, the movement was an urban phenomenon much as dispossession was a product of urban poverty. As-Sadr's message appealed more to Shi'is unable to convert newly acquired wealth and education into social status than to radical revolutionaries. By the late 1960s, Amal had become the party of choice for wealthy Shi'i émigrés investing in agro-industries and the booming real estate market (Norton 1987; Picard 1993, 2000).

Nonetheless, rooted in a struggle against dispossession, Shi'i political mobilization in the 1970s continued to invoke Marxist and religious fervor.

Revisionist readings of Shi'ism were recast into a political ideology preaching revolution against injustice. Drawing on cultural referents rooted in Shi'i political history and ontology, As-Sadr proclaimed:

> Today, we shout out loud the wrong against us, that a cloud of injustice has followed us since the dawn of history. Starting from today, we will no longer lament or cry! They called us al-rāfiḍūn.[7] We are men of vengeance who refuse tyranny and revolt against it. (Quoted in Picard [1993, 13])

With the mysterious "disappearance" of its leader in 1978 and the defeat of the radical left in the war, Amal parted with its founder's oracle. As-Sadr's intertwining of religious revisionism and political activism, however, would continue to define the path of Shi'i politics to date.

HEZBOLLAH AND SHI'I POLITICAL ACTIVISM

By the mid-1980s, a coterie of junior sheikhs inspired by As-Sadr as well as the triumph of the Islamic Revolution in Iran embarked on articulating a holistic political project in Lebanon. The project would further interweave Shi'i religiosity and notions of resistance into the community's political life. According to its symbolic founding father, the Islamic Resistance is not just an armed struggle against Israel. Inspired by Khomeini, Sheikh Ragheb Harb (d. 1984) envisaged al-muqāwama (Resistance) as shaping the worldview of its people, dubbed mujtama'al-muqāwama (the Resistance Society). In pursuit of this, Harb invoked "the community" as a sector, appealed to the charity of wealthy Shi'is, and mobilized the youth in volunteer-based self-help initiatives. In response to Israel's invasion in 1978, he and his colleagues initiated community-based schools, hospitals, and orphanages to cater to fighters, their families, and the Shi'a at large. Within a short span of time, the militant sheikhs were convinced that development is as much an arena for resistance as the battlefield is. Drawing on Islamic principles of takāful ijtimā'i (social solidarity) and ta'āḍud (collaboration), they initiated faith-based organizations including microcredit facilities funded through donations from the religious seminaries and wealthy expatriates (Qassem 2002). In punishment for his role as imam of the Resistance, Harb was assassinated by Israeli forces in 1984. His martyrdom inspired his colleagues to issue an Open Letter to the Oppressed in Lebanon and the World. The letter is considered the founding manifesto of the Islamic Resistance in Lebanon: Hezbollah. Committed to resisting the United States and Israel, the party inherited a network of community- and faith-based welfare organizations.[8]

Competing over the allegiance of the Shi'a, Amal and Hezbollah engaged in violent confrontations in 1988–1989 resulting in a geographic and socio-economic subdivision of power. The postwar political order instated under Syrian tutelage in 1991 allowed the two factions to replace this enmity with a precarious rivalry. The rapprochement between Amal and Hezbollah was consolidated with the formation of a strategic alliance between Syria and Iran. According to this formula, Amal became embedded in state and public sector institutions channeling resources to its constituency through clientelistic arrangements. Hezbollah, by contrast, consolidated the model of Shi'i political activism based on faith-community-based organizations. These organizations serve two functions. First, they mobilize resources toward the provision of social services, reconstruction, and economic development. Second, they provide avenues for the promulgation of the religiously informed worldview of the Islamic Resistance (Harb 2008; Mervin 2008; Le Thomas 2010). It must be noted that Hezbollah is far from uncontested in shaping the Islamic milieu in Lebanon. Interrogating the relationship between the party and Shi'i sheikhs reveals that while Hezbollah coalesced influential neighborhood sheikhs, many remained autonomous. The former are exemplified by the likes of Sheikh Ali Daamouche in Zokak El-Blat as well as a plethora of sheikhs in Dahiya. Lebanon's top Shi'i authority, Ayatollah Muhammad Hussayn Fadlallah (d. 2011), on the other hand, represented a parallel path. While he influenced Hezbollah's worldview, Fadlallah's independence was revealed in the realms of politics and society (Browers 2012; Saouli 2014). In addition to defining the cognitive territory of the Islamic milieu, he oversaw the largest network of faith-community-based organizations operating in parallel to (or in complementarity with) Hezbollah-run organizations.

FRAMING SHI'I POLITICAL ACTIVISM

In post–civil war Lebanon, Hezbollah-led Shi'i political activism was perceived to be the pawn of a Syrian-Iranian geopolitical project opposed to pro-US, Saudi-brokered regional agendas. Sectarian and geopolitical polarization quickly developed their Lebanese incarnations as the rift between the "Axis of Defiance" and the "Axis of Moderation" deepened. This was exacerbated by the political crisis set into motion by the assassination of former prime minister and symbol of postwar reconstruction, Rafic Hariri, in 2005.

Spearheading the two axes were the Future Movement and Hezbollah. The two rivals were, strategically, constructed as binary opposites: Sunni versus Shi'i; "secular" versus Islamist; pro-US versus anti-US. Their economic visions were also constructed according to this binary logic. Rafic Hariri was celebrated for a postwar reconstruction process committed to the logics of the global neoliberal shift and the structural adjustments prescribed by Western donor states and international financial institutions. In contrast, Hezbollah's opposition to urban development projects in Dahiya was seen as defiance toward US-led globalization. In juxtaposition to Hariri's bias toward global corporate interests, Hezbollah mobilized community- and faith-based organizations, furthering the view that it constituted an alternative to neoliberal globalization. However, nuanced inquiries into Hezbollah's involvement in welfare provision, urban governance, and faith-based development problematize this totalizing and reductionist narrative (see Harb 2000, 2008).

HEZBOLLAH AND POST-2006 RECONSTRUCTION

On July 12, 2006, Hezbollah carried out a cross-border operation, killing eight Israeli soldiers and kidnapping two. Dubbed Truthful Promise, the operation aimed to secure the release of Lebanese and Arab detainees by way of a prisoner exchange. The operation unleashed a wrathful Israeli response that ended only after thirty-three days of aerial bombardment. The war revealed what Israeli generals refer to as the Dahiya Doctrine, a military strategy pertaining to asymmetric warfare in urban settings. According to the strategy, disproportionate force is employed against civilians to punish them for supporting Hezbollah (Byman 2013). Hezbollah's stronghold, Haret Hreik in Dahiya, bore the brunt of Israel's bombardment. For the Lebanese, too, Dahiya is Hezbollah turf. Literally "the suburb," Dahiya is constructed in the official discourse as Beirut's periphery, invoking imaginaries of a Shi'i ghetto notorious for building and zoning violations and home to a population brainwashed by Hezbollah. This normative and reductionist representation acquired a spatial dimension because of the lopsided logics of post–civil war reconstruction reinforcing spatial segregation (Harb 2003, 2007; Deeb 2006).

On the first day of the ceasefire, Nasrallah's televised victory speech was broadcast over the wreckage that had become of Haret Hreik, the heart of Dahiya. Not unaware of the magnitude of the carnage, Hezbollah Secretary-General Sayyid Hassan Nasrallah pledged to rebuild Dahiya "more beautiful than it was." In pursuit of that, Hezbollah instituted an agency charged with overseeing the reconstruction. Dubbed Wa'ad (the promise), the agency provided a space within which a reorganized Dahiya was imagined, planned, and operationalized with the help of Lebanese and foreign architects and urban planners commissioned to implement and realize the project (Al-Harithy 2010; Fawaz 2014).

WA'AD: AN ALTERNATIVE MODEL OF RECONSTRUCTION?

In line with a general tendency to read religious (especially Islamic) activism as an alternative to neoliberalism, Hezbollah is considered "the most influential urban actor in Beirut's politics of inclusion" and its interventions a form of radical planning (Roy 2009). In juxtaposition to post–civil war reconstruction, however, Wa'ad did not adopt a tabula rasa approach. This stands in contrast to the general postwar reconstruction of the Beirut Central District, which demonstrated little regard for the social fabric of the city and resulted in the displacement of large populations from the city center and its immediate environs.

Hezbollah's reconstruction effort, by contrast, professed its commitment to on-site resettlement of those displaced by war. In conversations and interviews I conducted, officials from Hezbollah and Wa'ad insisted that the reconstruction of Dahiya is not a market-driven endeavor, but a political one: "The Resistance cannot be considered victorious in its war with Israel unless residents of war-affected neighborhoods regain their lives and the social fabric in Dahiya is restored." According to Wa'ad managers, the institutional setup and modalities of engaging local communities ("beneficiaries") in planning and executing the reconstruction project demonstrate the party's concern for social and urban development (interview with Hassan Jeshi, managing director of Wa'ad, 03.03.2010). In the following sections, the chapter critically examines the institutional setup and modalities governing the engagement of neighborhood dwellers in planning and implementing the project. It questions the extent to which the project may be considered a critical and radical departure from the neoliberal model of urban planning.

Institutional Setup and the New Urban Coalition

The reconstruction project was born in a highly polarized political environment. The July War failed to bring the Lebanese belligerents closer. Instead, the country entered a phase of political uncertainty with Hezbollah boycotting the government. Breaking the consociational tradition, this set into motion a protracted political stalemate, paralyzed the country, called into question the constitutionality of the government, and fueled a series of violent street fights.

Amidst this tumultuous political environment, Wa'ad was officially launched in a conference held in the Haret Hreik Municipality in May 2007. According to its master plan, the project would operate outside national state institutions and with limited involvement of local authorities (Harb and Fawaz 2010). The decision to exclude state institutions reflected Hezbollah's distrust of the central government as well as a public opinion unfavorable to government-led urban interventions. The government, committed to its neoliberal tradition, envisaged its role as limited to relief and the facilitation of a privatized reconstruction process (Hamieh and MacGinty 2011). Post-2006 reconstruction was conceived as independent of the labyrinthine state bureaucracy and, it was hoped, immune to its clientelistic mechanisms.

Wa'ad was initiated as a consortium bringing together the party's reconstruction arm, Jihad al-Bina', party-affiliated associations, subcontractors, and professionals in urban planning and architecture. To plan and execute the reconstruction process, the project set up two administrative arms. The first brought together architects, investors, and real estate developers with representatives of Hezbollah and the local authorities. The second consisted of a liaison office charged with arranging temporary resettlement and managing residents' participation in project planning. This participation, Wa'ad's managing CEO noted, "is based on a community meeting convened in Hezbollah's assembly hall" in November 2006. In it, the agency offered residents the option to either wait for state compensation and undertake reconstruction independently or sign off compensation rights to Wa'ad. The latter granted the agency authority to pool together compensation payments earmarked by the Lebanese government and donor states from donations mobilized by Hezbollah to finance a comprehensive redevelopment of Dahiya (interview with Jeshi, 03.03.2010).

This modality of "engaging" residents must be differentiated from "participation in project planning" as conceptualized by urban scholars. The latter involves collective decision making based on discussions reflecting the needs and concerns of neighborhood dwellers (Arnstein 1969; Rahnema 1993). This, Harb and Fawaz (2010) argue, was not the case in post-2006 reconstruction where residents were informed of their options. Effectively, residents' engagement was reduced to narrow choices about building finishes. For managers of Wa'ad, however, the liaison office offered an avenue to communicate dwellers' concerns to real estate developers and the latters' technical and economic concerns to dwellers (interview with Jeshi, 30.09.2014). Throughout the reconstruction process, residents were instructed to communicate with subcontractors and real estate developers only through Wa'ad's Liaison Office for Residents' Affairs. The agency, its managers explained, committed itself to negotiating on behalf of residents in disputes with government agencies and authorities, acting as a go-between (interview with Mounir Makki, director of the Wa'ad Liaison Office for Residents' Affairs, 30.09.2014). Effectively, this rendered the agency an arena where conflicts between social and economic policy would be mitigated.

Whether Wa'ad demonstrated a stronger bias toward the cost-benefit calculations of its subcontractors or the sociopolitical agenda driving the reconstruction process is hard to assess. Suffice to say that the institutional setup

of Hezbollah's reconstruction agency resembles urban revitalization strategies widely recognized in association with neoliberal urban policy. These
strategies entail governing large-scale urban development projects through
quasi-private and highly autonomous agencies empowered by a significant
redistribution of policy-making powers, competencies, and responsibilities.
This results in autocratic forms of governance whereby decisions are crafted
outside the scope of democratic institutions. Neoliberal modalities of city
making involve forging new urban coalitions based on institutional fragmentation. This governance is achieved by subordinating state institutions to
quasi-private agencies (Swyngedouw et al. 2002).

Interactions between Wa'ad and local state institutions in Dahiya demonstrate similar patterns. As the project neared completion, the question of
public infrastructure and communal spaces cast a shadow over residents'
ability to return to the intervention site. While the agency initially envisaged
a limited role for the municipalities concerned, this had to change in order to
circumvent Wa'ad's limited mandate restricted to privately owned property
whose claimants signed off authority to the consortium. This jurisdiction
does not allow Wa'ad to implement changes at the urban level. Therefore,
the agency engaged local authorities in quasigovernmental institutional
frameworks reinforcing their role as proactive enablers, partners, and clients.
Essentially, this resulted in the emergence of a new urban coalition replacing longstanding structures of negotiating urban policy (Al-Hamarneh 2013).
In Dahiya, this coalition is based on synergies between Hezbollah-dominated
municipalities, a small circle of decision makers, and elite fractions of civil
society.

Moreover, while classical understandings of neoliberalism suggest minimal state involvement, empirical evidence suggests the contrary. The synergy
between Wa'ad and municipal authorities demonstrates the involvement of
more state in realizing the reconstruction. Indeed, Dahiya municipalities and
the Union of Municipalities of Beirut Suburb allowed the agency to overcome
bureaucratic and political hurdles, expand the redevelopment plan beyond its
mandate, and channel state funds and contributions by international donor
states/organizations toward infrastructure projects.

According to Haret Hreik's deputy mayor, this politico-institutional setup
allowed Wa'ad to implement changes to public urban spaces, influence
re-regulation and zoning policies, and guide public investments in urban
infrastructure. Ahmad Hatoun, who also oversees the Association for Local
Economic Development Agency in Beirut Southern Suburb, added that "this
allowed for the involvement of international organizations [such] as the
Kuwait Fund [for Arab Economic Development], the European Union and
the United Nations" (interview with Ahmad Hatoun, deputy mayor of Haret
Hreik, 30.09.2014).

Disciplining Dahiya

Neoliberal urban policy is seen as dominated by capitalistic interests and criticized for its democratic deficit. That is to say, production and consumption patterns and economic interests are the driving factors guiding urban development rather than sociopolitical concerns (Jacobs 1961, 1969; Castells 1977; Harvey 1993). The institutional setup of Wa'ad's urban intervention may, indeed, resemble that of neoliberal urban policy globally. However, we must not overlook the fact that reconstruction and revitalization in Dahiya are also driven by a sociopolitical agenda embedded in Shi'i political activism and the Resistance project.

Dominated by Hezbollah, the reconstruction project served to reinforce the party's image as sole protagonist in Dahiya and emphasize its exceptional character as the "capital of the Resistance." Conceived as more than just a promise to restore the built environment, Hezbollah's urban intervention was designed as an effort to modernize, reorder, and reorganize Dahiya. The politico-institutional framework within which this takes place involves a complex nexus of entities and actors operating, intersecting, and diverging across different scales and categorical imperatives—a space within which a reorganized Dahiya is imagined and realized. This new Dahiya would reflect the perceived (and aspired) progress, embourgeoisement, and empowerment of the Shi'a.

In other words, post-2006 reconstruction provided an opportunity to address some of the issues that plagued Dahiya and project Hezbollah's political project on the urban environment. In conversations I conducted with Wa'ad planners and architects, they cited the agency's interventions in designing architectural models and dictating exterior décor as evidence of the conscious effort to "beautify Dahiya." In addition to aesthetic projections of Hezbollah's political project, scholarly accounts also draw attention to structural and legal-institutional means through which the party exercises sovereignty over Dahiya and its residents (Fawaz 2014). Other accounts describe projections of Shi'i political activism through the public practice and display of a particular middle-class urban piety (Deeb 2006; Harb and Deeb 2013). Together, these accounts paint an image of the complex triangulation of pastoral, disciplinary, and biopolitical projections of the Shi'i Islamic milieu in Lebanon.

However, it is my contention here that the Hezbollah-led socio-urban transformation could not be implemented through physical projections and structural coercion alone, but through the diffusion of "hegemonic ideas," to rephrase Dobbin, Simmons, and Garrett (2007, 454). The reconstruction effort required the formation and stewardship of rules regulating the public realm; rules that are "totalizing" and "individualizing," at the same time—to invoke Foucault's (1991) notion of "governmentality."[9] To grasp how the process of urban revitalization in post-2006 Dahiya rendered space a political matter to be "organized" and society material to be "disciplined," the following section examines the discursive combination of piety and notions of public order as exemplified by the Civil Campaign for the Promotion of Public Order. This combination is an articulation of a pious-neoliberal discourse designed to regulate the micropolitics of everyday life and achieve the large-scale management of people and spaces.

AL-NIZAM MIN AL-IMAN (ORDER IS OF THE FAITH)

Better known by its religiously informed slogan, Al-Nizam min Al-Iman (Order is of the Faith), the campaign was launched by civil associations affiliated with Hezbollah in November 2009. Patronized by Hezbollah MP Mohammed Raad, it is described as a "national endeavor to bring public order to Dahiya and promote a culture of law amongst its residents," as he declared in the inaugural speech in Dahiya (19.11.2009).

The campaign addresses an audience beyond Hezbollah's reconstruction area in Haret Hreik, appealing to residents of Dahiya in its broadest sense and Shi'i-majority regions countrywide. According to its general coordinator, the campaign capitalized on postwar reconstruction to address issues that plague Dahiya's congested residential, commercial, and symbolic heart. In his view, "the reconstruction process meant new building designs and a new urban plan . . . which must eliminate the chaos that prevailed" (interview with Hussein Fadlallah, Campaign Coordinator, 15.04.2010). Serious violations of shared and public properties, and building and zoning regulations in Dahiya had occurred between 1983 and 1994 in the context of the civil war (Fawaz 2014).

Inspired by the scale of the reconstruction effort, Jam'iyat Qiyam, an association for religiocultural studies, initiated a public awareness campaign, which operates under the patronage of Sayyid Hashim Safieddine, Nasrallah's cousin, heir-apparent and chairman of Hezbollah's Executive Council. The campaign, Al-Nizam min Al-Iman, promised to raise awareness and promote the value of order. In pursuit of this, it mobilized a complex nexus of entities and actors operating and intersecting under Hezbollah's broad umbrella. Exploiting the web of connections constituting Shi'i political activism in Lebanon (and beyond), the campaign mobilized Hezbollah-affiliated media, educational institutions, religiocultural associations, and sheikhs.

Responsible for the production of textbooks for Hezbollah-run educational institutions, the Cultural Islamic Al-Maaref Association published in 2010 a textbook of sixty-two pages called An Overview of Public Order. It was made compulsory in primary schools operated by the Islamic Religious Education

Association. Simultaneously, the Hezbollah-affiliated Lebanese Arts Association, Risālāt (messages) produced audiovisual material for the campaign. By early 2010, the messages and slogans appeared on billboards promoting public order as inalienable from "piety" and the "Resistance." Billboards were strategically distributed on major urban arteries in Dahiya including the (Old) Airport Road and Sayyid Hadi Nasrallah Avenue and on intercity highways in South Lebanon and the Bekaa. Together, faith-based organizations and radio and television stations associated with Shi'i political activism weaved and promulgated a message: "order is of the faith." The campaign collaborated with Hezbollah-run municipalities, Union of Municipalities of Beirut Southern Suburb, the Islamic Health Association, and civil defense forces.

Piety and Neoliberal City Making

In its articulation, the campaign constructs normative understandings of public order. Its inaugural propaganda video features Hezbollah deputy secretary-general, Sheikh Naim Qassem, explaining that "the universe demonstrates the necessity of some order . . . without which no flora nor fauna could exist." Against the backdrop of sensational music, and images of wildlife and natural scenery, Qassem's message bestows an epistemological normativity to the message that "order is of the faith." Quoting sayings attributed to Prophet Muhammad and his cousin Ali, the revered imam of Shi'i Islam, the campaign video on Al-Nizam min Al-Iman further underlines that "order" and "discipline" are not only "natural," but also divinely ordained. As quoted in the video, in his final speech, Ali instructed his followers "to submit to God and keep [their] affairs in order." This, the video concludes, proves that "order" and taqwa (submission or piety) are inseparable. The campaign's coordinators insisted that Dahiya is not exceptional: "Like other societies, its residents are naturally dispositioned toward order." The focus on Dahiya, they explained, reflected a desire to bring about order complementing the ambitious reconstruction effort.

Testifying to the synergy between reconstruction, the campaign, and Hezbollah's sociopolitical project, the party's secretary-general dedicated his bi-nightly Muharram speech on December 23, 2009, to the question of public order. The speech was delivered as part of the rituals associated with Shi'is' commemoration of Imam Hussain's martyrdom in the epic Battle of Karbala in 680 AD. In his speech, Nasrallah enumerated the salient problems and social ills that plague Lebanon. The list covered everything from traffic and illegal use of sidewalks to sanitation, building violations, drug use, and the theft of state electricity. Addressing these concerns, Nasrallah reiterated an Islamic orthodoxy: "Between chaos and order, the faithful must choose order." He went on listing religious opinions (fatwa) of contemporary Shi'i jurisprudential authorities where he particularly emphasized the opinions of Sayyid Ali Khamenei, Supreme Leader of the Islamic Republic in Iran, and the spiritual and political leader to whose authority Hezbollah subscribes.

For Khamenei, the faithful are "religiously obligated" to behave in accordance with the law. Failure to do so, the campaign propaganda video on Al-Nizam min Al-Iman warns, undermines violators' credentials as pious Muslims. One fatwa the campaign propaganda material refers to, considers "ablution and prayers performed using water, electricity or land unjustly and illegally usurped null and invalid in the eyes of God." Reiterating this view, Qassem warns in the campaign video: "Beware! If the state cannot hold you accountable for transgressions against public order, God Almighty will! Because order is of the faith." In promoting this religiously sanctioned order, Al-Nizam min Al-Iman links volunteerism with resistance and, thus, with reward in the hereafter. For example, the campaign coordinates with Hezbollah-affiliated Al-Mahdi Scouts and faith-based schools to mobilize Shi'i adolescents for on-the-ground campaigns to beautify Dahiya, advocate "civilized behavior," and engage in activities of a civil and urban nature.

FISSURES AND RUPTURES IN THE PIOUS NEOLIBERAL LOGIC

In short, while post-2006 reconstruction transformed space into a political matter to be organized, the campaign for public order—Al-Nizam min Al-Iman—addressed society as material to be "disciplined." Its message constructs a pious-neoliberal subject expected to act in line with understandings of "order" and "development" anchored in neoliberal developmentism and yet wedded to religiosity. Despite its ability to mobilize a complex nexus of entities/actors constituting Shi'i religious activism in Lebanon, the campaign reveals several disarticulations and fissures in its logics.

Responsibilization of the Individual and Society

Al-Nizam min Al-Iman demonstrates an understanding of problems salient in Dahiya as primarily a repercussion of individual (mis)behavior. The problem of "chaos" and the responsibility to achieve "order," thus, are contingent on the individual and the community rather than on structural factors. Charged with promoting the campaign's message beyond the audience of mosque-goers, Sheikh Najib Saleh articulates this viewpoint:

> While the state must enact and enforce laws, responsibility for public order is individual. . . . A pious individual must respect and abide by the law in

accordance with the teachings of Islam and the infallible imams. Then, comes the collective duty of the community to uphold public order. (Informal conversation, Haret Hreik/Dahiya, 28.09.2014)

When confronted with the popular opinion that state negligence toward Dahiya and the Shi'a lies at the heart of the problem—an opinion central to Shi'i religiopolitical activism since the mid-twentieth century—he appropriates the rhetoric of his ancestors as done on Assirat TV on September 9, 2014:

Indeed, state negligence is the prime cause for the social ills we see in Lebanon. Dispossession, deprivation and social injustice are the core of the problem. But there is no Islamic justification for violating the law . . . Nowadays, people use state negligence as an excuse for their trespasses. A pious Muslim is accountable before God and . . . state negligence does not make theft any less a sin in the eyes of God Almighty.

Essentially, Saleh's discourse exemplifies a shifting of responsibility from the state to the individual—a tendency widely recognized in association with neoliberal ideology. This deresponsibilization of the state is in line with the neoliberal global agenda in that it depoliticizes the problem, isolates it from the broader context, and conceives solutions from an individual or communal entrepreneurial perspective.

This responsibilization of society "goes hand in hand with . . . invocations of 'the community' as a sector" (Hart 2004, 92). While such invocations are not new to Lebanon's confessional political culture, Al-Nizam min Al-Iman bestows upon it neoliberal intonations wedded to a particular middle-class religiosity. The message is not anchored in the secular-democratic route to neoliberal development, but in a religious narrative.

Incoherencies and Disarticulations

Certainly, Al-Nizam min Al-Iman's message is not without its antagonists, especially among Lebanon's Shi'i community, which—to use Dabashi's words—embodies "the layered polyfocality of many worlds that have come its way" (2011, 318). For Lebanon's Shi'is, the historical struggle against dispossession and the influence of transnational revisionism are all but ancient history. This is evident in the way the campaign's message was received by local communities in Dahiya and peripheral regions of South Lebanon.

Under the patronage of Sheikh Najib Saleh, Al-Nizam min Al-Iman organized a series of televised public meetings in villages in South Lebanon intended to promote public order in the historic homeland of Lebanon's Shi'i community. South Lebanon is the historic homeland of the Shi'i struggle against the excesses of Lebanon's politico-economic system and is the heartland of the resistance. These meetings moved preaching beyond the space of the mosque and into everyday spaces, to paraphrase Atia (2012).

Set in the border village of Blida overlooking the Galilee, one televised meetings featured Saleh preaching public order and the teachings of Shi'i Islam's religious authorities on the topic. Unsurprisingly, villagers invited to Saleh's show repeatedly interrupted the sheikh. Their main concern, it seemed, was not what is order, but "who is responsible?" (Fiqh Al-Mujtama' 09.09.2014). The staged talk show turned into a heated disagreement. On the one hand, there were proponents of the idea that "the system" is responsible for the trespasses of local communities, corruption, structural imbalances, state negligence, and uneven development. "The authorities are to blame!" one hajj said in a thick local dialect. "If the state neglects its citizens and does away with justice, how can we ask people to uphold public order?" another asked. On the other hand, men and women exhibiting a particular middle-class form of piety associated with Hezbollah's urban elite disagreed. One woman said in a refined Beirut dialect, "Our imams teach that public order is a divine ordinance . . . Violators think they can wash themselves sinless by blaming the system but it doesn't work that way with God Almighty." Another concurred: "Violators are raised in households with a deficit in religious instruction . . . Their parents are to blame!"

A focus group discussion I conducted with young residents of Dahiya on May 13, 2010, revealed more radical disagreement with Al-Nizam min Al-Iman's message. While my interlocutors identified as pious Muslims and as adherents of the Resistance project, they expressed discomfort with the idea that public order is an individual responsibility. For them, Dahiya suffered repeated Israeli aggressions and state negligence: that is why its "inhabitants have to find alternative ways to survive." Singling it out as a space of chaos, they noted, is political in that it seeks to undermine "the Resistance." One respondent accused "the system" of stigmatizing Dahiya and its inhabitants to "conceal systemic corruption and injustice." Despite their empathy with the violators' motives in parting with the law, however, they were unequivocal in noting that public order is both a religious duty and a social demand. "Dahiya has been neglected by the state but we have grown used to that," a university student said. They expressed the opinion that Dahiya could become "more beautiful than before" only through community action, volunteerism, and self-help. This religiously informed entrepreneurial behavior, they believed, would counteract state negligence, attract investments, promote business, boost the economy and, ultimately, make life in Dahiya better. Evidently, taking the campaign's message beyond the space of the mosque, where one-way preaching is the dominant pedagogical method, and into everyday spaces helped uncover some of the fissures in the logic of its pious-neoliberal discourse. In addition, it revealed the disarticulations of contemporary Shi'i political activism as it struggles to combine its leftist legacy with the influences of neoliberal globalization.

SHI'I PIETY AND NEOLIBERALISM IN BEIRUT: A CRITIQUE

This chapter examined the evolution of Shi'i activism in Lebanon from its inception as a religiopolitical movement inspired by the radical left in the mid-1970s to its contemporary neoliberal turn. In doing so, it traced the birth of Shi'i activism to the emergence of the ḥussayniyya (community centers) as a space for mobilization and sheikhs as agents of this mobilization, as a result of which the movement acquired religious as well as political fervor. Generally framed as radically antisystemic, Shi'i activism drew inspiration from religious revisionism as well as progressive critiques of Lebanon's politico-economic system. Aggravated by Israeli invasions, it developed into a political project in defiance toward US-led globalized politics of intervention. In their resistance to dispossession and deprivation, Shi'i activists initiated faith-based enterprises invoking Islamic principles of community action, charity, and solidarity. Comprising a complex nexus of entities and actors operating autonomously of the state, they pursued development, empowerment, and communal aggrandizement. Framed in juxtaposition to political parties deemed pro-US, Shi'i political activism spearheaded by Hezbollah became commonly recognized as a "counterforce" to the dominant neoliberal configurations championed by Western governments and international financial organizations.

However, more nuanced accounts of Shi'i activism, such as developed here, problematize this totalizing and reductionist metanarrative. As this chapter has shown, Hezbollah is spearheading a political project aimed at consolidating the Shi'i community's political and economic gains through, among other things, redevelopment and revitalization strategies in Dahiya. Examining post-2006 reconstruction in war-affected neighborhoods, the chapter argues that the party produces strategies widely recognized in association with neoliberal developmentism. In its urban intervention, the party forged an assemblage of relations that were then criticized for their democratic deficit and the subordination of state institutions to quasi-private agencies.

This combination of piety and neoliberal developmentalism is in line with what Atia (2012, 809) calls pious neoliberalism: "a narrative of Islam that is in sync with neoliberal development ideology and yet wedded to religion." Crucially, it reveals spaces of compatibility between "the Resistance" and neoliberal economic rationale and demonstrates how the weaving together of Shi'i piety, the Resistance, and neoliberalism "leaves neither intact." This inquiry into interactions between neoliberalism and the Hezbollah-led

Resistance project has shown that the urban reconstruction project described in this chapter is not merely a circumstantial modification of a fundamentally singular original template nor is it resisting neoliberalism. Instead, it concurs with Roy's (2011, 310) proposition that modernity, developmentalism, and neoliberalism are "thoroughly hybrid": while they emerge through global circulations and experiments, they are embedded in local contexts, not merely global or borrowed.

As this chapter argues, while Hezbollah's urban intervention and the concomitant articulations of pious-neoliberal discourses regulating the public realm are inflected by strategic global influences, investments, and patterns of capital accumulation, they are homegrown. In other words, Shi'i pious-neoliberalism in contemporary Lebanon draws on a globalized "management-speak" that has become the retort to escalating social ills, to paraphrase Atia (2012; see also the chapter by Upadhyay, Wilkinson, and Ukah for similar developments). Al-Nizam min Al-Iman's rhetorical emphasis on proactiveness, individual responsibility, and self-help is contingent on the Resistance project and anchored in its unique cultural referents and technologies of governance as much as it draws on the neoliberal ideology. Furthermore, I have argued that the hegemonic coherence of pious-neoliberal discourses must not be exaggerated. Designed to regulate the micropolitics of everyday life and achieve the large-scale management of people and spaces, they also constitute discursive spaces of contestation.

CONCLUSION

Since 2006, the Shi'i community in Lebanon has witnessed significant transformations shaped by Hezbollah's two promises: to secure the release of detainees in Israeli prisons through armed resistance, and to rebuild and redevelop Dahiya "more beautiful than it was." In its two promises, the party reveals spaces of compatibility between a political project of perpetual defiance toward US-led globalized politics of intervention and development models premised on a hybrid re-creation and recasting of neoliberalism. The discursive combination of religion and piety with economic rationale in the course of the post-2006 reconstruction demonstrates how neoliberalism in Dahiya is contingent on and interacts with Hezbollah's Resistance project. I have demonstrated that members of the Resistance society are instructed to behave in a proactive and entrepreneurial fashion but also to "pave the road to Jerusalem," achieve victory against "the Great Satan" and, ultimately, come closer to God. Piety and resistance, thus, may entail perpetual defiance to US-led globalization, but do not necessarily mark a rupture with the precepts of its economic rationale.

NOTES

1. Fieldwork conducted for the purpose of this chapter was carried out with the support of a research grant awarded to the author by the Arab Council for the Social Sciences and funded by the Swedish International Development Cooperation Agency.

2. *Matawila* (singular: *metwali*): derogatory reference to Shi'i individuals invoking classist and sectarian prejudices.

3. In this chapter, Shi'i (singular) is used to denote an individual adhering to Shi'i Islam while Shi'a is used to denote the collectivity (e.g., the Shi'a of Lebanon). I also use Shi'i in the adjective form.

4. On the role of Shi'i clerics in political mobilization, see Shanahan (2005); Harik (2007); Louër (2008); Mervin (2008).

5. From Imam Musa As-Sadr's Ashura sermon delivered in Yater (Bint Jbeil, South Lebanon) on January 3, 1974. Transcript (in Arabic) obtained by the author.

6. An English translation of the Charter is published as Appendix A in Norton (1987).

7. *Rāfiḍūn* (singular: *rāfiḍi*): a derogatory reference to the Shi'a invoking their "rejection" of the early Caliphs of the Sunni-Arab empire.

8. On Hezbollah's emergence and ideology, see Qassem (2002); Saad-Ghorayeb (2002); Mervin (2008).

9. Here, I substitute technocratized neoliberal understandings of "governance" and "governmentality" with the repoliticized definition proposed by Hyden et al. (2004).

REFERENCES

Al-Hamarneh, Ala. 2013. "From Urban Governance to Urban Governmentality: Framing Urban Developments in Gulf Cities." Paper presented at the International Geography Union Regional Conference, Kyoto, Japan, August 2013.

Al-Harithy, Howayda, ed. 2010. *Lessons in Post-War Reconstruction: Case Studies from Lebanon in the Aftermath of the 2006 War*. New York, NY: Routledge.

Arnstein, Sherry. 1969. "A Ladder of Citizen Participation." *Journal of the American Institute of Planners* 35: 216–24.

Atia, Mona. 2012. "A Way to Paradise? Pious Neoliberalism, Islam, and Faith-Based Development." *Annals of the Association of American Geographers* 102 (4): 808–27.

Brenner, Neil and Nik Theodore. 2002. "Cities and the Geographies of 'Actually Existing Neoliberalism.'" *Antipode* 34 (3): 349–79.

Browers, Michaelle. 2012. "Fadlallah and the Passing of Lebanon's Last Najafi Generation." *Journal of Shi'a Islamic Studies* 5 (1): 25–46.

Byman, Daniel. 2013. *A High Price: The Triumphs and Failures of Israeli Counterterrorism*. New York, NY: Oxford University Press.

Castells, Manuel. 1977. *The Urban Question: A Marxist Approach*. Cambridge, MA: MIT Press.

Castree, Noel. 2006. "From Neoliberalism to Neoliberalization: Consolations, Confusions and Necessary Illusions." *Environment and Planning A* 38 (1): 1–6.

Dabashi, Hamid. 2011. *Shi'ism: A Religion of Protest*. Cambridge, MA: Belknap Press.

Deeb, Lara and Mona Harb. 2013. *Leisurely Islam: Negotiating Geography and Morality in Shi'ite South Beirut*. Princeton, NJ: Princeton University Press.

Deeb, Lara. 2006. *An Enchanted Modern: Gender and Public Piety in Shi'i Lebanon*. New York, NY: Princeton University Press.

Dobbin, Frank, Beth Simmons, and Geoffrey Garrett. 2007. "The Global Diffusion of Public Policies: Social Construction, Coercion, Competition, or Learning?" *Annual Review of Sociology* 33: 449–72.

Fawaz, Mona. 2014. "The Politics of Property in Planning: Hezbollah's Reconstruction of Haret Hreik (Beirut, Lebanon) as Case Study." *International Journal of Urban and Regional Research* 38 (3): 922–34.

Foucault, Michel. 1991. "Governmentality." In *The Foucault Effect: Studies in Governmentality,* edited by G. Burchell, C. Gordon, and P. Miller. Chicago, IL: University of Chicago Press.

Hamieh, Christine S. and Roger MacGinty. 2011. "Reconstructing Post-2006 Lebanon: A Distorted Market." In *Rethinking the Liberal Peace: External Models and Local Alternatives*, edited by Shahrbanou Tadjbakhsh, 181–94. New York, NY: Routledge.

Harb, Mona and Lara Deeb. 2011. "Culture as History and Landscape: Hizballah's Efforts to Shape an Islamic Milieu in Lebanon." *Arab Studies Journal* 14 (2): 10–41.

Harb, Mona and Mona Fawaz. 2010. "Influencing the Politics of Reconstruction in Haret Hreik." In *Lessons in Post-War Reconstruction: Case Studies from Lebanon in the Aftermath of the 2006 War*, edited by Howayda Al-Harithy, 21–45. New York, NY: Routledge.

Harb, Mona. 2003. "La Dahiye de Beyrouth: parcours d'une stigmatisation urbaine, consolidation d'un territoire politique." *Genèses* 51: 70–91.

Harb, Mona. 2007. "Deconstructing Hizballah and Its Suburb." *Middle East Report* 242: 12–17.

Harb, Mona. 2008. "Faith-Based Organizations as Effective Development Partners. Hezbollah and Postwar Reconstruction in Lebanon." In *Development, Civil Society and Faith-Based Organizations*, edited by Gerard Clarke, Michael Jennings, Timothy M. Shaw, 214–39. New York, NY: Palgrave Macmillan.

Harik, Judith P. 2007. Hezbollah: *The Changing Face of Terrorism*. London: I. B. Tauris.

Hart, Gillian. 2004. "Geography and Development: Critical Ethnographies." *Progress in Human Geography* 28 (1): 91–100.

Harvey, David. 1993. *Social Justice and the City*. London: Edward Arnold Publishers.

Heydemann, Steven. 2004. *Networks of Privilege: The Politics of Economic Reform Revisited*. New York, NY: Palgrave Macmillan.

Jacobs, Jane. 1961. *Death and Life of Great American Cities*. New York, NY: Random House.

Jacobs, Jane. 1969. *The Economy of Cities*. New York, NY: Random House.

Larner, Wendy. 2000. "Neo-liberalism: Policy, Ideology, Governmentality." *Studies in Political Economy* 63: 5–25.

Le Thomas, Catherine. 2010. "Socialization Agencies and Party Dynamics: Functions and Uses of Hizballah's Schools in Lebanon." In *Returning to Party Politics: Political Party Development in the Arab World*, edited by Myriam Catusse and Karam Karam. Beirut: Lebanese Center for Policy Studies.

Leitner, Helga, Jamie Peck, and Eric Sheppard. 2007. *Contesting Neoliberalism: Urban Frontiers*. New York, NY: The Guilford Press.

Louër, Laurence. 2008. *Transnational Shia Politics: Religious and Political Networks in the Gulf*. London: Hurst & Company.

Mervin, Sabrina, ed. 2008. *Le Hezbollah: état des lieux*. Paris: Sindbad.

Norton, Augustus R. 1987. *Amal and the Shi'a: Struggle for the Soul of Lebanon*. Austin, TX: University of Texas Press.

Peck, Jamie and Adam Tickel. 2002. "Neoliberalizing Space." *Antipode* 34 (3): 380–404.

Picard, Elizabeth. 1993. *The Lebanese Shia and Political Violence*. Geneva: United Nations Research Institute for Social Development.

Picard, Elizabeth. 2000. "The Political Economy of Civil War in Lebanon." In *War, Institutions and Social Change in the Middle East*, edited by Steven Hydemann. Berkeley, CA: University of California Press.

Qassem, Naim. 2002. *Hezbollah, al-manhaj, al-tajribah, al-mustaqbal* [Hezbollah, the method, the experience, the future]. Dar al-Hadi, Beirut.

Rahnema, Majid. 1993. "Participation." In *The Development Dictionary*, edited by W. Sachs. London: Zed Books.

Roy, Ananya. 2009. "Civic Governmentality: The Politics of Inclusion in Beirut and Mumbai." *Antipode* 41 (1): 159–79.

Roy, Ananya. 2011. "Postcolonial Urbanism: Speed, Hysteria, Mass Dreams." In *Worlding Cities: Asian Experiments and the Art of Being Global*, edited by Ananya Roy and Aihwa Ong. Hoboken: Wiley-Blackwell.

Saad-Ghorayeb, Amal. 2002. *Hizbu'llah: Politics and Religion*. London: Pluto Press.

Saouli, Adham. 2014. "Intellectuals and Political Power in Social Movements: The Parallel Paths of Fadlallah and Hizbullah." *British Journal of Middle Eastern Studies* 41 (1): 97–116.

Shaery-Eisenlohr, Roschanack. 2008. *Shi'ite Lebanon: Transnational Religion and the Making of National Identities*. New York, NY: Columbia University Press.

Shanahan, Rodger. 2005. *The Shi'a of Lebanon: Clans, Parties and Clerics*. London: Tauris Academic Studies.

Swyngedouw, Eric, Frank Moulaert, and Arantxa Rodriguez. 2002. "Neoliberal Urbanization in Europe: Large-Scale Urban Development Projects and the New Urban Policy." *Antipode* 34 (3): 542–77.

Traboulsi, Fawwaz. 2007. *History of Modern Lebanon*. London: Pluto Press.

Chapter 11

Religion and Corporate Social Responsibility

Taming Neoliberalism?

Michael MacLeod

Capitalism's most visible representative is the successful corporation, an organized business enterprise that accumulates profits through its productive activities. With the entrenchment of neoliberal economic policies throughout the developed world in the 1990s, large multinational corporations became much more numerous and, by all accounts, more powerful agents in the global spread of capitalism. A "pro-business" environment of less state regulation (e.g., the removal or reformation of environmental laws) and more mobility by capital (e.g., removing restrictions on finance) sparked an increasingly vocal anti-corporate-led globalization movement, famously manifest in the protests against the Multinational Agreement Investment (MAI) in 1997–1998 and later in Seattle at the World Trade Organization meetings in 1999. This opposition remains, albeit in a more localized or muted fashion (Smith 2014; Dwyer 2013; see also the chapter by Smith and Smythe in this volume). Instead of challenging neoliberalism and attempting to put the genie of global capitalism back in the bottle, a more subtle (and, I would argue, more substantive) direction has developed in the last two decades that primarily seeks to reform capitalism from the inside: making corporations more accountable by enhancing private (as opposed to public) authority of regulation. Business self-regulation—encouraging corporations and industries to voluntarily manage their affairs in a manner consistent with the wider expectations of society—has become a dominant motif in modern capitalism with neoliberal-influenced governments reluctant to impose state-led regulation for fear of capital flight. Its primary manifestation in the business world is called "corporate social responsibility" (henceforth CSR) and its dramatic rise in recent decades has led to intense debates concerning its purpose and effectiveness (May, Cheney and Roper 2007). While CSR is a highly contested concept—derided by neoclassical economists for interfering with the principles of free enterprise and by critics on the left as a mere pub-lic relations strategy or, worse, a neoliberal strategy in disguise—its modern manifestation definitely correlates with the rise of neoliberalism and its per-ceived negative social and environmental impacts.

Historically, the idea that businesses have wider obligations to society than merely making profit reaches back to the origins of capitalism. It was not until the twentieth century, however, that there was a more specific articula-tion of firms having a "social responsibility" to citizens, not coincidentally during periods when corporations as institutions were recognized as being increasingly powerful entities within the two major capitalist economies, the United States and Great Britain (Carroll 2009). In the United States, the 1971 report by the Committee on Economic Development (CED), a public policy group composed of both business people and educators, produced a seminal publication, *Social Responsibilities of Business Corporations*, which noted the dramatically changing social context and proposed that the social contract between business and society needed to be transformed so that firms would take into account issues such as the environment, minority rights, and poverty (CED 1971). But it was during the 1990s that CSR began to become much more visible in business practices globally, with the rise in the number of firms producing annual CSR reports, the creation in 1992 of a prominent global nonprofit organization (Business for Social Responsibility) that represented the initiatives and professionals associated with CSR, and the well-publicized success of corporations that made social and environmental concerns central to their pro forma business mandate (Carroll 2009). Even the United Nations became involved when it helped create the "Global Compact" in 2000, a principles-based initiative in which now over 10,000 corporations have signed on to agree to advance UN-based goals concerning the environ-ment, human rights, labor, and anticorruption. More recently, in 2014, the UN created a "Guiding Principles Reporting Framework" as a guideline for corporations to report on how their activities impact human rights. It is now not unusual for the world's largest multinationals to portray themselves as committed to the spirit (if not the letter) of these emerging notions of social responsibility: "At Unilever, our vision is to build a company that represents the new capitalism, in which business exists to serve—not take from—soci-ety" is but one recent example how powerful firms want to showcase their commitment (Unilever 2015, 5).

The pervasiveness of CSR has led some to call it "one of the more striking developments of the past several decades in the global political economy" (Levy and Kaplan 2008, 432). Others contend that CSR constitutes a broadly based social movement (Waddock 2009) that has produced a high degree of "institutionalization of CSR" within and among firms with prob-able long-lasting effects on the international community (Moon 2003, 266).

A key driver promoting corporate responsibility that often gets overlooked is the rise of socially responsible investing (SRI), including investors mobilized by their religious faith who dominated the early years of SRI in the 1970s, and whose influence has helped shaped the discourse over corporate power.

In this context, the increasing activism of shareholders, especially by institutional investors (including mutual funds, investment advisory and management firms, and public and private pension funds, all of which hold and invest capital on behalf of millions of citizens and employees in the United States and other countries), rose dramatically after the 1970s. Some of this investor activism is based on the idea of "socially responsible investment"—defined as a process that considers the social and environmental consequences of investments, in addition to using traditional financial criteria. Also called "ethical" investment, socially responsible investment (SRI) has evolved quickly from a niche investor option to a broader movement within the investment community to redefine fiduciary duty (the obligation to obtain the best returns possible for clients) and incorporate concerns—such as climate change—into financial analysis that would have been unheard of just a decade or two ago. Since the 1990s, SRI has been the fastest growing segment of the financial market and some argue that the CSR movement is a direct response to the dramatic rise and influence of SRI. Companies are increasingly being pushed to shift their behavior by shareholder advocacy and activism; in other words, they are "two sides of the same coin" (Fung, Law and Yau 2010, 2). As with CSR, SRI's rise is correlated with a neoliberal policy environment in which greater opportunity for corporate success is matched with a deep concern about the long-term sustainability of global capitalism.

The role of religion and religious belief surrounding the evolution of social responsibility in the financial sector is a much underexplored story. Faith-based activism has a long history of challenging capitalism, including in the birthplaces of the market economy: Europe (particularly the United Kingdom) and the United States. While Christianity's influence has long been linked to the creation or reinforcement of the "spirit of capitalism" (Weber 2001; Novak 1990; see also the chapters by Wilkinson, Ukah, and Upadhyay, this volume), the core convictions of many Christians and denominations have long sat uneasy with the functioning of the "free market" and the actions of powerful businesses. During the eighteenth century in England, John Wesley, the founder of Methodism, warned against industries that polluted the soul (alcohol) and the environment (tanning). In America during the same period, the Quaker movement helped spearhead the end of slavery by mandating members to cease investing in the slave trade. As capitalism matured and spread to every corner of the world, religious leaders have articulated deep concerns about its economic, moral, and social impacts.

In the 2009 encyclical *Caritas in Veritate* ("Charity in Truth"), Pope Benedict XVI argues that in a global context, businesses have a greater responsibility than ever to ensure that their activities consider the impact on people and the environment. He posits that the very success of the market economy depends on this transformation (Donadio and Goodstein 2009).

This chapter examines how the modern CSR movement and, more specifically, its principal driver, SRI, have been shaped by religiously motivated individuals and institutions. The argument made here is that the primary goal of religious involvement in CSR and SRI has been to reform neoliberal capitalism from the inside, in effect to moderate neoliberalism by articulating concerns about its social and environmental impacts and to change corporate behavior accordingly, not to oppose, let alone replace, capitalism. There is one caveat, however: although CSR is, as noted above, an increasingly global practice, the focus here is largely on how people and institutions of faith in Western countries have utilized their power and influence in responsible investment practices. Christianity does not have a monopoly on religiously inspired attempts to reform capitalism but since modern CSR and SRI originated in the West, faith-based activism has been more developed in advanced capitalist societies (see Kwayu in this volume for an interfaith example including Islamic activists).

The analysis proceeds as follows. First, the rise of the idea and practice of CSR and its relationship with neoliberalism is explored. Although some portray CSR as an embodiment of neoliberal practices and policies that further legitimizes corporate power and deepens capitalist social relations, the contention here is that at its core, CSR is best viewed as a corrective to the excesses of neoliberalism. Second, we assess SRI as a key driver of CSR and analyze the role and influence of religion and religiously motivated individuals and institutions on the evolution of modern SRI. It is difficult to see how SRI could have become as powerful a force without faith-based investor activism playing a central role; moreover, the goals of these investor activities are ultimately concerned with reforming—taming—neoliberalism, not resisting it. "CSR works *within* the container of corporate capitalism to *reform* it" (Baue 2010, emphasis in original).

CSR AND NEOLIBERALISM

In this section, the emergence of CSR is assessed through the lens of political economy, that is, understanding CSR as a socioeconomic phenomenon as opposed to a strictly business or management tool or issue. Until recently, mainstream scholarly analysis of CSR was dominated by management theories and debates over the business case for or against it and ignored the larger context of how CSR relates to global governance, power, and economic globalization (Gjolberg 2011). From a political economy perspective, CSR is part of the changing power dynamics between business, government, and society, and the responses this creates within and among these actors. Karl Polanyi, in his seminal *The Great Transformation*, argues that the rise of market liberalism in the nineteenth century and its insistence on the unfettered power of the market to create prosperity, stability, and freedom created a significant backlash against capitalism and the social and environmental costs it imposed on society in the 1930s, for example, visible in the widespread unemployment resulting from the economic crisis. The resulting societal response was what he referred to as a "double movement": the power of market liberalism becomes checked by society through a "network of measures and policies . . . integrated by powerful institutions" and even recognized those in business as necessary to sustain the market economy itself (Polanyi 1944/2001, 76). The ultimate purpose of this movement, Polanyi argued, was to "re-embed" the market economy into society and its relations (rules, customs, and institutions) rather than leaving society at the mercy of the laissez-faire system and its dictates.

Balancing the power of capitalism and the market economy, on the one hand, and protecting society from the externalities and costs that the market imposes, on the other, has been a constant theme in both scholarship and policymaking at the domestic and international levels. John Ruggie, an international relations scholar and later a United Nations Special Representative who helped develop the above-noted UN Global Compact and the new UN human rights framework for business, adapted these insights in a pioneering work of his own. He introduced the concept of "embedded liberalism" to describe the institutional framework that capitalist countries devised after the Second World War, in which a new liberal international order was complemented by individual state governments who provided social safety nets and adjustment assistance in varying degrees, conditioned by their respective political cultures (Ruggie 1982). This "grand bargain" helped create a long-lasting period of economic expansion and relative political stability, at least within the Western capitalist world, from the 1950s into the 1990s (Ruggie 2008).

Today, however, the spread of global capitalism seems to be outmatching the ability of governments and existing institutions to adequately check the market and its externalities. In the 1980s, neoliberalism—focused on privatization, deregulation, and increased liberalization of trade and investment—helped lay the foundation for an environment in which multinational corporations could operate more freely across borders, invest capital, and create global supply chains that produced and distributed vast amounts of goods in a post–Cold War world. The resulting prosperity came at a price, as the social and environmental costs of globalization provoked both a backlash to resist neoliberalism (e.g., in the rise of anticorporate globalization) and, significantly, a reconsideration of how to allow a globalized market economy to develop yet ameliorate its most negative effects on citizens and the environment, the ability to reform (or tame) neoliberalism. It is clear that the traditional governing institutions in society have become increasingly unable or unwilling to embed global market liberalism into shared societal values and expectations (and have, in fact, attempted to help reconstruct those values so as to fit with the demands of neoliberalism).

It is in this context that we should understand and explain the remarkable rise of CSR as a foundational basis for the functioning of modern business. At its heart, CSR can be viewed as a way to improve accountability of the most significant economic actor in capitalism, the corporation, which has become steadily "disembedded" from society (see, e.g., the chapter in this volume by Aikande Kwayu and the power of businesses to expatriate profits). CSR initiatives such as corporate sustainability and human rights reports that are voluntary but also self-regulatory initiatives such as the Equator Principles for banks, the Responsible Care program in the chemical industry, or the Forest Stewardship Council promoting sustainable forestry practices, to name but three prominent examples, are found not only within the business world itself but also within civil society, with nongovernmental organizations actively seeking to shape and coordinate with large corporations, sometimes closely involved and other times from more of a distance. Representatives from both business and civil society, in other words, are seeking to hold corporations more accountable. As neoliberal policies and practices empower business firms as a largely unfettered agent of global capitalism while states reduce their traditional regulatory governance and oversight of corporate activities, the rise of CSR can be seen as a reaction to this corporate power. CSR is thus now part of a contemporary "double movement" to tame neoliberal globalization: "In Polanyi's terms, [CSR] is an attempt to establish a more socially embedded form of economic governance" (Levy and Kaplan 2008, 443).

This is by no means an uncontested argument. Indeed, some recent critical scholarship by sociologists, political scientists, and legal scholars argues that CSR is little more than a reflection of neoliberalism. For example, CSR has been critiqued as a "neoliberal strategy in disguise" (Savevska 2014), that its discourse and practices are products of the "neoliberal imagination" (Shamir 2008), and that CSR "is the mirror image of the neoliberal policy framework" in its minimalistic approach to government intervention, among other factors (van Aartsen 2013, 42). To be sure, there is an affiliation between the development of both; in an increasingly regulatory vacuum with limited state control over global corporate practices (neoliberalism), corporations themselves are taking steps (CSR initiatives) to gain trust and legitimacy in the eyes of the public, to maintain a social license to operate in the global economy (Gjolberg 2011). And it is true that modern CSR practices arose first and more dramatically in the countries with liberal market economies (the United States and the United Kingdom) as opposed to the coordinated market economies found in Europe and Japan (Matten and Moon 2008).

What get missed, however, in these arguments are two important factors. First, the link between CSR and neoliberalism is more complex than what critics on the left portray. Modern advocates of CSR started to articulate their concerns over market fundamentalism and the power of unchecked capital long before neoliberalism took full flight in the 1980s. Throughout the 1950s and 1960s, the idea that corporations needed to assume greater concern and responsibility for society grew strong enough within certain business circles to draw fierce opposition from the two figures who became (and remain) the ideological icons for neoliberalism: Friedrich Hayek and Milton Friedman. Both of these men associated "CSR with socialism and [saw] it as a subversive, collectivist force that promotes conformity [running] counter to the achievement of individual freedoms" and tried to warn the corporate world away from any consideration of it (Vallentin 2012, 2). Friedman's famous 1970 article in *The New York Times Magazine* made a simple argument— "the social responsibility of business is to increase its profits" (Friedman 1970)—and since then, CSR advocates have battled with those like Friedman who they consider to be conservative reactionaries opposed to the explicit inclusion of social and environmental considerations into business practices. Thus, far from CSR and neoliberalism being a simple convergence of like-minded policies and principles—as those on the critical left argue—there is ample reason to believe that the two can be seen as opposing forces with quite different core assumptions. Indeed, CSR challenges us to rethink the interaction among the state, markets, and civil society, and is driven by moral and philosophical understandings that are not found in neoliberal thought or policies (Lebano 2010).

Second, what also gets missed in the critical analysis of CSR and neoliberalism is the essentially contested and evolving nature of both concepts. This is where a constructivist approach to international political economy is helpful, one that emphasizes the socially constructed nature of actors and processes in world politics (Abdelal et al. 2010). Constructivism posits that relevant actors—states and/or nonstate actors—interact to produce a set of expectations and common understandings that in turn give rise to a set of "norms"—intersubjectively held expectations of appropriate behavior by an actor (Finnemore and Sikkink 1999). The modern CSR movement has become so prolific and embedded within different social structures and the actors themselves that it can be argued that CSR should be understood as an emerging socially constructed norm in world politics: that is, we are witnessing a convergence of expectations around what constitutes proper behavior for corporations in society, domestically and globally (Risse 2002). The role of "norm entrepreneurs"—agents who advocate different ideas about appropriate behavior from organizational platforms that give their ideas credence—are critical elements in building new ideas of appropriate behavior in the global capitalist economy. In this vein, our focus should be on understanding the social construction of CSR, how it came about historically and what its intentions are for the global economy, that is, who pushed it and why.

In the next section, we assess how SRI and the SRI community (persons and institutions) have been critical in creating a norm of responsible behavior for corporations, and especially how faith-based investors have acted as innovative and persistent "norm entrepreneurs." Their role was an early and critical driver of responsible investment. By using market and ownership pressures, as well as "framing and shaming" businesses through shareholder advocacy, SRI has been attempting to reshape and reconstitute the identities of corporations in the global political economy, as well as the investor community as a whole.

SRI AND FAITH-BASED SHAREHOLDER ACTIVISM

The rise of CSR is closely related to the growth of SRI in the last few decades. Like CSR, there is no one commonly accepted definition of SRI. It usually refers to financial investment that takes account and incorporates social, ethical, and environmental factors. In essence, it is a process of identifying and investing in companies that meet certain standards of appropriate corporate behavior or of avoiding (and/or influencing) those companies that do not meet such criteria. SRI "embeds CSR in the functioning of shareholder capitalism" (Steurer, Margula and Martinuzzi 2008, 7), representing a broad field of investor practitioners and practices that has evolved into a key driving force for pushing changed corporate behavior and having "responsible" corporations in the global economy.

Practically, SRI is reflected in two broad types of activities by investors. The first, shareholder advocacy (also referred to as "shareholder engagement"), includes dialogue between investors and boards or other management of companies to alter corporate behavior as well as the use of proxy voting (using the rights of shareowners at annual corporate general meetings to bring visibility to an issue). The second, investor screening, concerns how shareholders make decisions on their initial investments in the first place, that is, what criteria are used to buy shares. Historically, "negative" screening refers to preventing or divesting (selling) investments in problematic businesses (tobacco companies) or countries (Burma, or Myanmar) and is often a more visible form of shareholder activism. The best known example was the divestiture of companies doing business in South Africa to support the anti-apartheid movement in the 1970s and 1980s. While shareholder advocacy is a more popular method for investor activism, investor screening in the form of divestment remains an important option for some investors to register their disapproval of both specific and general corporate behavior. Frustration with the climate change issue, for example, has recently resulted in a divestment movement that is increasingly visible worldwide (BBC 2015).

While both proponents and critics of SRI sometimes overstate its significance in financial markets—the former to emphasize their influence, the latter to emphasize the threat (Kurtz 2008)—it is, nevertheless, clear that SRI has grown dramatically in size, complexity, and importance in recent years. Since the mid-1990s, the growth in the number of SRI-dedicated mutual funds and their holdings in the United States alone has outstripped the universe of professionally managed investment assets by about 40% and the value assets subject to a form of socially responsible investing strategy are estimated to be up to 17% of the overall total of investment assets under management in the country (up from only 1–2% in 1995), according to some sources (USSIF 2014). One estimate is that in the United States in 1995, there were only 55 mutual funds that engaged in SRI with $12 billion in assets; by 2012, this had grown to 493 funds with assets of $569 billion (Glassman 2012). There are similar trends within most advanced industrialized countries.

While statistics indicate that socially responsible investing remains a "niche" investment tool within the financial community, the influence of SRI and the activism of its leading proponents has had a broad impact on investor attitudes and the general disposition toward corporate behavior. The very meaning of "fiduciary responsibility" (the obligations that an investor has to a client to earn as much of a return as possible on the capital he or she has been given) is being redefined within the investment community as a result of a long process of contestation over what factors can and should be considered as financially acceptable "risks" (Hawley and Williams 2005). What constitutes appropriate behavior for investors (and corporations) now includes factors not previously considered by traditional investors, such as climate change or human rights. Amy Domini, one of the pioneers of SRI in the United States, argues that the decision to invest in a socially responsible way allows us to (re)define the role of the corporation in society that takes into account financial rewards and also broader ethical questions relevant to society as a whole (Domini 2001). In a speech she made when receiving an honorary degree from Yale Divinity School, Domini, a life-long Episcopalian, pointed to religious motivation as the spark for her involvement in SRI: "For me, finance and capitalism are not exempt from God's will. Investors are not innocent in the actions of [what] they enable. Right is right and wrong is wrong" (Domini Social Investments 2007).

Domini's sentiments are not uncommon in the Christian church. Beginning in the late 1960s, the actions of church members and faith-based organizations became critical of the emergence of the modern CSR movement. Socially responsible investing became the primary vehicle for expanding what was acceptable (or unacceptable) corporate behavior. Religious belief was the first rationale for this rise in SRI and remains an important force today (Kurtz 2008). The first modern ethical investment fund, the Pax ("peace") World Fund, was founded in 1971 by the Reverend Luther Tyson, a long-time staff member of the United Methodist Board of Church and Society. It was created specifically to exclude (screen) from its portfolio any company with links to the arms industry, reflecting the anti-Vietnam War activism of the time. The fund also promoted fair employment practices and other socially responsible goals. In the same year, a Baptist Minister from Philadelphia, Leon Sullivan, was appointed to the Board of Directors at General Motors, which at the time was the preeminent American multinational corporation. Seeing an opportunity, the Episcopal Church sent its Presiding Bishop to GM's annual meeting, where he asked the board to consider withdrawing from running operations in South Africa to protest against the apartheid regime (GM employed the largest number of blacks in the country at the time). Reverend Sullivan pledged to create an accountability system that would spur corporations to help end institutionalized slavery. In 1977, his Sullivan Principles were among the first modern corporate codes of conduct designed specifically to instill an ethos of social responsibility in modern businesses, albeit with respect to the particular problem of apartheid. Much later, in 2011, on the heels of *Caritas in Veritate* and the global recession, the Vatican was said to be considering a "Catholic" version of the Sullivan Principles, to "reshape an amorphous economy that spans the entire globe, often defying control by anyone" (Allen 2011).

Religiously motivated investors helped pioneer the new types of shareholder engagement that arose between investors and corporations starting in the 1970s. As noted, shareholder activism occurs when owners of equity in publicly traded companies use their power to facilitate change in corporate behavior, using either shareholder resolutions at annual general meetings of corporations or by engaging in private dialogue with the management of companies on various issues. The trend line for both types of shareholder activism over the last few decades, and especially in the last fifteen years, shows (a) a substantial increase in the number of resolutions and/or in the frequency/intensity of the communication between (institutional) shareholders and (b) a growing concern beyond traditional corporate governance issues (such as executive compensation) toward the core concerns associated with SRI, especially human rights and environmental sustainability.

In part, these developments reflect a structural change in the United States (and other developed economies) whereby the influence of individual investors has been superseded by that of institutional investors, which now control trillions of dollars of investment capital. Individual investors once owned 93% of all US stocks (in 1950), but their share has steadily declined and is now less than 30%. Conversely, the proportion of US public equities managed by institutions grew from 7% in 1950 to about 67% in 2010; institutional investors are even more significant in their ownership in the largest American corporations, owning about 73% of the outstanding equity in 2009 (cited in SEC 2013). The institutional investment sector includes both large actors—such as public pension funds (e.g., the California Public Employees Retirement System, CalPERS, with hundreds of billions of dollars in assets) and some private pensions (e.g., TIAA-CREF)—and also hundreds of smaller asset holders, including many faith-based funds and investment firms, such as the Christian Brothers Investment Service (Catholic), Amana Mutual Funds (Muslim) and Guidestone Funds (Baptist), among many examples.

In addition to the creation of many specific religiously motivated investment funds, faith-based activism has also been leading in the collective mobilization of resources to promote greater social responsibility of business. This has mainly occurred in Anglo-Saxon countries and within the Christian church community. In the United Kingdom, the Church Investors Group (CIG), officially created in 2004, began in 1973 as an informal ecumenical gathering of those with trustee responsibility for church investments to come together to research and discuss ethical issues related to investment in the United Kingdom and worldwide. Since then, its membership has grown to include representatives of all the main denominations in the United Kingdom and Ireland, including pension funds, charitable trusts, and religious orders. As of 2015, it had 55 members representing investors with collective assets of over $25 billion; one of its main activities is to engage large corporations directly, inviting them to make presentations on their CSR policies to church investors. The CIG describes its essential mission thus: "We seek to increase the witness and influence of the Church in society by empowering each other to reflect the moral stance and teachings of our faith in our investment portfolios" (CIG 2014). Another similar organization in the United Kingdom, the Ecumenical Council for Corporate Responsibility, was created in 1989 as a church-based investor coalition and membership organization working for economic justice, environmental sustainability, and corporate and investor responsibility.

In Canada, the Task Force on Churches and Corporate Responsibility (TCCR) was created in 1975 as an ecumenical coalition of Canadian churches to promote social and ecological responsibility in Canadian-based corporations and financial institutions (SHARE 2005). One of the Task Force's first efforts was to assist church shareholders in influencing banks to stop making loans to the apartheid regime in South Africa. When banks refused to discuss the loans, the TCCR coordinated the efforts of church shareholders, who began to attend the banks' annual meetings to raise their concerns in a public forum about the banks' complicity in the apartheid system. Later, in the 1990s, the organization was at the forefront of efforts to convince corporations and investors to divest from Sudan because of its ongoing civil war and the genocide in Darfur. It was successful in hastening the departure of Talisman Energy, a Canadian company, from Sudan (this author was a consultant for Talisman during this period). In 2001, the TCCR became part of a new coalition with nine other ecumenical social justice coalitions, called KAIROS: Canadian Ecumenical Justice Initiatives, to continue advocacy work about corporate responsibility. Today, this advocacy includes monthly reports on SRI and coordination with investor coalitions, although shareholder activism is historically less prevalent in Canada than in its neighbor to the south, for a variety of regulatory and cultural reasons (SHARE 2005).

The Interfaith Center on Corporate Social Responsibility (ICCR)

Probably the best known religiously motivated organization promoting CSR through SRI is the US-based Interfaith Center on Corporate Responsibility (ICCR), founded in 1974. Established by the National Council of Churches, its original mandate was to advise and guide member churches on the ethical dimensions of its financial investments. It was originally composed of Catholic and Protestant churches, but Jewish groups also joined later. Within a few years of its creation, the ICCR was engaged in a highly publicized and controversial battle with multinational corporations about their marketing of infant formula to mothers in developing countries. Since then, the ICCR has developed into an international coalition of more than 300 faith-based institutional investor members including denominations, religious communities, pension funds, healthcare corporations, foundations, and dioceses with combined portfolios worth over $150 billion. Its activities include producing reports, engaging in dialogue, and submitting shareholder resolutions on issues as diverse as excessive executive compensation (Disney Corporation), protecting indigenous rights (Halliburton), reducing the use of toxic chemicals in hydraulic fracturing (Chevron Corp), disclosing the financial risks of climate change (Valero), and ending human trafficking (Hilton and Hyatt hotels) (Rheannon 2010).

The process of determining how the ICCR engages with corporations is relatively straightforward. Each summer, the organization holds meetings in which members and other interested parties (e.g., institutional investors who are not members and also organizations with similar goals such as the

"As You Sow" Foundation) to determine issues and topics for possible share-holder resolutions at the following year's annual company meetings (most are held in the spring). Companies with a particular stake in the issue are identified, and letters are sent to their executive management asking questions about potential risks. If the response is deemed insufficient, proxy resolutions are announced as forthcoming at the spring annual meeting. Issues are prioritized according to direct input from investors (members and affiliates), and also in conversation with civil society groups. In the last decade, climate change has become a leading subject for shareholder activists, including faith-based organizations, but other issues such as fracking (hydraulic fracturing), human rights, and labor issues are also high on the investor agenda. The most obvious manifestation of this shareholder activism is the increasing number of shareowner resolutions introduced in recent years. In 2015, the ICCR was responsible for just over half (227) of the record number (433) of shareholder resolutions introduced at corporate meetings by investors, and this despite the fact that it much prefers to hold private dialogue with individual corporations to press its case—and companies often responded to the threat of proxy votes by deciding to engage directly with investors behind the scene (Kropp 2015).

Although ICCR sometimes publicly downplays the faith-based aspect of its political power, it is clear that the related imagery is useful in its campaigns: "You haven't seen shareholder activism until you see a nun battling it out with CEOs. They can be devastating" (cited in Frel 2005). The executive director of the ICCR, when asked about their activities said: "Why do investors of faith work so hard to encourage CSR? If we study the teachings of our faith traditions, we really have no choice" (Laura Berry, cited in Rheannon 2010). One of the key members of the ICCR is the Tri-State Coalition for Responsible Investment, an organization of 40 Catholic dioceses and congregations in the New York City metro area. Its executive director, Sister Pat Daly, is well known within the corporate and investor communities and her involvement in shareholder advocacy is often referred to by major corporations as the impetus to taking dialogue seriously; indeed, her religious identity (and the faith-based nature of a significant number of proxy resolutions in the United States) has been shown to be positively correlated with getting responses and commitments to change from businesses such as the Ford Motor Company (Forbes 2010).

RELIGION AND NORM CHANGE

Religious organizations and their representatives are likely more effective in bringing about such reactions because they are considered to be more socially legitimate than other activist groups, and in the US context this may be key since the country has much higher rates of religious affiliation than other Western capitalist countries (van Buren 2005). A more recent study sponsored by the International Interfaith Investment Group—a Dutch-based organization similar to the ICCR known as 3iG, except with members of all faiths involved globally—provides evidence that shareholder engagement by religious investors is particularly effective because faith institutions are persistent, utilize their grassroots and extensive networks to understand community concerns, and combine this with their faith beliefs that they bring into the boardrooms of influential corporations through their shareholder advocacy (van Cranenburgh et al. 2012).

The goal of faith-based investor activism is clear, according to those involved: "We're not here to put corporations down, we're here to improve their sense of responsibility" (Sister Nora Nash of the ICCR, cited in Roose 2011). Religious organizations and individuals helped pioneer the advent of the modern SRI movement, which in turn sparked the rise of CSR. Although both developments pre-date the rise of neoliberal policies in the 1980s, the efforts and successes by faith-based investors helped set the pattern for other, nonreligious-based shareholder activism that has blossomed in the neoliberal era. Specifically, the collective action by investors modeled by the ICCR was emulated in 1989 when the CERES (Coalition for Environmentally Responsible Economies) organization was created, bringing together investors and civil society groups, followed by the creation of dozens of other similar investor coalitions and institutions since the year 2000 (such as the Carbon Disclosure Project, the Investor Network on Climate Risk, the Investor Environmental Health Network, the Responsible Endowments Coalition, the Conflict Risk Network, the UN Principles for Responsible Investment, among others) (MacLeod 2014). Not only did faith have a critical role in shaping the creation and development of modern SRI; faith-based shareholder engagement with corporations also remains a critical feature of current investor activism, so much so that the corporate world still takes notice when religions mobilize. In 2015, the *Wall Street Journal* reported that the publishing of the "Laudato Si" encyclical on the environment by Pope Francis is "unleashing a new wave of shareholder activism by Catholic investors" that corporations needed to respond to (Chasan and Murphy 2015).

CONCLUSION

This chapter has focused on several underexplored dynamics in the global political economy: the steady rise of CSR in the modern era and its hegemonic influence in the business section since the 1990s, the emergence of SRI as an original driver of this CSR and its continued relevance as a force in the financial sector, and the role and influence of religion and religiously motivated individuals and institutions in creating and shaping corporate behavior through its influence over SRI. The wider context for all of the developments, of course, is the dominance of neoliberalism—the set of ideas and policies that since the early 1980s has resulted in the steady disembedding of the state from the market, and in so doing has made corporations even more powerful entities in society. At its core, neoliberalism "obscures possible tensions between corporate and societal interests" and promotes the idea that businesses, in essence, can do no wrong (Vallentin 2012, 7).

Increasing the power of corporations and elevating the role of the marketplace has had an important consequence: it has now shifted the public political domain beyond that of state-societal interaction to corporate-societal interaction (Crouch 2011). Corporations have become so powerful, in other words, that they cannot avoid increased public attention and the desire for a new type of global governance to hold business accountable for all this power. In Polanyian terms, this is the reaction of societal forces—even within the business community itself—trying to reign in corporate power to address the externalities that have been more dramatically apparent in a business-dominated environment where traditional state-led governance is now weak or nonexistent. The modern CSR movement fits precisely within this context. It began even before neoliberalism emerged in the 1980s, but clearly in the one country where corporate power was least restrained: the United States. Not coincidentally, those whose ideas formed the central economic justification for the later rise of neoliberal policies (Friedman and Hayek) were also the earliest opponents of CSR, fearing it would weigh modern corporations down with societal oversight. They were correct in their fears but CSR-related ideas, discourse, and activities did not come to dominate global business until neoliberalism itself became entrenched in the Western world in the 1990s.

Without the influential role of faith-based activism, however, the CSR movement might not have developed in the manner or the extent that it did. Religiously motivated individuals and organizations played a critical part in utilizing their moral and ethical power in pioneering modern `socially responsible investing. Even before SRI became a more popular investment tool for the public as a whole in the 1990s, religious investors had mobilized their collective resources to counteract corporate power and activities that were deemed morally and socially inappropriate. Faith-based shareholder advocacy began to be used by the US-based ICCR in the early 1970s and has increased substantially since the 1990s, with the use of shareholder resolutions designed to provoke corporations into dialogue on issues such as climate change or human rights. The success of this organization has been emulated in the creation of many other investor governance networks, and the ICCR today remains the central nexus in the promotion of responsible investment in the United States, with similar efforts in Canada, the United Kingdom, and Europe.

To the extent that the global political economy is dominated by neoliberal economic ideas and policies, it is also subject to an ongoing contestation of this hegemony by efforts to re-embed corporate power back into society. Ultimately, the goal of these particular forces—CSR and its key driver, SRI—is to reform neoliberalism, to mitigate its worse effects. Although the influence of faith and religion is often overlooked in this struggle, the analysis in this chapter tells us that there are dynamics at play in the corporate world that should be explored with much greater attention and not ignored.

REFERENCES

Abdelal, Rawi, Mark Blyth, and Craig Parsons. 2010. "Introduction: Constructing the International Economy." In *Constructing the International Economy*, edited by Rawi Abdelal, Mark Blyth, and Craig Parsons, 1–20. Ithaca, NY: Cornell University Press.

Allen, John. 2011. "Vatican to Craft Catholic Sullivan Principles." *National Catholic Reporter*. Last modified March 1, 2011. http://www.ncronline.org/blogs/ncr-today/vatican-craft-catholic-sullivan-principles.

Baue, Bill. 2010. "Is Capitalism Broken? And Could the Corporate Social Responsibility Movement Re-Design It?" *CSR Wire*. Last modified February 16, 2010. http://www.csrwire.com/commentary_detail/1743-Is-Capitalism-Broken-.

BBC. 2015. "Can the Divestment Movement Tame Climate Change?" Last modified June 15, 2015. http://www.bbc.com/news/science-environment-33115298.

Carroll, Archie. 2009. "History of Corporate Social Responsibility." In *The Oxford Handbook of Corporate Social Responsibility*, edited by Andrew Crane, Abagail McWilliams, Dirk Matten, Jeremy Moon, Donald S. Siegel, 19–46. Oxford: Oxford University Press.

CED (Committee for Economic Development). 1971. *Social Responsibilities of Business Corporations*. Arlington, VA: The Conference Board.

Chasan, Emily and Maxwell Murphy. 2015. "Pope Francis Inspires Catholic Investors to Press Environmental Demands." *The Wall Street Journal*. Last modified July 9, 2015. http://www.wsj.com/articles/pope-inspires-catholic-investors-to-press-environmental-concerns-1436434201.

CIG (Church Investors Group). 2014. *The CIG Annual Report*. United Kingdom.

Crouch, Colin. 2011. *The Strange Non-Death of Neoliberalism*. Cambridge, UK: Polity.

Domini, Amy. 2001. *Socially Responsible Investment: Making a Difference and Making Money*. Chicago, IL: Dearborn Trade.

Domini Social Investments. 2007. "Amy Domini Accepts Honorary Degree at Yale Divinity School." Last modified October 10, 2007. https://www.domini.com/why-domini/domini-news/amy-domini-accepts-honorary-degree-yale-divinity-school.

Donadio, Rachel and Laurie Goodstein. 2009. "Pope Urges Forming New World Economic Order to Work for the Common Good." *New York Times*, July 7. Accessed July 24, 2015. http://www.nytimes.com/2009/07/08/world/europe/08pope.html.

Dwyer, Mimi. 2013. "Where Did the Anti-Globalization Movement Go?" *The New Republic*, October 25. Accessed July 20, 2015. http://www.newrepublic.com/article/115360/wto-protests-why-have-they-gotten-smaller/.

Finnemore, Martha and Kathryn Sikkink. 1999. "International Norm Dynamics and Political Change." In *Exploration and Contestation in the Study of World Politics*, edited by Peter Katzenstein, Robert Keohane, and Stephen Krasner, 247–77. Cambridge, MA: MIT Press.

Forbes, Melissa. 2010. "Climate Change, Cars and Catholic Nuns." Unpublished working paper, University of Michigan. Accessed July 15, 2015. http://sitemaker.umich.edu/mesoc/files/forbes_mesocworkshop_09_29_2009.pdf.

Frel, Jan. 2005. "Tis the Season for Shareholder Activism." *Corpwatch*. Last modified May 4, 2005. http://www.corpwatch.org/article.php?id=12195.

Friedman, Milton. 1970. "The Social Responsibility of Business is to Increase Its Profits." *The New York Times Magazine*. September 13, Page SM17.

Fung, Hung-Gay, Sheryl A. Law, and Jot Yau. 2010. *Socially Responsible Investment in a Global Environment*. Cheltenham: Edward Elgar Publishing.

Gjolberg, Maria. 2011. "The Political Economy of Corporate Social Responsibility." PhD diss., University of Oslo.

Glassman, James. 2012. "Five Mutual Funds for Socially Responsible Investors." *Kiplinger*. Last modified May 2012. http://www.kiplinger.com/article/investing/T041-C016-S001-5-mutual-funds-for-socially-responsible-investors.html.

Hawley, Jim and Andrew Williams. 2005. "Shifting Ground: Emerging Global Corporate Governance Standards and the Rise of Fiduciary Capitalism." *Environment and Planning A* 37: 1995–2013.

Kropp, Robert. 2015. "Record Breaking Number of Shareowner Resolutions in 2015." *Social Funds*. Last modified March 21, 2015. http://www.socialfunds.com/news/article.cgi?sfArticleId=4127.

Kurtz, Lloyd. 2008. "Socially Responsible Investment and Shareholder Activism." In *The Oxford Handbook of Corporate Social Responsibility*, edited by Andrew Crane, Abagail McWilliams, Dirk Matten, Jeremy Moon, and Donald S. Siegel, 249–80. Oxford: Oxford University Press.

Lebano, Adele. 2010. "The Concept of Corporate Social Responsibility: A Philosophical Approach." Working Paper No. 508. The Hague, NL: International Institute of Social Studies.

Levy, David and Rami Kaplan. 2008. "Corporate Social Responsibility and Theories of Global Governance: Strategic Contestation in Global Issue Areas." In *The Oxford Handbook of Corporate Social Responsibility*, edited by Andrew Crane, Abagail McWilliams, Dirk Matten, Jeremy Moon, and Donald S. Siegel, 432–51. Oxford: Oxford University Press.

MacLeod, Michael. 2014. "Mobilizing SRI Through Investor Governance Networks: The Politics of Collective Investor Action." In *Socially Responsible Investment in the 21st Century: Does It Make a Difference for Society*, edited by Celine Louche and Tessa Hebb, 23–42. London: Emerald Group Publishing, Critical Studies on Corporate Responsibility, Governance & Sustainability.

May, Steve, George Cheney, and Juliet Roper, eds. 2007. *The Debate Over Corporate Social Responsibility.* Oxford: Oxford University Press.

Matten, Dirk and Jeremy Moon. 2008. "Implicit and Explicit CSR: A Conceptual Framework for a Comparative Understanding of Corporate Social Responsibility." *Academy of Management Review* 33: 404–24.

Moon, Jeremy. 2003. "Socializing Business." *Government and Opposition* 38: 265–73.

Novak, Michael. 1990. *The Spirit of Democratic Capitalism.* Madison, WI: Madison Publishing.

Polanyi, Karl. 1944/2001. *The Great Transformation: The Political and Economic Origins of Our Time,* 2nd edn. Foreword by Joseph E. Stiglitz; introduction by Fred Block. Boston: Beacon Press.

Rheannon, Francesca. 2010. "Caring for the Gift of Creation: Religion and CSR." *CSR Wire.* Last modified October 13, 2010. http://www.csrwire.com/csrlive/commentary_detail/3087-Caring-for-the-Gift-of-Creation-Religion-and-CSR.

Risse, Thomas. 2002. "Transnational Actors and World Politics." In *Handbook of International Relations,* edited by Walter Carlsnaes, Thomas Risse, and Beth Simmons, 255–74. Thousand Oaks, CA: Sage.

Ruggie, John. 1982. "International Regimes, Transactions and Change: Embedded Liberalism in the Postwar Economic Order." *International Organization* 36 (2): 379–415.

Ruggie, John. 2008. *Embedding Global Markets: An Enduring Challenge.* Aldershot, UK: Ashgate.

Savevska, Maja. 2014. "Corporate Social Responsibility: A Promising Social Innovation or a Neoliberal Strategy in Disguise?" *Romanian Journal of European Affairs* 14 (2): 63–80.

SEC. 2013. "Institutional Investors: Power and Responsibility." Speech by Commissioner Luis A. Aguilar, US Securities and Exchange Commission, April 19. Accessed August 9, 2015. http://www.sec.gov/News/Speech/Detail/Speech/1365171515808.

Shamir, Ronen. 2008. "The Age of Responsibilization: On Market-Embedded Morality." *Economy and Society* 37: 1–19.

SHARE (Shareholder Association for Research and Education). 2005. *The Promotion of Active Shareholdership for Corporate Social Responsibility in Canada.* Vancouver, BC (reprint of 1996 original).

Smith, Noah. 2014. "The Dark Side of Globalization: Why Seattle's 1999 Protesters Were Right." *The Atlantic,* January 6. Accessed July 20, 2015. http://www.theatlantic.com/business/archive/2014/01/the-dark-side-of-globalization-why-seattles-1999-protesters-were-right/282831/.

Steurer, Reinhard, Sharon Margula, and Andre Martinuzzi. 2008. "Socially Responsible Investment in EU Member States: Overview of Government Initiatives and SRI Experts' Expectations Towards Governments." Report to the European Commission, Vienna. Accessed July 30, 2015. http://www.sustainability.eu/pdf/csr/

policies/Socially%20Responsible%20Investment%20in%20EU%20Member%20States_Final%20Report.pdf.

Unilever. 2015. *Enhancing Livelihoods, Advancing Human Rights.* Accessed July 1. http://www.unilever.co.kr/Images/sd_Unilever-Human-Rights-Report-29-June-2015_tcm244-429448_tcm109-430270.pdf.

Vallentin, Steen. 2012. "Neoliberalism and CSR: Overcoming Stereotypes and Embracing Ideological Variety." Paper presented at the 28th EGOS Colloquium in Helsinki, Finland, July 2–7.

van Aartsen, Constantijn. 2013. "CSR in Times of Neoliberal Hegemony." LLM Master Thesis, Maastricht University.

van Buren, Harry J. 2005. "Care for People and Creation: The Role of US Christian Institutional Shareholder Activists in Extractive-Industry CSR." *Greener Management International* 52: 77–90.

van Cranenburgh, Katinka, Jennifer Goodman, Celine Louche, and Daniel Arenas. 2012. "Believers in the Boardroom: Religious Organizations and their Shareholder Engagement Practices." Report by 3iG.

Waddock, Sandra. 2009. "Making a Difference? Corporate Responsibility as a Social Movement." *Journal of Corporate Citizenship* 33: 35–46.

Chapter 12

Taxing the Rich

Interfaith Activism in Tanzania's Mining Sector

Aikande Kwayu

Tanzania saw a policy shift from the socialist regime of the 1960s through the late 1980s to the neoliberal regime dominant today. The country adopted the Bretton Woods-instigated Structural Adjustment Programs (SAP), which, in general, have four basic elements: currency devaluation; reduction of the state intervention in the economy; elimination of subsidies in an attempt to reduce expenditures; and trade liberalization (Riddell 1992, 53). One key aspect of this shift was an increase in exports with a specific focus on the mining sector. However, while mining exports increased, the state's revenue from mining did not. This was partly due to tax policies that favored multinational mining companies. The policies included tax incentives and exemptions for new investors, low taxes for existing investors, and low royalties for minerals. The 2012 Annual Report of Tanzania's Controller and Auditor General (2013, 65) stated: "Tax exemptions are a necessary tool for investment promotion and economic growth." Ironically, the Bretton Woods institutions came to observe that tax exemptions in developing countries often lead to a "race to the bottom" as a result of the fear that if they do not grant them to multinationals, they will simply go to neighboring countries (IMF, OECD, UN and World Bank 2011, 24). Tax policies in Tanzania, in addition to tax exemptions, have loopholes that allow tax evasion and avoidance leading to significant illicit financial flows. It is estimated that Tanzania loses around US $1.87 billion in tax revenues every year. Global Financial Integrity, a USA-based think-tank, reported that illicit flows from Tanzania totaled US $18.73 billion from 2002 to 2011. All these have led to a low tax revenue base contributing to the government's inability to provide public services.

The changes in policies from socialist to neoliberal are also reflected in the gradual but institutional changes in mining policies from the 1980s to the 2000s. The chronology of the evolution of mining policies, which will be presented in a later section, is a manifestation of policy changes in Tanzania. These policy changes led to a mixed impact of high economic growth of 7% average over a decade after the millennium with persistent poverty levels stagnating at over 30% of the population in the same period. That rang an alarm bell in the ears of civil society. Beginning in 2000, we see increased activism and policy advocacy in the country. Policy Forum (see www.policyforum-tz.org), an umbrella organization that brings together about hundred civil society organizations in the country was, for example, established in 2002 with the specific aim of increasing informed civil society participation in decisions and actions that determine how policies affect ordinary Tanzanians, particularly the most disadvantaged (Policy Forum 2015). Faith institutions are among the civil society organizations in the country that are actively and specifically involved in advocating against mining policies in Tanzania that do not benefit the poor. In 2002, an interfaith initiative known as Interfaith Standing Committee on Economic Justice and Integrity of Creation (ISCJIC) commissioned a landmark study on the effect of tax exemptions on mining companies in the country. This Committee, which includes members from the Protestant Churches, the Catholic Church, and Muslim groups, was the beginning of a continuous effort by the group to advocate against unfair tax policies that favor the few rich at the cost of the many poor. In light of this interesting initiative and for the purposes of understanding the place of the varied roles of religion and religious groups in neoliberalism, this chapter analyzes the specific activism by the Committee by examining how it has framed (Keck and Sikkink 1999) its argument against neoliberal policies. It demonstrates how the Committee came to be the most organized and effective opposition to the neoliberal mining regime in Tanzania and how it managed to frame and present an effective critique of these negative policies over the last few years.

To this end, the next section of the chapter provides the policy context by explaining the change from socialist to liberal policies in Tanzania. Following that, the chapter looks at the evolution of mining policies that, as will be noted, reflected the nascent neoliberal policies in the country. In doing so, the chapter examines the impact of these policies, which led to an outcry from civil society. It goes on to explore and examine the role of faith institutions as part of civil society by analyzing advocacy roles played by, in particular, the ISCJIC.

THE SOCIALIST (UJAMAA) POLICIES IN TANZANIA

In 1967, under the leadership of President Julius Nyerere, Tanzania launched the Arusha Declaration, which institutionalized socialist policies in the country. The policies were customized to the Tanzanian context. Collectively known as *Ujamaa*, these policies promoted self-reliance and unity among other socialist policies that fought against what Nyerere called the exploitation of man by man. While the policies had a significant economic impact, they more closely resembled social-political policies that influenced social relations in Tanzania, arguably, more than economic policies. Peace and stability in Tanzania are largely attributed to its Ujamaa policies. Tanzania is an island of peace surrounded by chaotic neighbors because of the ideals that were formed and embedded in the implementation of Ujamaa policies (Erickson 2012). Some scholars have argued that Tanzania created peace and stability at the cost of its economy (Scott 1999; Johnson 2000), but the country managed to provide universal primary education during the formative years of Ujamaa policies. According to the Organization of Economic Co-operation and Development (OECD 2008), between 1962 and the 1980s, in keeping with its socialist goals of self-reliance, the Tanzanian government vigorously pursued a universal primary education program with some remarkable results. According to Lewis (2007), "the schools were reorganized as economic, social, and educational communities that practiced self-reliance" (50). The gross enrollment rate in primary education rose from 35% in the late 1960s to around 98% in the 1980s (OECD 2008). This one example of the ability to provide universal access to primary school indicates that Ujamaa policies were not entirely responsible for the economic misperformance in Tanzania. Other factors such as huge external debts and the subsequent cumulative high interest rates burden—the Volcker Shock (Klein 2007)—have more explanatory power to account for the economic failure in the country than the Ujamaa policies that were meant to enhance self-reliance.

THE EMERGENCE OF NEOLIBERALISM IN TANZANIA

The adoption of the SAP in the mid-1980s and the subsequent liberalization policies saw a steady increase in economic growth. This was due to increased foreign direct investment, expansion of service industries (finance and banking), and tourism. The peak was in the 2000s, when the economic growth rate average was 7% from 2001 to 2011 (URT 2011). However, the poverty rate only declined from 35% to 33% in the same period (URT 2011). The situation is a paradox reflected in the increasing inequality vividly evident in Tanzania. For many activists, this is an unfortunate and unacceptable situation in a country that possesses the third largest gold mining sector in Africa, oil and gas reserves, and wildlife and game reserves that are world wonders. However, the paradox should not be a surprise in a neoliberal economic system. Inequality resulting from high economic growth amidst persistent poverty is becoming an increasingly known quality of neoliberalism. Brubaker and Mshana (2010) have argued:

> In the present world economic system there is not much need for many people's contributions. Both the labour power and the purchasing power parity of the world's underclass seem to be dispensable. Since 1980–1990 inequality has increased at a very high rate. Presently all domestic and international statistical indices of inequality are much higher than before the beginning of 1989. From that year until the world economic crisis of 2008-2009, the world went through a period of high growth. However, the proceeds were not used to reduce poverty, lessen inequality or sustain ecology. (24–25)

Neoliberalism's main argument that the free market encourages efficiency, and hence economic growth, does not address its weakness or failure to create jobs. Stiglitz (2013) in his latest book *Price of Inequality* argues that "unemployment—the inability of the market to generate jobs for so many citizens—is the worst failure of the market, the greatest source of inefficiency, and a major cause of inequality" (xii). Failure to create employment for youth in Tanzania as well as the lack of pro-poor growth policies has partly led to the increased levels of inequality. How this inequality came about can be studied by taking a closer look at the mining sector that is very important for Tanzania. The section below presents the chronology and evolution of these policies. The presentation reveals the move from strict protectionist policies to gradual favorable low-tax policies under neoliberalism that have attracted multinational mining companies.

EVOLUTION OF MINING POLICY IN TANZANIA

Mining policy and legislation in Tanzania can be traced to the early years of British colonial rule. In 1929, the British colonial government in Tanganyika (the former name for Tanzania before the 1964 union with Zanzibar Island) passed a Mining Ordinance. This, according to Bryceson and Jonsson (2014), provided an opportunity for small-scale miners to acquire prospecting rights. Bryceson and Jonsson continue to argue that gold export in Tanganyika rose to four tonnes in 1938, making it the largest contributor to the colonial territory's economy as it contributed to almost 20% of export earnings (Bryceson and Jonsson 2014, 13). In the 1940s, large deposits of diamonds were discovered in Mwadui, Tanganyika, by a geologist named John Williamson who subsequently founded Williamson Diamond Mining that started operations soon after. By the 1950s, diamonds contributed to 3% of the GDP and 15% of export earnings (Bryceson and Jonsson 2014, 13). In 1961, Tanganyika gained independence. Nyerere was optimistic about the country's development based on the three-year development plan (1961–1964) he had set up. The failure of this plan, partly as a result of inadequate foreign assistance (Coulson 1982) and other tensions of international politics of the time, turned Nyerere toward the left politically in the interests of making Tanzania self-reliant. This, in turn, led to the Arusha Declaration of 1967 explained above.

Within the context of the Declaration, Nyerere sought to preserve natural resources until the time when Tanzanians were ready, in terms of capacity, to harness those resources. Nyerere stated: "We will leave our mineral wealth in the ground until we manage to develop our own geologists and mining engineers" (cited in Chachage 2010, 4; Bryceson and Jonsson 2014, 13). The focus was thus on increasing agricultural production. However, with the stagnant economic growth of the 1970s attributed to the global oil crisis and other factors including the war between Tanzania and Uganda in 1978, the country had to look for remedies, of which mining was an option. Thus, the country reviewed its mining policies and legislation, and the *Mining Act* was passed in 1979. This Act allowed Tanzanians to register mining claims in areas designated for prospecting mining activities that did not require large investment expenditures and specialized equipment (Bryceson and Jonsson 2014). This expanded the sector. However, there was still more potential for an effective mining industry. Thus we see the development of the mining policy known as *The National Mineral Policy* in 1983. This policy outlined the procedure for granting investors mining rights (Kulindwa et al. 2003).

At the same time, the country was also facing enormous external pressure from the World Bank and IMF to reform its economic policies via SAP as Tanzania's public debt had increased as a result of the Volcker shock, and the country was faced with a debt crisis. Eventually, in 1985, Tanzania bowed to the pressure and adopted the SAPs. Upon the adoption of these reforms, Nyerere voluntarily left office, giving way to another president, Ali Hassan Mwinyi, to take over and implement the reforms. From then on and throughout the 1990s, the country passed significant legislation and amendments to accommodate the reforms. This legislation was both economic and political. Political reforms included the change from a one-party system to a multi-party system. Economically, the country adopted liberalization policies in accordance with the SAPs whereby foreign direct investment was invited and privatization of the public enterprises encouraged. Following this, another Mining Act was passed in 1998. Kulindwa et al. (2003) argue that this Act paved the way for foreign mining investment. There were also political efforts to invite and encourage investors. President Benjamin Mkapa warmly extended his invitation in 2001: "I invite you to Tanzania. Let us forge a profitable and smart partnership—we, in Tanzania with our mineral resources and you, with your capital, technology, know-how and managerial skills" (quoted in Lange 2006, 1). Indeed, the investors accepted the invitation; the World

Bank reported that mineral exports in Tanzania increased from less than 1% of export revenue in 1990 to 50% in 2005 (Bryceson and Jonsson 2014). Data from Tanzania's Ministry of Energy and Minerals show that from 1997 to 2007, a total of 6,478 licenses were given for primary prospecting and prospecting; 10,637 licenses for mining; and 1,064 licenses for trading minerals (Bomani Report 2008). However, while the mining sector boomed, benefits to the citizens and the country in general were minimal. Chachage (1995) provides the statistics of this gloomy situation. In 2004, for example, gold exports were worth US $593.2 million but the government collection of revenues in the form of royalties and taxes was only about US $27 million. This was a puzzle that could only be explained by the nature of neoliberalism, whereby economic growth does not necessarily correlate with poverty reduction. Those with capital benefit more than those that are without, and as gathered from President Mkapa's statement cited above, it is the investors who have capital. In neoliberalism, as has been well expounded by Piketty (2014), inequality is created because of the fact that returns on capital are larger than the returns on labor. This is partly because capital owners are given policy preferences that ensure maximum profit at the expense of the general public. Such policy preferences include tax exemptions, as has been the case in Tanzania where mining companies enjoyed tax incentives from the government.

Tax Incentives to Mining Companies

The paradox in relation to the mining boom and the persistence of poverty was attributed to the tax incentives given to foreign companies including mining companies. In total, overall tax exemptions in Tanzania went from Tanzanian Shillings (TShs.) 201 billion in the first half of the 2000s, to a record high of TShs. 1.8 trillion in 2011–2012 (CRC Sogema 2013, 25). By 2011–2012, according to the Tanzania Revenue Authority (TRA) estimations, tax exemptions were approximately 4.4% of the country's GDP (CRC Sogema 2013, 26). The 2010–2011 data show that there were many beneficiaries of these tax exemptions including the mining companies in the top five. The mining companies benefited from 11% of the overall tax exemptions in the country (CRC Sogema 2013, 33). Following these tax exemptions and policies favorable to the mining sector, the country itself benefited very little from the generous wealth created by multinational companies extracting minerals in the country. Neoliberal advocates praised the system. For example, McDonald and Roe (2007) pointed out:

> Since 2001, annual gold production has continued to grow rapidly and now routinely exceeds one million ounces per annum. This impressive upsurge in mining activity means that the sector now accounts for over 40% of the

country's exports, around 75% of its foreign direct investment (FDI) (some $300 million annually in recent years as against total FDI of only around $10 million per annum a decade earlier) and a rising share of government tax revenues (currently 3.6%) and GDP (currently around 3.2%). (7)

Such arguments are a puzzle because if the mining sector accounted for 40% of the country's exports and 75% of foreign income earnings, why did it contribute to only 3.2% of the GDP? Such differences showed how mining production had little impact on the country's GDP. This led to a public outcry and advocacy activism led by civil society including faith institutions.

FAITH INSTITUTIONS AGAINST NEOLIBERAL POLICIES IN TANZANIA

Because of persistent poverty and increased inequality amidst enormous wealth creation in the mining sector, faith institutions found themselves in an urgent situation to provide services. Since Independence in 1961, faith institutions have been at the forefront in the fight against poverty by providing education and health services. For this reason, faith institutions have had close relations with the government over the years. During the Ujamaa period, the relations between the government and faith communities were very good because the principles of Ujamaa were compatible with the values of faith communities.

Whereas the non-religious civil society organizations were either suppressed or incorporated into the ruling party (de-factor and de-jure), religious organizations were silent, partly because some of the basic principles of the ideology of the day (Ujamaa and Self-Reliance) and related policies were more or less similar to religious principles such as those of equality, humility and the spirit of sharing. (Mukandala et al. 2006, 341)

In the wake of the failure of Ujamaa policies and the adoption of the liberalization policies, faith groups were set aback by the persistent poverty and increased inequality. With their active presence in the fight against poverty, the religious groups came to understand the structural factors that perpetuate poverty amidst economic growth. These include policies that encourage economic growth but with insignificant effect on poverty reduction. Such has been the situation in Tanzania, where economic growth has been on the rise but with no effect on the majority of its people who live below the poverty line. In light of this, the three main religious representative bodies in Tanzania including the Christian Council of Tanzania (CCT), the Tanzania Episcopal Church (TEC), and the Muslim Council of Tanzania/Baraza la Waislamu

Tanzania (BAKWATA) came together in 2008 and formed an *Interfaith Standing Committee on Economic Justice and Integrity of Creation* (ISCJIC) to fight against the unfair neoliberal policies.

The Interfaith Standing Committee on Economic Justice and Integrity of Creation (ISCJIC)

The ISCJIC is a body formed by the three main faith bodies in Tanzania mentioned above. The CCT represents twenty "traditional" Protestant churches including the Lutheran Church, Anglican Church, and Mennonite Church, among others. The TEC represents the Catholic Church, the single biggest denomination in Tanzania in terms of population and believers. The National Muslim Council of Tanzania (BAKWATA) is the mainstream body that represents Muslims, who belong to Shia, Sunni, and Sufi divisions, in Tanzania. It has been pointed out that two of these bodies, CCT and BAKWATA, were established with the help of the government in the immediate postindependent era. Olsson (2011) argues that Ujamaa policies managed to disarm unwanted religiopolitical mobilization and effectively incorporated religious organizations and religious values into the national project. Here Olsson (2011) concurs with Westerlund's (1980) argument that the government did this in two main ways: first, by directing unwanted, primarily Muslim, religious institutions not to mix politics and religion and second, by encouraging, primarily Christian, mission churches to play their part in developing the nation. As a result of this control, the religious institutions that were established during the initial years of Ujamaa policies are still well connected to the state and they, arguably, carry with them political authority.

Moreover, Liviga argues that "religion played a major role in Tanzania's quest to build a socialist society in the 60s and 70s. The two major religions in the country—Islam and Christianity—did not oppose the Ujamaa ideology and in fact supported it by encouraging their followers to obey government orders" (cited in Mukandala et al. 2006, 329). The government was thus instrumental in institutionalizing this allegiance by assisting in the establishment of religious bodies, which acted as representatives of followers. Both CCT and BAKWATA were established during the administration of Nyerere. As a result, some believers, in particular Muslims, do not pay allegiance to BAKWATA as they consider it more political and a government body more than an Islamic body. On the other hand, as Olsson (2011) observes, BAKWATA argues that Muslim alternative groups such as BARAZA KUU (The Supreme Council of Islamic Organizations) and other groups such as UAMSHO (a perceived radical Muslim group that considers BAKWATA as illegitimate because of its close ties with the government) should not be allowed to exist when BAKWATA is the only legitimate representative of Muslims in Tanzania. He further observes that representatives from BAKWATA, CCT, and TEC describe alternative Muslim and Christian groups in terms of religious fundamentalists whose actions are a threat to the nation's sociopolitical stability (Olsson 2011). In this, he maintains that BARAZA KUU, which was founded in direct opposition to BAKWATA, sees it as the Muslim wing of the ruling Chama Cha Mapinduzi government, controlled by the influential Catholic and Protestant organizations and CCT (Olsson 2011). Knowledge of the origins of these three bodies and their historical connection to the state helps explain why they are the only three bodies forming an interfaith committee on such a crucial economic matter.

The section below discusses advocacy initiatives carried out by the ISCJIC in regard to mining. Here attention focuses on two published studies commissioned by the committee. These are *A Golden Opportunity*, published in 2008, and *The One Billion Dollar Question*, published in 2012; other advocacy initiatives are also studied (e.g., the criticism of Canadian mining companies). This is followed by a critical analysis of each publication. Specifically examined is the advocacy strategy used by the Committee and how it framed its message against neoliberal policies in the mining sector of Tanzania. Keck and Sikkink (1999) explain that framing is a way of presenting issues to make them comprehensible to the target audience, to attract attention and encourage action. Similarly, McAdam, McCarth, and Zald (1996) define framing as "conscious strategic efforts by groups of people to fashion shared understandings of the world and themselves that legitimate and motivate collective action" (6). The Committee commissioned studies to determine and identify the negative impact of mining sector tax exemptions to the country's economy. The studies were part of a framing strategy, as they not only provided scientific arguments for advocacy but also justified and provided legitimacy to the proposed changes.

ADVOCACY INITIATIVES CARRIED OUT BY ISCJIC

Advocacy initiatives are efforts carried out with the aim of influencing (mostly improving) policies (Hudson 2001; Edwards 1993; Bryer and Magrath 1999). There are many ways to carry out advocacy. These include undertaking studies and publishing their findings, lobbying policymakers, training, policy analysis, and campaigning for certain policies. The ISCJIC uses many of these ways when trying to improve policies. In the case of mining, it has so far commissioned two studies. These studies were financed by the Norwegian Church Aid (NCA) and carried out by independent consultants. The findings and publications were well publicized in various websites including the

Policy Forum and in a number of newspapers in the country. In addition to the studies, as noted earlier, the Committee carried out other advocacy activities. One key example was the criticism of Canadian mining companies.

Canadian Extractive Industries in Tanzania

In November 2009, ISCJIC delivered a press statement titled *The Negative Impacts of Canadian Extractive Industry Operating in Tanzania*. The statement highlighted the general paradoxical problem of being rich in resources, yet experiencing rising poverty levels. Specifically, the statement touched on the issue of local communities that were removed from their land to give way to the mining operations of Canadian mining companies in Geita town located in the Lake Victoria Zone of Tanzania. The removal was accompanied by severe human rights abuses such as forced evictions from ancestral and traditional lands without adequate compensations. The Committee's statement then highlighted another paradox of the difference between values espoused by the Canadian government such as being a true friend and development partner of Tanzania, on the one hand, and the practices of its companies, on the other hand. As the statement noted, in areas where the Canadian extractive industries are located in Tanzania, there is not any visible development (ISCJIC 2009). The statement called on the government of Canada to uphold its values by, first, developing transparent, inclusive, and human welfare-centered policies to govern the extractive industry from Canada in other countries; second, by instructing the Canadian extractive industries to adopt the public participatory strategy; and, lastly, by supporting the governments in Africa to have sustainable and development-oriented policies for all partnering countries in the extractive industry.

The Committee took the issue of the removal of the residents of Geita town very seriously and followed up with the local district officials who confirmed that the mining company gave the communities US $400,000 for compensation. The Committee found out that the company had paid US $1.2 million to the government for compensation. The ISCJIC followed up to ensure that the communities were being compensated (Munga 2012). In addition, other initiatives taken by the Committee members included media publications at both the international and local levels. For instance, in 2012, Bishop Stephan Munga, the then ISCJIC chairman, wrote a moving article in the internationally renowned global development blog for the Guardian (United Kingdom) about the importance of transparency in mining (Munga 2012). Bishop Munga is also a member of the Tanzania branch of the Extractive Industry Transparency International (EITI). Its website asserts that EITI is the global standard promoting open and accountable management of natural resources. It seeks to strengthen government and company systems, inform public debate, and enhance trust. It is supported by a coalition of governments, companies, and civil society working together. In addition to media and publicity, the Committee also partners with international NGOs such as Tearfund (Unearth the Truth Campaign) in carrying out advocacy at the international level.

The Role of Naming, Shaming, and Framing Strategies

The Committee thus engages with networks beyond the Tanzanian border in "framing and shaming" strategies that have the potential for a *boomerang* effect as described by Keck and Sikkink (1999; see also Gready 2004). In advocacy studies, *boomerang* refers to the setting in motion of a process of mutually re-enforcing internal and external legitimacy and pressure (Gready 2004). More specifically, Keck and Sikkink describe how national NGOs facing a repressive and unresponsive government "bypass their state and directly search out international allies to try to bring pressure on their states from outside. This is most obviously the case in human rights campaigns" (quoted in Gready 2004, 346). For example, the membership of Bishop Munga in EITI is an example of the boomerang effect of the Committee's advocacy work, as EITI also exerted pressure on the Tanzanian state. Thus, boomerang effects characterize the work of transnational advocacy networks in assisting NGOs in Tanzania to get their messages through to their own states. They do so through advocacy work beyond the state level in international forums and through international organizations, which put pressure on domestic governments that are thus "framed, named and shamed" internationally. This is also an example of how corporate social responsibility activism as described in the chapter by MacLeod can be made more effective in the Global South. As he outlines in his chapter, religious activists may be more effective in this context as they enjoy a broader credibility and moral authority. Besides these advocacy activities, two studies of the Committee on the mining sector, *A Golden Opportunity* and *The One Billion Dollar Question*, were the most thorough and influential in the country. The sections below discuss each of these publications.

Report from 2008: *A Golden Opportunity*

This report from 2008 looks at two dimensions of mining issues: the economic dimension and the ethical situation. It examines the failure of mining corporations to contribute to the country's economy. This can be seen in the fact that between 1997 and 2005, Tanzania exported gold worth more than US $2.54 billion but the country only received US $28 million a year from royalties and taxes. The country thus lost at least US $265.5 million through low royalty rates, government tax concessions, and tax evasion. These negative impacts in economic terms were the consequences of low tax revenue brought about by the 1998 Mining Act, which led to low tax rates for foreign investors, and minimal governmental and popular democratic scrutiny with regard to corruption. The report argues that because of the World Bank–supported economic reforms, the country offered a number of tax incentives to mining companies. Among the incentives offered was a 3% royalty on gold exports, the ability of mining companies to offset 100% of their capital expenditure (i.e., mining equipment and property) against tax in the year in which it is spent, and low taxes on imports of mining equipment. These reforms were a continuation of structural adjustment policies discussed in earlier sections of this chapter. The Mining Act of 1998 further consolidated these incentives.

A second problem is the prioritization of large-scale mining that has come at the expense of small-scale artisan miners. The issue of unemployment is worth noting here. The report notes that six major gold mines in Tanzania employ a total of 7,135 people. This is a relatively low number and reflects the fact that most of the small-scale artisanal miners lost their jobs when these mining companies came in. In this respect, the report observes that in the 1990s, there were 500,000 to 1.1 million small-scale artisan miners, but in 2006, there were only 170,000. The report shows that people in gold mining areas are barely benefiting from the increase in foreign direct investment. This fact further highlights the negative impact of neoliberal policies and what Stiglitz calls the failure of markets to provide employment (Stiglitz 2013). Another important observation noted in the report is the disparity between the pay Tanzanians employees in mining receive and that of the CEO. It is reported that the Tanzanian miner received between US $128 and US $240 per month while the CEO of Barrick Gold received US $9.4 million per year in 2006.

Generally, the report observed that minerals account for nearly half of the country's exports and the country is the third largest gold producer in Africa after South Africa and Ghana. It then asks where the mineral wealth is going. This is the complex question that defies simplistic answers. However, it is a relevant and urgent question for policymakers and Tanzanians if the country wants to fight poverty seriously. It is thus obvious that the economic reforms that embraced neoliberalism in the country have proven to be ineffective in fighting poverty. The GDP growth at 7% over the last few years has only benefited the few elites at the cost of the majority, thus leading to rising inequality. Based on the observation, the report recommended amendment of the mining law and stopping the signing of new contracts until this is done. It furthermore demanded that gold mining companies should declare and make publicly available information on how much they make and the taxes they pay and other remittances. Lastly, Tanzania should join the EITI.

It is noteworthy that the first and the third recommendations above were taken into consideration and were implemented as has already been high-lighted above: the country joined EITI and in 2010, a new Mining Act was passed. The new Mining Act brought with it changes in taxes. The tax exemptions went down to 8% in the year 2011–2012 (CRC Sogema 2013, 33), reflecting the impact of the new legislation. However, the fact that the ISCJIC engaged in another study and published its finding in 2012 is an indication that despite the above changes, there was need for continuing advocacy work. The 2012 study was titled *The One Billion Dollar Question: How Can Tanzania Stop Losing So Much Tax Revenue?* The section below summarizes this publication.

Report from 2012: *The One Billion Dollar Question*

The aim of this study was to establish the magnitude of tax revenue losses in Tanzania and to recommend measures to minimize such losses. The report shows that in 2009–2010, Tanzania collected US $2.8 billion in taxes. It argues that exemptions to corporations have deprived Tanzania of average TZS 458.6 billion (US $288 million) a year between 2008–2009 and 2010–2011. It particularly notes that mining companies pay around US $100 million a year, which is less than 7% of the value of mineral exports. It then argues that the taxes are low because of tax incentives. The report further observes that employees of the companies rather than the companies pay 65% of mining taxes. Furthermore, it argues that illicit capital flow from Tanzania ranges from US $94 milion to US $660 million a year and losses from trade mispricing equal US $109–US $127 million a year. In terms of tax revenue losses, the illicit flow could cost the Tanzanian government up to US $300 million a year. In light of the above, the report recommended, first, the removal of tax incentives; second, the provision of a publicly available tax expenditure analysis that would look at the "transfer of public resources that is achieved by reducing tax obligations . . . There are five types of tax expenditures, which are tax exemptions, tax deductions (allowances), tax deferrals, tax relief, and tax credits" (CRC Sogoma 2013); third, a review of the Mining Act (2010) and renegotiation of the terms of all mining agreements; and fourth, a fair tax on the oil and gas sector. It concluded by calling for more open government.

The above recommendations indicate a coherent follow-up from the 2008 report. Some of the recommendations in 2008 were implemented by the government; yet there was still room for improvement. For example, the 2008 report recommended a need for a Mining Act, which was enacted in 2010. However, the 2012 report saw the need for reviewing the Act for improvements. The country was still losing too much revenue from mining. It is also important to note that there have been calls from different groups including opposition members of Parliament to cut off or at least to reduce tax incentives. In 2013, for example, Zitto Kabwe, the then chairman of the Parliamentary Committee on Public Accounts and shadow finance minister, highlighted the gloomy fact that the amount of tax exemptions given by the Tanzanian government, US $1.1. billion, equals the amount that Tanzania borrowed from China to build a 500 km gas pipeline (Manson 2013).

ANALYSIS OF ADVOCACY INITIATIVES
IN TANZANIA AND THEIR LIMITS

It is evident that advocacy initiatives carried out by the ISCJIC have been successful. Although it is difficult to measure exactly the influence of their contribution toward creating awareness of revenue loss out of mining, it is evident that some of the recommendations they made in the first report in 2008 were taken into consideration and were implemented by the government, such as joining the EITI and reviewing the Mining Act. This shows that the government is apparently listening to those calls and since 2013, it has also promised to work on reducing the tax exemptions. In the financial year 2013–2014 Budget Speech, the Minister of Finance stated that the government would review the Tanzania Investment Act Section 38. This was in order to reduce tax exemptions for deemed capital goods and to continue enhancing the capacity of government officials to curb tax evasion and avoidance by big companies, especially in the communication, minerals, and gas sectors including transfer pricing (Policy Forum 2013). Following this, in October 2014, the Government signed a contract with mining companies to set new terms for royalty rates and payments (Binala 2014).

It is important to note that these initiatives by the religious activists were a contribution to similar efforts by other civil society organizations such as the Policy Forum, which as discussed earlier, is an umbrella organization for 100 civil societies in Tanzania. This enormous civil society activism from both secular and religious forces was thus able to bring to the fore the huge loss of revenue to the country from the mining sector as one factor that explains the persistent poverty amidst economic growth. In framing poverty in Tanzania as a result of misguided policy, the activists also provided obvious solutions to the problem. In this context, it stands out that the ISCJIC has not relied only on its moral authority but also undertaken evidence-based advocacy. It went beyond rhetoric and carried out research. Such evidence-based strategies are crucial in framing as they ensure legitimacy in the eyes of the public and the targeted audience. The two studies used experts who analyzed technical data and presented their findings in a way that was comprehensible to the general public. The reports were also updated on the basis of changes in terms of policy. For example, the 2008 report has a second edition, which reflects the findings of the Bomani Commission, which was set up in 2008 by the president to review mining policies and advise the government on the mining sector.

That said, it does not mean that advocacy initiatives have only been received positively. On the contrary, there have also been several difficulties. Advocating against mining is a direct counterattack to some of the donor countries with political and financial influence in Tanzania. The multinationals operating in Tanzania belong to countries that provide foreign aid and fund development projects. For example, Barrick Gold is a Canadian company and the government of Canada provides significant funding toward development in Tanzania. In fact, the Canadian government has been criticized for tying development aid to mining in developing countries (Brown 2013). Aid is used as a commercial and public relations instrument by mining companies in developing countries (Brown 2013). This insensitivity and double standard of the Canadian government and its mining industry was displayed when it stopped funding some of the development projects undertaken by CTT because of CCT's advocacy initiatives against Barrick operations in Tanzania. In turn, the advocacy initiatives themselves are also funded by foreign donor countries, which might also have certain interests as their companies are also operating in Tanzania. For example, the 2012 study and report were funded by the NCA, which receives most of its funds from the Norwegian government that also owns Statoil. Statoil has operations in Tanzania's gas and oil industry. Having said that, it is crucial to note that it is impossible to carry out advocacy work in a vacuum. Advocacy is about engagement and interaction toward better policies. It is thus important for the ISCJIC to use the boomerang effect and to work with foreign governments and NGOs with a similar mindset toward good policy development that will ensure the trickling down of mining wealth to everyone in Tanzania.

WHERE TO GO FROM HERE

It is arguably the case that there are many factors that have pressured the government toward a hard stance on tax exemptions. The advocacy efforts by faith groups as well as other groups in the society have played a significant role in raising awareness, but other factors such as problems with donors in a situation of desperate dependency have also awakened the government. In late 2014, the donor community, which includes embassies of the OECD countries and representatives of multilateral organizations including the European Union and World Bank in Tanzania, froze some of their budget support because of corruption cases in the country. Such shocks in the government's face turn out to be a disciplining whip for the government to look into other sustainable and independent ways of raising fiscal revenue. Nevertheless, there is more to do. In reacting to the agreement between the government and mining companies, Zitto Kabwe (2014) noted in his blog:

> As a country we still generate peanuts from mining sector. With mineral exports valuing US $1.7 billions, revenues (royalty, taxes and other levies) to government coffers averages only $150 millions. The largest sources of revenues are royalty and employees taxes. We must think outside the box and introduce fiscal measures that maximizes government revenues without negatively impacting investments.

But it is not only the government that needs to improve the way it operates. There are also areas in which faith institutions and, in particular, the ISCJIC could improve their advocacy work. First of all, the ISCJIC needs to step up mobilization of its believers or followers. The three faith institutions (CCT, TEC, and BAKWATA) that make up the ISCIJC have the largest number of followers in the country. In fact, they command the majority of the population. If the believers get to know the work of this committee, they might be able to exert more pressure on the government to adopt fair policies. It is for this reason that the ISCJIC needs to publish their reports in Kiswahili also. Both of the reports are published only in English, thus making it harder for the majority of Tanzanian citizens to read them. Third, more open advocacy needs to be carried out through media such as TV, radio programs, and social media networks including Twitter, Facebook, Instagram, and blogs. Lastly, the ISCJIC might benefit from forming a coalition with other partners in the same fight such as members of parliament and other civil society organizations. The ISCJIC needs to follow the example of the Jubilee Debt Campaign, which involved not only churches and faith-based institutions but also citizens, civil society organizations, parliamentarians, and media companies (see Shawki 2000). Nevertheless, it needs to be emphasized that interfaith initiatives in Tanzania have come to be respected as key to addressing some of the main problems in the country. It is impressive to see that different faiths have managed to come together in the fight against neoliberal policies in Tanzania. Such initiatives must be supported and continued in order to improve the situations of the many in Tanzania who have been excluded from the benefits of the global economy.

CONCLUSION

This chapter has highlighted the impact of neoliberal policies in Tanzania with regard to the mining sector. With the adoption of the liberalization policies, Tanzania experienced a paradox. There was increased exploration and export of mining with huge earnings and subsequent GDP growth, but it was accompanied by persistent poverty. Between 2000 and 2010, the country's GDP growth was 7% on average while poverty declined only by 2%. Today, 33% percent of Tanzanians still live in poverty.

The adoption of neoliberal policies in Tanzania was a critical departure from the socialist policies (Ujamaa) launched during the 1967 Arusha Declaration. These advocated for equality, universal access to education, and other social welfare policies. In this, the policies were compatible with the values of faith institutions in the country. During the Ujamaa period, the relationship between the government and faith groups, particularly CCT and BAKWATA, was very cordial. As we saw above, these faith institutions encouraged their believers to be loyal to the government. As a result, there is a perception that the two faith institutions were government-established. This is also due to their continued relationship with the government and the insurgence of "radical" religious groups that do not necessarily agree with the mainstream groups represented by CCT and BAKWATA. Nevertheless, the interfaith council was able to intervene effectively in the public debate on poverty amidst economic growth and wealth for a small minority. As this chapter has shown, their advocacy initiative led to improved policy and to a "reformed" neoliberalism, even though there were certainly other factors involved as well that account for the change in the policy of the government toward the mining companies. Nevertheless, the fact that there were domestic actors criticizing the government for its negligence provided one crucial impetus for change in the mining policies.

REFERENCES

Binala, Jaston. 2014. "Tanzania Seals New Tax Deal with Mining Firms." *The East African*, October 11. Accessed August 20, 2015. http://www.theeast-african.co.ke/news/Tanzania-seals-new-tax-deal-with-miners-drops-15pc-waiver-/-/2558/2483144/-/8xnhsjz/-/index.html.

Brown, Stephen. 2013. "Undermining Foreign Aid: The Extractive Sector and the Commercialization of Canadian Development Assistance." *Open Canada*, September 16. Accessed August 20, 2015. http://opencanada.org/features/undermining-foreign-aid/.

Brubaker, Pamela and Mshana Rogate, eds. 2010. *Justice Not Greed*. Geneva: WCC Publications.

Bryceson, Deborah Fahy, Eleanor Fisher, Jasper Jonsson Bosse, and Rosemarie Mwaipopo, eds. 2014. *Mining and Social Transforming in Africa: Mineralizing and Democratizing Trends in Artisanal Production*. New York: Routledge.

Chachage, Chambi. 2010. "Mwalimu in our Popular Imagination: The Relevance of Nyerere Today." In *Africa's Liberation: The Legacy of Nyerere*, edited by Cassam A. and Chachage Chambi, 3–6. Oxford: Pambazuka Press.

Chachage Seithy, Loth. 1995. "The Meek shall Inherit the Earth but not the Mining Rights: Mining and Accumulation in Tanzania." In *Liberalised Development in Tanzania*, edited by Gibbon Peter, 37–108. Uppsala: Nordic Africa Institute.

Controller and Auditor General (CAG). 2013. *Annual General Report of the Controller and Auditor General on the Final Statements of the Central Government for the Year Ended 30th June, 2012.* Dar-es-Salaam: National Audit Office.

Coulson, Andrew. 1982. *Tanzania: A Political Economy.* Oxford: Clarendon Press.

CRC Sogema Inc. 2013. *Tanzania Per Tax Exemption Study, Proposed to the Ministry of Finance of Tanzania.*

Curtis, Mark and Lissu Tundu. 2008. *A Golden Opportunity: How Tanzania is Failing to Benefit from Gold Mining.* Dar-es-Salaam: CCT, BAKWATA, and TEC.

Curtis, Mark and Ngowi Prosper. 2012. *The One Billion Dollar Question: How Can Tanzania Stop Losing So Much Tax Revenue?* Dar-es-Salaam: CCT, BAKWATA, and TEC.

Erickson, Alicia. 2012. "Peace in Tanzania: An Island of Stability in Sub-Saharan Africa." *Research Discourse* 3 (1): 18–31.

Gready, Paul. 2004. "Conceptualising Globalization and Human Rights: Boomerangs and Borders." *The International Journal of Human Rights* 8 (3): 345–54.

ISCJIC. 2009. "The Negative Impacts of Canadian Extractive Industry Operating in Tanzania." *Press Statement.* Accessed August 20, 2015. http://www.miningwatch.ca/sites/www.miningwatch.ca/files/TEK-BAKWATA-CCT_statement_0.pdf.

IMF, OECD, UN, and World Bank. 2011. *Supporting the Development of More Effective Tax Systems.* Report to the G-20 Development Working Group.

Johnson R. W. 2000. "Nyerere: A Flawed Hero." *The National Interest* 60. http://nationalinterest.org/article/nyerere-a-flawed-hero-552.

Kabwe Zitto. 2014. "Tanzania Mining Companies Migrating to the Mining Act 2010 and a Lusaka revolution" *Zitto na Demokrasia Blog*, October 12. https://zittok-abwe.wordpress.com/2014/10/12/tanzanian-mining-companies-migrating-to-the-mining-act-2010-and-a-lusaka-revolution/.

Keck, Margaret E. and Kathryn Sikkink. 1999. "Transnational Advocacy Networks in International and Regional Politics." *International Social Science Journal* 51 (159): 89–101.

Klein Naomi. 2007. *The Shock Doctrine: The Rise of Disaster Capitalism.* New York: Henry Holt and Company.

Kulindwa Kassim, Mashindano Oswald, Shechambo Fanuel, and Sosovele Hussein, 2003. *Mining for Sustainable Development in Tanzania.* Dar-es-Salaam: Dar es Salaam University Press.

Lange Siri. 2006. CMI Report. *Benefit Streams from Mining in Tanzania: Case Studies from Geita and Mererani.* Bergen: Chr. Michelesen Institute.

Lewis Suzanne. 2007. *Education in Africa.* Philadelphia: Mason Crest Publishers.

Manson Katrina. 2013. "Tanzania Faces Tax Exemptions Dilemma." *Financial Times*, June 12. Accessed August 20, 2015. http://www.ft.com/intl/cms/s/0/3cfe4802-d354-11e2-95d4-00144feab7de.html#axzz3RXO8dB4k.

McAdam, Doug, John McCarthy, and Zald, Mayer. 1996. *Comparative Perspectives on Social Movements: Political Opportunities, Mobilizing Structures and Cultural Framings.* New York: Cambridge.

Mukandala, Rwekaza, Othman Said Yahya, Mushi Samwel, and Ndumbaro Laurian. 2006. *Justice, Rights, and Worship: Religion and Politics in Tanzania.* Dar-Es-Salaam: REDET.

McDonald, Catherine and Roe Alan. 2007. "The Challenge of Mineral Wealth: Using Resource Endowments to Foster Sustainable Development: Tanzania Country Case Study." *ICMM Report*, www.icmm.com.

OECD. 2008. *African Economic Outlook Report: Tanzania*, Paris: OECD.

Piketty, Thomas. 2014. *Capital in the Twenty-First Century.* Cambridge, MA: Harvard University Press.

Policy Forum. 2013. "Tax Policy Brief." Accessed August 20, 2015, http://www.policyforum-tz.org/sites/default/files/Taxpolicybrief.pdf.

PwC. 2012. *Corporate Income Taxes, Mining Royalties and Other Mining Taxes: A Summary of Rates and Rules in Selected Countries; Global Mining Industry Update.* Accessed August 20, 2015. http://www.pwc.com/en_GX/gx/energy-utilities-mining/publications/pdf/pwc-gx-miining-taxes-and-royalties.pdf.

Riddell, Barry. 1992. "Things Fall Apart Again: Structural Adjustment Programmes in Sub-Saharan Africa." *Journal of Modern African Studies* 20 (1): 53–68.

Scott James. 1999. *Seeing Like a State: How Certain Schemes to Improve the Human Condition Have Failed.* New Haven: Yale University Press.

Stiglitz Joseph. 2013. *The Price of Inequality.* London: Penguin Books.

United Republic of Tanzania (URT). 2011. *Poverty and Human Development Report*, Dar-es-Salaam.

Westerlund, David. 1980. *Ujamaa na Dini: A Study of Some Aspects of Society and Religion in Tanzania 1961–1977.* Stockhom: Almqvist & Wiksell International.

Chapter 13

Greed and Climate Change

Confronting Economic Globalization in the US Religious Environmental Movement

Justyna Nicinska

The reemergence of religion into the public sphere has raised questions about the nature of the secular state, and religion's role in public discourse (Casanova 1994). It also raises questions about what constitutes "religion" and how to adequately comprehend this religious resurgence as a force in political and economic spheres. Can religious actors engage in a democratic society and serve as multiple interest groups in charting its course? As discussed in the introduction to this volume, a constructivist approach to studying religion can avoid the pitfalls of narrowly defining religion in either essentialist or orientalist terms. In viewing religion as a human construct, religion and religio-social movements are defined based on the actor's interpretation.

This chapter explores the growing religious environmental movement in the United States with a specific focus on its climate change activism. Their activism has led them to question the current state of global capitalism and to propose significant transformations to the prevalent economic model of neo-liberal globalization. The remarkable aspect of the religious environmental movement in the United States is that it cuts across faiths and comprises an interesting coalition of religious denominations that at times can have divergent views on other societal questions. However, as my case study shows, the religious environmental movement is increasingly at the forefront of morally driven action and faith-based investment campaigns. It seeks to embed a humanitarian and environmental ethic into the capitalist system while challenging the assumptions and benefits of unlimited growth and material wealth as representative of the good life.

The underlying message of holism, interconnectedness, and moral obligation to care for the "Earth community" is shared by members of the religious environmental movement and reflected in their framing. They are informed by scientific findings concerning climate change and other ecological problems. However, their main driver for engaging in activism is a spiritual, morally driven belief that caring for God's creation is a religious mandate, a "confessional" issue. In other words, for this social movement, the high social cost of climate change and the disproportionate impact of Global North countries in the production of greenhouse gases is a pivotal *moral* issue. This moral imperative drives the religious environmental movement to challenge the current capitalist model, how worth is assessed, and to seek alternatives, such as those offered through divestment, sustainable practices, and reduced consumption. As a result of their values, religious groups are increasingly playing a key role in this social discourse calling for action on climate change and to move away from highly consumptive lifestyles, through their ideologically driven frames. This way of "framing" the issues is summarized by Gus Speth who identifies the root causes of the ecological crisis as "pride, apathy and greed" with the solution lying in a "cultural and spiritual transformation" (in Bingham 2009, 9).

This chapter will provide an overview of the religious environmental movement and will locate it within social movement theory. It will describe *collective action frames*, their purpose, and their application by the movement. Concrete examples of how frames are applied to climate activism by the movement will be illustrated. In the final sections, this chapter will illustrate how this religious environmentalism can be distinguished from the broader secular environmental movement, along with the religious diversity found within it. A special focus here will be on the role of evangelical activism within religious environmental activism and—contrary to the prevailing assumptions—the growing role of evangelical groups in addressing climate change as a major societal issue.

THE ORGANIZATIONAL MAKEUP OF THE RELIGIOUS ENVIRONMENTAL MOVEMENT

The focal points of this study are religious environmental groups and organizations engaged in climate change activism in the United States and how they have coalesced into a religious environmental movement. Smith and Pulver define such groups as "organizations who engage in environmental work from a spiritual or religious perspective" (Smith and Pulver 2009, 146). For the purposes of this chapter, these religious environmental groups (often referred to as REG in this chapter) are defined as faith-based nonprofit organizations, places of worship (churches, temples, and congregations of various denominations), and religious groups engaged in ecological programs, specifically with an inclusion of climate change in the scope of their activities. The US-based religious environmental movement is composed of diverse organizations (congregations, church organizations, and grassroots-based NGOs) and individual activists who focus on a faith-based approach toward climate change, share similar values, and frame the issue in terms of moral action. Many of them are led by individuals with multiple affiliations, for instance, to their particular congregation or faith as well as to a nongovernmental organization. These activists come from all over the United States and represent both conservative and liberal perspectives. Taken together, they have become part of a growing social movement calling for a profound transformation of neoliberal capitalism and for a reduction in material consumption.

Members of this movement included in the study were predominantly Christian, but there were also interfaith organizations (Christian, Jewish, Muslim, Hindu, Baha'I, and other faiths). Following the constructivist understanding of religion proposed in the introduction, their notion of faith and how it linked with ecology were self-defined. This means that what constituted a religious environmental organization was based on that organization's own construction of its religiosity and identity rather than relying on a predetermined definition. To this end, their specific interpretations or frames are analyzed and set against the wider context of a social movement's response to neoliberal globalization. This was achieved between 2011 and 2013 by undertaking semi-structured interviews with subject matter experts as well as through observations of activists' events, public discussions, and document analysis. It is important to point out that only organizations that seek to promote environmentalism were selected for this study. While there are a number of faith-based NGOs that deny anthropogenic (human caused) climate change and are in outright opposition to environmentalism, they constitute a minority among the religious environmental groups (Nicinska 2013, 74). They were not included in this study as the object of research was to understand how religious groups frame their activism to combat climate change in religious terms.

One notable grassroots organization, Interfaith Power and Light (IP&L), was founded by Reverend Sally Bingham and expanded from the 1990s to the present to include most US states. IP&L's primary mission is a religious response to global warming, which makes it one of the main organizations focused exclusively on climate change and energy issues. With its state-affiliated model it also has a strong local presence across the United States (Interfaith Power and Light 2015). Another example of an REG is the National Religious Partnership for the Environment (NRPE), an umbrella interfaith-based NGO originally composed of four mainline US religious organizations. Its constituent members include the United States Conference of Catholic Bishops, the National Council of Churches, the Coalition on Environment and Jewish Life, and the Evangelical Environmental Network (NRPE 2015).

These members offer a very diverse representation of US religious organizations. This includes the Protestant, Eastern Orthodox, Peace Churches, and African-American denominations, Jewish and Catholic faiths, as well as evangelical Christians and progressive and conservative positions. Evangelicals are often portrayed as being anti-climate change, and these groups (including EEN, Blessed Earth, Restoring Eden, and A. Rocha) illustrate the increasingly strong position of evangelical organizations on climate change as a moral issue that must be addressed.

RELIGION, ENVIRONMENTALISM, AND SOCIAL MOVEMENTS

The unique niche of the religious environmental movement rests on its core foundation of social justice (or fairness in the evangelical interpretation), combined with a sense of duty to care for the earth and its inhabitants as a religious mandate. Religious environmental groups, as part of a social movement, engage in conflictual collective action in challenging existing regulations and protesting projects, such as the Tar Sands oil pipeline. They share norms, values, and networks that create a common identity, which leads to a greater sense of cohesion. As a result, it is now possible to classify religious environmentalism as a distinct social movement, though one with clear linkages to the wider environmental and social justice movements. The field of social movements offers valuable insight into the study of environmentalism, especially in understanding the mobilization and drivers of social change. Della Porta and Diani (2006) define social movements as "a distinct social process, consisting of the mechanisms through which actors engage in collective action, namely involvement in conflictual relations with clearly identified opponents; linked by dense informal networks; and sharing a distinct collective identity" (20–21). By conflictual relations, Della Porta and Diani refer to engaging in political or cultural conflicts either in support of or in opposition to social change, where conflict denotes an oppositional relationship between actors seeking power over the same issue. Della Porta and Diani note that social movements consist of more than social movement organizations (SMO) engaged in collective action, and also include individual actors and collectivities, who are, nevertheless, connected to the other actors by a shared collective identity (21–22). The implication is that the religio-social movement studied here is composed of organizations, institutions, and individuals and, collectively, they and their practices make up the religious environmental social movement in the United States whose frames will be presented in the second part. These frames are a significant component of this social movement's identity and unique role.

Smith and Pulvar note that religious environmental groups function as primarily ethics-based organizations (Smith and Pulvar 2009). This means that morals, values, and beliefs play a strong role in the organizations' operating principles and motivation, as they do for many secular organizations, although the specific expression of these ideologies may vary. While the main focus of environmental groups is about the larger issue of the transformation of lifestyles and the "greening" of beliefs, there are also some issue-specific groups. For example, IP&L concentrates on a religious response to global warming as their core issue. Yet, while this specific focus defines their mandate, it does not prevent them from working for broader societal and lifestyle transformation. In addition, many groups engaged in the religious environmental movement that focus on issue-specific themes also link to those with individual and community-level transformation. Together, they seek to transform lifestyles by emphasizing consumption of local produce and teaching people how to cook from scratch, as well as encouraging their members to value less materially-oriented living as a source of happiness and stability (Sleeth 2012; observations and personal communication with experts 2011–2012). Today, we can say that the various religious environmental groups can be described as a growing social movement. There is evolving identity formation and shared culture along with the aim to challenge dominant social norms. For some of the groups, this will take the form of protest, while for others it will be implemented through challenges to consumerism. Doherty and Doyle (2006), as well as Schlosberg and Bomberg (2008), note that environmentalism and the environmental movement are not monolithic, but composed of varied approaches, actors, and coalitions. The movement involves a heterogeneous set of groups. There are representatives of major religious organizations, such as the Catholic Church, the National Association of Evangelicals, faith-based NGOs, and both conservative and liberal US political perspectives. Especially noteworthy is the fact that the highly polarized US political environment has generated environmental activism from a "less expected" source of conservative evangelicals, who have sought to frame climate change in terms of "creation care" (Bomberg and Schlosberg 2008, 345–46). As Bomberg and Schlosberg observe, support from evangelical groups may lead to interesting alliances with mainstream environmental groups, as explored further below.

FRAMES: HOW TO UNDERSTAND CLIMATE CHANGE FROM A RELIGIOUS PERSPECTIVE?

A significant emphasis in researching environmental and other movements rests on the understanding of frames. Benford and Snow (2000) define *collective action* frames as "action-oriented sets of beliefs and meanings that inspire and legitimate the activities and campaigns of a social movement organization (SMO)" (614). Several authors have made use of framing analysis to understand the environmental movement (Schlosberg and Bomberg 2008). In movements where ideas and values play a central role in the creation of a "discursive commons," it is centrally important to study how they relate their concerns to the public. Brick and Cawley argue that the creation of discourse commons can lead to the formation of "discursive bridges" between different ideas, which may lead to transformations at various levels (Brick and Cawley 2008, cited in Schlosberg and Bomberg, 191–92). The way that environmental groups draw on ideology and frame their cause offers new insights into the diverse forms a social movement can take in order to challenge dominant paradigms. Framing is relevant in assessing religious environmental groups' approach toward activism, given that much of their emphasis rests on transforming the way in which the human-ecology relationship is portrayed. As will be seen below, various frames have come out of the religious environmental movement: care for God's creation, love for neighbors, concern for the poor and the outcast, and issues of justice or fairness.

Snow et al. (1986) analyze the support of and participation in SMOs through the use of what they call *frame alignment processes* in their study of religious organizations. They identify four types of such processes: frame bridging; frame amplification; frame extension; and frame transformation. They note that social movements can apply only some or all of these processes with varying levels of success (467–76). As illustrated throughout this chapter, religious environmental groups utilize these four frame alignment processes to express their value-based message on faith and ecology in terms that are best suited to their target audience and in this manner amplify existing values. For instance, evangelical and Catholic groups frame mercury air pollution in terms of a pro-life issue, where caring for the "unborn" is extended to providing a healthy environment. This way they have established a bridge linking the general concern for the unborn and the specific environmental issue that resonates with their members and inspires further action. *Frame bridging* applies to the linkage of two issue areas under one cause or sentiment pool, a tactic that is utilized by a variety of SMOs, including religious environmental groups, in establishing a connection between religiosity and environmentalism (Snow et al. 1986, 467–68). In this sense, two concepts, which were previously viewed as disconnected or not related, are linked to establish a new way of dealing with the cause of the SMO. Simultaneously, some religious environmental groups engage in *frame amplification* (including value and belief amplification) in building on the existing ideologies of potential supporters and amplifying either their religious or ecological components (469–70). Evangelical Christians' framing of their environmental campaigns in terms of creation care is a means to extend accepted norms into the more contentious realm of environmentalism. Frame extension is also applied, for instance, in how faith-based development NGOs have extended their human rights mission to include a component of "climate justice." *Frame transformation*, defined by Snow as dividing into domain-specific and global-interpretive frames (473–76), is also observable in religious environmental groups, especially in the sense of more sweeping, global frames, which relate to the relationship of faith, ecology, and human connectivity more generally. In addition to these processes, networks need to frame issues in a certain context that makes their cause meaningful, a process called *frame resonance*. This relates to how an organization interprets its information in a way that impact public understanding (Keck and Sikkink 1998). Issue framing is a significant process for religious groups as they try to convey environmental messaging in a different context, which they perceive to have greater resonance with their audience and the general public.

As Billings and Samson have observed, though, frames will not adequately reflect what drives social movements without understanding their ideologies (Billings and Samson 2012). Such ideologically structured action is reflective of activism by religious environmental groups. The frame analysis adopted here has sought to include ideology in the construction of frames to carve out their deeper meaning. Shawki concludes, in analyzing the Jubilee 2000, that coherently expressed frames that resonate with notions of justice and moral values can lead to successful outcomes for social movements (Shawki 2010). The chapter by MacLeod in this volume likewise demonstrates the role of religious beliefs and conviction in obtaining a successful outcome of norm transformation.

One prominent frame utilized by many groups in the religious environmental movement is related to extending social justice to include the impact of climate change and other forms of environmental degradation. This is important as social justice has a strong foundation in most religious belief systems. In this case, the groups under study apply frame extension, bridging, amplification, and transformation. It is also critical to use local examples and to extend the global consequences of climate change to reflect local realities and amplify the scope of the problem, thus localizing climate justice. In other words, without framing their message in a personally meaningful way in relation to their larger belief system, it is harder to sway their target audience. Religious environmental groups amplify their message to show that environmental degradation, much of the time, impacts poor people most severely. It is also significant for the religious environmental movement to transform how "the environment" is perceived by their audience to illustrate that environmental justice is not just about "polar bears and tree frogs," but to acknowledge that "humans are a part of the environment and that when bad things happen to the environment, bad things also happen to people" (personal communication, interfaith REGs, May 13, 2012). As one minister noted in the same context, "There's nothing in my personal faith tradition that says I'm allowed to live a lifestyle that continues to harm other people." However, for many people, without experiencing direct negative impacts, it is hard to gain support for larger changes. In this context, it is important to note that US Evangelical Christian groups frame "justice" differently. Justice, as noted by some evangelical leaders, can be a contentious term because of its historical association with the US liberal movement. As a result, the evangelical creation care movement frames social justice as a matter of fairness, loving your neighbors, and loving the poor and, the least of these (Ball 2010).

The religious environmental movement strongly emphasizes that US culture has become dominated by consumerism where the possession of material goods acts as a measure of worthiness and happiness. In their messaging they try to convey that money does not buy happiness and that people could benefit from reducing consumption and, instead, focusing more on the quality of life as opposed to the possession of many goods. To quote one member: "Nobody is anybody because of what you've got. As Jesus said, a person's worth can't be measured in terms of the abundance of your possessions and in America we've tried to do that and we need to forget it and it doesn't work anyway because nobody ever is satisfied, if that's what you're trying to measure yourself by" (personal communication, interfaith REGs, May 8, 2012).

Religious environmental movement activists also express that they work within a broader accountability and longer timeframes than immediate needs and electoral cycles. They find that religious beliefs can resonate deeply with people and be a more powerful motivator than continuing to look solely at the financial and scientific bottom line, and rather "to hear from voices that address our imaginations, and our souls, and our conscience" (personal communication, Interfaith REG co-chair, May 16, 2012). This is also evident in the evangelical context, though evangelical leaders engaged in creation care would not advocate against development or having a good life but, instead, would acknowledge the need to give natural resources their "Sabbath rest" and doing so in a sustainable manner (Ball 2010, 94–95). As summarized by an evangelical theologian:

> There are clear indications in different scriptures that the non-human creation is not just for human use and consumption, it is that God intends for people to use it . . . nothing wrong with shaping it and developing it and using it in those kinds of ways—always with the respect for sustainability . . . but there are other passages that talk about that it should be for the glory of God . . . so the created order is not just for human consumption. (personal communication with Evangelical theologian and organization leader, May 16, 2012)

In framing the debate about consumption, one member of an evangelical environmental group noted that defining the problem as overconsumption in the United States is "like putting lipstick on a pig—I just call it greed" (personal communication with Evangelical REG leader, 2012). According to these evangelicals engaged in creation care, these are very basic terms used in framing the consumption discussion as what should be an acknowledged Christian sin. Blessed Earth, another NGO, which does not use the term climate change, focuses on fostering lifestyle changes and living practices in support of creation care, but also in a transformation of high-paced material consumption-oriented Western lifestyles (observation 2012). For instance, Nancy Sleeth's book *Almost Amish* presented a set of practices aimed toward simplifying lifestyles, using fewer resources, and spending more time with family and friends (Sleeth 2012). In this way, Sleeth (2012) did not frame her message as one of deprivation, but, rather, one of enrichment and spiritual growth through practices such as "keeping the Sabbath" and taking a day of rest. Framing messages in a way that people can relate to and one that is relevant to their faith is paramount when tackling a topic such as climate change, especially in the United States where climate skepticism remains high. At times, that means not leading with climate change as the first message, but instead talking about local air pollution, or the savings to be had by increasing energy efficiency: generally "meeting people where they're at" rather than confronting climate denial outright (personal communication, interfaith REG member, May 21, 2012).

THE RELIGIOUS ENVIRONMENTAL MOVEMENT IN THE CONTEXT OF SECULAR ENVIRONMENTALISM

The role of religious organizations in social movements has been explored by several authors. Barbara Yarnold (1991) and others explored what factors led to religious engagement in social movements and the implications of their engagement. She notes that religious organizations can help to facilitate the spread of a social movement's core ideas to the general public and policymakers in part through their use of an "established communications system," in the form of their congregations (1–3). Historical examples of this type of engagement from religious organizations are the civil rights movement and black Protestant churches in the United States, where positive law conflicted with natural law in the rights of African Americans (25–30). Yarrow's findings regarding the role of religious organizations in communicating the core concepts of a social movement to the public and policymakers are reflected in the study of the religious environmental movement. As the chapter illustrates, in addition to communicating core ideas, religious groups also serve in framing a movement's messaging in a way that is aligned with and resonates within a given social group's or political system's deeper beliefs. The statement below by Gus Speth, Dean of Yale's School of Forestry and the Environment, while addressing a meeting of thirty evangelical leaders, since dubbed the "Thomasville Rebellion," illustrates how belief can complement scientific approaches as it reaches citizens from a different perspective:

> Thirty years ago, I thought that with enough good science, we would be able to solve the environmental crisis. I was wrong. I used to think the greatest problems threatening the planet were pollution, bio-diversity loss and climate change. I was wrong there too. I now believe that the greatest problems are pride, apathy and greed. Because that's what's keeping us from solving the environmental problem. For that, I now see that we need a cultural and spiritual transformation. And we in the scientific community don't know how to do that. But you evangelicals do. We need your help. (Bingham 2009, 9)

In general, SMOs engaged in the religious environmental movement do not separate human and nonhuman creation in their messaging about the vulnerable. While some environmental groups may focus more on the nonhuman aspect, the niche that religious groups fill aims to bridge that void, with human beings seen as an interrelated part of the "environment" (personal communication, interfaith REG, June 7, 2012). For the faith community, a key issue is always working to "integrate issues within a wider frame," meaning that religions have multiple aspects of social justice including climate change as well as other concerns, such as health care and unemployment. Unlike groups focused exclusively on the environment, they have to take multiple aspects of an issue into consideration. They work to link climate change with poverty, human health, and concerns that relate more to traditional ministries that are familiar and understandable to their audience.

In the context of the religious environmental movement, groups such as the NRPE, IP&L, Religious Witness for the Earth, GreenFaith, and the National Religious Coalition on Creation Care emphasize a holistic perspective, which focuses on the wider aspect of climate and environmental issues within an intergenerational time scale and moral-bound perspective. This holistic approach is perceived as the unique contribution of the faith community to environmental discourse. In their work with secular environmental NGOs, religious environmental groups are thus able to address the widespread perception that environmentalism is seen as "caring more about polar bears than people" (personal communication, Catholic REG member, October 2011). In other words, the secular groups are perceived as not framing their message in a way that clearly includes human beings as part of the environmental equation. The Sierra Club and World Wildlife Fund, among others, have ongoing partnerships with many faith groups (Sierra Club 2008) and welcome their engagement. As one participant observes:

> I don't know where they come from, what motivates them (secular ENGOs). I just know their particular job is to work on environmental issues; our particular job is to work to protect all of God's creation . . . we are God centric not human centered, so there is no such thing as a resource for human consumption, it is a gift from God . . . we rarely use the word environment, it's creation, it's God's creation, it's God's world . . . (personal communication, Christian REG, June 7, 2012)

Movement members also point out that the ideological divide in the country along political lines can prevent the other side on the fence from accepting the message of climate science. The particular advantage, therefore, of religious organizations is that their membership is often composed of both sides of the aisle, or they can relate the environmental issues back to key issues relevant for their believers and make them more palatable. Consequently, they will frame their message relative to their core teachings and emphasize how environmental issues are a part of their core faith values.

In their interaction with the mainstream environmental movement, religious environmental movement organizations view their role either as being part of multiple and overlapping movements or as a more distinct faith-based environmental movement. They view their voice as adding a novel approach toward ecological degradation and climate change, and the majority view themselves as overlapping with the wider environmental movement, but not as a subset of it. As noted by one activist:

> It's prudent with such an overwhelming amount of evidence that we have to change our lifestyle, that climate change is an indictment on the consumer mentality and our addiction to fossil fuels; it cannot be sustained and every issue has hidden in it moral and ethical questions that often are part of the subconscious of the environmental movement, but we are able to bring those principles up to the forefront which is how religion is unique from the environmental movement; we do things because the scriptures and our principles and our theology lead us to those conclusions, and so ours is an extension of the life of religion into the life of society. (personal communication, Interfaith REG, May 2012)

Some groups note that while the fundamental message may be similar from a religious or secular viewpoint, the way it is framed and portrayed is where the key differences lie. Many religious environmental movement organizations view their approach to be broader than that of some secular groups even though many of their goals align. Religious environmental organizations can involve multifaith partnerships with the diversity of views that reflect that broad constituency. They see their approach toward creation care as inclusive of "things that crawl and fly" as well as all people and places, including ecological issues as well as issues of equity, resources, and the economic transition. They seek a "reinvigoration of religious life in the United States and around the world" (personal communication, Interfaith REG, March 23, 2012). As one leader observed:

> It would be great if the climate crisis weren't happening, but we'd still be at this because for us it's about becoming more fully ourselves as religious people. In addition to doing what's right and making and caring for vulnerable people and caring for real places and real people that are hurting. So, it's dual for us and I don't know that we share that necessarily with all our secular friends and allies and that's fine. (personal communication, Interfaith REG leader, May 23, 2012)

Those involved in the nexus of faith and ecology work to build bridges between their organizations' core missions of caring for the vulnerable and providing community services, and highlighting environmental issues. Religious environmental groups view their role as one of participating in both a distinct faith-based movement that can overlap with the wider environmental movement while galvanizing a moral- and faith-driven response.

EVANGELICAL CHRISTIANS AND CREATION CARE: "WHAT WOULD JESUS DRIVE?"

One intriguing aspect of the religious environmental movement is the engagement of evangelical Christians, who are often perceived as having a climate-change-denying stance closely aligned with a conservative Republican Party platform. As the findings in this chapter illustrate, however, some evangelical Christians in the United States are a part of the religious environmental movement, which they define as "creation care" to indicate their understanding of the need to address climate change and other issues. Their involvement has grown in scope to include prominent evangelical leaders and organizations.

Evangelical environmental groups primarily view their role as that of fostering a creation care movement one that has similar goals to the wider environmental movement but uses different frames and messages to reach its audience. Many of these groups profess acting as a bridge between the two worlds of secular environmentalism and evangelical Christianity, some from a lifestyle transformation/education approach, and others through more direct political action (personal observation 2012).

Evangelical environmental groups observe that the culture experienced a shift from the early 1990s to the present in support of creation care. Initially, they received criticism from some evangelicals suggesting that they should not get involved with an issue that was perceived by some as too liberal, secular, or even pantheistic. By the year 2000, conservative evangelical groups were coming out with their own creation care statements (Evangelical REG organizers, personal communication 2011 and 2012). For example, the Evangelical Climate Initiative (ECI) is a group of over three hundred senior evangelical leaders, including prominent figures like Rick Warren, who believe that the United States needs to address global warming. They support that effort in a way that would "create jobs, clean up our environment and enhance national security by reducing our dependence on foreign oil" (ECI 2006). The ECI calls for action on climate change. It also affirms that climate change was human-induced. It encourages a market-based approach, such as carbon trading. The latter has received support from several energy companies as noted on their website in a statement in 2013. Recently, over 170 senior evangelical leaders signed a letter praising President Obama's environmental activism and showed their support for action on mitigating pollution from coal-powered plants (Alexei Laushkin, email message to author, August 3, 2015, and EEN 2015).

In researching evangelical Christians and climate change, McCammack (2008, 119–42) looked at both conservative and liberal evangelical groups, noting that strong divisions still exist among evangelicals on how to approach climate change and whether it is a moral issue worthy of activism on a similar scale to abortion or gay rights. However, as Greenberg further points out, political conservatism in the United States is not monolithic. In fact, he demonstrates that conservative values used to promote frugality, as well as conservation and stewardship, and do not really correspond with the present emphasis on consumption. At present there is an "emerging green conservatism" in the United States that is described as being "elastic." Greenberg points to "green outliers" including prominent evangelical leaders also mentioned by McCammack, like Richard Cizik, and Reverends Ted Haggard and Jim Ball of the Evangelical Environmental Network, who are advocating green thought and "creation care" as central to conservative ideology (Greenberg 2006, 85–111). This is evident in the support of notable evangelical Christian climate scientists, like Jim Houghton and Katherine Hayhoe, who have sought to combine their expertise with a moral call for action (Houghton 2004; Hayhoe and Farley 2009).

Evangelical environmental groups work to show how a literal interpretation of the scriptures supports the care for creation and stewardship of the earth, and contains many edicts against its destruction. In this way, they counter the views of Dominion theologists who believe that life on earth will end with the return of Jesus and that the increasing environmental destruction makes the return of Christ more likely (Hendricks 2005). Evangelical groups involved in the religious environmental "creation care" movement have the advantage of appealing to values and beliefs, in particular religious beliefs, so that they can tap into people's "hearts," which can bring a deeper level understanding than just seeing the "facts." In this way, Evangelical environmental groups aim to develop a strong base of supporters for creation care in their community. They also see that with the United States being a major contributor of greenhouse gases, much of their emphasis should be national in order to foster more meaningful progress. One evangelical leader noted that the United States is one of the largest emitters and also the largest economy in the world and that it has the ability to combat global warming. Therefore, given the political impact of evangelicals in the United States, their "unique role and responsibility" lies in persuading US policymakers to protect the poor from the consequences of climate change (personal communication, Evangelical REG leader, November 11, 2011).

One of the leading organizations in the creation care movement is the Evangelical Environmental Network (EEN), a ministry that has focused on providing an evangelical response to climate change. It is striving for greater support in the evangelical community, emphasizing the biblical role of creation care, and it is also calling for comprehensive climate legislation (Evangelical Environmental Network 2015). Its reverend, Jim Ball, launched an innovative campaign with the question: *What Would Jesus Drive?* This campaign demonstrated that the EEN did not oppose "development" but, instead, chose to highlight living life as Jesus would. Hence, the campaign was aimed at improving US fuel efficiency standards and encouraging the use of more fuel-efficient cars (personal communication, EEN, November 2011). It was a highly successful media campaign with over 4000 media stories (Evangelical Environmental Network, WWJDrive 2015). The *What Would Jesus Drive?* campaign framed personal transportation choices as a moral issue for Christians, linking fuel inefficiency in cars with their negative health and environmental consequences, thus bridging two previously unconnected frames in their message.

For Evangelical organizations, creation care is framed as "a matter of life." One example of how this frame was extended includes the Mercury and the Unborn campaign already mentioned above, in which EEN partnered with Catholic groups such as the Catholic Coalition on Climate Change to advocate for more stringent coal power plant standards proposed by the EPA, which would limit the amount of mercury released into the air. EEN and the United States Conference of Catholic Bishops argued that caring for the unborn (both are antiabortion) means more than opposing abortion; it also means making sure the fetus and the mother are not exposed to harmful pollutants, thus justifying support for this regulatory measure (personal communication with campaign members, 2011–2012; Mercury and the Unborn 2011; Evangelical Environmental Network 2015; and Christian News Wire 2011). While some organizations actively pursue legislative reform, others such as Blessed Earth refrain from engagement in direct political action with the belief that "the system will take back what the culture hasn't granted" (Blessed Earth, personal communication, May 2012). Their approach is to tie creation care with other conservative values believing that those who believe in a literal interpretation of the Bible should take note of the message about caring for the Earth, as well as living simply, fulfilling their needs without taking too much.

CONCLUSION

The US religious environmental movement has shown considerable growth in the number and diversity of participants, and activism over the last ten years. It is anticipated that this movement will not be transient and will continue to expand and evolve over the next decade. The scope of its impact and influence in transforming neoliberalism and existing sociopolitical structures should continue to be evaluated. This is especially relevant for the United States, where religiosity has not declined to the same degree as elsewhere and where relative to other Western countries, religion has a central role in the public discussion (Haynes 1998, 10). As this chapter has shown, the religious environmental movement perceives its role as being part of multiple environmental movements, which are, to a certain extent, connected. This is evident in how evangelical groups refer to a "creation care movement"; others prefer to define it as the "faith and ecology movement" as well as the "faith-based climate movement," while many participants in the religious environmental movement increasingly make linkages with the divestment movement (personal observation, 2012–2013; see also the chapter by MacLeod in this volume). Grassroots mobilization is a critical part of achieving wider societal transformation over many years for the religious environmental movement, as well as influencing political elites, with some progressive groups increasingly focusing on resisting neoliberal capitalism (personal communication, Interfaith REG, 2012).

The challenge for the US religious environmental movement is to link a complex issue such as climate change with specific collective action frames that reflect the specific ideology of their membership and that resonate with their target audience to mobilize support. Religious environmental activists approach this by "breaking down" the overwhelming problem of climate change into localized applications linked with their values and beliefs, as well as by adapting messages that are faith-specific and actionable, such as the practice of carbon lent, Sabbath, and bridging local food sovereignty with large-scale climate impacts.

It should be noted that this movement in the United States is connected to a broader global movement, with many faith traditions and world religions taking a prominent stance in calling for action on climate change. Examples of this include the encyclical on climate change by Pope Francis and the Islamic Climate Declaration issued in 2015 (McGrath 2015; Faiola, Boorstein, and Mooney 2015). This also reflects the perspective of religious environmental activists with their emphasis on the "glocal"—meaning a localized focus on activism and change coupled with a global understanding of the consequences of climate change and other ecological issues. This is seen in their conceptualization of "Love thy neighbor" as a moral obligation to care for human and nonhuman creation at home as well as in other parts of the world. This moral obligation is strengthened by their conviction that affluent states contributed more to greenhouse gas emissions and are thus more responsible for action considering that countries in the Global South are suffering from the consequences of global warming, already visible in drought and changes in the growing season.

The model religious environmental activists promote is one of localization, which is not synonymous with localism or with the opposite of globalization, but transitions focused on a specific place within the context of a broader regional, national, and global framework (De Young and Princen 2012). In essence, this type of transformation to low consumption and self-sufficiency sought by the activists requires a large-scale societal shift in values that relates to ecological holism, but is also intimately linked with human well-being and quality versus quantity of life. In its relation to neoliberal globalization, the religious environmental movement thus aims to transform the most extreme policies of this paradigm. For many progressive members of the movement, this means replacing neoliberal capitalism with a system that promotes equity, investments that are measured and evaluated in terms of their societal and ecological footprint, and a move toward an "ecological civilization" where material wealth is not prioritized over ecological health. This differs from the evangelical (creation care) approaches, where this transformation is based on lifestyle choices, that is, the car one drives, and technological adaptation that favors sustainability. The evangelical movement favors market-oriented approaches toward achieving these outcomes. They are thus reflective of the need to transform neoliberalism, but not necessarily capitalism.

In this sense, we can conclude that religious environmental activism actively resists economic globalization and neoliberal capitalism, which it sees as a driving force of ecological degradation, social instability, and injustice. However, it is important to note that it does not oppose capitalism as such but, rather, favors its transformation. The term "spiritual capital" reflects this broader view of economic progress. As defined by Jonathan Porritt, spiritual capital is growth in spiritual terms, growth as human beings in learning and quality of life as opposed to continuous material consumption (personal observation, Christian Ecology Link 2012 annual meeting). This ties in with the idea of the indigenous movement as detailed in the chapter by Scauso that similarly redefines key values such as growth in order to signal the need to lead a less destructive lifestyle. For religious activists, "the good life" is not constrained to wealth, but they take a holistic and nonmaterial approach toward defining a fulfilling and successful life. This holds true for both progressive and conservative elements of the religious environmental movement, where a focus on community, quality of life, and interconnectedness is emphasized over consumption. Consumption without sustainability and moral consideration is viewed as greed and a sin.

REFERENCES

Ball, Jim. 2010. *Global Warming and the Risen Lord: Christian Discipleship and Climate Change*. Washington, DC: Evangelical Environmental Network.

Benford, Robert D. and David A. Snow. 2000. "Framing Processes and Social Movements: An Overview and Assessment." *Annual Review of Sociology* 26: 611–39.

Billings, Dwight B. and Will Samson. 2012. "Evangelical Christians and the Environment: 'Christians for the Mountains' and the Appalachian Movement Against Mountaintop Removal Coal Mining." *Worldviews* 16 (1): 1–29.

Bingham, Sally G., ed. 2009. *Love God, Heal Earth: 21 Leading Religious Voices Speak Out on Our Sacred Duty to Protect the Environment*. Pittsburgh, PA: St. Lynn's Press.

Bomberg, Elizabeth and David Schlosberg. 2008. "US Environmentalism in Comparative Perspective." *Environmental Politics* 17 (2): 337–48.

Reverend Cizik, Richard. 2009. "What If." In *Love God: Heal Earth: 21 Leading Religious Voices Speak Out on Our Sacred Duty to Protect the Environment*, by Reverend Canon Sally G. Bingham. Pittsburgh, PA: St. Lynn's Press.

Christian News Wire. December 21, 2011. "Evangelicals Praise EPA's Mercury Rule for Protecting Unborn Children." Accessed August 15, 2015. http://www.christiannewswire.com/news/4606218515.html.

De Young, Raymond and Thomas Princen, ed. 2012. *The Localization Reader: Adapting to the Coming Downshift*. Cambridge, Massachusetts and London, England: Massachusetts Institute of Technology Press.

Doherty, Brian and Timothy Doyle. 2006. "Beyond Borders: Transnational Politics, Social Movements and Modern Environmentalisms." *Environmental Politics* 15 (5): 697–712.

Evangelical Climate Initiative. 2006. "ECI Statement." Accessed August 15, 2015. http://www.aeseonline.org/aeseonline.org/Evangelical_Climate_Initiative.html.

Evangelical Environmental Network. 2015. "Ministry Overview." Accessed August 15, 2015. http://creationcare.org/ministry-overview/.

Evangelical Environmental Network. 2015. "Mercury and the Unborn." Accessed August 15, 2015. http://creationcare.org/mercury-and-unborn/.

Evangelical Environmental Network. 2015. "Public Letter on Clean Power Plan." Accessed August 15, 2015. http://creationcare.org/climate-realists-energy-optimists/public-letter-on-clean-power-plan/.

Evangelical Environmental Network. 2015. "What Would Jesus Drive—Welcome, Introduction and Background." Accessed August 15, 2015. http://www.what-wouldjesusdrive.info/intro.php.

Faiola, Anthony, Michelle Boorstein, and Chris Mooney. 2015. "Release of Encyclical Reveals Pope's Deep Dive Into Climate Science." *The Washington Post.* Accessed August 19, 2015. http://www.washingtonpost.com/local/how-pope-franciss-not-yet-official-document-on-climate-change-is-already-stirring-controversy/2015/06/17/ef4d46be-14fe-11e5-9518-f9e0a8959f32_story.html.

Greenberg, Nadivah. 2006. "Shop Right: American Conservatism, Consumption, and the Environment." *Global Environmental Politics* 6 (2): 85–111.

Hayhoe, Katherine and Andrew Farley. 2009. *A Climate for Change: Global Warming Facts for Faith-Based Decisions.* New York, Boston, Nashville: Faith Words.

Haynes, Jeff. 1998. *Religion in Global Politics.* London and New York: Longman.

Hendricks, Stephanie. 2005. *Divine Destruction: Wise Use, Dominion Theology, and the Making of American Environmental Policy.* Hoboken, NJ: Melville House Publishing.

Houghton, John T. 2004. *Global Warming: The Complete Briefing.* Cambridge, UK: Cambridge University Press.

Interfaith Power and Light. 2015. "Mission-History." Accessed August 15, 2015. http://www.interfaithpowerandlight.org/about/mission-history/.

Keck, Margaret E. and Kathryn Sikkink. 1998. *Activists Beyond Borders: Advocacy Networks in International Politics.* Ithaca and London: Cornell University Press.

McCammack, Brian. 2008. "Hot Damned America: Evangelicalism and the Climate Change Policy Debate." In *Religion and Politics in the Contemporary United States*, edited by Marie R. Griffith and Melani McAlister, 119–42. Baltimore: Johns Hopkins University Press.

McGrath, Matt. 2015. "Islamic Call on Rich Countries to End Fossil Fuel Use." *BBC.* Accessed August 19, 2015. http://www.bbc.com/news/science-environment-33972240.

Mercury and the Unborn. 2011. "An Evangelical Call to Stop the Mercury Poisoning of the Unborn." Accessed August 15, 2015. http://mercuryandtheunborn.org/.

National Religious Partnership for the Environment. 2015. "Partners." Accessed August 15, 2015. http://www.nrpe.org/partners.html.

Nicinska, Justyna. 2013. "Religious Environmental Groups and Global Climate Change Politics in the United States and the United Kingdom: What Motivates Activism?" PhD diss., Rutgers, State University of New Jersey.

Schlosberg, David and Elizabeth Bomberg. 2008. "Perspectives on American Environmentalism." *Environmental Politics* 17 (2): 187–99.

Shawki, Noha. 2010. "Issue Frames and the Political Outcomes of Transnational Campaigns: A Comparison of the Jubilee 2000 Movement and the Currency Transaction Tax Campaign." *Global Society* 24 (2): 203–30.

Sierra Club. 2008. "Faith in Action." Accessed June 11, 2013. http://www.sierraclub.org/ej/downloads/faithinactionreport2008.pdf.

Sleeth, Nancy. 2012. *Almost Amish: One Woman's Quest for a Slower, Simpler, More Sustainable Life*. IL: Tyndale House Publishers.

Smith, Angela M. and Simone Pulver. 2009. "Ethics-Based Environmentalism in Practice: Religious-Environmental Organizations in the United States." *Worldviews* 13 (24): 145–79.

Snow, David A., E. Burke Rochford, Steven K. Worden, and Robert D. Benford. 1986. "Frame Alignment Processes, Micromobilization, and Movement Participation." *American Sociological Review* 51 (4): 464–81.

Yarnold, Barbara M. 1991. *The Role of Religious Organizations in Social Movements*. New York/Westport, Connecticut/London: Praeger.

Chapter 14

Faith, Global Justice, and Resistance to Neoliberalism

From the World Social Forum to Occupy!

Peter J. Smith and Elizabeth Smythe

This chapter critically examines the role of religion and faith-based organizations in resisting neoliberalism, especially its global dimension, which has been viewed negatively by social justice activists around the world, especially since the financial crisis of 2008.[1] It examines activists' role in the Global Justice Movement (GJM) through involvement in two sites of resistance namely, the World Social Forum (WSF) and the Occupy Movement, in particular Occupy Wall Street (OWS). Both the WSF and OWS represent different sites of resistance and are linked to the coalitions of nongovernmental organizations (NGOs) and social movements that engaged in protests against key international institutions of global governance since the 1980s. The desire to go beyond resistance to articulate alternatives to neoliberal globalization is reflected in the creation of the WSF in 2001 to coincide with, and in contrast to, the World Economic Forum, the annual gathering of powerful corporate and state actors in Switzerland. The WSF global event was held annually from 2001 to 2005 and then subsequently once every two years in a city in the Global South, gathering thousands of global justice activists under the theme "Another World is Possible!" For those studying transnational social movements and for the GJM, it is a key site of resistance to neoliberalism and a public space where alternatives can be discussed and articulated. Occupy! on the other hand, was a one-time event that emerged spontaneously in New York and elsewhere as a reaction to the global financial crisis of 2008 and involved actions that are harder to classify.

Today, as Ulrich Beck (2000) notes, the global cannot be separated from the local and thus local activism must be seen in the larger context of opposition to global neoliberalism, most evident at the WSF. We argue that religious opposition to, and criticism of, neoliberalism, is a salient aspect of the GJM and Occupy. Indeed, Slavoz Žižek (as quoted in Murtola 2012, 331) argues that in terms of anticapitalist resistance, "St. Paul had it right using religion to rock the foundations of authority." Yet, most social scientists studying transnational social movements and global justice have ignored the role of faith-based groups partly because this challenges their perceptions of religion in society. In taking up the invitation from the introduction, this chapter argues that while religion has served political-economic forms of domination and control, it is ultimately socially constructed and has also served as a means of resistance to empire (see also chapter 2 on the two sides of religion). We begin our analysis with a discussion of the secularization thesis and its political and economic significance, including the relationship of the state to religion.

SECULARIZATION, POLITICS, RELIGION, AND CAPITALISM

Concepts of secularization in the social sciences all share the belief that as society becomes more modern, religion will fade away and disappear (Shah and Philpott 2011). This decline of religion is often linked to the Treaty of Westphalia of 1648 when the state's legitimate monopoly of power and coercion in society subordinated religion's role in societal discipline. Once privatized, religion became politically marginalized, often through state policies. Laicism, meaning opposition between state and religion, created a series of hierarchical polarizations or dualisms, which subordinated religion and put it in a cultural and intellectual box from which it has struggled to emerge (Hurd 2011, 75).

Religion became separated from the secular sphere in a variety of ways. The secular and the sacral were not mutually relational in any way, with religion subordinate to the secular and public. Religion was seen to be focused on the transcendent while the secular was concerned with the things of this world, the immanent. To be secular was to be rational, to be religious was to be irrational and emotional, a source of violence, and a danger to the political sphere.[2] Being premodern, religion had to be pushed aside to make way for the modern in politics and economics. Today, however, there is increasing acknowledgment that secularism did not triumph and that religion is on the rise, gaining political influence around the world (Shah and Philpott 2011). The boundary between the secular and religion was never as demarcated as many claimed.

The fact that the boundary between religion and politics and other spheres of the social world has never been fixed requires a definition of religion that rejects dualistic thinking. Wilson (2012) provides a more historically constituted and nuanced one defining it as "an internally logical set of ideas and beliefs about the nature of existential reality (encompassing the immanent as well as the transcendent) that shapes and is shaped by both individual and community, identity and action, and which *may* be facilitated and practiced through institutional arrangements, rituals and/or symbols" (20). It moves away from such confining dualisms as public and private, secular and sacred, acknowledging that institutional arrangements are less constitutive in some religions. Thus defined, religion can transcend the public-private divide and be viewed as relevant to politics, public life, capitalism, and global justice.

The recognition that these dualisms were never accurate to begin with has led a new generation of scholars to question the artificial line between politics, socioeconomic life, and religion. In terms of Christianity, the focus is on a comparison of empire now and empire then, that is, the Roman Empire. What emerges is a view of early Christianity in conflict with empire, a conflict that resonates today, but which is at odds with Christianity's association with empire in the modern period, 1500–1900. An ahistorical approach to Christianity's origins created a blind spot claims Hal Taussig (2005):

> How New Testament scholarship, most Christian interpretation over the last millennium, and countless assemblies of worship and research could have missed the contrast with Roman imperial power at the heart of early Christianity defies imagination. One can only account for this unbelievable ignorance as a haunting tribute to the power of denial and the complicity of Christendom in imperial domination over the past 1,200 years. (2)

Horsley (2003), Crossan and Reed (2004) interpret the teachings of Jesus and Paul as challenging the Roman empire's political-economic and religious ideological structures. Early Christianity appears as a counter-imperial liberation movement; a role they argue that it can serve again today. In this scholarship we see a different Paul from how he is commonly portrayed, as a conservative who transformed the teaching of Jesus into a state supporting religion of empire (O'Grady 2013). This recent scholarship argues that only seven of Paul's thirteen letters were written by Paul himself and in these seven a more radical Paul appears. The six remaining letters, were, in fact, ghost written, an acceptable practice at the time and these are the letters where Paul appears as conservative, if not, reactionary (Borg and Crossan 2009).

According to Borg and Crossan (2009) Paul placed loyalty to Christianity over loyalty to Rome with a radical message of freedom and social, religious, and gender equality. Crossan and Reed (2004) see the imperial structures of Rome and those of today as analogous maintaining "We are, at the start of the twenty-first century, what the Roman Empire was at the start of the first century" (412).

With the exception of the Jubilee debt campaign the recent study of religion's resurgence has focused more on its political dimensions in international politics (Rees 2011) than on its relationship to contemporary capitalism. However, according to Mark C. Taylor (as quoted in Davis and Crockett 2007, 7), "global capitalism is inseparable from a global religious revival." Taylor's analysis is supported by the work of Wilson and Steger (2013) who argue that "'globalization'—understood as neoliberal economic globalization—is contributing in many ways to an increasing questioning of secular rationalism as the main arbiter of acceptable knowledge in contemporary global politics" (482). What is being produced as a result are "multiple religious globalisms—religiously infused political ideologies that inspire the faithful to pursue a particular vision for society—that operate as both supporters of and loci of resistance to dominant forms of neoliberal globalization" (482). Following Wilson and Steger, this chapter focuses on religion as a source of resistance to neoliberal globalization. Religion, we argue, can work for a fairer and more just economic system. This is evident at both the WSF and OWS. The WSF Charter of Principles (2001) makes it attractive to progressive religious groups (which to date have been primarily Christian), challenging neoliberal globalization as it proclaims its adherence to democratic debate and opposition to neoliberalism and any form of imperialism (see the chapter by Kwayu in this volume for an example of progressive Islamic activism). Given its openness to movements and groups, however, the WSF has not been without divisions among religious groups on important issues in the GJM as we indicate below.

Resistance to neoliberalism can be seen as forming part of what Karl Polanyi (1886–1964) described as a countermovement in his book *The Great Transformation*, which argued that economies are imbedded in society and culture. As the market tried to separate itself from society, society's natural response was to resist and seek means to protect itself in the form of a countermovement. Religion's role in this activity has been ignored by social scientists or has met with skepticism.

The Global Justice Movement—Resisting Neoliberal Globalization

The WSF and OWS are two manifestations of a decades-old countermovement against neoliberalization, which has its roots in the Global South but today resonates in the global North as a result of recent policies of austerity and restraint. Both the WSF and OWS are parts, one global, the other local, of what is described as the GJM defined by one analyst as "the loose network of organizations . . . and other actors engaged in collective action of various kinds, on the basis of the shared goal of advancing the cause of justice (economic, social, political, and environmental) among and between peoples across the globe" (Della Porta 2007, 6).

The GJM is a form of resistance to a global political economy dominated by corporate rule, which is aided and abetted by states. As the economy globalized in the 1970s and 1980s, so did resistance to it. The expansion of the free market, disembedded from social and political regulations, generated a countermovement consisting of subaltern classes, workers, and unions seeking social protection from the excesses of the market. A countermovement of resistance against neoliberal globalization is reflected in the Zapatista uprising of 1994 in Chiapas, Mexico; the Battle of Seattle in 1999; protests at meetings of institutions of global governance; and the creation of the WSF in 2001. These protests produced a particular logic and culture of grassroots participation and horizontality, or lateral organizing involving decentralized, loosely knit networks with open, nonhierarchical democratic decision-making processes. These became part of the culture of both the WSF and the Occupy Movement along with their innovations in the creation of new forms of political space.

WSF and Faith Groups

The creation of the WSF was a response to neoliberal globalization, but at the outset it appeared to exclude faith groups. According to its Charter of Principles (2001), the WSF is a space of opposition to neoliberalism but also a "plural, diversified, non-confessional . . . context"—that is, a secular space. The WSF participants and the spiritual aspects of movements and groups associated with the forum tell a different story.

The WSF and Religion

The WSF began in 2001 in Porto Alegre, Brazil, but subsequent global events have been held in India and Africa as well. Participants have numbered between 70,000 and 150,000. Today the WSF and the continental, regional, national, and local forums it spawned (Smith and Smythe 2011) have been key focal points in resisting neoliberal globalization. Initial analyses suggested that the WSF was evolving along secular lines (Lechner 2005) and religion was seen as a source of violence, fundamentalism, and oppression (Daulatzai 2004, 562). We argue, in contrast, that the presence of religion at the WSF deserves to be taken more seriously because religion played a role in the founding of the WSF, most participants at the WSF view themselves in religious, not secular terms, and religious institutions have always been active at the WSF providing critical analyses of neoliberalism. Moreover, spirituality with its emphasis on affect, emotion, authenticity, relating to others, and interconnectedness with one another and the Earth has been part of the GJM and the WSF process. Using a case study of the World Council of Churches

(WCC) below, we illustrate the presence of religious organizations and the way in which their critiques of neoliberalism formed an important element of the ideas generated in the forum process.

Religion and the Founding of the WSF

Religion has been present at the WSF since its inception. Here place matters. Brazil welcomed the first WSF partly because of the role of religion in creating a receptive host political culture. During the military dictatorship (1964–1985), the Catholic Church "became the most legitimate institution leading civil society opposition" (von Sinner 2007, 174). It became theologically progressive giving rise to liberation theology, which suffused the ideas of individuals, organizations, and social movements associated with the WSF. For example, Francisco (Chico) Whitaker is credited with conceiving the WSF as an open space for the convergence of social movements and NGOs opposed to neoliberal globalization. Long associated with the progressive wing of the Catholic Church in Brazil, Whitaker takes his theological inspiration from Archbishop Helder Câmara and the Liberation theologian Leonardo Boff. Since 2001, Whitaker has served on the Brazilian Catholic Bishop's Justice and Peace Commission, one of the eight organizations credited with organizing the first WSF. He has been associated with the Brazilian Worker's Party (PT), an amalgam of trade unionists, intellectuals, and proponents of liberation theology founded in 1980 and one of the first sponsors of the WSF in Porto Alegre. One leading organization of the first WSF, the Landless Rural Worker's Movement (MST), has been heavily influenced by liberation theology (Reitan 2007, 153). Thus, while religion embodied as an institutional actor was not a driving force behind the WSF, its cultural presence animated many of the key actors who were.

Religion and WSF Participants

Despite the claim that the WSF space is secular, surveys show it is occupied by participants, particularly from the Global South, who identify themselves in religious terms. A survey in Porto Alegre in 2003 indicates that 62.6% of respondents claimed to be religious.[3] Keeping in mind that about 85% of all participants were Brazilian, this is no surprise. A later survey of WSF 2007 participants found that over 90% of those that identified themselves as very religious came from the Global South (many of them African).

Of the WSF participants in the sample from the South (333), approximately 70% (268) were somewhat or very religious (Transnational Social Movement Research Working Group 2007).

Religious Organizations and the Forum Process

In addition to the religiosity of WSF participants, the role of religious organizations involved in the GJM in providing rational critiques, analyses of, and alternatives to, neoliberal globalization deserves more attention. Religious organizations, primarily Christian, have played an active role at the WSF from the outset, providing program content through seminars and workshops, often in cooperation with other organizations. This role was enhanced by the 2004 decision of the WSF's governing International Council to adopt a more bottom-up consultative and self-organizing process for the program. Involving 1,800 groups and organizations, it resulted in eleven themes, which served as a basis for organizing more than 2,500 Forum activities. While the themes included human rights, pluralism, and diversity, faith groups saw the seventh theme involving "Ethics, cosmo-visions and spiritualities—resistances and challenges to a new world" as welcoming their presence, and ecumenical organizations began appearing at the WSF in greater numbers.

It was, however, the 2007 WSF in Nairobi, Kenya, that brought faith-based organizations to the forefront. A cursory view of the program shows the strong presence of Christian Churches. The Catholic charity *CARITAS* had a large European delegation, which, along with the *All African Council of Churches* (Protestant), created the Caritas-AACC ecumenical platform. Many other Christian churches had a strong presence as did faith-based development and ecumenical organizations such as the *Economic Justice Network*, the *Ecumenical Advocacy Alliance*, *Catholic Overseas Development Agency UK* (CAFOD), the *Maryknoll Office for Global Concerns*, and the *World Council of Churches*. Local Nairobi churches and those across Africa facilitated and mobilized African participation at the forum. Local churches demonstrated their deeper community roots than many of the NGOs by mobilizing people from the slums. A series of workshops, "Voices from the Slums," were sponsored by churches and parishes in Nairobi. Their focus was not a narrow religious one but included issues of debt, global poverty, the right to water, HIV/Aids, and human rights.

Spirituality, Reason, and the Forum Process

While surveys have demonstrated the religiosity of forum participants and WSF programs show how faith organizations have been involved in providing analytical content and proposals for alternatives at forums, the broader question of spirituality and its role at the WSF has not been fully addressed. It needs to be if we are to fully grasp the extent to which a religious/secular division fails to capture the full reality of the GJM. Usually thought of as a sense of an interconnection with others and the Earth itself, which brings meaning to life, spirituality is usually seen as encompassing, but going beyond, organized faith or religion. Geoffrey Pleyers (2010), in his book *Alter-Globalization: Becoming Actors in the Global Age*, provides a suggestive analytical tool for grasping this aspect of the GJM. Within the alter-globalization movement (i.e., the GJM), he sees two distinct trends, one the "way of subjectivity" and the other the "way of reason," embodied in distinct types of actors opposing neoliberal globalization.

Subjectivity refers to the irrational side of political activism emphasizing creativity, the experiential, the relational, and the emotional. Reason emphasizes knowledge, rationality, expertise, and hierarchy. Each becomes a basis for resisting neoliberal globalization. Those practicing the way of subjectivity do so in terms of artistic celebration, for example, street theater, parades, dancing, and music. While Pleyers does not acknowledge it, feelings of joy, connection, and liberation are signs of spiritual experience. Those associated with the way of reason are found in larger NGOs and movement organizations that stress the importance of rationality, expertise, and knowledge in critiquing, analyzing, and formulating alternatives to neoliberal globalization. They are likely to be top-down, hierarchical, and led by experts (Pleyers 2010, 13).

While the way of reason and of subjectivity are analytical categories in practice, as Pleyers acknowledges, it is not a case of dualisms, of either/or, but of both/and. Emotional and experiential politics are not antagonistic to or bereft of the exercise of reason. Similarly, large NGOs are not devoid of emotion and passion. These trends are intertwined in both types of organizations and present at social forums, but often in tension with each other. Horizontally based activists are frequently critical of the hierarchical practices of large NGOs (Smith et al. 2008). Pleyers's categories can be used to analyze the role of spirituality in challenging neoliberalism in the social forum process as they reject the reason-emotion/spiritual duality of religion and modern politics.

Spirituality is often unrecognized by social scientists as being a dimension of many activists opposed to neoliberalism. The exception seems to be in the acknowledgment of the growing assertion of indigenous spirituality, which the WSF, especially since the 2009 meeting in Belém, Brazil, has reflected (Becker and Koda 2011). In contrast to their hostility to faith-based groups, the presence of indigenous people and their spirituality has been embraced and celebrated by social scientists studying the WSF. The indigenous peoples of Latin America reject dualistic thought as the Scauso chapter in this volume indicates. The Zapatistas, indigenous peoples in Chiapas, Mexico, whom Pleyers (2010) classifies as fitting into the way of subjectivity, also reject dualistic thinking (Marcos 2013). Yet, the Zapatistas have inspired global activists, influenced horizontal organizing and the creation of the WSF itself, especially its slogan, "Another World is Possible" (Smith et al. 2008; Marcos 2013). As our case study of the WCC and its role at the WSF indicates, the critiques of neoliberalism that have been informed by faith or religious teachings are increasingly incorporating other spiritual perspectives.

The World Council of Churches and the WSF

One of the most prominent faith-based organizations at the WSF is the WCC, a large ecumenical movement representing 560 million Christians, the majority residing in the Global South. Founded in 1948, it includes more than 340 churches, denominations, and church fellowships in over hundred countries and territories with a focus on issues of social justice (WCC 2011). It is particularly interesting to examine not only because of its ecumenical nature and cooperation with a range of faith-based organizations and social movements but also because it focuses on both the rational and spiritual sides of resistance. The WCC has increasingly identified with the WSF and its struggle against neoliberal globalization as evident in a number of documents. As one document (AGAPE 2005, 1) states:

> From the very beginning of this process, the WCC has made a clear distinction between globalization as a multi-faceted historic process and the present form of a pernicious economic and political project of global capitalism. This form of globalization is based on an ideology that those groups and movements involved in the World Social Forum have described as "neoliberalism."

In stressing the rational side, the WCC rejects such dualisms as the economy and ecology, man and nature, and, instead, sees them as interrelated. In its initiatives on globalization, it has collaborated with the Lutheran World Federation (LWF) composed of 145 member churches in seventy-nine countries representing over seventy million Christians (WCC 2015). Like the WCC, the LWF has been engaged in issues of economic globalization and has been a regular participant at the WSF.

Although present from the start, it was in 2003 that the WCC began to assume a higher WSF profile presenting workshops on water, economic globalization, peace, violence, and youth. Framing its participation as a "spirituality of resistance," program organizer Rogate Mshana argued for a "need to recover the long tradition of a Christian spirituality critical of power. It is a spirituality which has given those without power the strength and courage to oppose those who abuse it" (as quoted in WCC 2003). At the forum, the WCC acted under a broad ecumenical umbrella including the WLF and a coalition of Latin American and Brazilian churches, participation that expanded with the addition of the theme of spirituality in 2005.

In its critiques of globalization, the WCC (2005) linked itself to the WSF in the *Alternative Globalization Addressing Peoples and Earth (AGAPE)*. AGAPE was prepared under the direction of the WCC Secretariat but in response to local pressures (Rogate Mshana, email message received by co-author Smith, April 19, 2011). The document identifies the WSF as the major expression of resistance to neoliberal globalization and presents a detailed analysis and critique of neoliberal globalization, positing alternative values and possibilities. Neoliberalism, it claims, "is an economy of death" (4). It proposes, instead, a life-affirming vision of "an Earth community where all peoples live in just relationships with each other, with all creation and with God" (37), a vision that is clearly spiritually grounded. Neoliberalism, it asserts, is but the latest version of empire to which resistance is necessary. In calling for an "economy of life," it aligns itself closely to the indigenous concept of *buen vivir* discussed in the Scauso chapter in this volume (see also the conclusion).

Speaking of the necessity of "eco-justice," and of seeing the economy and ecology as interrelated and inseparable, the WCC moved beyond the notion of Third World debt to the idea of ecological debt highlighted in the 2007, 2011, 2013, and 2015 WSFs. The ecological debt is one that the North owes the South: the debt accumulated by Northern, industrial countries toward Third-World countries on account of resource plundering, environmental damages, and the free occupation of environmental space to deposit wastes, such as greenhouse gases (Acción Ecológica, quoted in Bullard 2010).

As defined above, it reframed the nature of debt and Northern responsibility for it. Issues such as just trade, just finance, an economy of life, and the financial collapse in 2008 are also addressed in a critical, empirical manner, often in conjunction with other social movement actors. WCC has worked with the *Fellowship of Christian Churches in West Africa*, the *Ecumenical Advocacy Alliance*, the *United Methodist Church of the Ivory Coast*, the *Third World Network*—Africa, and *SEATINI* (the Southern and Eastern Trade Information and Negotiation Institute). For example, they all held a workshop at the 2011 WSF in Senegal entitled "Economic Partnership Agreements Imposed on the African Continent," which provided detailed analyses of one-sided trade and investment agreements negotiated between groups of African countries and the European Union noting their devastating impact on the African continent. Here the analyses parallel those one might see in any critical NGO report.

The case of the WCC shows that a deeper understanding of religious participation in the WSF incorporating rational critiques as well as acknowledging spirituality is needed. Participation of religious organizations at the WSF shows no signs of diminishing. The programs of the 2013 and 2015 WSF's in Tunis, Tunisia, are cases in point. The context reflected, as the WSF often does, the major issues of the locale in which it is imbedded. Networks of faith groups in North and West Africa and from across Europe worked with other social movement actors providing content to workshops addressing a wide variety of issues from climate justice to land grabbing in Africa. Islamic and other faith groups addressed questions such as whether a separation of religion and state is necessary to preserve democracy, the issues of democratic transition, the rights of women, especially discrimination and violence in an Islamic context.

Notwithstanding the above, some words of caution are in order. As the 2010 Pew foundation study cited earlier indicated, both Muslim and Christian faiths in the Global South remain traditional and patriarchal regarding the role of women and LGBT groups as do some conservative religious groups in the United States. It is around issues of gender and sexuality that the presence of some churches within the GJM and the WSF have been viewed with concern. In Nairobi, gender equality, female genital mutilation, reproductive rights (especially abortion), HIV/AIDS prevention, and questions around sexual orientation and human rights generated tension between some religious organizations and feminists and LGBT groups. Most provocative was the statue of a visibly pregnant young teenage girl, hung on a cross Jesus-like, by Danish sculptor Jens Galschiott titled "In the Name of God" and dedicated to all of the victims of fundamentalism. Some churches in the Global North such as the Catholic Church, though critical of neoliberalism, remain staunchly patriarchal regarding women, a position that is anathema to many participants at the WSF. Nanga, for example, described the anticapitalism of Caritas, a global Roman Catholic charity, in essence as false, stating that "participation by reactionary Christianity threatens feminist and LGTB movements" (Nanga 2009, 289).

The WSF and the Occupy Movement represent different levels of scalar responses of the GJM to neoliberal globalization, one global, one local. While WSF participants are not disconnected from the local, they engage with transnational networks when these can serve local causes (Tarrow and Della Porta 2005). Participants in the Occupy Movement, on the other hand, operated primarily on the local scale fueled by populist anger regarding the global financial collapse brought on by practices of, and state policies encouraged by, Wall Street.

Like the WSF, social scientists have paid scant attention to the presence of religion and spirituality in the Occupy Movement. From a European context where few people identify as religious (though many continue to believe in God), this not surprising (Pew 2010). In the United States, however, where 57% of the population identify themselves as religious, a figure more in line with countries from the Global South, one would expect greater engagement from faith-based groups. Indeed, there was.

RELIGION AND OWS

While the origins and character of Occupy have been discussed elsewhere,[4] we note that it was inspired by the Arab Spring and the *Indignados* movement in Spain, both of which represent efforts to create new forms of public space organized around horizontalist principles. Despite the claim that the Occupy Movement was global, we argue that it was decidedly regional, centered primarily in the north, especially the United States and Europe. Using online blog data, the *Guardian* newspaper mapped the Occupy protests of October 11, 2011. While the protests took place in 951 cities in 82 countries around the world, they were overwhelmingly focused in the United States and Europe (*Guardian* 2011). The Occupy Movement in the United States was particularly strong, reflecting the dissatisfaction with growing inequality among many Americans. Of the 747 protests on the global day of protest on October 15, 2011, for which there is a record, 425, or 57%, occurred in the United States, a figure only rivalled in per capita terms by Canada, with 63 protest events, or 8% of the total. Thus, approximately two-thirds of "global protests" occurred in North America (calculated from the *Guardian* data set).

Our focus is on OWS. Wall Street can be said to be "a metonym for global financial capital . . . a symbol of injustice . . . a frame through which direct actions were planned" (Gluck 2012). OWS represented local opposition to this global symbol connected to injustice, a theme that resonated strongly with religious activists at OWS.[5] Strong religious involvement in progressive causes has been an important part of American history. Religion offered a moral sanction for independence from the British Empire, inspired the anti-slavery movement, supported the New Deal, and permeated the civil rights struggle. Relegating religion to the private sphere is an inaccurate depiction of American public life. While the United States is secular, religion plays an important role in American civil society and in efforts to influence public policy.

A belief that religion should be in the public square also informed religious activism at OWS. This is evident in anonymous interviews conducted by one of the co-authors of this chapter (Smith) in 2012. According to one rabbi, "all religions have a mandate for social and economic justice," and "if religion is not engaged in the public square it is a fossil." When it was suggested to one Black church leader that reverends should stay in the pulpits and congregations in their pews, the response was "This is insanity. Churches are violating the Gospel if they are not out in the world." A reverend in an activist church agreed, stating, "If you are only preaching in the pulpit you are not doing much." For a Buddhist monk, "religion is concerned with social order, justice, mutual respect, preservation of the natural order" and "must enter into public discussions." The separation of public and private made no sense to one seminarian who noted that "religion is already in the public square, we live in a pervasively religious country." The rabbi made one important caveat on the role of religion in public life—that "religion and state should be separate but not faith and the issues of the day."[6]

The creation of OWS as a public space was seen as an important opportunity for religious activists as "it opened up a public square to address the issues of the day" (personal interview with Reverend Michael Ellick of Judson Memorial Church, July 2012). For Ellick, a key supporter of OWS, there had been too many failures to create space and transcend a focus on single issue politics. Ellick recognized the importance of reimagining politics, of creating public spaces of diversity and drawing people to them. Here, the emotional/spiritual side of political engagement discussed previously is important. Ellick, for example, stressed the significance of spectacle evident in Occupy in terms of street theater, poetry, and symbolism as necessary to attract an audience and media attention. He helped organize and lead an interfaith march from Judson Memorial Church to Zuccotti Park where an interfaith service was to be held. At the center of the march was the golden calf, a symbol of greed and idolatry in the Muslim, Christian, and Jewish traditions.

The calf, which resembles the Wall Street bull, represented the greed of the one percent. The symbolism worked. According to Reverend Jennifer Butler: "In the streets, the cheers and prayers were overwhelming. Photographers and TV crews flocked to us" (2011). According to Butler, the image went viral, framing in moral terms for many what Occupy was all about: condemning greed and injustice; it helped to give rise to the network of Occupy Faith groups across the United States (Ellick interview). Religious leaders made a point of wearing religious garb to signify both the presence of faith in the movement and to show a progressive alternative to conservative religions so dominant in US mass media. This progressive-conservative split "has become an increasingly important framework within which people construct their religious identities and express their values and beliefs—across a range of religious traditions" (Lynch 2007, 17) (see also Nicinska, this volume).

Faith groups present at OWS also performed support functions crucial to any social movement. Churches and Muslim organizations supplied shelter and resources—food, tents, showers, and social media support. When OWS was raided, churches took in the displaced for up to two months. Churches helped mobilize congregations to march to Zuccotti Park bringing, for example, African-American churches into a space that was overwhelmingly white and middle class. Religious activists also performed an important educational function. Several interviewees reported going back to their more conservative congregations using their experiences at OWS to explain what the Occupy Movement was all about.

When asked what religious values motivated them all interviewees stressed the importance of social and economic justice. Protestant activists drew from the Gospels and the Prophets of the Old Testament—Jeremiah, Amos, Micah, and Isaiah—to draw attention to issues of justice, poverty, and debt forgiveness. Some spoke in terms of religion as liberation, that "God is the God of the oppressed." The emphasis on social and economic justice by interviewees drew upon male figures in the Bible and omitted feminist perspectives. However, in an interfaith service on November 13, 2011, in Zuccotti Park, theologian Traci West drew upon Mary of Nazareth's announcement in the Gospel of Luke that "God has lifted up the lowly, God has brought down the powerful from their thrones." West spoke directly to those women neglected by the existing economic system, stating:

> If you are a poor single mother on welfare, if you cannot feed your family no matter how many part-time jobs you have, you feel lowly and defeated and no greedy, corrupt politician cares, listen to the radical Christian gospel of economic equality from a poor, unwed, pregnant prophet of God. (West 2011)

Interviewees in the Jewish tradition drew extensively from the Prophetic tradition of the Old Testament, with its emphasis on the need for justice and alleviation of poverty. The Muslim interviewees stressed that justice was at the heart of Islam. These religious activists were strongly supportive of OWS.

The OWS, however, like the WSF, was a space of tensions. Increasingly full of the homeless, drug dealers, and others dropped off by the police, it became "a grimy earthly place" (anonymous interview 2012). According to one female activist, "it had become dysfunctional and dangerous" (interview 2012). When the evictions came, they were brutal and violent. Many young seminarians who formed part of what became known as *Protest Chaplains*, performing pastoral work at OWS, rushed down from their seminary wearing clerical garb to form a cordon between the police and the occupiers but were beaten back.

The evictions were by all accounts traumatic and a great loss to movement building. Yet it can be said that OWS and the Occupy Movement spawned considerable religious activism which, while reduced, has not faded away. Many activists reported they were still politically engaged, moving out into the communities fighting foreclosures and slum landlords, organizing rent strikes and often getting arrested when doing so. In the aftermath of Hurricane Sandy, many members of the Occupy Movement, religious activists, and churches organized relief efforts in hard-struck areas. *Occupy Faith NYC*, an interfaith group, has continued to meet, organize, and participate in direct action. While Occupy has been criticized for a lack of specific proposals, groups such as Occupy Faith have been specific about their intentions and policy proposals, drafting, almost a year after the evictions, a mission statement. The statement opens by saying: "Roused by Occupy Wall Street, Occupy Faith New York sets forth a moral and faith-based imperative for the regional and global movement for change," one that is more reformist than radical. Occupy Faith pledged to work for a "fair tax policy," "promote fair wages for all," work to "get money out of politics and limit the power of corporations," and take part in direct actions (Occupy Faith Statement, October 10, 2012). Specific actions targeted at the American context were coupled with a continuing commitment to global justice. Occupy, like the WSF, created a space where global justice activists could challenge neoliberalism but go beyond critiquing it and articulate alternatives.

CONCLUSION

This chapter has examined the role of religion and spirituality in resisting capitalism through the struggle of the GJM against neoliberal globalization. Using two key sites of struggle, the WSF and OWS, we show that this role has been largely ignored by those studying the GJM. Others like David Korten (2008) concur, noting at the 2007 United States Social Forum that spirituality plays an important role in this political activism and "yet we never talk about it" (352). One reason is the dominance of analyses of the GJM, the Occupy Movement, and the WSF by secular intellectuals. This produces a blindness, an occlusion of sociological reality. Santos (as quoted in Daulatzai 2004) has called this disconnection "the sociology of absences," that creates nonexistence of an entity when it "is disqualified and rendered invisible, unintelligible or irreversibly discarded." A counterhegemonic movement such as the WSF should address these absences, he argues, noting the need to recognize the "role of spirituality in the social struggles for a better world" (571). Yet, the WSF and its International Council remain silent on the issue of religious presence at the WSF preferring to maintain a veneer of secularity. In terms of sheer numbers and demographics, religious organizations cannot be ignored. Those striving for change must confront the reality of the religious presence in the Global South (Knighton 2006, 71).

We acknowledged, however, that religion is not always a source of unity in the struggle. As indicated above, there have been divisions even within Christian churches and between churches, faith groups, and other social justice movements around issues such as gender and sexuality. At the WSF in Tunis 2013 and 2015, soon after the Arab Spring and elections that brought Islamist party majorities in Egypt and Tunisia, tensions between the secular and Islamic groups in relation to the rights of women were evident. Even in the case of economic injustice and globalization, Christian churches are hardly unified. In his analysis of *Poverty, Wealth and Ecology*, Rogate Mshana (2007) of the WCC admitted:

> Economic concerns have emerged as a divisive issue for the churches. The AGAPE process in particular revealed that many of the old North–South tensions and conflicts remain. Differences in analyses and recommendations among churches and ecumenical partners stem largely from divergences in ideological standpoints that are, in turn, determined by social and historical locations.

This chapter also addressed the issue of dualism and the role of spirituality in the GJM showing how the subjective, irrational, emotional, and spiritual, side of political activism was evident in both the WSF and OWS. Consistent with a reviving indigenous movement and its emphasis on spirituality, the rights of Mother Earth, and living well, and the increasing emphasis on the way of subjectivity in political activism at the WSF, the WCC, as we indicated, developed stronger, holistic critiques of neoliberal globalization in addition to its detailed reasoned critiques. Rejecting the growth model, emphasizing a solidarity economy and the Earth as a living entity, the WCC engaged the debate on the "civilizational crisis" of hegemonic Eurocentric modernity. The critique is grounded on theological premises and biblical interpretation.

Our analysis also indicated the different forms of resistance in the two sites of struggle. In contrast to the WSF, OWS was more about direct action, occupation of a space, and confronting the one percent, reacting in a hostile, but peaceful way, to the economic crisis. With the exception of the Jubilee debt campaign, discussed in the introduction to this volume, where the link to the Sabbath-Jubilee Christian tradition is readily acknowledged by social scientists, the role of religion and spirituality in the GJM's resistance to neoliberal globalization is not. Our two cases of the WSF and OWS indicate why it is important to pay more attention to religious activism, its opposition to neoliberal globalization, and its concrete alternatives for a more just and humane world order.

NOTES

1. The authors gratefully acknowledge the support of the Social Sciences and Humanities Research Council and the Coolidge Fellowship Program in Social Movements and Religion, Union Theological Seminary/Columbia University, July 2012. An earlier version of this chapter was presented at the Conference on the Social Sciences and the Christian faith sponsored by the Centre for Scholarship and the Christian faith, Concordia University of Edmonton, May 3, 2013.

2. This section of the chapter is indebted to the work of Erin Wilson (2011a) and (2011b).

3. *Source*: Survey of the Profile of WSF Participants IBASE (2003).

4. See, for example, the online articles from *Cultural Anthropology*, sponsored by the *Journal for the Society of Cultural Anthropology*, July 2012, http://www.culanth. org/?q=node/641.

5. This section draws upon interviews of twelve religious activists from Protestant, Catholic, Jewish, Muslim, and Buddhist faith traditions conducted in July 2012 by Smith, supplemented by online research and secondary sources. The exception is Reverend Michael Ellick of Judson Memorial Church, whose media prominence made it difficult to keep his name anonymous.

6. All quotes in this paragraph are taken from personal anonymous interviews by Smith, this chapter.

REFERENCES

Beck, Ulrich. 2000. *What is Globalization?* Walden, MA: Blackwell Publishers.

Becker, Marc and Ashley N. Koda. 2011. "Indigenous Peoples and Social Forums." In *Handbook on World Social Forum Activism*, edited by Jackie Smith, Scott Byrd, Ellen Reese, and Elizabeth Smythe. Boulder, CO: Paradigm Press.

Borg, Marcus J. and John Dominic Crossan. 2009. *The First Paul: Reclaiming the Radical Visionary Behind the Church's Icon*. San Francisco: Harper One.

Bullard, Nicola. 2010. "Climate Debt as a Subversive Political Strategy." *Committee for the Abolition of Third World Debt*. http://cadtm.org/Climate-debt-as-a-subversive.

Butler, Reverend Jennifer. 2011. "The Golden Calf and Occupy Wall Street." *Huffington Post*. October 13, 2011. http://www.huffingtonpost.com/rev-jennifer-butler/golden-calf-occupy-wall-street_b_1009455.html.

Crossan, John Dominic and Reed, Jonathan L. 2004. *In Search of Paul: How Jesus's Apostle Opposed Rome's Empire with God's Kingdom*. San Francisco: Harper.

Daulatzai, Anila. 2004. "A Leap of Faith: Thoughts on Secularistic Practices and Progressive Politics." *International Social Science Journal* 56 (182): 565–76.

Della Porta, Donatella. 2007. "The Global Justice Movement: An Introduction." In *The Global Justice Movement: Cross-National and Transnational Perspectives*, edited by Donatella Della Porta, 1–28. Boulder: Paradigm Publishers.

Glück, Zoltán. "Between Wall Street and Zuccotti: Occupy and the Scale of Politics." Fieldsights—Hot Spots, *Cultural Anthropology Online*, February 14, 2013, http://www.culanth.org/fieldsights/67-between-wall-street-and-zuccotti-occupy-and-the-scale-of-politics.

The Guardian UK. 2011. "Occupy Protests Around the World: Full List Visualized." http://www.guardian.co.uk/news/datablog/2011/oct/17/occupy-protests-world-list-map?newsfeed=true#data.

Horsley, Richard A. 2003. *Religion and Empire: People, Power, and the Life of the Spirit*. Minneapolis: Fortress Press.

Hurd, Elizabeth Shakman. 2011. "Secularism and International Relations Theory." In *Religion and International Relations Theory*, edited by Jack L. Snyder, 60–90. New York: Columbia University Press.

Knighton, Ben. 2005. "Multireligious Responses to Globalizations in East Africa." *Transformation* 23 (2): 76–85.

Korten, David. 2008. "Spirituality and the Transformative Moment." *Solidarity Economy: Building Alternatives for People and Planet. Papers and Reports from the U.S. Social Forum 2007*, edited by Jenna Allard, Carl Davidson, and Julie Matthaei, 345–52. Chicago, IL: ChangeMaker Publications.

Lechner, Frank J. 2005. "Religious Rejections of Globalization." In *Religion in Global Civil Society*, edited by Mark Juergensmeyer, 115–35. Oxford: Oxford University Press.

Lynch, Gordon. 2007. *The New Spirituality: An Introduction to Progressive Belief in the Twenty-first Century*. London: I.B. Tauris.

Lutheran World Federation. 2015. "About." https://www.lutheranworld.org/content/about-lwf.

Marcos, Sylvia. 2013. "Presentation at World Social Forum." Tunis, Tunisia. March 27, 2013.

Mshana, Rogate. 2007. *Poverty, Wealth and Ecology*. World Council of Churches, online, http://www.oikoumene.org/fileadmin/files/wcc-main/documents/p3/poverty_24p.pdf.

Murtola, Anna-Maria. 2012. "Materialist Theology and Anti-capitalist Resistance, or, 'What would Jesus Buy?'" *Organization* 19 (3): 325–44.

Nanga, Jean. 2009. "The World Social Forum in Africa." In *World Social Forum Challenging Empires*, edited by Jai Sen and Peter Waterman, 276–91. Montreal: Black Rose Books.

O'Grady, Selina, 2013. *And Man Created God: Kings, Cults, and Conquests at the Time of Jesus*. New York City: St. Martin's Press.

Pew Forum on Religion and Public Life. 2010. "Islam and Christianity in Sub-Saharan Africa." http://www.pewforum.org/2010/04/15/executive-summary-islam-and-christianity-in-sub-saharan-africa/.

Polanyi, Karl. 2001. *The Great Transformation: The Political and Economic Origins of Our Time*. Boston, MA: Beacon Press.

Pleyers, Geoffrey. 2010. *Alter-Globalization: Becoming Actors in the Global Age*. Malden, MA: Polity Press.

Rees, John A. 2011. *Religion in International Politics and Development*. Northampton, MA: Edward Elgar.

Shah, Timothy Samuel and Daniel Philpott. 2011. "The Fall and Rise of Religion in International Relations: History and Theory." In *Religion and International Relations Theory*, edited by Jack L. Snyder, 24–59. New York, NY: Columbia University Press.

Smith, Jackie and Marina Karides, Marc Becker, Dorval Brunelle, Christopher Chase-Dunn, and Donatella Della Porta. 2008. *Global Democracy and the World Social Forums*. Boulder, CO: Paradigm Press.

Smith, Peter J. and Elizabeth Smythe. 2011. "(In)Fertile Ground? Social Forum Activism in its Regional and Local Dimensions." In *Handbook of Social Forum Activism*, edited by Jackie Smith, Scott Byrd, Ellen Reese, and Elizabeth Smythe, 29–49. Boulder, CO: Paradigm Press.

Tarrow, Sidney and Donatella Della Porta. 2005. "Conclusion: 'Globalization,' Complex Internationalism, and Transnational Contention." In *Transnational Protest and Global Activism*, edited by Donatella Della Porta and Sidney Tarrow, 227–46. New York: Rowman & Littlefield.

Taussig, Hal. 2005. "Prologue: A Door Thrown Open." *Union Seminary Quarterly* 59 (1).

Transnational Social Movement Research Working Group. 2007. University of California, Riverside.

von Sinner, Rudolph. 2007. "The Churches' Contribution to Citizenship in Brazil." *Journal of International Affairs* 61 (1): 171–84.

Wilson, Erin K. 2010. "Beyond Dualism: Expanded Understandings of Religion and Global Justice." *International Studies Quarterly* 54 (3): 733–54.

Wilson, Erin K. 2012. *After Secularism*. New York, NY: Palgrave Macmillan.

Wilson, Erin K. and Manfred B. Steger. 2013. "Religious Globalisms in the Post-Secular Age." *Globalizations* 10 (3): 481–95.

World Council of Churches. 2003. "'Spirituality of Resistance' Key Theme of WCC's Contribution to World Social Forum." February 26, 2011. http://www.oikoumene.org/en/press-centre/news/spirituality-of-resistance-key-theme-of-wcc-s-contribution-to-world-social-forum.

World Council of Churches (Justice, Peace and Creation Team). 2005. *Alternative Globalization Addressing Peoples and Earth (AGAPE)*. Geneva. https://www.oikoumene.org/en/folder/documents-pdf/agape-new.pdf.

World Council of Churches. 2011. "Who Are We?" http://www.oikoumene.org/en/who-are-we.html.

World Social Forum. 2001. Charter of Principles. http://www.fsm2013.org/en/node/204.

Chapter 15

Indianismo and Decoloniality

Voices of Resistance

Marcos Scauso

In the years between the 1970s and the 2000s, much of Latin America followed the Washington Consensus. This economic formula promoted a homogenizing notion of development intended to fit all (De la Barra and Dello Buono 2009, 3), but it led in many cases to social inequality, unemployment, social exclusion, poverty, and political discontent (Petras and Veltmeyer 2005, 222). Few groups in Latin America experienced the severe costs of these policies as much as the indigenous populations, but what is remarkable is that even fewer have been as active and radical in their resistance (Escobar 2010). One of the most paradigmatic cases of radical resistance emerged in Bolivia with the Indianista movement.

Indianismo, the underlying worldview of the movement, started to emerge during Bolivia's neoliberal era beginning in August 1971, when the dictatorship of Hugo Banzer Suárez took control of the government and harshly repressed many forms of collective action. His government proceeded to implement the structural adjustment policies by the International Monetary Fund and World Bank (Ticona 2013, 2000). Also during this decade, indigenous activists began exploring the works of Indianista intellectuals and they also entered the halls of Bolivian universities (Rivera 1999, 153; Ticona 2011).

In the 1980s, Bolivia transitioned to democracy and deepened the application of neoliberal policies after the 1985 presidential election of Victor Paz. His government exacerbated the streamlining of Bolivia along neoliberal lines and its integration into the global economy through the strict application of the notion of development promoted by the Washington Consensus. This is the context in which the Indianista movement expanded its political force by taking control of one of the principal unions of Bolivia, namely the Confederación Sindical Única de Trabajadores de Bolivia (Rivera 1999, 153).

While working together with other social movements, in the year 2000, they vehemently resisted the privatization of water during the water wars. In the city of Cochabamba, "water warriors" started mobilizing in large numbers once the company *Aguas de Turani* (a subsidiary of the Bechtel Corporation) raised the prices for water after signing a 40-year lease with the government. After much repression, the use of tear gas, political arrests, and the intervention of the national government, the company decided to leave the country and the governor of Cochabamba resigned. In 2003, a similar political action took place during the gas wars. Initially, the movements' demands were the simple cancellation of the deal to export gas through Chile, but they quickly became more comprehensive to include the resignation of President Gonzalo Sanchez de Lozada, the liberation of political prisoners, justice for the killings of activists and civilians because of the repressive usage of police force, and a move away from the neoliberal model of development (Assies 2004). These events and struggles are often considered to mark the end of the neoliberal era in Bolivia. They helped to unify the different social movements active throughout the country, which collectively put Bolivia on a different path and ensured that an outright neoliberal government could no longer hold on to power.

The analysis in this chapter focuses on the decolonial aspects of Indianismo, which seeks to dismantle the very basis of the domination and the hierarchical mentality that is reinforced today through neoliberal globalization, but which is, for most activists, a direct continuation of the colonization process. Indianismo entails a project that intends to transform the colonial system of oppression and to construct a space where the diversity of indigenous peoples can flourish. The core of the Indianista discourse is teased out through the description of the notion of *complementarity*. This worldview understands the cosmos as a relationship between incomplete and different parts that make up a harmonious whole. Indianismo practices a discourse that seeks to connect *difference* and *equality*. Indianismo is, then, a radical discourse that questions the deepest levels of the colonial mentality imposed for hundreds of years upon the Americas and beyond (Todorov 1982). It seeks to dismantle the very basis of the domination and the hierarchical mentality that is reinforced today through neoliberal globalization.

The analysis in this chapter utilizes Foucault's notion of archeology (Foucault 1972) and does so by concentrating on the *rules* that emerge from the regularities of a discourse practiced on different occasions (Foucault 1972, 48). In this sense, the main focus of this chapter is centered on a set of practices connected to each other by the internal logic of a *discursive formation*. In order to follow this methodology, the chapter starts with an analysis of the notions of *Pachamama* (Mother Earth) and *buen vivir*, which is sometimes translated as "live well" (*sumak kawsay* in Quechua or *suma quamaña* in Aymara). This section illustrates the Indianista opposition against neoliberal globalization, but it also begins to show a much deeper level of resistance based on a form of decolonial mentality. Second, the chapter describes the definition of neoliberalism that Indianismo is constructing as the "other" against whom it struggles. Third, the philosophical section seeks to unveil the core of the Indianismo to be found in the notion of *complementarity*, which gives coherence to the entire project. On a more concrete level, it transforms life from its ontological roots onward. Complementarity is, then, the core of the discourse uniting everything else. It provides a starting point that connects equality and difference in order to oppose the *homogenizing tendency of neoliberal globalization.* The final section of this chapter utilizes this archeological analysis to follow the inner logic of Indianismo and also to draw out its internal limitations or boundaries. This discussion leads toward the description of the most radical element of Indianismo—namely, its notion of *reflexivity*, its ability to reflect critically on itself as well as on how it relates to everyday life in order to transform itself accordingly.

PACHAMAMA AND BUEN VIVIR

Following a Foucauldian discourse analysis, the notions of *Pachamama* and *buen vivir* emerge as two of the key elements in Indianista thinking. *Pachamama* comes from Aymara religiosity and it translates to Mother Earth. The Aymara people represent at least 17% of the population of Bolivia that is fifteen years old or older (Instituto Nacional de Estadística). Despite different definitions of *Pachamama*, in the Indianista discourse practiced, for example, by Evo Morales and social movements such as Vía Campesina, she is the entity that represents the complexity of the relationships and existence of all beings as well as things on earth. *Pachamama* is thus the result of the coexistence of all things on Earth, which create a single organism (for similar ideas from within Christianity, see the chapter by Nicinska). *Pachamama* is not only the addition of the parts but also the whole that results from the organic relationship between everything on earth. In this sense,

> We do not live on Earth. We are Earth, part of Earth. Between living beings and inert beings; between the atmosphere, the oceans, the mountains, the surface of earth, the biosphere and the anthroposphere there rule interrelations. There is no addition between all these parts. Instead, there is an organic relationship between them. (Zaffaroni 2015, 88, author's translation)

This notion decentralizes earth by taking away humanity's role of domination (Mardones Hernandez and Garcia 2015, 5). Here, humans appear as equal parts of *Pachamama* and thus do not obtain a special status in any hierarchical cosmic order. As a result of the Pachamama discourse, a respect for life and its diversity emerges from the underlying acceptance of the equality of all beings that are woven together in an organic relationship on Mother Earth.

In order to protect life, then, this project seeks a balance between the satisfaction of the necessities of different beings through reciprocity. As Zaffaroni mentions, Pachamama, or Mother Earth, appears as a giant community that encompasses the entire biosphere. Its complex links creating a balance in nature in order to protect the diversity of life. In this way of thinking, actions of one entity on Mother Earth inevitably affect, but also complement, the actions of others.

This discourse of Pachamama has now given rise to a new legal and constitutional discourse, first in Ecuador, then also in Bolivia, under which Earth or nature is given legal standing. This juridical form of environmentalism seeks to protect the biosphere and to put it in a sustainable balance that would help to avoid its depletion by the "fundamentalism of the market" (Zaffaroni 2015, 113). The new Bolivian constitution mentions Pachamama's rights in, for example, Articles 33 and 34. These articles state that peoples have the right to live in a protected environment where there is an equilibrium with nature. These articles also establish the right of anyone to take legal actions to defend Mother Earth, should practices destroy the precarious natural equilibrium.

The notion of *Pachamama* is often deployed by governmental policies in Bolivia, social movements such as Vía Campesina or CONAIE (Confederation of Indigenous Peoples of Ecuador), the government of Ecuador, and intellectuals of decoloniality (e.g., Mignolo 2012; Escobar 2010). Evo Morales, the indigenous leader of one of the branches of the movement who was elected president in 2005, even went so far as to speculate on their universal applicability. He proclaimed that the rights of *Pachamama* need to be universal because the isolated actions of one country cannot stop the global overconsumption of resources (Morales 2012). This way of thinking led Morales to assert that the developed nations of the North have a climate debt to the South. In Evo Morales' view, highly controversial but adopted as a part of the World Social Forum discussions, the countries of the North have developed their economies and have become wealthy through a form of colonialism that exploits natural resources belonging to the South or even to the whole of humanity. From his point of view, the overutilization of resources and the production of greenhouse gases have to be seen as one of the material bases that enabled development in the Global North. Since these resources have been depleted solely in order to increase the standards of living in a particular region, the North ought to pay back the debt stemming from the exploitation of these resources and in this way allow the South to develop policies to deal with climate change. This discussion shows that the discourse of Pachamama has consequences for the global development discourse. In order to restore the balance that has been undermined by the overdevelopment of the North, there needs to be compensation to establish a more sustainable equilibrium of living standards. It shows that Earth is a single organism affected negatively more by one party than the other.

In neoliberal notions of development, human beings merely appear as actors to be satisfied through rational choices of consumption. But this model assumes that resources are endless and that Mother Earth can be exploited without any consequences. Against the neoliberal economic assumption of unlimited growth and consumption as the only path toward development, the Indianista notion of Pachamama reminds people that nature is an organism that cannot be exploited endlessly without being destroyed (Mardones, Hernandez, and Garcia 2015, 4). From this perspective, humanity has taken on a suicidal path that is threatening its survival as a whole (5). Insofar as Earth ought to be a balanced organism, the depletion of resources by humans is now coming back to haunt that humanity. The idea of natural limits to growth and the need to restore balance also appear in Evo Morales' discourse. He points out that the world suffers a crisis related to the neoliberal model of development, which is based on the endless search for profit through, for example, the unfair distribution of wealth enabled by the policies of international financial institutions (Evo Morales, G77 speech 2014). In his view, this form of capitalism leads the world toward an ecocide and ultimately is a form of suicide (Evo Morales, Conferencia Mundia 2014).

According to Indianismo, the solution to this crisis derives from reconceptualizing development through Pachamama thinking. The name of the project is *buen vivir* and it seeks to create a model through which different peoples can have more equality while respecting their differences and avoiding the destruction of Mother Earth. To develop a better understanding of this project, the notion of Indianista environmentalism is used here to illustrate the deeper connection that this project seeks to establish as a basis of resistance against neoliberalism.

Insofar as Earth is a limited organism, humans ought to seek the satisfaction of their necessities in *moderation*, without depleting other species, thus maintaining a balance with the reproduction of life in diversity. *Buen vivir* thus relates humanity to the environment without locating it as the apex of a hierarchy. It is a way of life that leads to the encounter and enjoyment of heterogeneity in all its aspects. Insofar as Earth is understood as a single organism, each tiny part complements other parts. This makes humans only a part of the community.

The consequence of this Pachamama thinking extends to a new way of looking at world politics from an environmental perspective. Evo Morales, for example, promotes this idea as a universal project that may solve the global crisis of neoliberal capitalism (Evo Morales, UN 2014). He condemns opulence, luxury, and overconsumption (Evo Morales, Ten Commandments 2012). His discourse also expands into the political arena, where direct participation and the redistribution of wealth appear as key tools utilized by the "warriors" of *buen vivir* in order to decrease asymmetry, hierarchy, and, thus, domination. This is why, for example, the Bolivian Constitution of 2009 establishes that political participation can take place not only through elections, but also through direct types of influence, such as referenda, the citizenship initiative for legislation, assemblies, and other deliberative forums (Bolivian Constitution 2009, Articles 11, II, 1). In the cultural realm, Evo Morales highlights that the political project of *buen vivir* entails a struggle against colonialism, which still homogenizes life on earth in its new incarnation in the form of neoliberal globalization (Evo Morales, G77 speech, 2014). This has been integrated into the new Bolivian constitution that asserts that the diversity of indigenous peoples ought to be protected against the racism of colonialism (Bolivian Constitution 2009, 7).

It is necessary to clarify here that, notwithstanding Evo Morales' proposals and some of his actions, many of his domestic policies and speeches have contradicted this Indianista discourse. While the relative enhancement of the respect for diversity in Bolivia since 2006 can hardly be questioned, the tension between development and Indianismo still creates conflicts in the relationship between diversity, equality, and the overarching policies of the Bolivian state (Ari 2014, 186). Mining, road construction, the expansion of oil as well as gas production, and other developmental programs often affect the lands and livelihoods of indigenous communities. The most paradigmatic case of this tension occurred in 2011, when Evo Morales' government started working on the construction of a road across the ancestral territories known as *Territorio Indígena Parque Nacional Isidoro Secure* (TIPNIS). Many movements successfully resisted the construction of this road, which ultimately had to be cancelled. Evo Morales also lost the support of several social movements such as CONAIE, which wrote a public letter reminding him that, in the path toward development, ancestral rights and *Pachamama* always come first (Umberto Cholango in The Links blog, 2011). The leftist blog NACLA concluded that "the TIPNIS struggle and the subsequent conflicts with militant mineworkers have revealed the government's anti-indigenous, anti-union proclivities, while new alliances with agrobusinesses have betrayed its core peasant constituency" (Emily Achtenberg in the NACLA blog 2013). In another publication, the same blog mentioned that the economy of Bolivia continues to be extractive and thus still seeks to increase its revenues from the income produced by the exports of raw material. Felipe Quispe, another leader of the indigenous movement, even characterized Evo Morales as a neoliberal president hiding behind an Indianista, communitarian, and leftist mask (Felipe Quispe, interviewed by Jimena Costa, 2012). These examples show that there is a discrepancy between the Indianista discourse and some of the policies of the government. They also signal the existence of different interpretations of Indianismo. Nevertheless, this particular set of Indianista practices need further study since they form an important example of a radical alternative to neoliberal globalization, even if its implementation, predictably, will run into many difficulties and obstacles. The remainder of the chapter is dedicated to the understanding of the inner patterns and rules of this discourse.

NEOLIBERALISM AND INDIANISMO

Indianismo is understood here as radical because it reaches and criticizes one of the deepest levels of neoliberalism, namely its hierarchicalizing mentality of singularity—the notion that there is no alternative and that there is only one way of doing things, one of the key criticisms directed at the structural adjustment policies of international financial institutions. In the neoliberal globalization project, the *individual* appears as a consuming subject that uses nature to satisfy its endless desires. Here, humanity is located above the rest of Earth and this position justifies a limitless form of progress through dominance, not only over nature but, necessarily, also over countries. Neoliberalism thus promotes "massive and excessive consumption of products in the belief that 'to have' more is 'to live better'" (Evo Morales, Ten Commandments 2012). This notion evokes the comprehension of the *world* as a single capitalist society that ought to produce in order to satisfy this individual. Consequently, *development* is understood as a single line of progress toward massive consumption and production. The closer a society is to the satisfaction of the consuming individual and the mode of production required for this form of life, the higher it is in the neoliberal hierarchy. This is where the Washington Consensus recipe—Williamson's (1990) famous summary of key neoliberal proscriptions—seeks to mold policy. Based on the notion of competition and specialization, neoliberalism supposedly creates the conditions necessary for a country to export in the sector where it has its biggest comparative advantages. Through this path, countries are supposed to move up in the different stages of development so that they can reach the levels of Europe or the United States.

One of the problems of this discourse is that, at least in Bolivia, it did not achieve its promise. According to Evo Morales, the neoliberal discourse has put the entire country (and also the planet) in a dangerous crisis. During the G77 plus China Summit in 2014, Evo Morales asserted: "This unfair manner of concentrating wealth and this predatory way of destroying nature are giving rise to a structural crisis that is becoming unsustainable over time" (Evo Morales 2014). Additionally, neoliberalism increased poverty, wealth concentration, hunger, and inequality in Bolivia (Evo Morales 2014). The key problem with neoliberalism, however, is that its policies assume that there is a single form of truth. Just like the rest of the discourse, truth itself is ordered hierarchically. The differences between knowledges and truths are ordered based on a particular conception of epistemology, which judges all differences as inferior or superior. The archeological description of neoliberal epistemology exceeds the scope of this chapter, but it is now possible to understand how Indianismo seeks to build a radical form of resistance that reaches the roots of neoliberalism to eradicate it.

From the notion of Pachamama discussed above, Indianismo seeks to construct a project that views each part (individual, community, people, nation, state, continent) as conforming an organic whole. This discourse enables a space where each community can have its own truth and the differences between communities do not entail a hierarchy. Insofar as each entity is a part of an organic whole, each community is understood as an equal member of the organicity of *Pachamama*. From this point of departure, Indianismo creates a *project of heterogeneity*. It fights to resist homogenization and to enable the diversity of life.

The political aspect of this Indianista project thus evokes a notion of *oppression* stemming from the colonial process of homogenization through Westernization in its latest neoliberal phase. Colonial powers enact this form of neoliberal singularity through different mechanisms. First, neoliberalism is understood as an ideology that generates homogeneity through the universalization of the consuming individual, Western reason, and its notion of development, which entails a single path of history toward European modernization (Caba and García 2014). This hierarchicalizing idea organizes differences between communities, peoples, countries, and knowledges through the various stages of development that are vertically ordered in the phases toward modernization. This is why neoliberalism is both homogenizing and hierarchicalizing. On the other hand, the deleterious effects of neoliberal policies increase inequality and poverty, which sustain these hierarchical positions and reproduce the Western order of things.

Indianismo struggles for the possibility of respecting the differences of each part (community, nation, people, culture, etc.) by understanding them as equals in the relationships that shape Pachamama. This is neither a neutral philosophy nor a form of relativism. Instead, it is a political weapon that allows for heterogeneity and brings differences to light (Fernández and

Sepúlveda 2014, 5). While certain core elements are widely shared, there are, however, different interpretations of Indianismo in the Bolivia of today.

In the Indianismo of the earlier Fausto Reinaga, one of the most important intellectuals and ideologues of Indianismo in Bolivia during the 1970s, this struggle entailed a strategy of subversive rebellion through a guerrilla war against the colonial order (Reinaga 1970, 5). This Indianista war was meant to fight homogenization in general and it included a strong opposition against *mestizaje*, which was viewed as a state-run Westernizing strategy of forced assimilationism (Feldman 2015, 2). According to Javier Sanjinés, mestizaje is "the process by which the Spanish and Indian have intermixed, creating a racial and national synthesis" (Sanjinés 2004, 2). This ideology was the racial basis for the unification of a nation under a single European dream. In contrast to this, Indianismo sought to create a separation between the Western (White) and the Indianista Bolivia. The fight would create the division into two republics. One of them would be a space that would allow expression of the Indio identity. Felipe Quispe, for example, continued to promote this notion of separatism during the water wars from 2000 onward (Ari 2014, 167). According to Quispe, the Indianista project entailed a radical transformation called *Pachakuti* (transformation of Earth), which would be achieved through a revolution (Felipe Quispe, interviewed by Jimena Costa, 2012).

Other intellectuals and activists thought of this project in different terms. Many took the notion of diversity and sought to struggle for a broader project of *decoloniality*. In his later work, Fausto Reinaga himself moved away from the notion of an Indianismo based on the separation of two republics in Bolivia. After his writings during the early 1970s, he started to think that this form of relationship belonged to the entire cosmos and thus the whole world had to seek a transformation toward what he called the *Amaútico* community. *Amauta* translates to "master" or "wise" in Quechua and it was the Inca title given to teachers in the Empire. Here, Amautas understand the cosmos and thus reach the truth of the organic relationship between all the parts of the cosmos. Reinaga takes this into account and makes it a universal philosophy that encompasses the entire world in the formation of a *community* (Ticona 2013, 221). This is the project of the Indio, which is understood here not as a biological race or an authentic form of identity that anteceded colonialism; instead, it was the *pensamiento* (mentality) of liberation that could create a worldwide space of peace through the struggle against occidental Westernization (Reinaga 1978, 55).

Many scholars and intellectuals followed this broader notion of decoloniality. For example, the well-known intellectual of decoloniality from Colombia, Arturo Escobar, concluded that the indigenous movements of Bolivia struggled for the creation of a space of *relationality* that was a task for the whole world (Escobar 2010, 46). He pointed out that this space would enable

a nonhierarchical form of coexistence that would avoid the abolition of difference (Escobar 2010, 33). Similarly, Walter Mignolo, a recognized researcher
of colonialism and resistance, also claimed that Fausto Reinaga constructed
a notion of epistemological decoloniality, which had its own project in the
search of a space for "harmony and reciprocity, rather than living in competition and meritocracy" (Mignolo 2012, 25). Finally, María Isasi-Díaz and
Eduardo Mendieta mentioned that these indigenous struggles, as well as other
voices that emerged throughout the world, constructed a space "of all life"
(Isasi-Díaz and Mendieta 2012, 4). Although sometimes contradictory, Evo
Morales' deployment of Indianismo is also closer to this definition.

It is necessary to clarify here that decoloniality does not seek a "foolish
postmodernism" by enabling all differences in relativism (Estermann 2014,
5). Instead, it seeks to fight against "monoculturalism" and in this battle it
retains a strong critical element (Estermann 2014, 5). It, furthermore, enables
different peoples to coexist without imposing single forms of identity upon
each other. In this sense, as Estermann points out, decoloniality entails a
struggle against the asymmetry, domination, and inequality of homogenizing
mentalities. It is not just a promotion of "ethnicism" or "folklorism."

Many aspects of this discourse have acquired political force thanks not
only to the work of intellectuals of decoloniality or grassroots movements,
such as Vía Campesina, but also to governments that promote many aspects
of these ideas. Evo Morales mentioned during a UN summit in 2014 that
"colonialism is the brutal and archaic form of domination destroying humanity. It is the mother of fascism, racism and all discrimination. The possibility
of overcoming it entails the respect for the free determination of the peoples
of the world and the exchange of knowledges in complementarity and solidarity" (Evo Morales, G77 speech, 2014). In this struggle, indigenous peoples
are the ones pointing in the direction that Bolivia and the world ought to follow (Bolivian Constituton 2009, 4). Here, the enemy is *domination* in general
because it imposes a single form of mentality that orders the whole world in
a hierarchy. In this sense, Evo Morales mentions: "We are fighting not to
dominate anyone. We are fighting to ensure that no one becomes dominated"
(Evo Morales, G77 speech 2014). This possibility is not reached through a
form of culturalist relativism, but through a political project that aims toward
equality and difference at the same time.

PHILOSOPHY AND DISCOURSE: THE
COSMOS AND COMPLEMENTARITY

By focusing on a set of Indianista *practices*, this section follows archeologi-
cally the *patterns* that connect the previous notions and make up a *discursive*

formation (Foucault 1972, 38). The advantage of using Foucault's archeology is that it seeks to find the *patterns* of a discourse. It does not focus on the particularities of the material bases of a discourse such as a movement, an author, or a president. It analyzes a voice in its own logic by concentrating on particular discursive events that are connected through these internal rules. What is, then, the core of the discourse? How does Indianismo reach the deep roots of colonialism in order to undermine its basis and build a different as well as radical project?

As previously mentioned, Indianismo defines Pachamama from an interpretation of a *religiosity* that is practiced today by many of the peoples that live in the cities of El Alto and La Paz, as well as around the Lake Titicaca. One key element of this religiosity is the possibility of respecting and valuing differences. The key notion here lies within the comprehension of *complementarity* that links the multiple entities that coexist in the world. Complementarity is the philosophical equivalent of the organicity of Pachamama discussed above.

This organic relationship between all things on Earth takes place at two levels. On the one hand, it is understood as part of a *reciprocal* relationship (reciprocity), which entails that the action of one being affects the totality of Earth and all other things. A concrete expression of what this entails is that the satisfaction of the necessities of one part of Pachamama may directly threaten the survival of another on Earth. This notion is used, for example, in the previously mentioned definition of Pachamama in environmentalist circles and has found its concrete expression in the move to give legal standing to Earth or nature. On the other hand, the relationship of Pachamama goes much deeper in the definition of *complementarity*, which encompasses the "being" of entities or their identity. This ontological notion finds incompleteness (deficit) in each single coherent identity and completeness only in the organic aggregate of differences. For example, the great variety of ethnic differences in Bolivia makes up a more complete whole when looking at Bolivia in the context of a plurinational state. Plurinationality means that all peoples or nations of Bolivia should coexist in equality. Each community or nation is thus valued because it is different, but it is also humbled because it is only part of the whole. No single nation is perfect by itself and thus superior; instead, each difference complements the other in the formation of a heterogeneous yet unified Bolivia. It is important to note here that Bolivia has an extremely complex demographic composition. Within the 40% of the population that was fifteen years old or older and considered itself indigenous in the 2012 census, there were more than thirty-seven ethnicities (Instituto Nacional de Estadística 2012). Through this constitutional notion of plurinationality, they are legally protected from the homogenizing tendencies of central governments imposed, for example, through neoliberal adjustment programs and their notion of economic development. In this sense, the 2009 constitution of Bolivia establishes that the state seeks the happiness of all through the possibility of *buen vivir* in equality, liberty, reciprocity, dignity, and complementarity (Bolivian Constitution 2009, Article 8). This form of equality seeks to create a space where single notions of nationhood or development can be resisted through, for example, the protection of the autonomy of indigenous peoples, the official recognition of thirty-seven languages, the respect and guarantee of religious freedoms, the possibility of establishing forms of self-government, and the respect of different forms of land property (Bolivian Constitution 2009).

The differences between identities thus complement each other and make up the organic totality of the cosmos. In this sense, the cosmos finds its harmony in the complementarity that is possible only insofar as heterogeneity or differences coexist. The very characteristic of the cosmos is, thus, heterogeneity. This idea places a religious value on *difference* as the only transcendental characteristic shared by all. Everything shares the fact that everything is different. Insofar as difference is the basis that enables complementarity, then, each single part cannot be perfect by itself; it requires others to complete the deficit that it finds in itself. It requires others to be a complementing part of the community of the cosmos. Within this *capacity* to complete others and being completed by others, all parts in life appear as equals; all differences appear as valued; and diversity appears as the characteristic of the universe. As a result, each community is different, but it does not seek to expand onto others because only by living with the difference of others can it coexist in the perfect cosmos of organic heterogeneity. In sum, complementarity is the relationship of equality that all things share because through their differences they make up the organic whole. Each singularity is thus imperfect, incomplete, or in deficit by itself, but it is also equally valued in that it is a part of the whole.

This religious notion of complementarity thus seeks to build a radical understanding of equality that is then extended onto all things in the universe (Mamani-Bernabé 2015, 72). Here, each nation or community is also a singularity that lives within a collective form of complementarity (Mamani-Bernabé 2015, 66). This notion of communitarianism entails that each community may have its own history, genesis, organization, political order, traditions, identity, future, and truth that need to be taken into account when planning for economic development projects such as mining or road construction. At the aggregate level of inter-entity relationships, Indianismo builds a notion of truth in multiplicity that can cope with the equality of difference between peoples even when they contradict each other. This is a very radical element of resistance against the homogenizing effects of neoliberalism, and domination, in general.

These ideas were clearly opposed to colonialism in Fausto Reinaga's understanding of truth and reason. In his book *La Razón y el Indio* (Reason and the Indio), Reinaga criticizes the Western form of reason as a conception that locates human ideas and their coherency before the cosmos (Reinaga 1978, 66). According to Reinaga, European thought ever since Socrates has privileged human mentality over the complexity of the cosmos. In this anthropocentric mentality, the singular logic of a coherent philosophy is imposed upon reality and it acts as an ontological basis for domination. This is the basis of every totalitarian ideology that seeks to encompass everything through the lenses of a single and perfect logic. Neoliberalism, for example, builds an idea of the individual, the world, and development that is homogenizing through a hierarchical order by proscribing one type of macroeconomic policy, one type of trade regime, and one type of economy based on private property as well as the universalized idea of the consuming individual. In Indianismo thinking, each reason-based idea is incomplete, but also equal. Instead, truth emerges through the coexistence of different ideas in a nonhierarchical and complementary relationship (Reinaga 1978).

Through the logic of complementarity, Indianismo thus assumes the possibility of the coexistence of many truths. Insofar as difference is what gives equality to all entities and insofar as each reason-based idea is always incomplete by itself, each truth is valued in its difference and locality. Each community may have its own history, culture, knowledge, and truth. Each one is thus valued for its differences, but also humbled by its incompleteness. This is why Reinaga affirms that, in the Indianista project, the cosmos comes before reason (Reinaga 1978, 157). The very logic of the cosmos is the aggregate of radical differences and this truth delineates all other reasons. This connection between all the different entities of the cosmos is religious in that it is the transcendental characteristic of everything, but it is not centralized or managed by any one God. It is the result of the relationship between the differences of all entities, namely complementarity. It is the freedom of all life, the truth of all life, and the good of all life (Reinaga 1978, 27). This complicated notion is the political project of the "Indio." It is a *form of life* (Reinaga 1978, 21). The Indio, as shaped by Reinaga, is a mentality as well as a connection with the cosmos; it is the comprehension of heterogeneity in complementarity; and it is the political struggle against the *pensamiento único occidental* (singular occidental mentality) (Reinaga 1978, 22).

THE LIMITATION OF INDIANISMO AND THE NOTION OF REFLEXIVITY

As a discourse of struggle, Indianismo creates a separation against an "other" that is opposed or an enemy. This "other" is clearly delineated around neoliberal globalization, homogenization, domination, hierarchy, and colonialism.

Whom else, however, does this discourse marginalize? Insofar as Indianismo is understood as a discourse of diversity, everything that does not fit the logic of equality in difference (complementarity) is left outside of the boundaries of this project. Those who do not view the world or the cosmos in these terms are on the side of "otherness." This stance is justified against those voices that have hierarchicalized, dominated, and homogenized societies. The problem is, however, that it also marginalizes others who have suffered under these same colonial projects and remain in oppressed positions.

In the logic and purity of a single discourse, Indianismo seeks to build a space for diversity, but it also excludes everything that is *incoherent* with its logic. It creates a hierarchy based on diversity itself, whereby subjects are organized based on how far they are from homogenization and how close they find themselves to complementarity. This boundary has created an interesting debate around Indianismo and decoloniality.

It is in this context that some authors assert that these notions of decoloniality ignore marginalized populations. Silvia Rivera, for example, highlights that the notion of two republics creates a project that excludes one of the most marginalized sectors of Bolivian society, namely the *Cholas* (Rivera 2004, 10). *Cholage* is understood as a form of identity often represented by Bolivian women wearing high bowler hats and puffed skirts. This group of women finds itself caught in the middle of a process of mestizage and Westernization, which locates them in an ambiguous position between the Indio and the Western notions of civilization. Cholas are neither fully Western, nor fully Indianistas. They do not express complementarity, but they also do not simply express Western modernity. Both sides of the struggle thus exclude them (Rivera 2004, 11).

This exclusionary boundary can be further clarified through the definition of the Indio. As previously mentioned, Reinaga defines the Indio as a mentality that parallels the cosmos through the construction of a space where difference can persist in equality. Here, the Indio is *the* subject of complementarity and reciprocity. In a way, then, this notion of Indianismo creates a perfect discourse and logic that seeks to settle the problem of diversity through the universalization of the relationship of complementarity. To the contrary, those who do not fully respect difference are considered to be hierarchically lower in the scale of liberation, truth, and good. There are thus Indios, half-Indios, and non-Indios. Those who have not reached Indianness need to be pedagogically transformed to reach liberation. Felipe Quispe, for example, mentions that decoloniality entails changing our mentalities to Indianize ourselves (Felipe Quispe, interview by Jimena Costa, 2012). In a sense, then, Indianismo has its own internal logic that can also be conceived as hierarchicalizing in different terms. Complementarity is turned into a perfect code, a single logic, or a consistent ideology for equality and difference. This is why Reinaga locates the cosmos before reason and in this operation he gives Indianismo the logic of complementarity as its transcendental core. Silvia Rivera's problem with this discursive operation is that it also has its limitations and deficits.

This problem can also be found in the work of several intellectuals of decoloniality who hold on to the political project of complementarity more explicitly. These authors put more emphasis on the search for difference in equality by relegating the notion of the imperfection of singular truths. Estermann, for example, argues that this form of decoloniality is critical and liberating (Estermann 2014, 7). In this context, he underlines that the overexpansion that takes place while searching for a more perfect notion of diversity in order to include others, such as the Cholas, is a colonial trap that leads to postmodern relativism and, in effect, dismantles the political struggle of decoloniality (Estermann 2014, 6). In other words, if there were no internal logic for Indianismo and thus no hierarchy based on levels of Indianness, there would be nothing. Indianismo could not exclude the Cholas, but it would also stop opposing "others" such as colonialism. As previously mentioned, Escobar, Mignolo, Mendieta, and Isasi-Díaz also think of this space as a *task* for all. Here, the discursive logic of complementarity remains as the desirable project of transformation that needs to hold on to *a* logic in order to oppose colonialism and avoid relativism.

This criticism, however, has been taken into account by some of these authors themselves. Thus, many of these intellectuals explicitly understand that once the internal logic of a discourse is set, limitations emerge through the construction of an "other" and the exclusion of some. Mardones, Hernández, and García therefore argue that a project of resistance against neoliberalism and toward the construction of a society built on the notion of *buen vivir* has to include *communitarian reflexivity* in order to comprehend different forms of oppressions and problems (Mardones, Hernandez, and Garcia 2015, 12). Reflexivity is here defined as the ability to reflect critically on established truths and the willingness to change once new insights emerge. Escobar also asserts that the delineation of communities is always *in movement*; it creates different *pluriversal spaces* that never settle their boundaries permanently (Escobar 2010, 36).

In a sense, then, this discourse finds itself in a *philosophical tension* between a political struggle for diversity and its inevitable deficit. On the one hand, the moment of political struggle (opposition to an enemy) pushes the discourse to define a logic and to create boundaries of otherness that are always exclusive in some sense. Many of the authors, however, realize this limitation and have developed the idea of reflexivity to counter rigidity. On the other hand, the search for a perfect form of diversity leads to the colonial trap of postmodernism. Insofar as a discourse seeks pure diversity, then, it can create no boundary and no exclusion of any enemy. It can exclude no "other," not even domination. In this sense, a discursively perfect form of diversity would lose its critical edge and it would fall into the nihilism of relativism. This is why decolonial authors depart from the notion of reflexivity, which allows them to settle their project *momentarily* but also questions the very limitations that it may entail. This ontological stand allows them to struggle against colonialism while being cautious about the imposition of a new *orthodoxy* (Ashley and Walker 1999, 265). Decoloniality thus avoids universalizing a particular notion, but it also avoids relativism by understanding momentary forms of domination. This is how reflexivity unfolds onto the political project of decoloniality and Indianismo.

CONCLUSION

The notion of decoloniality that derives from Indianismo teaches a form of transformation related to politics, economics, culture, environmentalism, and truths. It starts from the idea of Pachamama as the organic relationship established between everything on Earth. Then it builds upon the possibility of *buen vivir*, which seeks a decolonial space where difference is located as the commonality shared by all, thus making all entities equal. In order to achieve this goal, Indianismo investigates the philosophical notion of complementarity, which views the cosmos as a relationship between incomplete and different parts that make up a whole of harmony. Each singularity (beings, communities, states, truths, etc.) is thus equal, different, and incomplete by itself.

Based on this notion of complementarity, Indianismo struggles against the imposition of the dominating hierarchy promoted by neoliberalism and its colonialism. This form of resistance thus seeks to increase equality between different peoples, and also between humanity and the rest of Earth. This project of *buen vivir* entails a radical transformation in that it starts from a notion of complementarity that enables a basis of equality for everything through the value given to difference. From this ontological platform, social movements and even governments aim toward a transformation in which each entity in the world has the same right to live and be. In order to be able to create this space, this project does not only need to resist the mentality of neoliberal progress, but it also needs to seek redistribution of wealth and power, which would undermine colonial as well as neoliberal domination. Indianismo thus seeks to fight the idea of unlimited progress, which makes resources scarcer for some than for others. It aims toward a world environmentally balanced and in which living well (*buen vivir*) is a possibility for all. Here, "all" not only includes humanity but also entails all the other species and objects that are part of the organic relationship of complementarity that makes up Earth and the cosmos.

However, insofar as Indianismo forgets that all singularities are incomplete, it views itself as universal and it builds discursive limitations that may exclude particular subjects, such as the Cholas. Despite this limitation, reflexivity is an intrinsic part of the core notion of complementarity. As previously mentioned, this notion views every single part of the cosmos as one difference among others. This makes each separate entity incomplete. Each single ideology thus cannot be perfect by itself, not even Indianismo. Reflexivity thus emerges from the Indianista notion of complementarity in order to promote an *anti-totalitarian* capacity to criticize and reform itself. As soon as Indianismo settles itself and appears to have a perfect solution (perfect code), the question of hierarchy, domination, and exclusion (the deficit of singularity within complementarity) makes it only a momentary solution. This is the most radical aspect of Indianismo, which is not a final utopia defined for once and for all. Instead, it is a voice of resistance built upon notions of reflexivity and transformation that come from a religiosity of diversity. In this discourse, religiosity, resistance, equality, difference and reflexivity, thus, go together.

REFERENCES

Ari, Waskar. 2014. *Earth Politics: Religion, Decolonization, and Bolivia's Indigenous Intellectuals*. Durham, NC: Duke University Press.

Ashley, Richard K. and R. B. J. Walker. 1990. "Introduction: Speaking the Language of Exile: Dissident Thought in International Studies." *International Studies Quarterly* 34 (3): 259–68.

Assies, Willem. 2004. "Bolivia: A Gasified Democracy." *European Review of Latin American and Caribbean Studies* 76: 25–43.

Caba, Sergio and Gonzalo García. 2014. "La denuncia al Eurocentrismo en el Pensamiento Social Latinoamericano y la Problemática de la Universalidad del Conocimiento." *Polis* 38: 1–15.

De La Barra, Ximena and Richard A. Dello Buono. 2009. *Latin America After the Neoliberal Debacle: Another Region Is Possible*. New York: Rowman & Littlefield.

Escobar, Arturo. 2010. "Latin America at Crossroads: Alternative Modernizations, Post-liberalism, or Post-development?" *Cultural Studies* 24 (1): 1–65.

Estermann, Josef. 2014. "Colonialidad, Descolonización e Interculturalidad: Apuntes desde la Filosofía." *Polis* 38: 1–15.

Fernández, Blanca and Bastien Sepúlveda. 2014. "Pueblos Indígenas, Saberes y Descolonización: Procesos Interculturales en América Latina." *Polis* 38: 1–7.

Foucault, Michel. 1972. *The Archeology of Knowledge and The Discourse on Language*. New York: Vintage Books.

Isasi-Díaz, Ada María and Eduardo Mendieta. 2012. *Decolonizing Epistemologies: Latina/o Theology and Philosophy*. New York: Fordham University Press.

Mardones, Juan I. Alfaro, Carmen de Jesús Fernández Hernández, and Manuel de Jesús González García. 2015. "La Transdisciplinariedad una Herramienta para Apuntar al Buen Vivir." *Polis* 40 (14): 1–15.

Morales, Evo. 2014. "Ciertas Naciones Cometen Ecocidio con la Madre Tierra." Speech, Conferencia Mundial sobre el Cambio Climático, Lima, December 9, 2014. http://peru.com/actualidad/politicas/evo-morales-ciertas-naciones-cometen-ecocidio-madre-tierra-noticia-307536.

Morales, Evo. 2014. "Our Liberation Is for the Whole of Humanity." Speech, G77 Plus China Summit, Santa Clara, Bolivia, June 14, 2014. http://links.org.au/node/3917.

Morales, Evo. 2014. "Discurso del presidente Evo Morales." Speech, United Nations General Assembly, New York, January 8, 2014. http://eju.tv/2014/01/discurso-del-presidente-evo-morales-en-la-onu-luego-de-recibir-la-presidencia-del-g77-ms-china/.

Morales, Evo. 2015. "Ten Commandments against Capitalism." Speech, Manifiesto of Isla Del Sol. Lake Titicaca. 14 August, 2015. http://links.org.au/node/3182.

Petras, James and Henry Veltmeyer. 2005. *Social Movements and State Power: Argentina, Brazil, Bolivia and Ecuador*. London: Pluto Press.

Quispe, Felipe. 2012. "Trayectoria Política de Felipe Quispe." Interview by Jimena Costa, Instituto Prisma.

Reinaga, Fausto. 1970. *Manifiesto del Partido Indio de Bolivia*. La Paz: PIB.

Reinaga, Fausto. 1971. *Tesis India*. La Paz: PIB.

Reinaga, Fausto. 1978. *La Razón y el Indio*. La Paz: Litografías e Imprentas Unidas.

Rivera, Silvia. 1999. "Sendas y Senderos de la Ciencia Social Andina." *Dispositio, Crítica Cultural en Latinoamérica: Paradigmas Globales y Enunciaciones Locales* 24 (51): 149–69.

Rivera, Silvia. 2004. "La Noción de 'Derecho' o las Paradojas de la Modernidad Postcolonial: Indígenas y Mujeres en Bolivia." *Aportes Andinos, Aportes sobre la Diversidad, Diferencia e Identidad* 11: 1–15.

Sanjinés, Javier C. 2004. *Meztizaje Upside-Down: Aesthetic Politics in Modern Bolivia*. Pittsburgh: University of Pittsburgh Press.

Ticona, Alejo Esteban. 2000. *Organización y Liderazgo Aymara, La experiencia indigena en la politica boliviana, 1979–1996*. AGRUCO, Agroecología Universidad Cochabamba, Universidad de la Cordillera.

Ticona, Alejo Estaban. 2011. *Bolivia en el Inicio del Pachakuti: La larga lucha anticolonial de los pueblos Aimara y Quechua*. Cochabamba: Akal Ediciones, S.A.

Ticona, Alejo Estaban. 2013. *El Indianismo de Fausto Reinaga: Orígenes, Desarrollo y experiencia en Qullasuyu-Bolivia*. PhD diss., Universiad Andina Simón Bolívar, Sede Ecuador.

Todorov, Tzvetan. 1982. *The Conquest of America: The Question of the Other*. Oklahoma: University of Oklahoma Press.

Zaffaroni, Eugenio Raúl. 2015. *La Pachamama y el Mundo*. Buenos Aires: Ediciones Madres de Plaza de Mayo.

Chapter 16

Religious Arguments in the Global Economy

Peter J. Smith

This book set out to explore the relationship between religious activism and neoliberal globalization. As the chapters indicate, the relationship is complex and varied even within similar religious traditions. There is, for example, no single relationship within Islam between religious activism and global capitalism, as the various chapters by Marei, Dreher, Bozkurt, Kwayu, and Webb indicate. As a consequence, the book chapters were divided among religious actors who emphasized the promotion or reform of, or resistance to, neoliberal globalization and not by religion per se. With these categories in mind, the conclusion performs three tasks: (1) it summarizes our major findings; (2) while doing so it also provides a critical analysis of one important argument in the literature about religion and globalization or neoliberalism; and (3) it points to directions in future research, particularly the relationship between spirituality and capitalism, a topic that deserves more attention.

MODELING VERSUS SOCIAL MOVEMENT ACTIVISM—A SUMMARY AND CRITIQUE

The perspective of this section is on the latest phase of economic globalization, also called neoliberalism. Its purpose is to twofold. It will summarize the key results of the chapters in the book and, in doing so, it will critically assess a leading interpretation of the impact of neoliberal globalization upon religion described as "modeling," an approach at variance with the approach of this book.

The "modeling approach" starts from a specific understanding of today's form of neoliberal capitalism. According to Castells (2010), the neoliberal economy is informational, global, and networked. By informational is meant that by means of digital technologies, corporations can create knowledge-based production systems capable of operating on a global scale. For the first time in history, international financial markets, international trade, and the production of goods and services can function on a global scale at all times. Not all economic activity is global or works in this fashion, of course, but this neoliberal global economy has now become the dominant social force in society working to ensure that all social phenomena including the state conform to its demands.

Beyer (2013) and Turner (2011) have put forward an argument that today religion is modeling itself on the digital neoliberal economy just described. By modeling is meant "a structural and semantic parallelism between any two systems" (Beyer 2013, 7). That is, according to this perspective, one sphere of a social system emulates features of another, in this case dominant, sphere. Increasingly, claims Beyer (2013), religion is modeling itself "in terms of production and consumption" as well as "in terms of information and entertainment" (16). On this Turner (2011) concurs:

> Modern religious formations are profoundly influenced by the globalisation of economic life, specifically by the commodification of everyday life. Religion becomes part of the global economic system in terms of the circulation of religious commodities (amulets, prayer books, pilgrimages and so forth), by the creation and promotion of religious lifestyles . . . by the adoption of modern communication technologies (the Internet, videos, cassettes, TV stations, computerization and so forth). (279)

What both Turner and Beyer are referring to is the commercialization and commodification of religion. In modeling religion on the economy, people will treat "the sources of religion more like Walmart that has customers" (Beyer 2013, 17). According to Turner (2011), "it is the commercial values of the secular world that shape religion rather than religious values that shape markets" (283). That society, in this case the economy, shapes religion is a perspective recognized in this book. However, as the chapter later indicates, Turner and Beyer have overstated their case. Religious social movements, like many other social movements, also employ digital technologies, mobilizing on national and transnational bases; in other words, they do not just run in parallel with the global economy. On the contrary, they influence and shape the global economic system itself. Furthermore, some movements demand reforms and present alternatives to neoliberal globalization. Here religious social movements are not so much shaped by neoliberalism as they are trying to shape it, reform it, or get rid of it altogether. In sum, not all religious social movements model themselves on, or conform to, the economy.

At the same time, however, there is ample evidence that religious social movements adapt to and accommodate neoliberal globalization, which would seem to validate Beyer and Turner's position. Here religious actors increasingly stress individualism and consumption, core values of neoliberalism. The emphasis on consumption as an aspect of religious life turns Weber's argument on its head. Weber had argued that Protestantism had an orientation emphasizing piety and abstention from consumption in favor of wealth creation. In our consumption-oriented world, gratification does not come in the hereafter but in the here and now. Prosperity and consumption thus become hallmarks of certain religious movements.

Religious social movements that accommodate and promote neoliberal globalization are described in this book by Wilkinson, Ukah, and Upadhyay. The first two focus on Pentecostalism. Upadhyay addresses the issue of the spiritual *guru* (religious teacher) as part of the formation of neoliberal corporate Hinduism. In terms of Pentecostalism, organizationally, like the network economy, it is networked and highly decentralized, and operates on a global scale. Casanova (2011) describes Prosperity Pentecostalism as "the most dynamic and fastest growing sector of Protestant Christianity worldwide and likely to become the predominant form of Christianity in the twenty-first century" (435). Indeed, Casanova claims, Pentecostalism is "the first global religion" (437).

Wilkinson's chapter provides an excellent introduction to Pentecostalism. He notes its American roots and influence on shaping its spread among Christians throughout the world. Pentecostalism, he notes, is not static but dynamic, changing over time and place. While it has roots in the United States, it has become global but not in a homogenous way. As Beyer (2013) acknowledges: "With globalization, the global includes its opposite, the local, such that when religion appears as the local, it is thereby also global, or better, glocal" (44). One would expect that, being glocal and decentralized, it would vary according to time and place. According to Wilkinson, "Pentecostalism is diverse and found throughout the world." While all Pentecostals may be from the same family, there are important differences within the family. Wilkinson, like Beyer and Turner, acknowledges that Pentecostalism is shaped by neoliberal capitalism but, he argues, it is not that straightforward. Rather, he maintains there is evidence that "Pentecostalism acts as a catalyst for the expansion of a new global economy" (67).

Ukah offers the reader an example of how Pentecostalism has adapted to the African, particularly the Nigerian, context. In his case study, which discusses how one "Pentecostal organization accommodates neoliberal practices through its engagement with the real estate market in Nigeria" (75), he argues that Pentecostalism "embraces and accommodates neoliberal global practices rather than challenging or resisting it, or even introducing countermeasures to it" (80). In his case study focusing on the Redeemed Christian Church of God in Nigeria, he describes how it has become entrepreneurial and an important market actor. What is particularly significant is the extent to which the Pentecostal church in Nigeria (and Africa) engages in commercial cultural production using the mass and social media to sell DVDs, books, devotionals, and mobile apps. Yet, despite this fact, there is little evidence in Nigeria or Africa that the expansion of Pentecostalism has done most Africans any good. In fact, claims Ukah, "there seems to be a negative correlation between increased Pentecostal penetration and expansion and economic well-being in Africa" (75).

Upadhyay's chapter, like Wilkinson's, argues that, in India, the corporate Hinduism he discusses is not merely shaped by secular structural forces in the global economy but, in turn, helps to shape it. On the one hand, they identify "with the more assertive and somewhat anti-Western political project of Hindutva" (93), as Upadhyay notes, but at the same time they have become important actors themselves using mass media and social media to sell their religious wares, providing spirituality workshops to companies so as to prepare them to function in the neoliberal market.

Marei's chapter on the role of neoliberalism and Hezbollah in Lebanon argues, as does Upadhyay's in the case of India, that it is not easy to categorize a religion, in this case Islam, as promoting or rejecting neoliberal globalization. One can interpret it as doing both. While neoliberalism has often been seen as an American-led project that is often monochromatic, Marei reminds us that local circumstances, place, and history, the glocal, have to be taken into account. He argues that one can adopt neoliberal logic but at the same time use it for one's own political projects. So, at one and the same time, "Hezbollah's Resistance project exemplifies a variegated neoliberalism that is homegrown, counterhegemonic, and alternative to mainstream configurations of neoliberalism" (168). That is, Hezbollah can be seen as promoting neoliberal capitalism while at the same time maintaining its enmity toward the United States.

Dreher's chapter provides another variation of an Islamic social movement, the Gülen or Hizmet movement, that originated in Turkey but now has become a global movement. While very different from Hezbollah, the Hizmet movement has also accepted the logic of neoliberalism. At the same time, it has worked to revitalize Islam in a nonviolent way and to protect its adherents from the perceived debilitating effects of the Western secularized version of neoliberal globalization. In sum, Hizmet is integrating itself into the Western globalization project but not unequivocally so. It promotes neoliberal globalization but offers its own version of reforms based on conservative values eschewing the consumptive focus of Pentecostalism.

Thus, there is little uniformity in terms of how religious social movements accommodate and promote neoliberal globalization. The modeling that occurs indicates that some religious social movements and churches (e.g., Pentecostalism) are much more comfortable with the consumptive aspects of neoliberalism while others such as Hezbollah and Hizmet de-emphasize consumption and try to create autonomy and insulate Islam from commercialization. Indeed, Hezbollah remains a critical opponent of the primary advocate of neoliberal globalization, the United States. Clearly, one size does not fit all. In Turkey, for example, the Justice and Development Party (AKP) relies on its Sunni Islam political base to remain in power. In doing so, the AKP employs an instrumental approach to Islam using it to establish neoliberal hegemony over the working class, as outlined in the chapter by Bozkurt.

In Beyer and Turner's discussion of religions modeling themselves on neoliberal globalization, there is little or no discussion of religions and religious social movements that may take a more critical stance to neoliberalism. These range from being mildly reformist to being sharply critical, offering strong resistance. Here the sense of religious autonomy and agency is much more visible, challenging any rigid notion of religion modeling itself on the economy. In Tunisia, for example, the democratic Islamist Renaissance Party—Ennahda—which started out as a suppressed opposition movement later became the governing party after the Tunisian Revolution of 2011. It has since lost power. Here, Tunisian circumstances have forced Ennahda to be pragmatic and compromising, recognizing that Tunisia must adapt to a globalizing world, but at the same time the party is mildly reformist, trying to mitigate its harsher social consequences. Indeed, as Webb notes, "Ennahda's longer term plans envisage a remoralized Tunisian economy and polity" (146).

Ennahda's reformist stance is, as noted, trying to accommodate neoliberalism but maintain its democratic Muslim integrity. More assertive in terms of reform is the corporate social responsibility movement as described by MacLeod, which has increasingly been influenced by faith-based groups, largely American, acting within their networks to make corporations more accountable. There is a recognition that corporations have become "disembedded" from their social responsibilities and by promoting socially responsible investment, faith groups are trying to "re-imbed" neoliberalism, bringing a greater degree of social control. What many faith groups want is a reformed, more humane neoliberal capitalism. While Kwayu does not use the terms disembed and reimbed, her chapter is also a case study in which interfaith groups—Catholic, Protestant, and Muslim—are working together to reimbed the mining industry in Tanzania, putting it more under the control of Tanzanians. All this to prevent them from expatriating so much of their profits, thus providing Tanzania with a more just portion of royalties that can be put at the service of alleviating poverty. What is particularly interesting about this interfaith activism, which has enjoyed a degree of success, is that it did not make its case on moral grounds but through the means of rigorous social scientific studies that validated their claims to the public and government.

Kwayu's chapter demonstrates that rather than modeling themselves on the neoliberal economy, interfaith groups in Tanzania have come out critically against neoliberal globalization. More precisely, instead of emphasizing religious modeling of the economy, a preferable approach might to be realize that as neoliberalism becomes the dominant force in society, religions must interact with it in either a positive way, adapting and accommodating it, if not promoting it, or a more critical way, reforming or resisting it. Resistance can come in a variety of forms.[1] In terms of resistance, the key for other religious social movements may be fear of climate change that threatens creation as a consequence of the notion of unlimited growth promoted by neoliberalism. It is this fear that is increasingly uniting a number of disparate groups, secular and religious, against the excesses of contemporary capitalism. Among religious actors across the political spectrum, including once staunchly conservative faith-based groups, there is considerable urgency in their activism, and their critiques much sharper.

This is particularly evident in Nicinska's chapter on the US religious environmental movement (REM). According to Nicinska, REM "seeks to embed a humanitarian and environmental ethic into the capitalist system while challenging the assumptions and benefits of unlimited growth and material wealth as representative of the good life" (229). Seemingly, the REM is emphasizing reform of neoliberalism, but this is not always the case (although there are some groups in REM promoting reform). Nevertheless, its emphasis on growth leads networked religious environment groups to insist that there must be "significant transformations to the prevalent economic model of neoliberal globalization" (229). Given the centrality of growth to neoliberalism, suffice it to say that the underlying message is that capitalism based on this model does not deserve to exist. This is because it is perceived as a threat to God's creation, which includes the human and the nonhuman, which are interconnected in a great web of life. The accent is clearly on spiritually driven activism informed by scientific evidence.

Spirituality is also a dimension of religious resistance found in the network-based global justice movement, specifically the World Social Forum (WSF) and the Occupy Movement. Like the REM, social movement actors, including Christian Churches, attending the periodic meetings of the WSF argue that neoliberal globalization is in need of transformation, if not replacement with an alternative economic system. Many faith-based groups, like other NGOs, provide scientific evidence in their indictment of the negative effects of neoliberal globalization using the internet as a means of distribution. Among the churches present at the WSF, the World Council of Churches rejects neoliberal globalization as a model for the economy, stressing "an economy of life" that has a distinct spiritual perspective closely resembling Scauso's discussion of *buen vivir*, our last case study in the book.

Indeed, Scauso's chapter offers the sharpest indictment of neoliberal capitalism but this time from an Indigenous perspective—one, I argue, that is finding increasing resonance in the global justice movement. This would not be the first time that an Indigenous movement has played a role in the resistance against neoliberal globalization. As noted in the Smith and Smythe chapter, the Zapatista movement of Mexico has been an inspiration for the global justice movement and the WSF. Scauso argues that Indianismo rooted in Bolivia "seeks to dismantle the very basis of the domination and the hierarchical mentality that is reinforced today through neoliberal globalization" (270). Indianismo, moreover, has a clearly spiritual dimension evident in his discussion of *Pachamama* (Mother Earth)—an "organic relationship established between everything on Earth" (271). If realized, Indianismo with its notions of Mother Earth and living well would require an alternative way of living that rejects neoliberalism and its growth fetish.

What the chapters by Nicinska, Smith and Smythe, and Scauso have in common is a recognition of the centrality of spirituality in terms of resistance and the need to reject neoliberal globalization as a model for the economy and for religion itself. This book has concentrated on religious social movements in terms of whether they promote, reform, or resist neoliberal globalization. Religion, it has argued, was a social construct, meaning that religion is what religious social movements make of it (see Introduction). What the remainder of this chapter does is focus greater attention on spirituality and its relationship to neoliberal globalization, arguing that it, too, is socially constructed and can both promote and resist neoliberal globalization. Key to this discussion is that a spirituality of resistance shared increasingly by social movements, nonreligious, Indigenous, and religious, is perhaps posing the greatest challenge to neoliberal globalization incorporating an alternative vision of how we should live together. Here, the spiritual, the political, and the scientific are coming together, in particular, on climate change, bridging the separation that had existed between religion and the latter two. As noted previously, spirituality is very much a contested term with its meaning changing according to time and place. As such, it is important to discuss how spirituality, variously interpreted, can be put at the service of global capitalism as well in opposition to it.

SPIRITUALITY AS A FACILITATOR OF GLOBAL CAPITALISM

By most accounts, spirituality, like religion, is difficult to define. According to Kourie (2006), "the persistent interest in the phenomenon of spirituality is all the more remarkable given the fact that there is no clear, unequivocal definition of the concept that is acceptable to all interested in the field"

(22). Because its vagueness leads to confusion, Kourie argues that "it will be helpful to have a working definition that will encapsulate the essence of spirituality, eliminate misconceptions surrounding the term and facilitate discussion" (22). She thus defines spirituality as "the 'ultimate values' that give meaning to our lives, whether or not they are religious or non-religious" (22). Carrette and King (2005) agree with Kourie that spirituality is difficult to define. However, they argue that spirituality is a historical, social construct, one that is contested. As a result, "searching for an overarching definition of 'spirituality' only ends up missing the specific historical location of each use of the term" (3). Furthermore, argue Carrette and King, there are advantages to its vagueness in the sense that "its *vagueness and ambiguity* allows it to mask the underlying ideologies that it is used to represent" (3). The claim that spirituality can mask underlying ideologies suggests its relationship to power.

The fact that spirituality is socially constructed means that its meanings have shifted over time. One interpretation is that whereas religion is associated with organized and institutionalized beliefs and practices (Taylor 2010), spirituality refers to qualities and aspirations of individuals and to the human dimension of one's spirit. For some, spirituality represents a search for the transcendence of the self associated with "piety" and "otherworldliness," implying a duality between matter and spirit. Spirituality viewed this way is not a relevant part of most people's lives. Today, however, spirituality is enjoying increasing visibility. According to Heelas (2012):

> Spirituality has run riot, on a nigh global compass. This is most visible in the wealthiest of countries. It is also in evidence among the wealthier echelons, the more cosmopolitan elites of less well-off nations the world over. A radical shift appears to under way, one from religious tradition where spirituality is ignored or marginalized to being emphasized within religious traditions and beyond. (3)

Spirituality is seen to be particularly relevant to the wider population in the sense that for many, it refers to one's personal growth, a search for the "ultimate values" and sense of belonging that give meaning to our lives. This search for ultimate values, meaning, and belonging in our lives can be religious or nonreligious. Thus one can be "spiritual without being religious." Spirituality in this sense is distinctly individualistic and private, analogous to the individualization and privatization argued to have occurred in religion with the rise of modernity and capitalism.

What is being referred to above is more often than not a form of post-Christian spirituality that broke from the moorings of the Christian tradition beginning in the 1960s. Houtman and Aupers (2007) along with Heelas (2006) trace this type of spirituality back to the counterculture of the 1960s. In turn, this spirituality formed the basis of the New Age movement of the

1980s, disembedding from the counterculture as it did so. There is no particular order or coherence to New Age spirituality. It is left to each individual to decide what the relevant, constituents parts of this spirituality are. Spirituality can thus be referred to as a "do-it-yourself religion," "pick and mix," or "spirituality à la carte" (Houtman and Aupers 2007). Spirituality in this sense is analogous to a religious supermarket.

Underlying this spirituality is a search for authenticity and meaning in one's life. Turner looks at this phenomenon from a global perspective, speaking of "the emergence of new spiritualities that are heterodox, urban, commercialized forms of religiosity typically outside the conventional churches, and often appealing to the new middle classes in the service sectors of the global economy" (Turner 2011, 225). Moreover, Turner asserts, these spiritualities cater "to the individual need for meaning" (225). Speaking of New Age spirituality in particular, Heelas (2006) argues that it is becoming "a growing presence within the heartlands of capitalism" (49), finding expression in the workplace in terms of training, workshops, courses, and seminars. This very much echoes the findings of Upadhyay (this volume) in terms of the commodification of Hinduism and its popularity among India's new middle classes. According to Carrette and King (2004), there has been "a silent takeover of 'the religious' by contemporary capitalist ideologies by means of the increasingly popular discourse of 'spirituality'" (2). As a result, the ethical and the religious have become subordinated to a neoliberal agenda, which promotes accommodation to, if not promotion of, consumerist values and corporate capitalism.

A SPIRITUALITY OF RESISTANCE

Moreover, spirituality as it appears above, clearly leans toward an anthropocentric view of the world in the sense that the emphasis is on the individual humans and their quest. It is precisely this anthropocentrism that divides this view of spirituality from more radical, critical views of spirituality that are more Earth centered. These critical views of spirituality emphasize that God or the Divine is not a separate entity but bound up with ourselves, the Earth, nature, and the cosmos (Lynch 2007). The same can be said for spirituality. The Earth, moreover, is sacred and we now speak of the sacredness of Mother Earth. In addition, there is an acknowledged need for a spirituality that recognizes the imperative of the existing ecological crisis we now face. No longer is the natural world to be exploited for human benefit.

Gordon Lynch (2007), for example, writes about the rise of a progressive spirituality claiming that "such a perspective rejects the anthropocentrism and pragmatic environmental concern for a deeper spiritual vision of the fundamentally interconnected nature of all reality in the proper understanding of the human place within this wider story" (37). Kourie (2006) argues that there is a "new" spirituality arising, particularly in Christianity, but not exclusively so, which stresses the interconnectedness of all life both nonhuman and human, which are both a part of nature. We see portents of this in the chapter by Nicinska on the growth of the REM. Driving the activism of REM, she notes, is spiritual belief. Its underlying message is one "of holism, interconnectedness, and moral obligation to care for the 'Earth community'" (229). REM argues that boundless material consumption and the notion of unlimited growth must be rejected.

THE RISE AND INFLUENCE OF INDIGENOUS SPIRITUALITY

In its own way, REM forms a part of what this chapter describes as a "spirituality of resistance." Perhaps nowhere else is the spirituality of resistance more exemplified than in the growing worldwide Indigenous movements that are increasingly working with environmental movements within what is now referred to as the Climate Justice Movement. In part, Indigenous activism has been sparked by neoliberalism, which encourages mass consumption and the opening of national markets, and the removal of barriers to international trade and investment. Mass consumption, in turn, requires finding and exploiting natural resources, which are increasingly located in remoter regions inhabited by indigenous peoples (Coates 2004, 216).

Indigenous resistance is thus found throughout the world. The focus in this section of the chapter extends the analysis of Scauso by indicating how ideas of *Pachamama* (Mother Earth) and *buen vivir* (living well, not better) are diffusing beyond Bolivia and Latin America finding parallels in other movements. In the indigenous cosmo-vision of the Indianista discourse of Bolivia, *Pachamama*, states Scauso, "is the entity that represents the complexity of the relationships and existence of all beings as well as things on earth" (271). All things are connected to one another, humans included, in a vast web of existence. Moreover, Mother Earth is sacred. *Buen vivir* refers to the fact that because what Mother Earth can provide is limited, we must be moderate in what we take from her and not deplete resources or species. Unlimited growth would destroy Mother Earth. *Buen vivir* rejects not only anthropocentrism, but it also rejects the duality of humans and nature. According to Alcoreza:

> The concept does not split mankind from nature and has an inseparable interconnection between the material life of reproduction and the production of social and spiritual life. Men and women, together with nature, are part of the Mother Earth and there is a communion and dialogue between them mediated by rituals in which Nature is understood as a sacred being. (Alcoreza 2013, 145)

This cosmocentric vision has a number of consquences. First, one cannot distinguish between the spiritual and the political. Second, it rejects the notion of patriarchy, and third, as noted previously, it rejects the neoliberal economic growth model.

Now, it should be said that *buen vivir* is not a concept particular to South America. Analogous principles to *buen vivir* exist in Indigenous cultures worldwide (Focus on the Global South 2013). The Indigenous peoples of the Philippines use a variety of native terms that equate to the "simple life." In Africa, "Ubuntu" has similar connotations to *buen vivir*. According to Nussbaum (2003), Ubuntu in Zulu "speaks to our interconnectness, our common humanity, and the responsibility to each other that flows from our deeply felt connection" (as quoted in Benedetta and Margherita, 3). In Canada, former chief, George Poitras, from Fort Chipewayan in northern Alberta, notes that the Cree term for the same concept as *buen vivir* is *miyo matsuwin* (Dillon 2014, 4).

THE DIFFUSION OF *BUEN VIVIR* (THE GOOD LIFE)

There are clear signs that the values associated with *buen vivir* are now becoming part of the discourse and value system of non-Indigenous organizations and movements. This is known as the process of diffusion. Diffusion refers to the incorporation of some idea, practice, or item by an individual, group, or movement (Wood 2011, 306). Diffusion requires specific means of communication and an opportunity to deliberate on the worth of the idea. As Jackie Smith (2014) notes, crises, economic and environmental, are creating spaces for Indigenous ideas and values to emerge as sources of inspiration and discussion. In terms of *buen vivir*, two opportunities for discussion and diffusion stand out. The first is the WSF. According to Smith (2014) WSF, Belém, in 2009 exposed a wider public to the discussion of Indigenous ideas and values. A second opportunity came in 2010 when the Bolivian government, in the wake of the failure in 2009 of the Copenhagen Conference on climate change, invited civil society organizations to Bolivia. Approximately 30,000 persons attended what became known as the World People's Conference on Climate Change and the Rights of Mother Earth. They debated proposals on recovering and integrating Indigenous practices and beliefs in the form of *buen vivir* producing the Universal Declaration of the Rights of Mother Earth.

The idea of *buen vivir* and the Rights of Mother Earth spread rapidly from that point, becoming adopted by a variety of organizations. For example, during the conference, the Global Alliance for Rights of Nature was formed by 18 organizations from around the world. Since that time, over 125 organizations have signed on to the Founding Principles of the Alliance, which rejects anthropocentrism:

The primary premise of the Alliance is that . . . humans must reorient themselves from an exploitative and ultimately self-destructive relationship with nature, to one that honors the deep interrelation of all life and contributes to the health and integrity of the natural environment. An essential step in achieving this is to create a system of jurisprudence that sees and treats nature as a fundamental, rights bearing entity and not as mere property to be exploited at will. Breaking out of the human-centered limitations of our current legal systems by recognizing, respecting and enforcing Rights of Nature is one of the most transformative and highly leveraged actions that humanity can take to create a sustainable future for all. (Global Alliance for Rights of Nature 2015)

The remainder of this section offers three examples of networks and organizations exemplifying the spread of *buen vivir* and Rights of Mother Earth. These include (1) Focus on the Global South, (2) the Health of Mother Earth Foundation (HOMEF) in Nigeria, and (3) the papal encyclical, *Laudato Si'* (2015).

Focus on the Global South

Focus on the Global South (Focus) is one of the most prominent organizations in the struggle against neoliberal globalization (Carroll 2015). It was established in 1995 "to challenge neoliberalism, militarism, and corporate-driven globalization while strengthening just and equitable alternatives" (Focus 2015b). Focus, headquartered in Bangkok, Thailand, is a combination of think-tank and advocacy organization critiquing and providing alternatives to neoliberal globalization.

Given its orientation, it is not surprising that Focus would be interested in *buen vivir*, which it views as an alternative paradigm to the economic growth model of contemporary capitalism. In recent years, Focus has been promoting *buen vivir* and its similarity to like concepts among Indigenous peoples of South East Asia. This is largely due to the fact that in 2012, Focus hired Pablo Solón, from Bolivia, as its executive director. Solón is known as a strong supporter of the Declaration on the Rights of Mother Earth and was one of the key organizers of the World People's Conference on Climate Change in Cochabamba, Bolivia, in 2010.

Not long after Solón arrived as its director, Focus in 2013 began a series of discussions with Asian Indigenous peoples, civil society organizations, and social movements to ascertain what could be learned from *buen vivir*. Considered among the strong points of the concept was the fact that it stressed harmony over growth, community over individualism, complementarity over competition, and integrity over morality. By integrity was meant emphasizing "living well"—to eat well, to care for nature, to listen to and respect others. Moreover, the report rejected the duality of spirituality and materiality stating that "for indigenous peoples all over the world the spiritual world cannot be separated from the material life" (Focus 2013, 7). At the same time, Focus (2015a) does not see *buen vivir* as related only to the experiences of Indigenous peoples in Latin America and South and Southeast Asia. Rather, it sees the concept as part of a counterhegemonic struggle, stating elsewhere: "We must take advantage of the growing doubts around the economic growth model to advance alternative paradigms such as *buen vivir* (living well). The challenge is how to articulate such paradigms to make them viable realities for the population at large" (Focus 2015a).

Health of Mother Earth Foundation

The HOMEF in Nigeria is a recently created ecological and advocacy organization with a focus on education "whose major objective is to overturn the current thought pattern which makes people in Nigeria, in Africa especially, accept the neo-liberal logic as the only way to do things" (Bassey 2013, 1). HOMEF focuses its advocacy work on the broad themes of fossil fuels (alternative energy, climate change, climate justice) and hunger politics. HOMEF has received quick prominence primarily because of its director, Nnimmo Bassey. Bassey is a widely known Nigerian activist, author, and poet. Bassey has been a strong supporter of *buen vivir* and the Rights of Mother Earth, including during his tenure as chair of Friends of the Earth International. For example, receiving, as chair of FOEI, the Right Livelihood Award in 2010 (otherwise known as the alternative Nobel Peace Prize), Bassey (2010) stated that "just as we have rights, so does the Earth" (2010). In terms of *buen vivir*, he sees analogous concepts in Nigeria such as *Eti uwem*. Bassey (2013) explains:

> *Eti uwem* is a concept in Ibibio, one of the several languages in Nigeria, which literally means *good life* or *good living*. Within it is the idea of living in harmony with nature and all peoples. It incorporates dignity, respect, rectitude, integrity, solidarity and contentment. Within this concept are the key principles of social justice, power relations and citizens' and communal ownership and control of local resources. It objects to speculation, exploitation, expropriation and destructive activities and, very importantly, no monetary price can be placed on life and nature.

Eti uwem, Bassey (2013) argues, is supportive of what he describes as "green democracy," by which he means "living well in a citizens-driven democracy."

The Papal Encyclical—*Laudato Si'*

Pope Francis' encyclical on the need to fight climate change and preserve the planet has reverberated around the world. While the encyclical has a variety of influences, this section pays particular attention to the impact of indigenous cosmology. This reflects the fact that new ideas, initiatives, and democratic creativity often come from marginalized parts of society and the globe to the center (Markoff 2003). This is true of concepts such as *buen vivir* and Mother Earth and also the ideas and values found in the pope's encyclical. In part, this may be attributed to the fact that Francis is from Argentina and is the first pope from the Global South. As Naomi Klein (2015, 2) notes, the Vatican under Francis is full of people with real power who come from the Global South. Moreover, Klein notes that the Catholicism of Latin America is distinctive, being "more influenced by indigenous cosmology . . . precisely because the genocide of indigenous people in Latin America was far less complete" than it was in North America (2).[2]

In publishing the encyclical, the pope had an advantage that other religious leaders and organization do not have. That is, globalization has elevated the presence of what is now a transnationalized church providing unprecedented public visibility for the papacy, which has "assumed eagerly the vacant role of spokesperson for humanity" (Casanova 1997, 133). In assuming this role, the Church has remained critical of capitalist globalization, demanding a more just economic system. Pope Francis builds upon this tradition and incorporates it into his encyclical, meaning, in effect, that it is about much more than the climate; it is about social justice, poverty, and how we should live together and inhabit the Earth.

The pope (2015), quoting Francis of Assisi, refers to the Earth as both his "sister" and his "mother" (3). He soon moves to a primary theme of the encyclical, that of interconnectedness and interdependence of all those who reside on the planet, itself a living entity, including humans who are not separate from nature but a part of nature. According to Francis, who explicitly rejects anthropocentrism, "everything is interconnected, and that genuine care for our own lives and our relationships with nature is inseparable from fraternity, justice and faithfulness to others" (52). So in our care for the planet, we must have a due regard for others, with justice as a guiding principle. Everything, he notes, is related, including justice and a healthy planet.

It is his regard for a healthy planet that leads Francis to sharply criticize the consumerism that is despoiling the planet and corroding our cultures in the pursuit of more and more things. Such an attitude is built upon a technocratic paradigm fostered by the present economic system that believes we have been put upon Earth to dominate it and extract from it what we desire. Here the Earth is not living but inanimate, a source of exploitation. This leads Francis to reject "this idea of infinite or unlimited growth . . . so attractive to economists, financiers and experts in technology. It is based on the lie that there is an infinite supply of the earth's goods, and this leads to the planet being squeezed dry beyond every limit" (79).

What is the alternative? While Francis does not use the concept of *buen vivir*, his thinking is very much parallel. According to Francis, we must accept the notion that "less is more" (162). "Christian spirituality," he maintains, "proposes a growth marked by moderation and the capacity to be happy with little. It is a return to that simplicity which allows us to stop and appreciate the small things." Transforming the present economic system, he admits, will not be easy but it must be done if we are to save the planet and ourselves. This transformation cannot be done following existing modes of thought. Rather, Francis argues:

> There needs to be a distinctive way of looking at things, a way of thinking, policies, an educational programme, a lifestyle and a spirituality which together generate resistance to the assault of the technocratic paradigm. Otherwise, even the best ecological initiatives can find themselves caught up in the same global-ized logic. (2015, 84)

Given that everything is connected, there can be no quick, technical fixes to each environmental problem. We need to go much deeper than what the ruling political and economic elites prescribe. Clearly, the encyclical calls upon us to rethink our relationship with Mother Earth anew. In doing so, it is now evident that indigenous cosmologies are enjoying a renaissance that is diffusing throughout the world enjoying unprecedented influence.

CONCLUSION

The pope's encyclical is clearly political, suggesting the need for systemic change in the economy and how we live and associate with one another. It is a reminder that it is almost impossible to radically separate religion, politics, and the economy into distinct spheres. They are most invariably related to one another in some way. How they are related is a focus of this book. Here, the emphasis was on religious social movement activists and their positions *vis-à-vis* neoliberalism as analyzed by contributors from various conservative, quantitative, liberal, Marxist, and critical theory perspectives. However, as the first chapter stated, "in order to understand the role of religious activists . . . we need to take into account the whole complexity of possible approaches to neoliberal globalization." This, in turn, called for a social constructivist approach that eschewed viewing religion(s) as reified and essentialist. Rather, what the book has validated is the importance of viewing religion and spirituality as historically constructed and contested concepts that are in flux and vary according to time, place, and cultural setting. In turn, one must expect that religious social movements in terms of their activism and position toward neoliberal globalization will take different and nuanced positions depending on whether they promote, act to reform, or resist by, for example, creating an alternative form of living.

This approach has a number of advantages. First, we believe it is empirically accurate, suggesting complexity and difference. Second, it moves away from Eurocentric approaches to the study of religion and religious activism. Here the historical impact of imperialism and colonialism matter in terms of the social construction of religion and religious activism. Third, the emphasis on complexity, difference, and nuance requires that one take a critical perspective on sweeping claims, for example, that today religion and spirituality are modeling themselves on neoliberal globalization omitting evidence to the contrary.

Finally, it suggests the centrality of religious activism and perspectives to public debate and discussion of neoliberalism and its role in society. Indeed, chapter 2 made it clear that neoliberalism itself can be viewed as a form of religion and theological expression. Here, it can be asked: Is not neoliberalism a form of market fundamentalism operating on a global scale, putting an emphasis on the market above all else in society? Is it not the one true faith as espoused by secularist apostles? Are we not asked to make sacrifices such as the imposition of austerity to protect and promote the market? Is not human, that is, state intervention into the market an "original sin" potentially disrupting the mysterious operation of the market, guided as it is by an "invisible hand"? In his analysis of "Theology, Spirituality and the Market," Mo Sung (2007) states that "faith in the market is an idolatrous faith which demands human sacrifices in the name of a human institution that has been elevated to the category of absolute. In this sense the laws of the market are the incarnation of the sacred in today's world" (75).

Religion, spirituality, and neoliberalism are thus hard to separate from one another and to ignore despite differing perspectives on their relationship. Indeed, religious and spiritual perspectives may rival, if not replace, modern ideologies and "isms" in their critiques and analyses of, and alternatives to, neoliberal globalization. Indigenous spiritualities and their diffusion, for example, combine in potent fashion rational analysis, moral criticism, emotive commitment, and an alternative vision that could seriously challenge the hegemony of neoliberalism itself.

NOTES

1. Resistance has more than one meaning. As the introduction to the book indicated, resistance is often used in a critical theory sense referring to emancipation. In another sense, it can refer to the daily and ongoing struggles against an oppressive

system. Slaves, for example, wanted to be emancipated but on a day-to-day basis resisted the slave system in a variety of ways, big and small. Today, there are parallels to both senses of resistance in terms of neoliberal capitalism.

2. An important caveat is in order here: The Catholic Church should not be seen as a progressive force historically when it comes to its relations with Indigenous peoples. In Canada, for example, the Catholic Church was responsible for the operation of residential (boarding) schools for Indigenous children who were coercively displaced from their homes. This removal resulted in physical, cultural, sexual, emotional, and spiritual abuse, if not attempted cultural genocide. In December 2015, Prime Minister Justin Trudeau stated he would ask Pope Francis to apologize for the Church's role in this regard. In addition, the Church has been slow to admit to sexual abuse of children elsewhere by its priests and has also been criticized for its *patriarchical* attitude toward women. Finally, at best it has an ambivalent relationship to LGBT rights.

REFERENCES

Alcoreza, Raúl Prada. 2013. "Buen Vivir as a Model for State and Economy." In *Beyond Development: Alternative visions from Latin America*, edited Miriam Lang and Dunia Mokrani, 145–58. Amsterdam: Transnational Institute.

Bassey, Nnimmo. 2010. "Acceptance Speech," Right Livelihood Award, Stockholm, December 6, 2001. http://www.rightlivelihood.org/bassey_speech.html.

Bassey, Nnimmo. 2013. "Between Eti Uwem and Green Capitalism (Green Democracy)." Health of Mother Earth Foundation, http://www.homef.org/article/between-eti-uwem-and-green-capitalism-green-democracy.

Benedetta, Crimella and Margherita Giordano. 2013. "Indigenous Voices: Enriching Contaminations between Buen Vivir, Ubuntu and the Western World." Study Paper in the Department of Economics, Roma Tre University, Rome.

Beyer, Peter. 2013. *Religion in the Context of Globalization.* New York: Routledge.

Carroll, William 2015. "Modes of Cognitive Praxis in Transnational Alternative Policy Groups." In *Globalizations*, published online January 19, 2015, pp. 1–19. doi:10.1080/14747731.2014.100123.

Carrette, Jeremy and Richard King. 2005. *Selling Spirituality: The Silent Takeover of Religion.* New York: Routledge.

Casanova, José. 1997. "Globalizing Catholicism and the Return to a 'Universal Church'." In *Transitional Religion and Fading States*, edited by Susanne H. Rudolph and James Piscatori, 121–41. Boulder, CO: Westview Press.

Casanova, José. 2001. "Religion, the New Millennium, and Globalization." *Sociology of Religion* 62 (4): 415–41.

Castells, Manuel. 2010. *The Rise of the Network Society, 2nd edition.* Malden, MA: Wiley-Blackwell.

Coates, Ken S. 2004. *A Global History of Indigenous Peoples: Struggle and Survival.* New York: Palgrave Macmillan.

Focus on the Global South. 2013. "Learning from our Roots, Advancing our Struggles: More Conversations on Vivir Bien." http://focusweb.org/content/learning-our-roots-advancing-our-struggles-more-conversations-vivir-bien.

Focus on the Global South. 2015. "The Paradigm: Deglobalisation." http://focusweb.
    org/content/paradigm-deglobalisation.
Global Alliance for Rights of Nature 2015. "Founding Principles." http://therightsof-
    nature.org/fundamental-principles/.
Heelas, Paul. 2006. "Challenging Secularization Theory." *Hedgehog Review* 8 (1–2):
    46–58.
Heelas, Paul. 2012. "On Making Some Sense of Spirituality." In *Spirituality in the
    Modern World*, edited by Paul Heelas, Vol. 1, 3–37. London: Routledge.
Houtman, Dick and Aupers Stef. 2007. "The Spiritual Turn and the Decline of Tradi-
    tion." *Journal for the Scientific Study of Religion* 46 (3): 3–37.
Klein, Naomi. 2015. "Naomi Klein on Visiting the Vatican and the Radical Eco-
    nomic Message Behind Papal Climate Encyclical." Interviewed by Amy Good-
    man, August 4, 2015. Democracy Now! http://www.democracynow.org/2015/8/4/
    naomi_klein_on_visiting_the_vatican.
Kourie, Celia. 2006. "The 'Turn' to Spirituality." *Acta Theologica* 27 (2): 19–40.
Lynch, Gordon. 2007. *The New Spirituality: An Introduction to Progessive Belief in
    the Twenty-first Century*. London: I.B. Tauris.
Markoff, John. 2003. "Margins, Centers, and Democracy: The Paradigmatic History
    of Women's Suffrage." *Signs: Journal of Women in Culture and Society* 29 (10):
    85–116.
Mo Sung, Jung. 2007. "Theology, Spirituality and the Market." In *Another Possible
    World*, edited by Marcella Maria Althaus-Reid, Ivan Petrella, and Luis Carlos
    Susin, 67–80. London: SCM Press.
Pope Francis. 2015. *Laudato Si' (Be Praised) On the Care of our Common Home*.
    Rome: The Vatican. http://w2.vatican.va/content/dam/francesco/pdf/encyclicals/
    documents/papa-francesco_20150524_enciclica-laudato-si_en.pdf.
Smith, Jackie. 2014. "Counter-hegemonic Networks and the Transformation of
    Global Climate Politics: Rethinking Movement-State Relations." *Global Dis-
    course: An Interdisciplinary Journal of Current Affairs and Applied Contemporary
    Thought* 4 (2–3): 12–138.
Taylor, Bron Raymond. 2012. *Dark Green Religion: Nature, Spirituality and the
    Planetary Future*. Berkeley, CA: University of California Press.
Turner, Bryan S. 2012. *Religion and Modern Society*. Cambridge: Cambridge Uni-
    versity Press.
Wood, Leslie. 2011. "Youth Camps and the Bolivarian Revolution." In *Handbook of
    World Social Forum Activism*, edited by Jackie Smith et al. Boulder, CO: Paradigm
    Press, 305–20.

Index

Notes on Contributors

Umut Bozkurt, PhD, is an assistant professor in the Department of Politics and International Relations at the Eastern Mediterranean University, Cyprus. Her research interests are state theory, critical political economy, and modern politics of Turkey and Cyprus. Her latest works focus on the political economy of the Justice and Development Party in Turkey and the nature of the economic relations between Turkey and North Cyprus.

Davis Brown (J.D. New York University, LL.M. George Washington University, PhD University of Virginia) is a professor of political science at Maryville University of St. Louis. He is the author of *The Sword, the Cross, and the Eagle* (2008) and other works on war ethics and security studies. Dr. Brown is the co-author of the new Religious Characteristics of States dataset, with Patrick James.

Sabine Dreher, PhD, Bremen University, has taught in the Department of International Studies at Glendon College, York University since 2008 and was Assistant Professor at Near East University from 2002 until her emigration to Canada. Her research focus is on the politics of neoliberal globalization. Her most recent publication includes "What Is the Hizmet Movement? Contending Approaches to the Analysis of Religious Activists in World Politics" (2013) *Sociology of Islam* 1: 257–76.

Michael MacLeod, PhD, George Washington University, is Associate Professor of Political Science at St Mary's University, Canada. Previously, he taught at George Fox University in Oregon, where he was Director of International Studies. His research focuses on the power and accountability of multinational corporations in emerging global governance, and specifically on how institutional investors have increasingly utilized their power to influence businesses on human rights and environmental sustainability.

Justyna Nicinska, PhD, completed her doctorate at Rutgers University Newark and currently works at the National Oceanic and Atmospheric Administration. US Department of Commerce. Her research interests include global environmental politics, social movements, and religious environmentalism. Her PhD thesis titled "Religious Environmental Groups and Climate Change Politics in the United States and United Kingdom: What Motivates Activism?" was defended in 2013.

Aikande Kwayu, PhD, is a research affiliate at the University of Oxford, Department of Education, and development consultant at BUMACO Ltd. Her recent publications include Amy Stambach & Aikande Kwayu, 2013, "Take the Gift of My Child and Return Something to Me: On Children, Chagga Trust, and Religion on Mount Kilimanjaro," *Journal of Religion in Africa* 43 (4): 379–95. She is also publishing for the *Continent Observer*, an independent online news media specializing in Africa's politics.

Fouad Gehad Marei, PhD, is a Lecturer at the Otto Suhr Institute for political Science at Freie Universität Berlin since 2013. Fouad is also the recipient of the 2015/2016 Research Grant Award of the Arab Council for the Social Sciences for his project *Resistance, Piety, and Development: Hezbollah's Capital of Resistance as Global City*. Fouad's broad research agenda focuses on state-society relations, globalization and development, and Islamist religious activism in conflict and post-conflict contexts with a particular interest in Lebanon and Syria.

Marcos Scauso, M.A., obtained his B.A. in sociology at the National University of Argentina; he finished his M.A. in International Relations at San Francisco State University, and is now a PhD candidate at the University of California, Irvine, in the Department of Political Science. His research interests are international relations, theory, and identity politics in Latin America.

Peter J. Smith, PhD, is Professor of Political Science at Athabasca University, Alberta, Canada. He has published recently on globalization, nonviolence and the global justice movement, indigenous and environmental resistance to North American pipeline development, the rise of the surveillance state, and trade politics in a variety of journals and books. He is also a co-author *of Global Democracy and the World Social Forums*, 2008 and 2014 editions.

Elizabeth Smythe, PhD, is a professor of Political Science at Concordia University of Edmonton, Alberta, Canada, where she teaches international and comparative politics. Her research interests include international trade and investment agreements, and transnational social movements seeking to influence or resist these agreements and their use of spaces, such as the World Social Forum, to articulate alternative visions of social justice. She co-edited *the Handbook on World Social Forum Activism* (2012).

Asonzeh Ukah (Dr. habil.) is a sociologist/historian of religion. He joined the University of Cape Town, South Africa, in 2013. He taught at the University of Bayreuth, Germany, from 2005 to 2013. He has done fieldwork in Nigeria, Cameroon, Uganda, South Africa, Germany, and England. He is the author of *A New Paradigm of Pentecostal Power: A Study of the Redeemed Christian Church of God in Nigeria* (2008) and has published numerous peer-reviewed essays in international journals (in English, German, and Spanish). He co-edited *Bourdieu in Africa: Exploring the Dynamics of the Religious Fields* (with Magnus Echtler, 2016). He is the Director of the Research Institute on Christianity and Society in Africa (RICSA), University of Cape Town, South Africa.

Surya Prakash Upadhyay, PhD, is Assistant Professor at the Indian Institute of Technology, Mandi, India. His research interests are mainly in the Sociology of Religion, with an emphasis on emerging forms of spiritualities in cities. His most recent publication is "Globalization, Mass Media and Proliferating 'Gurus': The Changing Texture of Religion in Contemporary India" with Rowena Robinson in *The Globalization of Turbulence*, edited by Prashant K. Trivedi, New Delhi Council for Social Development.

Edward Webb, PhD, is Associate Professor of Political Science and International Studies at Dickinson College, where he also co-founded the Middle East Studies program. His research interests are mainly in the politics of North Africa and Turkey, with emphases on religion, authoritarianism, education, and media. He is the author of *Media in Egypt and Tunisia: From Control to Transition?* (2014) as well as articles on secularization in Turkey and Tunisia, among others.

Michael Wilkinson, PhD, is Professor of Sociology and Director of the Religion in Canada Institute at Trinity Western University. His publications include *Canadian Pentecostalism: Transition and Transformation*; *A Liberating Spirit: Pentecostals and Social Action in North America*; *Global Pentecostal Movements: Migration, Mission, and Public Religion*; and *Catch the Fire: Soaking Prayer and Charismatic Renewal*.